W9-CKF-286

MODERN RADIO STATION PRACTICES

SECOND EDITION

Joseph S. Johnson
Kenneth K. Jones

San Diego State University

Wadsworth Publishing Company, Inc.
Belmont, California

Communications Editor: Rebecca
  Hayden
Production Editor: Larry Olsen
Designer: Nancy Benedict
Copy Editor: Paul Weisser
Technical Illustrator: Ayxa Art
Cover Illustration: Victoria Philp

© *1978 by Wadsworth Publishing*
Company, Inc.
© *1972 by Wadsworth Publishing*
Company, Inc., Belmont, California
94002. All rights reserved. No part of
this book may be reproduced, stored
in a retrieval system, or transcribed,
in any form or by any means,
electronic, mechanical, photo-
copying, recording, or otherwise,
without the prior written permission
of the publisher.

Printed in the United States of
America
  2 3 4 5 6 7 8 9 10—82 81 80 79 78

Library of Congress Cataloging in
Publication Data

Johnson, Joseph Steve, 1937–
  Modern radio station practices.

  Bibliography: p. 406
  Includes index.
  1. Radio broadcasting—United
  States. I. Jones, Kenneth Karl
  1919–   joint author. II. Title.
  PN1991.3.U6J6 1978   384.54
  77-20830
ISBN 0-534-00550-0

PREFACE

This book is about programing today's American radio station. It is not a complete management book, but it approaches programing from a management view. As several who have used the first edition requested, the production section has been expanded in this second edition. The book has also been updated, but the focus and purpose remain the same as the first edition.

This book will be of greatest use to the beginning broadcaster and to the student who wants to know about radio, either as a profession or for personal understanding. While much that is here will be elementary to the experienced broadcaster, it is hoped that the perspective on radio programing and the essential information regarding program decision-making will be useful to the professional as well as the student.

The book is a result of several years of practical professional experience combined with research from print and personal sources. We have tried to maintain a balance between theory and practicality. We have tried not to be too obvious or too general, while trying at the same time to avoid too much shop talk or specific transitory information of limited value.

The profiles and appendixes are presented as part of the text, not merely optional reference material. These sections provide many of the details that give more of a working knowledge of the medium.

Because radio is so dynamic, the reader must keep abreast of current developments through the trade press, through extensive listening to radio, and through constant observation of society.

For the person who wants to be a radio professional, it is important to gain an understanding of principles and concepts. Some of this understanding can be gained through reading. But producing radio programing is not a spectator sport. To learn how to play the game you must play it, not just observe or read about it.

We wish to thank those who assisted in the preparation of the book, including those professionals who allowed us to poke around their studios and who patiently answered our questions. Among them are: Dick Estell, WKAR; Mel Cody, KMPC; John Young and Dickie Rosenfeld, KILT; Roy Wood; Marlin Taylor, Bonneville Broadcast Consultants; Al Newman and Vic Ives, KSFO; Ray Nordstrand, WFMT; Stan Schweiger and Sherrie Sutton, WINS; Bert Wahlen; Ken Gross, Pulse Pacific; Terry D'Angona, Dimensions Unlimited; Jim Holton, NBC; Jerrell Shepherd, KWIX; Marnie Mueller, WBAI–FM; Bruce Marr and Jim Simon, KABC; Harold Niven, NAB; Mike Stark, Russ Hamnett, and Tom McManus, KPBS–FM; Bernard Koval, KFI; Jack Williams, Pacific Recorders; Lee Carroll, Studio West. Dale Franzwa (Brooklyn University) and Marge Iverson were of particular help as sources for research papers prepared when they were students at SDSU, used in the production section. We also appreciate the thoughtful suggestions made by those teachers who read the manuscript for this edition: Jeryl R. Davis, Washington and Lee University; Carolyn D. Fisher, Orange Coast College; Lynn S. Gross, Loyola Marymount University; Jean M. Longwith, San Antonio College; and Ernest Martin, Jr., University of Kansas.

J. S. J.
K. K. J.

CONTENTS

1

Radio: The Newest Medium   1

2

Success Factors   13

What Makes a Program Interesting? 25

Production 67

Programs 111

The Physical and Operational Plant 32

Music on Radio   157

News   167

Promotion   186

10

Sales   204

11

Research   214

12

Governmental and Nongovernmental Controls   224

13

Criticism   240

Station Profiles   245

CHAPTER 1

Radio:
The Newest Medium

Radio celebrated its fiftieth year in 1970. Yet, paradoxical as it may seem, radio broadcasting is the newest of the electronic media on the basis of its programing. Television, which took over radio's original format in 1954, forced radio to find a new, more marketable format. Radio, compelled to reevaluate and readjust its role and mission, is thus the newest medium—and a solvent and healthy one. As we enter the final quarter of the twentieth century, there are more radios than people in the United States. The recent and projected technological developments, the growth of FM, the growth of syndication and the resurgence of networking, the continuing development of new programs and formats, and the attractiveness of radio as an advertising medium, all make radio a vital aspect of modern human experience with an enormous impact on our thoughts, our perceptions, and our actions.

The Size and Scope
of Radio Broadcasting

Radio's importance to listeners can be indicated by comparing how much time they spend using the medium with time spent using other media. Studies show that the average American spends the following number of hours per year using each medium:

Watching television—between 1,000 and 1,200 hours per year. (The figures vary from study to study. The TV set is on in the average home roughly seven hours a day, but individual viewing is roughly three hours a day.)

Listening to radio—between 900 and 1,000 hours per year. (Radio listening is more individual than watching television. Television is more a group behavior.)

Reading newspapers—approximately 300 hours per year.

Reading magazines—approximately 270 hours a year.

Attending movies—10 hours a year. (Less than half of the public goes at all. A small percentage of the public accounts for a large share of movie attendance. The audience is mostly dating age. This, of course, does not count movies on television.)

Attending live sporting events—less than 5 hours a year. (This includes amateur and professional.)

Attending live concerts—less than 5 hours a year. (This includes symphonies, rock concerts, barbershop quartets, and school groups.)

A recent RADAR[1] study of radio listening in the U.S. showed radio's weekly reach to include 92 percent of all persons 18 and over, 99 percent of all teenagers, and 94 percent of all people in the 25–49 age bracket. Radio sets outnumber people by a ratio of 1.7 to 1. The average American household owns 4.9 radios.

Further, during daytime hours people spend more time with radio than with any other medium. One major retail food chain found that 80 percent of adult women spend more time daily with radio than with television. Figure 1.1 shows the pattern of listening. From 6 A.M. to 6 P.M., people listen more than they watch. After 6 P.M., television attracts many more people than radio, of course, and over a week or a year reaches slightly more people. Also, television viewing is more concentrated, with fewer stations and programs attracting those larger audiences. It is no wonder that radio people, when addressing a group during daytime hours, like to ask the audience for a show of hands to the question: How many of you have watched television today— read a newspaper—listened to radio? It is virtually always a vote for radio.

The following statistics indicate the importance of radio in our economy.

Over $2.5 billion was spent for radio receivers in 1974. Radio set sales were up more than 400 percent over sales in 1952. About 99 percent of 1974 automobiles were radio-equipped. The car radio is used 62.4 percent of driving time. Transistor set sales were up 2,042 percent over 1952. FM set sales have increased to 54 percent of radio sales. The number of radios sold each year approximates the combined circu-

---

[1] Radio All Dimension Audience Research, a national study done for the four networks: CBS, NBC, ABC, and Mutual.

Average Quarter Hour Ratings
Monday–Friday, 6 : 00 A.M.–Midnight

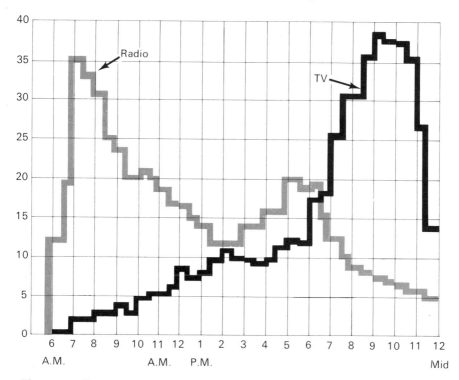

Figure 1.1 Recent all-media studies conducted by The Pulse, Inc., document that radio listening surpasses television viewing for two-thirds of the broadcast day. An illustration of radio's dominance is shown on the chart above, based on persons age 12+ from the Three-Stage All-Media Pulse Survey conducted in the New York area.

lation of all morning and evening newspapers. There are more radios in the United States than there are telephones in the entire world. Americans spent over $200 million for transistor radio batteries alone during 1974. Of the 25,000 radio stations in the world, the United States has approximately one-third. There are roughly five times as many radios per capita in the United States as there are in Europe, and sixteen times as many as in Asia or Africa.

The following news story indicates how people can get involved— too involved—with radio.

> Two Southern California teenagers were killed last month in separate accidents under roughly identical and equally bizarre circumstances, to wit: While strolling along railroad tracks on afternoons of perfect visibility they were struck from the front by diesel locomotives traveling at moderate speeds.

Despite the fact that neither young person had a history of deafness, there is strong evidence to indicate that neither had heard the oncoming trains until the instant before he was hit.

The only possible explanation for their failure to detect the approach of several tons of churning machinery on an otherwise quiet afternoon is the fact that both of the teens had transistor radios plugged in their ears.

Broadcast advertising has consistently demonstrated an annual growth faster than that of total advertising expenditures or the economy of the country. For several years after the television boom, radio suffered through transitions in program formats and sustained either real losses or losses in percentage of advertising revenue spent in the medium. But in recent years radio revenue has increased by a greater percentage than has television revenue or that of other competing media. In 1976, radio had its biggest percentage growth-year since 1944 and its greatest dollar growth-year ever.

While radio's story is positive, it should be seen in perspective. Statistics for 1976 show approximately $31.2 billion spent for advertising in all media, national and local. Radio gets less than 10 percent of that total figure, roughly 37 percent of television's share, and newspapers get as much as radio and television together. All advertising accounts for 2.9 percent of the nation's personal consumption expenditures (PCE), while radio advertising accounts for .21 percent of PCE—a fairly low amount to support something we use for a thousand hours a year.

The average annual revenue per station is only $225,000, demonstrating that individual stations are small businesses. Three out of every four dollars gained in revenue are from local advertising. Just over one dollar in five comes from national and regional spots, less than one radio advertising dollar in twenty comes to the network, and less than one radio advertising dollar in one hundred winds up as station revenue from network compensation.

Radio's cost per listener reached makes it an effective advertising medium. Reach and frequency analyses show that most advertisers using other media can improve their advertising efficiency by putting at least part of their advertising money into radio.

Radio Compared to Other Media

What makes radio, limited as it is to sound, so popular? How has it been able to restructure itself in the face of the initially overwhelming competition from television programing? Why is it that, in an age that looks forward to concentrated communications using highly sophisticated techniques such as electronic transmissions for point-to-point mail service, individual computer drops, and photophones, the broadcasting of an aural signal alone should be so indispensable and pervasive? It is because radio has specialized, serving more specific tastes in an informal, intimate way. Even if television had not appeared, radio, forced by competition to do what it can do best, would have moved in that direction. Even though radio is a prime purveyor of that most popular communication—music—it is not purely an entertainment service. It has become an extensive personal information system, bringing pertinent data to the individual which he can use in his own sphere of activity. Radio information is now and here in time and place.

The average American wakes up to radio. It is our constant companion while preparing to meet the demands of the day. We plan our activities around the information we learn from radio. Radio tells us about our community and the events that will significantly affect our activities. We learn what is unique about the day and what is available from the community through radio.

Radio Treats the Listener as if He Were Blind

Radio demands nothing from the listener during a broadcast except that he listen. Hence, the listener is free, manually and visually, to do other things while listening. Radio is the only advertising-supported medium that gives this freedom. Thus, radio listening is a flexible activity and may be combined with many other activities.

Radio Broadcasting Is Bound by Time

Any given message monopolizes listener time for its duration and, hopefully, also gains listener attention. When the message is finished it is gone, dead, unless repeated again for numerous recalls and additional information. Print is quantitative. If you take out an ad in the local daily newspaper or a local magazine, you may obtain as many copies for an historical archive as you wish. But time is ephemeral, and all you may have of a tangible nature after your broadcast is a billing record from the station or, better yet, a rating record commenting on the number of listeners your message reached. Print, like television, is eye-oriented. Radio is ear-oriented. There is no "middleman" in print. The reader scans at his own pace, referring back to portions of the message he finds either extra interesting or difficult to understand. Radio broadcasting does not have this objectivity. Radio em-

ploys an interpreter who exerts influence on a very subjective basis
into the objectivity of the content of the message.

Radio Is Personal, Subjective, and Intimate

It is a personality medium. It is intensely human in dealing with the
events and ideas of the day on a person-to-person basis. It works emotionally. Radio never has been a medium for an audience of millions;
rather, it has been, and is, a medium of millions of one-person audiences. Radio broadcasting had been in service for over twenty years
before two men clearly revealed this intimate, highly emotional quality
of the radio communicator. Arthur Godfrey could attest to the thousands of women who have written him concerning their most cherished
dreams, confident that Arthur knew each of them as closely as they
knew him from listening to him each day. Just after World War II,
Dave Garroway's "1160 Club" on WMAQ in Chicago set the tone for
later disc jockeys' lighthearted requests of their listeners. The story of
Garroway's advice to listeners, that the best way to hear his program
was to sit directly in front of the radio set with the volume turned up
as full as the neighbors could stand (resulting in a strong comment
from the Chicago Police Department), may not be entirely apocryphal.
Sales boomed for products that Garroway and Godfrey talked about
on the air. Godfrey was one of the first radio personalities to endorse
the products he advertised. It is a truism that advertising can bring
you to the product only one time. Nevertheless, the power of strong
radio communicators like Godfrey and Garroway was such that many
a product was apparently purchased a second and third time entirely
because of their endorsement.

Radio Is Mobile

Because of the engineering developments in the miniaturization of
broadcast equipment, radio has become as mobile as its audience.
Sociologists tell us that a dominating characteristic of modern America
is the extreme mobility of the individual in our country. A young
executive with a national corporation may, in the course of his career
with that firm, live in, work in, and become a visible part of half a
dozen major cities throughout the country. He and his family may
find themselves a part of both coasts, living at various times in the
supermegalopolis areas of "San-San, Mil-Cle, and Bos-Wash." Because
of the cross-pollination of many regions, and because of the immediate
impact of television, all regions of the nation are becoming more alike.
Key West, Florida, has much in common with Seattle, Washington,
with Presque Isle, Maine, and with San Diego, California. Radio is an

immediate common denominator linking one region of the country to another and yet focusing on that which is unique and singular in a particular region. One way for a traveler to feel a part of a new area is to listen to the radio of that community, for radio must, by its very nature, reflect as a social mirror the likes and interests of the people it serves.

People are mobile in terms of their interests and vocations. The educational community has the almost impossible task of preparing the individual for changing careers two and one-half times, on the average, in his lifetime. A career change is not just a change of jobs within a corporate structure or employment moved to a different location; it is a total change of responsibilities and duties involving separate knowledge and separate applications of knowledge. Obviously, such an involved citizenry must avail itself of the fastest and most complete information service available. Radio can help to provide this service.

Personal mobility has brought about technological developments in radio broadcasting unique to this medium. The relatively low frequency, long wavelength transmission is ideal for reaching remote areas within the country. Radio is the lifeline for ranchers in remote agricultural areas. Alaska has depended upon the bush pilot and his radio communication system to develop the interior regions of the state.

The development of the car radio makes it possible for the individual to be in touch with the community while in transit. Development of transistors to replace the vacuum tube has allowed portable radios to accompany the individual anywhere. Radios are more numerous at the beach and on the street than they are in the living room. Sports fans take their radios with them to the game so they can tune in on the expert opinion that helps them understand, interpret, and enjoy the action.

This characteristic mobility has influenced radio in its program selection. When radio was primarily an entertainment medium listened to mostly in the living room of the home, programs were developed in quarter-hour, half-hour, and hour time segments. People were usually stationary while listening to network programs. If a person began listening to a radio drama, it was fairly certain that he planned to listen to the program all the way to its end. The networks could schedule programs based on the fixed attention of their audiences. A modern, mobile radio audience can no longer guarantee a fixed-time availability. It is difficult to become involved in a 30-minute whodunit mystery while driving to a destination that requires twenty minutes of driving time. Would the listener sit in the car until the program is over? More likely, the listener would not become involved in the story in the first place. Thus, it was necessary that open-ended programs, laced together by the personality of a host-communicator, become the standard fare of radio broadcasting. Music and news are its staple items. The average length of much of the music is two and one-half minutes. The news headlines featured every hour are only slightly longer. A commercial message runs no longer than a minute. Consequently, the mobile listener may tune out whenever his schedule demands his attention, secure in the knowledge that the news item will be repeated and that he probably will hear his favorite musical selection again later in the day. NBC's "Monitor" was one of the first to innovate the segment approach to programing for a busy mobile audience—a far larger audience than even NBC imagined.

Radio in Historical Perspective

There are certain responsibilities required of any medium considered to be "mass communication." It is totally impossible to program for a large and heterogeneous audience without distinct compromises in program content, style, and approach. The price is often boredom and contempt from the more sophisticated and intelligent members of the audience. What is banal and condescending to one portion of the audience might be intriguing or bewilderingly complex to another segment of listeners.

The development of motion pictures replaced the large theatrical road-show extravaganza as the principal vehicle for mass entertainment. Motion pictures were better able to reach audiences of all backgrounds and ages, and the stage was forced to be more provocative, more specialized, and less of a mass entertainment. The advent of radio was less a threat to motion pictures than it was to the newspaper. Since radio could not involve the visual element, entertainment programing over radio tended to supplement motion picture fare, as it has sporting and other events. On the other hand, newspapers and news magazines believed they would be particularly threatened if radio were allowed to transmit news. Concerned with what seems now to be a most naive fear, newspaper publishers believed no one would ever read about the news again if they were allowed to hear the news first over radio. Long suppressed by publishers in its effort to transmit news, radio finally gained news freedom during World War II. The only loss suffered by the newspapers was the financially draining "extra" edition, which publishers had wanted to get rid of anyway. In fact, radio news sparked renewed interest in news, whether reported on radio, in papers, or in news magazines.

Television had the most devastating influence on both motion pictures and radio. Motion pictures reacted first by attempting to keep their movies and stars off television schedules. Then, motion pictures began producing the large, terribly expensive and lavish pictures emphasizing spectacle in wide screen opulence. This ploy succeeded in destroying the "C" movies, and many of the personnel from "C" pictures transferred to television. Through the influence of foreign films and the work of the new wave of cinema directors, the motion picture soon assumed the same freedom to treat meaningful social themes with explicit adult frankness that the legitimate theatre had assumed after motion pictures became the prime mass-entertainment medium. Today, motion pictures are, for the most part, in financial health and have little fear of extinction by television programing, although few films are produced for a general mass audience.

For radio the impact of television was even more traumatic. Television seemingly could do anything that radio could do, and more. Television could program with the same immediacy of radio. Television was organized and operated by the same large electronic corporations that developed the radio broadcasting industry and utilized the same operational philosophies and procedures. The fact that television could protect network radio from disappearing, because of mutual ownership, was small solace to the independent radio station and the network-affiliated station that did not have a television operation to assist it during this transition period. Radio had either to look for new audiences to serve or to discover how to serve old audiences in new ways. Radio chose the latter and rediscovered its potential in new and firm ways.

Radio first abdicated its position as a mass-entertainment medium by transferring its emphasis to a personalized entertainment and information service. It gave up premium listening time in the entertainment slot of 7:00 to 11:00 P.M. (see Figure 1.1). Radio recognized that the head of the household would be available primarily during early morning hours and driving time; that women would be a primary target for daytime listening; and that teenagers represented a large potential audience through popular music and its stars. Radio acknowledged that television could cover national and world spectacles far better than it could, but that the price structure of television made it difficult to cover the local scene quickly and thoroughly. In its instinct for survival, radio recognized that it could do this job better, quicker, and cheaper, and it was geared to the advertising dollar available for local advertising. It realized that it was an extremely adaptable medium, able to change its message within minutes of broadcast time to suit any circumstance.

So, network programing became of relatively little consequence for radio compared to the heavy reliance television stations placed upon network affiliation—except for international and national news. The Associated Press and United Press International news wires and the

news bureaus of larger station groups in strategic cities fed information to the independent stations, thus allowing them to compete on
equal terms with the network-affiliated stations programing national
and world news. It is noteworthy that the resurgence of radio networks
is based on the development of ·specialized networks such as ABC's
four networks, Associated Press Radio, United Press International
Audio, the Mutual Black Network, and National Public Radio.

Radio's Formats

A prime characteristic of modern radio station operation is that it
can react to local needs. Radio talks about its own community, reflecting the personality of its own people. And, of greatest importance,
radio is frcc to program to specific audiences. No longer must each
station be all things to all people like its television counterpart. A radio
station may choose a specific kind of audience and concentrate on
filling the needs and interests of that particular audience. For instance,
each urban area has multiple audiences. Certainly, teenagers are interested in Top-40 and rock stations. Others prefer country music. Classical and fine arts stations find a measurable audience, as do all-news
and conversation station formats. Nearly everyone tunes in popular
music stations at some time or other during the week. An advertiser
can determine the demographics of the audience he wants to reach
and can find a radio station that programs to that audience at a cost
he can afford. And that is the formula for the success of modern radio
station operations—specialization. It does the job for the small advertiser in the local marketplace.

Today, it is unlikely that a major city will be dominated by a single
radio station. There is much more likely to be a stand-out radio station
for each major program category. Whenever too many stations using
one kind of format start chewing into each other's audiences, the
stations suffering the most usually seek to escape their competition by
changing formats. And when any single station shows audience shares
significantly larger than its competitors, one or more stations will try
to duplicate its format and take some of its listeners.

Radio: A Medium of
Personal Expression

Radio is a medium through which personal statements can be made.
It is a medium in which one person can write, produce, engineer (when

the union will let him), perform, and come up with a finished product exactly as he wants it, hampered only by his own limitations. Few opportunities exist for that kind of expression in the other mass media. Most efforts in other media are done by groups, and groups have to compromise. People in radio are not free of compromises, but they have fewer of them to make. That is one reason why working in radio can be fun and invigorating for many people—if they have the right situation.

Radio and the "Wired City" Concept

Cable television's existing services, along with projected innovations, have suggested to some that cable is the future of communications.

The demands already made upon communications services have almost devoured the available radio frequencies. Each communications service requires its own frequency in the location where it performs its services. Landmobile radio has overrun the channels available to it. More and more utilities are demanding radio frequencies to provide communication links among their services. Fortunately, compared to television, radio requires relatively little spectrum space; AM radio needs 10 kilohertz (KHz) per channel, and FM requires 200 KHz per channel. Compared to television's requirement of 6 *mega*hertz (MHz) per channel over a spread of eighty-one VHF and UHF channels, radio's space is small in ratio to the number of stations available throughout the country able to use these frequencies.

The very nature of radio broadcasting eliminates the use of the "wired city" concept. Radio is a medium for a mobile audience. Television demands a static audience. Cable television using a wired closed-circuit concept can serve a television audience, but it is doubtful that a closed-circuit system can adequately serve radio audiences. Mobile audiences demand a medium that can reach them when they are unavailable to television.

Radio broadcasting has established its place as the newest medium in the communications spectrum by pinpointing the specific services it can perform in our society. Tempered by competition and forced to reconsider its value to a communication-oriented world, radio broadcasting has readjusted and redefined its contribution. Radio is fired and glazed and fully prepared to provide services required in the decade ahead.

Suggestions for Further Learning

1. Through personal observation, note the ways people with whom you come in contact use radio. Analyze your listening habits and others'. What appeals to people? When and why do they listen?

2. Make your own study, similar to that made by Pulse (see Figure 1.1). Do your results match closely with those shown on the chart?

CHAPTER 2

Success Factors

Success in American radio takes different forms. Success can be measured by audience size and by the influence exerted in the community. Success can be the admiration of other professionals or critics who think that the station is doing a professional job. But that which is the most pervasive and desired objective of management is financial success. The other kinds of success are important, too, but they are intangibles that bring only comments from listeners, party invitations, and "ego-warmth." While many in station management would like to be loved and rich, most are just willing to settle for a balanced budget.

Every kind of station needs to attract listeners to generate support funds. All station managers secretly wish that everybody would listen to their stations all the time. Since there are so many competing media and competing stations, and since you cannot reach everybody with one kind of programing, the attempt is to attract the largest possible audience that will generate the largest possible revenue. Stations try hardest to appeal to those who buy the products of the advertisers— the mass adult audience between about 20 and 55 years of age. Usually, it is only when stations are unsuccessful in reaching that audience or when competition is very strong that stations are willing to settle for a less marketable segment. They may seek other segments such as the younger or older, or the rich or the poor, unless in a given area or under given circumstances one of those audience segments predominates. Under very competitive situations, the stations will fragment that middle group of 20-to-55-year-olds, choosing to emphasize male or female appeals, or aiming for the under-30 age segment, or the over-40s, or only the more affluent.

Since radio leans heavily on demographics, and since the total number of listeners is not as important as the *total marketable audience*, radio serves the very young and the old less willingly than the young and middle-aged married persons who buy so many of the mass-produced products of potential sponsors. In radio, it is considered something of a curse to have an audience composed primarily of teen-agers or old persons, especially the poor old. The young are preferred over the old because the youth are potential consumers, even though they are only a minor market segment at the time.

The ingredients that enable a station to attract listeners and sponsors are discussed in the following sections.

Music

Music is the staple of modern radio programing. It is an inexpensive source of programing, and it is also highly desired by the audience. Almost everyone likes music. To be sure, not everyone likes the same kind of music, and choosing the music which appeals to the desired listeners is not an easy matter. The type, amount, quality, setting, presentation, and competition are all factors for the programer to consider in the selection of music.

Music is personal and emotional. An individual's tastes are dependent upon education, experience, personal qualities, social position, and ambitions, among other factors. People choose to listen to the music they hear because of availability, personal taste, and social utility.

The type of music and the way it is programed are particularly important to the station because the music greatly affects the type and number of listeners the station will get. A radio station exists for other people, not strictly as a catharsis for the owner, manager, or programer. Therefore, even the esoteric stations have a built-in tendency away from music that is too selective, since every station is interested in maximizing its audience. Those stations that have chosen to specialize do so because it is a way of maximizing their audience. The country music station operator specializes because hopefully he will attract all of the people who like country music. Secretly, the station operator wishes that everyone liked country music. Unless he is in an area where country music is preferred by more people than any other type of music, he probably would switch his format if he could compete with the stations that were programing the majority music. Stations specialize not always because they want to but because they have to.

The music preferred by more of the adult consumers than any other is the melodic popular ballad. There is very little correlation between record sales generally and the adult American public's preferences. Among adults, rock music and country music are disliked more strongly than other forms. Opera is also largely disliked. The more esoteric classics and jazz pieces are not widely accepted. Polkas, band music and marches, Hawaiian, Dixieland, and other specialized types have relatively small acceptance. People do not seem to mind subtle jazz of a commercial nature with slight improvisation of familiar themes. They do not, as a whole, like wholesale improvisation.

These statements are generally true of the adult public, but there are local situations and specialized publics where such is not the case. A sizable minority of our society prefers country music over all other forms. Teenagers listen to almost nothing but rock music. Opera fans are among the most vocal devotees to be found for any form of music. Among the better educated some of the more esoteric forms are relatively more popular than among the population as a whole. But, generally speaking, what most people prefer is melodic music slightly on the bland side, with heavy reliance on "standard tunes," no clear preferences for either vocal or instrumental music, and with a slight preference for male over female singers.

Whether such preferences will continue, or for how long, remains to be seen. Most adults are not devotees of rock music, but teenagers have adopted it as their own. Country music is on the increase. On the one hand, people who are raised on one type of music may not quickly abandon it. On the other hand, many types of behavior and tastes do change with age. Children watch cartoon shows on television and read comic books, but few adults do. Certainly, some of the appeal of teen music for teenagers is having their own music that adults do not prefer. The social utility of fitting in with the group and group preferences is especially strong among the young. It appears that the beat itself is not the prime reason for adult dislike of the teen music. More important is that adults interpret the music as having juvenile or unintelligible lyrics, a lack of melodic quality in many of the voices and instrumentation, youth-oriented thematic materials, and repetition.

In recent years the general audience attitude to rock music has softened, and rock has broadened its appeal by borrowing greatly from other music, becoming more diverse, more sophisticated, and more adult. Rock is the preferred dance music and the main support of the record industry. It is much less important to television (especially prime time), Las Vegas, club and concert entertainment, and most of America's top-rated radio stations. (See Music Glossary, page 381.)

News

Some stations in markets with a large number of stations do not program any news at all, specializing only in music. Such operations are extreme in their specialization, for there are few people who never want any news or who want nothing but news. Stations which broadcast no news generally are acknowledging that other stations are doing the news job better than they could.

News is an important element for most successful stations. As a medium of communication, radio's most important job is relaying the news. Few top-rated stations in either audience ratings or advertising rates do not have a strong news effort. It is in the area of news that the networks perform their greatest service in radio today. While other network programing, generally stated, is simply a drug on the market; the news resources of the networks, with their Washington and overseas bureaus and their professional writing and on-air presentations, can add greatly to many stations' programing and service.

People do not spend as much time listening to news as they do to music. Once they learn that the world is still functioning, what the weather is forecast to be, and whether their favorite ball team won, they may prefer to listen to music rather than hear the news repeated. But, more than any other reason, people first turn on the radio in the morning to get the news. People frequently prefer something more than headline capsules and five-minute summaries, although the detail of newspapers usually is not expected or even desired. News efforts vary considerably, according to the type of station.

Personalities

This is an area where there are divergent points of view, more so than in other areas. Many stations with top ratings, and especially those with high advertising rates, use the strong personality approach. Many others feel it is important that the station, not the on-air individual, should have the personality.

Those who use the personality approach feel that, in a business where so much programing can be duplicated by other stations, strong, identifiable personalities can make the difference. These stations stress the warm, human sounds of one person talking to another as if face to face. They also note that many advertisers react favorably to an identifiable person who can push their products in addition to entertaining and informing people over the air.

The drawbacks to the personality approach are several. Personalities can be very expensive, especially the good ones. Anonymous voices can be shuffled in and out without much effect, but the loss of a major personality that a station has been building up for years can be a big blow to a station which has promoted him and invested in his success.

Strong personalities often find that they are stars and sometimes do not take direction very well. Also, many disc jockeys cause controversy for the station with their off-air behavior. If they get to be big names on radio, DJs often seek further fulfillment or fortune by going into television or moving to another market. Strong personalities can begin to feel that they are more important than the stations they work for. Many earn more money than their immediate superiors or even more than the station manager. Many managers do not like to deal with show-business types, preferring the orderly businesslike ways of more sedate types of businesses.

In spite of the drawbacks, however, most of the top-rated stations with ad rates at the top of their markets play the personality game because there is nothing as effective in reaching people as other people. "Name" stars can make a difference.

Talk Other than News

This factor applies not only to stations which emphasize talk programing, such as the telephone talk stations, but to all stations. The ratio of talk to music is an important factor in all music programing. Too much extraneous talk hampers the music programing. Many people will listen to a show because of the personality, because he has interesting views or is funny or presents interesting people; but they may protest if he presents too much of such material in what is supposed to be a music show. How much talk, what type it is, how it is programed, and at what hour are all factors that affect the success of a station.

Consistency

Consistency applies to both the quality and the type of programing. To illustrate its importance regarding the *type* of programing, consider the following example. Suppose that, in a market of fifty stations, a station decides to change its format radically. The first likely effect is that the station will lose most of the listeners it had. It then must try to get new listeners from the other fifty stations. Many of the listeners to those other stations are happy with what they have and will not change. Since most listeners do not "dial around" very much, the station with the new format will have to do a lot of something just to attract attention. The attraction of new listeners will most likely be very slow unless the potential audience is one which is experimenting with radio and is receptive to change. The group that is least resistant to change is the young. Most stations would prefer an older audience with more money to spend, but this audience is more set in its habits and listening patterns. Audiences are built very slowly, but they can be lost almost overnight.

The station builds the audience by doing the same thing (with minor variations) every day so that listening patterns can be established. Except in small markets where it is easier to keep track of radio schedules because there are few stations, it is difficult to build an audience if there are great paradoxes in the daily program schedule. Varying programs or program parts must be compatible with the overall sound. Abrupt shifts in appeal or interest generally are not desirable. Even sports coverage and other special events must be considered carefully and fit into the overall image.

Consistent *quality* is also desirable. A station which has high quality one day and sounds like a poor carbon copy of itself the next day faces the same problem that the maker of any product faces who has poor quality control—the station may lose its audience. Radio, in dealing with emotional and qualitative elements, is more prone to variation than a computer-operated production line, and no performer is always at his peak; but consistency is very desirable for maximum success.

Consistency, however, must be balanced by a willingness to change. In radio, more than in other media, the only constant is change. A controlled, disciplined change that retains the familiar touch, while embracing the new, is most likely to succeed. Of course, for an unsuccessful station, a whole new image may be desirable. A new image, however, must be carefully planned and sustained over time to build an audience and achieve success.

The Ability to Localize

Since radio is a local medium, the ability to localize programing is crucial, although not entirely tangible. A station must reflect an awareness and concern for its coverage area.

This local concern can be manifested in several ways. An awareness of the local conditions and a concern for them in what is broadcast on the air is the most obvious. Legitimate public service, boosting the local community, participation, and generally showing concern and pride help to build the desired image. The community should feel that the station is "one of us." Many large corporations with successful stations have gone into new markets exuding confidence that they would "show the local rubes a thing or two about radio." The corporations often have lost money because the locals gave them a good education about the individuality of the community, and because the locals had a different attitude. The ability to relate to the local market, or segments of it, is dependent upon having an attitude of service and upon understanding local needs and conditions. A station's concern is especially shown in the on-air sound of its news coverage, its air personalities, its public service efforts, and even its commercials. Listeners also get a "feeling" for a station through its promotions and in the participation of station personnel in civic affairs.

Promotion

Radio operations employ two kinds of promotion: audience promotion and sales promotion. Audience promotion—basically advertising—includes efforts aimed at listeners through on-air promotion as well as promotion aimed at nonlisteners through off-air promotion. All of the advertising techniques that sell soap, politicians, and goodwill generally will also sell radio. The potential is as large as the budget. An advertising campaign can use newspapers, television, billboards, skywriting, bumper stickers, sweat shirts, and messages in fortune cookies. Getting station exposure among nonlisteners is important, but also important is to continue to sell regular listeners with high-quality, carefully selected promotional aids.

Unfortunately, many stations' promotion campaigns are limited to contests. Management sometimes tries to buy listeners with contests. Contests can be helpful, but they can also detract if not run carefully. Some contests are big-money giveaways. Others use relatively smaller prizes but make the fun of the contest the focus of the effort, such as a contest which asks listeners to come up with clever or humorous bits than can be aired with credit to the listeners.

Promotion also takes the form of slogans, station identifications, and announcements. Many stations have produced musical signatures that try to capture the spirit of the station.

It would be easy to underestimate the word-of-mouth exposure that comes from having a capable and happy staff that is proud of their jobs and their station. Having employees who show their pride in their organization and who tell their friends and relatives about their station starts a chain reaction that can reach a surprising distance into the community.

Nothing can make up for a bad product. Advertising can enhance a great product, and it can help a mediocre product if the competition is not too strong. But it will kill a bad product that has strong competition.

In addition to audience promotion, sales promotion aimed at the potential advertiser or advertising agency is necessary. Even though people in the advertising business are aware of all the techniques used to sell products, they still admire a good campaign by a station, and they can be sold by the same techniques they themselves use.

An important adjunct to sales promotion is the audience-rating business. Although ratings are used by programers to aid them in making decisions, their primary use is by advertisers. Ratings made by companies such as Pulse, Hooper, and Arbitron can be used to sell the station's time. Salesmen accentuate strong points in the ratings to sell potential advertisers. Of course, if the station does not get good ratings, it must rely on other strategies.

Often, surrounding many other things that cannot be measured quantitatively, a certain "halo effect" exists that only partly can be explained rationally. Many stations have this quality or syndrome. It exists when the public's or advertisers' opinions are manifested in ratings, opinions, or images that are greater than the qualitative and competitive factors would seem to warrant. Some stations so dominate their markets that they are, in effect, above the competition. The image is built upon favorable word of mouth and based upon superior quality, but it is partly an irrationality on the part of the public. It is part truth and part myth, a charisma, a bigger-than-life projection, a star quality. Clever promotion can be a major contributing factor, and, in fact, is what much of Hollywood was built on.

Sales Effort

Sales personnel often remind others involved in station efforts that if it were not for sales none of them would be working. While very few salesmen can get by without a strong product, all stations need, at the very least, someone to take sales orders and, usually, someone to pound the pavements and knock on agency doors. The importance of the sales effort in a station can be shown by the fact that more station managers come up through sales than any other branch of the station organization. Broadcast sales demand considerable creativity and initiative.

A national sales representative acts as a station's sales agent in metropolitan centers where national advertising is bought. Selection of and coordination with this representative are important to a station's financial success.

Competition

As in other fields of endeavor, success in radio does not always demand greatness; it merely requires being the best in the market or just remaining competitive. Stronger competition requires a stronger effort to succeed. In radio, competition not only may generate a lot more hustle, but may dictate the type of station to operate. Many formats and program schedules are the result of counterprograming —that is, providing an alternative service or programing strengths against weaknesses of the competition. Many chain operations (several stations under one ownership) that use a particular style or format in most of their stations are forced by a strong competitor to alter their programing in a given market because the competitor is more successful with the preferred format. How skilled a station is at competitive strategy greatly affects its success.

Resources

The finances that enable a station to survive periods of general economic recession, to withstand pressure from a tough new competitor, or to move quickly into new areas are obviously the key resources needed for operation. A good signal that gets into the entire coverage area is another integral resource, as is a good frequency. A tradition and a name built up over a period of time among the public and advertisers, as well as potential employees, is a further resource. News mobile units, helicopters, fully equipped production studios, good working conditions, and a favorable location all add to the satisfaction of both the public and the employees. The impression of being a first-class station is always good for public relations and sales.

The most successful stations are strong in all of the areas mentioned in this chapter. Successful stations that are weak in one or more areas do exist, although there are not many in the large competitive markets; it happens only where the competition is also weak in one or more areas.

Budgets

Budgetary needs vary by station type, size, and market. However, figures compiled by the NAB and FCC give an indication of practices in use generally. Program department expense does not fluctuate as much by station size as it does by type of station. In all-sized markets, the program department expense averages from 30 to 35 percent of total station expenses. Some types of stations will run dramatically higher and others lower. Selling expense ranges from 13 to 25 percent of total expense. Small stations have a smaller percentage of selling expense because they have fewer agency and national representative commissions. FM stations, though mostly small, also have, on the average, high sales costs—among the highest in the industry (perhaps because FM has been harder to sell). Engineering costs range from 9 to 16 percent of total expenses; the larger stations have the higher cost percentages. The reason is that small station announcers work "combo"—that is, they do their own board work and take transmitter readings themselves. In large stations, unions require a separation of duties, with engineers "operating the board" as well as taking meter readings. Among the least expensive of station operations are the records, music licensing fees, and outside news services—all vital programing elements. Most expenses go for station salaries.

Modern radio displays a variety of formats, quality, and effectiveness. Most radio stations are very small businesses. The variation can be shown graphically by comparing a large metropolitan station having over a hundred employees with a small automated station having only one full-time person and a few contracted services. It is possible to operate a radio station with automation gear that is maintained by an engineering service. A telephone-answering service can employ a telephone girl with a third-class FCC license who can dial the transmitter to take remote meter readings. The music can be purchased from a programing service. The lone full-time employee (can we call

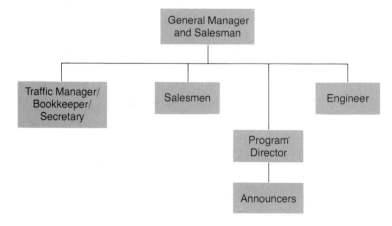

Figure 2.1 Small Station Organization

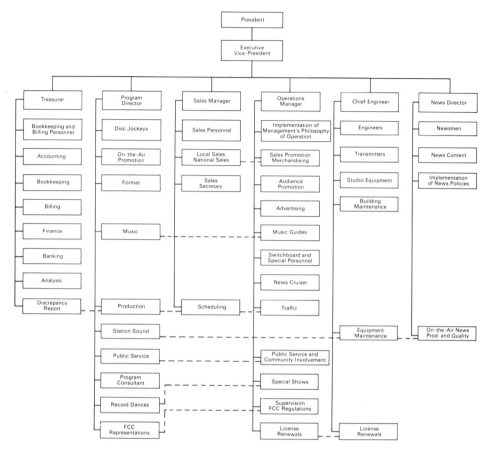

Figure 2.2 Large Station Organization

him the manager?) oversees the operation, sells and produces all of the commercials, and keeps the station operating. Another way to demonstrate the variation in radio stations is with an organization chart for a small station and a large one (see Figures 2.1 and 2.2.) In this book we are not insensitive to the variation between the small and the large station. But we are more interested in discussing principles that apply to *most* stations, regardless of station or market size.

In this chapter we have identified a number of areas to which the station operator must give attention. In later chapters we will elaborate upon many of these areas.

The Competitive Environment

As we have noted, stations do not exist in a vacuum. Their success or lack of success is dependent upon a number of factors. Some are programing factors. Some are revenue factors. Some are promotion factors. Another way of looking at only those factors which have an impact on listening is shown in Figure 2.3.

Figure 2.3   The Competitive Environment

Suggestions for Further Learning

1. Using the headings of this chapter as a checklist, analyze the radio stations in your market. Where is each strong and weak? Make a list of recommendations that might bring each station up to par in each area. Would it be worth the cost?

2. What appeals do you note on radio stations in your area that are very local or unique to your area?

3. Relate the success factors mentioned in this chapter to the Station Profiles starting on page 246.

CHAPTER 3

What Makes
a Program
Interesting?

The one factor that all successful radio programs or stations have in common is the ability to engage and retain the listener's interest. That is usually accomplished by finding and presenting programing that people are already interested in. Successful programs normally relate to previous experiences of the audience. The producer or programer must know whom he is trying to reach and how he can appeal to the experience and interests of this target audience. Beyond choosing materials that serve existing interests, there are a number of elements that can maximize listener interest.

Continuity

Most people do not like to rethink and explore continually but prefer to establish a routine. Even in an area with fifty radio stations, most listeners do all of their listening to no more than three stations. People build up listening habits. A station's consistency in quality and style allows the listener to build up these habits over time. There is security in the familiar voice, in familiar stations, and in language as people are accustomed to hearing it. The air personality can become an old friend. Changes, except at very unsuccessful stations, should be evolutionary rather than revolutionary. A station that finds a successful formula and sticks to it is almost always more successful than a station that changes its style often.

Variety

Variety may seem in opposition to continuity, but it really is not. Continuity is important, but so is variety; the two must find a comfortable balance, and the point of balance depends on the type of station. Variety is important for the pace. A well-paced show never sags or leaves listeners exhausted; it is a balance between too much tension and too much relaxation. Contrast between the old and the new, the serious and the comic, and the fast and the slow all help retain interest. Since the human mind tends to alternate between focusing and wandering, like the tides that ebb and flow and the heart that beats and relaxes, listeners adapt better to a program which has places for relaxing as well as places demanding optimum attention. There must be ascending and descending curves of tension; purposeful variety is what constitutes timing. The deliberate regulation of tempo, pitch, and emotion gives impact, whether in drama, music, or a commercial announcement.

Economy

Most programs need a good editor, for what is left out is equally important as what is retained. Every element should be purposeful. Radio is an intimate medium, one which needs understatement if it is to wear well. Radio must be conditioned to long-term success, not simply short-term popularity. Radio will be difficult to listen to over time if its elements are constantly overplayed. Slight understatement wears best.

Grace

Grace is the elegance of skill possessed by so many of the great artists and athletes; grace is the form that convinces spectators that, with a little practice, they too can be superstars—until they try duplicating that skill. This grace cannot result without exceptional skill and the polish added by careful preparation. Ease of presentation—grace—makes for easier listening, brings a smoother flow to the program, and instills a subtle, positive influence in the listener. Frequently, the main ingredient contributing to grace is thorough preparation, which gives a smoother feel to presentations because of the confidence that controlling more of the variables gives.

Novelty

Radio has constant need for the new and fresh, for the surprise that promises escape from the too familiar. But as people do like the security of their conventions, novelty, like variety, must be balanced with the familiar.

Human Interest

People are interested in themselves and others like them. Each of us, to a degree, wants the world to be reflected in our own image. The little personal, homey traits or comments that may not really amount to much can still have the effect of making the listeners like an announcer or a station.

Humor

Humor is a topic for a separate book. Suffice it to say that people like to laugh. For the most part, people like humor that makes them feel comfortable and does not threaten them. Although people have their private jokes in which they say the unsayable, most people do not like humor of a public nature that is at the expense of others. They react negatively to that humor which publicly pokes fun at another's cherished beliefs, his race, or his religion. People are "turned off" by what they feel is slapstick, vulgar, corny, or sick.

There is an endless supply of humor. There always will be new jokes because there always will be new fads, happenings, and experiences that can be joked about. Much of humor is based on exaggeration about everyday situations. A reverse angle or surprise ending to a commonplace event or familiar story can make people laugh. The incompatible, the absurd, the incongruous, and the unusual circumstance all can make people laugh. So much of the humor is dependent upon the manner of presentation, the personal sensitivity and characteristics of the humorist, and the appropriateness to the occasion. There are many types and levels of humor. Many different types of humor work for different kinds of people.

Involvement and Participation

The success of entertainers who involve the audience in the act is widespread. Radio is not a two-way medium, except for telephone talk shows. Radio cannot involve the audience in the way the hypnotist or folk singer can involve his live audience. Yet, in radio, as in other media, much of the real show takes place inside the spectator or listener. One kind of involvement is to stimulate the listener to think along with the announcer, or sing along with him, or take some action he advocates. Another kind of participation is community involvement. The people of the community are affected by hearing about the station's participation. They are also affected by hearing themselves speaking on news and other programs, or merely being mentioned. Audience participation can take many forms. The teenager who uses the station's music as a rallying point for social interaction is a kind of participant, as is the person who enters a contest or follows his favorite baseball team. The greater the interaction between the station and the community, the greater the station's chances for success.

Buildup

Attracting audience attention, establishing interest, and creating anticipation are all vital factors of "building up" a coming attraction. Ed Sullivan used the buildup for more than twenty years on his television show, announcing a top star several times during the show before the star finally appeared near the end of the program. When Larry "The Legend" Johnson hosted an all-night telephone talk program on WIND, Chicago, he would place a telephone call to a famous or an off-beat person, but it frequently would take three hours to get the call through; meanwhile, the anticipation built up. When he called "to see if the buzzards really do come back to Hinckley, Ohio," or to see "if there really are Pygmies in Peru," or when he started on Monday to make his phone call to Yugoslavia and it got through on Thursday, the phone call itself was not nearly as much fun as the "chase" getting there. The anticipation, "getting there," is much of the fun.

Using Spoken Language

One of the frequent mistakes of inexperienced radio newsmen and announcers who are quite capable of fluent *written* language is that they carry it over into radio where *spoken* language is demanded. On radio it is necessary to speak in language that will be understood readily by the listener. An announcer must not sound like a talking book. Extremely complicated sentences, phrases, and words are better left to print where the reader can reread, stop, think, and go on at his own pace. *Exacerbate, contumely,* and *troglodytic* are better left unsaid.

Personality

Individual performers need to express personality, and stations also need personality. Since so many stations are basically alike, the personality of a station makes the unique ingredient that separates it from the competition. A station and program host alike need to convince the audience that they are "good fellows," that the audience's interests and concerns are theirs as well.

Attitude is most important to radio communication. Since radio is direct, intimate, personal, and non-group oriented, the kind of communication that is most effective is the direct, face-to-face, informal, and friendly kind of presentation appropriate to a living room or patio. Such phrases as "Hello, out there" and "Good evening, everybody" and the attitude that accompanies such statements are out of place in modern radio.

A station's announcers should sound intelligent by always being well informed about whatever it is they are trying to communicate. If they can say interesting or entertaining things, and if they are friendly, warm, informal, relaxed, and natural, they are most apt to be successful. Announcers should talk *to* listeners rather than *at* them, sounding more interested in the listeners than in themselves. People like their air personality to be enthusiastic and cheerful in a way that does not sound forced. They like a sense of humor, but that does not mean air personalities constantly have to tell jokes or be funny.

Quintilian's old pronouncement about a good speaker being a good man speaking well has merit, because much of what a man is comes through on the air. Not all good air personalities lead exemplary lives, but off the air they must be, at least in part, what they seem to be on the air. Radio management prefers announcers to "be themselves" rather than to be actors, because acting and "being a personality" demand quite different approaches. If an announcer is on the air every day for five years, his steady listeners get to know him quite well. Highly important is an attitude of being honest with people, of wanting to communicate something—to reach out to other people. Basic sincerity is a desired characteristic for communicators, even for humorists. Another quality that complements sincerity well is liking people.

There was a time in American broadcasting when every on-air personality had to have a deep, well-modulated voice. Many announcers stuck their fingers in their ears to better hear the music of their own voices, enunciated like British actors, and functioned as unctuous mechanical men. Those days are gone. Now, the reverence for the sound of words and the staged approach has given over to informality. Today's audience is more interested in what is said than in hearing a display of virtuosity, although this is not to say that good voices are not important. Audiences still prefer soothing, pleasant, soft, deep voices. Sloppy pronunciation, nasal voices, and inarticulateness are not liked by audiences. Smoothness and polish are still desired. Understatement with emphasis on content and what is done with the voice rather than just the fact of having a good voice are emphasized today. Polish without ostentation is most effective.

People like good pronunciation, pleasant voices, and appealing mannerisms. They like to hear people who appear accurately informed, with clear, understandable deliveries. They like the sense of effortless skill that comes from professional competence. They like concise, clean, direct language.

Audiences do not like air personalities who are affected, monotonous, brassy, irritating, too sweet, or too folksy. They dislike an announcer with a superior attitude, a conceited snob, or one who is too sarcastic, hostile, or sharptongued. Audiences do not like a person who appears to be phony, who is too biased, who has a chip on his shoulder, or who is immature. They dislike announcers who are uninformed, overenthusiastic or overemotional, trying too hard to be funny, or who resort to off-color or tasteless jokes.

Since the announcer is the voice of the station while he is on the air—the intermediary between the listener and a good share of the message—he is one of the station's most important products. An inexperienced announcer working for a minimum wage is apt to give the station a less than professional sound.

An announcer contributes more to a station's personality than just his vocal presence on the air. He is usually the team captain of every program in which he is involved. He is in many cases his own engineer and operator, and is nearly always the producer in charge. Aside from a few large stations, the day of the separate radio producer-director is gone, with a few exceptions such as some special programs or commercial recording sessions done by an advertising agency. An announcer takes direction from his station manager, his program director, and, to a degree, the station's sales department in handling commercial matter. But he is generally the person with the million-dollar station at his fingertips. For this reason, radio may be thought of as an announcer's medium. It might be argued that radio and television are both salesmen's media because of the large role of advertising and because most managers come up through sales. The most important link to the people, however, is the announcer-producer.

Suggestions for Further Learning

1. Analyze three commercials that are heard on radio in your area. Which do you like best? Least? Which will do the most effective job of selling the product? Give reasons for each of your decisions.

2. Analyze a program hour. How many different voices are heard in that hour? What is the source of each? Network? Recording? Live? In your view, what do the voice changes do for the programing?

3. Choose an air personality you like, another you dislike. State your reasons in each case. Find someone who has different opinions. See if discussion brings new insights and appreciation for the other view.

CHAPTER 4

The Physical and Operational Plant

The modern radio station has changed as markedly in its physical operations as it has in its program content and format from the days of network dominance. The most important event to affect modern radio program production methods occurred even before the heavy pressures of television programing competition—the development of the audio tape recorder and playback units. With the tape recorder, radio was freed from studio production of programing. Programs can be edited after production instead of being pretimed and fully scripted before production, as they were when broadcasts were live before a studio audience. As in motion pictures and television, post-production editing and assembling of the final broadcast version for radio has become as important as preproduction planning and the production phase, either on location or in-studio. Although before tape it was possible, even with some awkardness, to record radio programs via disc and wire recording, it was virtually impossible to properly edit a radio program and totally impossible to record remote program materials with the necessary fidelity. Sound effects that now can be recorded authentically at the source of the sound were simulated in the studio by mechanical and electrical means. An entire element of the production team was built around the sound effects man's ability to recreate sound.

The tape recorder changed the daily production schedule. Most program elements now can be prerecorded, developed bit by bit, assembled in the control room (or separate production room), and offered for broadcast at the scheduled time originating from a tape playback unit.

The term "actuality" in news is applied because events can be recorded as they happen. Content is recorded using many production techniques to provide a constant flow of information about events as they occur. The audio tape recorder has been constantly refined so that today we have miniaturized, simply operated, high-fidelity units for remote production and highly sophisticated, multi-track, and even computer-directed units (such as the MCI, the Scully, the Stephens, and the Ampex ART-100) for studio production.

Studio programing in the sense of the large team production is all but obsolete. The radio-drama production team that consisted of director, engineer, sound effects man, announcers, actors, and musicians assembled for one program rarely exists today, except for a handful of syndicated and network programs. Drama, when performed for radio, is produced in recording studios capable of handling complex productions of all sorts.

Radio production is exceedingly personal. One man with a tape recorder can conceive a program, devise its format, record its content, and edit it into its final broadcast shape to be aired at a time most likely to reach the audience intended for that program.

An announcer has become less a continuity agent filling in information between programs and more a communicator who controls program material from various sources simultaneously and places it into an entertaining and informative format that makes immediate sense to the listener. A modern radio station must be constructed and equipped so as to allow the varying content fed to the station to be prepared for broadcast with the greatest versatility and immediacy.

Since broadcasting is evolving constantly, and since the student can be kept up-to-date through manufacturers' catalogues and brochures, this chapter will not delve in detail into the operation of equipment components. Rather, it will deal with the operational rationale in terms of programing for the broadcast system that has evolved to serve the contemporary radio audience.

Studio Layout

Whether a station is large or small, FM or AM, with separate announcer and engineer or a combination operation, basically the same kinds of equipment are necessary for the smooth, professional operation of the station. The studio is more of an electronic office than it is a studio, in the sense of production development. Figure 4.1 is a line drawing of the sophisticated broadcast facility of station KFI, in Los Angeles. Photographs of the studio layout (Figures 4.2 through 4.5) confirm that the modern radio station, incorporating all of the "state-of-the-art" hardware, must be "human engineered" as well, so that the broadcast facility may serve the human element. Modern radio stations with the right formats have married automation and the human element in a harmonious, relaxed studio atmosphere The result is

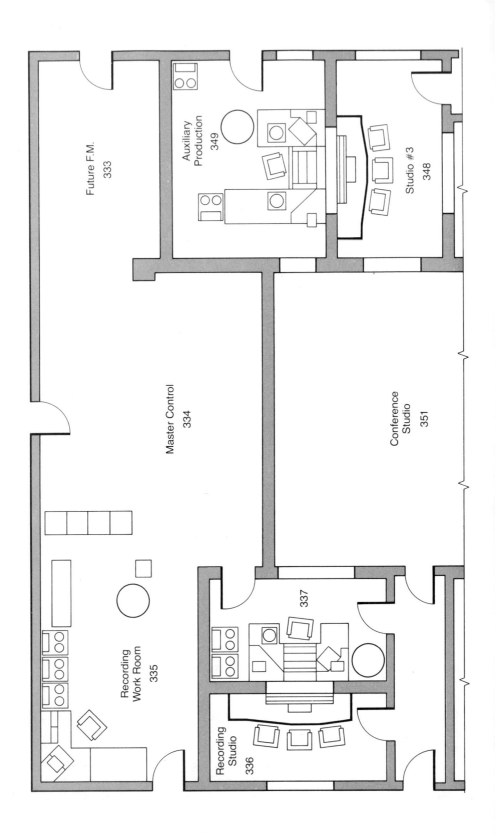

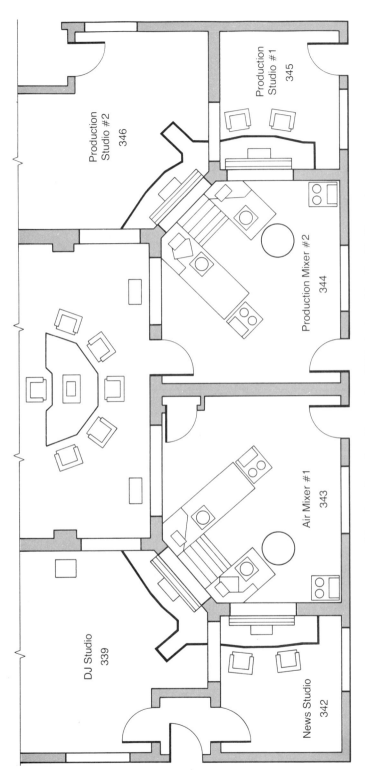

Figure 4.1 Line drawing of radio station KFI, designed by Pacific Recorders and Engineering Corp. Most programing originates in the Air Mixer #1/DJ Studio/News Studio shown lower left. The Production Area at right is an exact duplicate, and can be used for production or air. The large studio in the center is used for talk shows and shows with guests. Only the studio area is shown. News room, offices, etc. are not shown. Figures 4.2 through 4.5 show views of the studios.

Figure 4.2 Showing the Engineer/Operator in KFI Air Mixer #1. The DJ is in DJ Studio. The window to the right shows the Conference Studio.

freedom from the drudgery of routine performance that automation can do better, so that the talented broadcaster may spend his or her time more profitably to conceive, create, and enjoy the business of being broadcasters. You will note that the control and production facilities are usually large enough for one person (seldom more than two or three) to work in comfortably. The control room must have microphones of good quality, variable-speed turntables, cartridge tape units, and one or more reel-to-reel tape recorders. Stations that depend upon a large amount of talk programing undoubtedly will develop a news-and-discussion studio where panel-type programs may be produced. If a station's policy is to have the announcer read the news, then no separate news booth is necessary as long as the news area is easily available to the announcer-engineer so that he may return

Figure 4.3 Production Mixer #2. Production Studio #2 is at left, Production Studio #1 at right.

quickly to the broadcast control area. Some stations still have large studios. Although a studio may be used rarely for production, it can be, and often is, the only room in the plant large enough for staff meetings.

A sophisticated radio station serving a medium or large market well may have program lines, two-way radio, or telephone communication with the following sources:

1. Traffic cars and/or helicopters or airplanes
2. Weather bureau
3. Stock brokers and investment business houses
4. Police station headquarters and highway patrol

Figure 4.4   From the Engineer/Operator's chair.

5. Mayor's office and city hall
6. Recreation areas for beach and ski conditions
7. Sports arenas and stadiums
8. Telephone connection for listener participation

In addition to these sources, a station will have network lines if the station is affiliated with a network.

Commercials may be produced by advertising agencies or written and produced in the station. In metropolitan stations, virtually all spots come through an agency. In smaller stations and smaller markets, most of the material will be written and produced in the station.

A larger station, utilizing separate announcers and engineers, may have "intercom" systems that allow an announcer to monitor all

Figure 4.5 Loman and Barkley's view of their DJ show at KFI.

studios, talk via two-way radio, monitor network feeds, and talk with his engineer and other departments that are preparing and updating program material for him to use in the course of his broadcast schedule.

The modern studio is an acoustically treated workshop, sound-insulated from outside noise and vibration. The announcer has high-quality microphones for optimum voice fidelity.

Control Layout

A program control room may feed the program signal to a master control, or it may operate as a master control itself. Many large stations have decentralized the master control function in the interest of maximum versatility. Therefore, each control console should be as complete and versatile as possible. Many radio equipment manufacturers, such as Gates, Collins, McCurdy, and RCA, make consoles with the capability required of the modern radio station. A growing number of FM stations are broadcasting in stereo, and a few even are broadcasting four-channel quadraphonic stereo. All equipment must be capable of recording and playing back stereo programs and must be compatible with the monaural sound of the announcer and with monaural program material that is not available in stereo.

The control room is where all of the program elements are put together for broadcast. In addition to the console, there should be no less than two variable-speed turntables, two or three cartridge tape playbacks so that multiple commercial, public service, and promotional announcements or production effects may be played back to back, and two or three reel-to-reel tape recorders necessary for all production and on which entire programs can be recorded and played for broadcast. Programs may be delayed for later broadcast from such sources as the network feed or special telephonic feeds from the scenes of events. Or a Washington bureau may provide special materials to each station within a group ownership. These materials can be used as a program or be integrated into other programs.

An announcer's voice is almost the only sound that is broadcast live from a radio station. Even traffic alerts and news items may be recorded in their entirety and checked for appropriateness and quality. The lines from a traffic car or trafficopter can be "normaled" (fed directly without special switching) to tape recorders that automatically record information as it is sent down the line or from two-way radio. Telephone reports also can be recorded automatically if a station has the necessary equipment.

The heart of the broadcast operation is the control console. It must accept program materials from multiple sources and must be able to send the integrated program to multiple feeds. Regardless of the kind of console used, it must have monitor and cue facilities so that the operator can preview and hear the output of the console during all operations. Whether potentiometers (volume controls) have slide or rotary control, sound levels must be faded smoothly without distortion. Each console must have the capability of handling multiple microphone and turntable feeds, cartridge playbacks, reel-to-reel tapes, and remote lines.

Station WBEN, in Buffalo, and the Ward-Beck Systems of Toronto, in designing new, modern radio facilities, set about to totally support their broadcast personnel with digital electronics and automation technology. The console in Master Control incorporates a full random-access automation system. The board is designed to be operated either "combo" by the air talent or with an engineer at the console and talent in an adjacent studio. (See Figure 4.1 for KFI's studio arrangement.) A random-access sequencer, designed by Ward-Beck, is built into this console. This sequencer will start turntables, cart machines, and reel-to-reel playbacks while up to fifteen events can be fed into the sequencer at all times. Once the sequencer is armed to carry out a series of specific events, the talent can control all of its activities with three push buttons. CANCEL dumps whatever is in the sequencer, so that it can be rearmed with new commands. HOLD places the sequencer into a mode where it does not see its commands and therefore does not react to them. And RESTART produces a tone signal which will instantly restart the sequencer and play its next previously stored event. This system provides a maximum of support and a minimum of technical responsibility for the air personality. He goes on the air "live," with the sequence of events on his show all set up. He starts the sequence by pushing one button, and while it is running he is free to create his material for a later sequence. Some may fear such automation, but any program host who has ever cued up cut 15 on a reel-to-reel tape will love it.

The control consoles in the production studios are duplicates of the broadcast console, but also include controls for adding equalization and reverberation (for an explanation of equalization and reverberation, see pages 97–98 below). KFI and WBEN duplicate the consoles in each studio in exact detail so that personnel may interchange facilities without having to readjust their production techniques to fit the idiosyncrasies of different kinds of equipment requiring different operational procedures. Line-of-sight, microphone channels, and intercoms are maintained between all studios and announcing booths.

The control console must be able to send the program to its desired destination. Obviously, the signal is sent to the transmitter for broadcast. But it also may be fed to telephone lines that send the program to a distant destination, such as a network origination. The program may be sent to a recorder from which the program may originate in a later broadcast. Large-market stations record the signal for later aircheck and for FCC reference on special recorders recording at the speed of $15/16$ inch per second. Using a four-track tape machine, this recording can provide a record of (1) what is fed to the transmitter, (2) what gets transmitted, (3) all two-way radio communications, and (4) continuing time checks that help the station to find the information on the other three tracks.

Remote Facilities

The most important article of remote gear is the portable audio tape recorder such as those manufactured by Sony, Norelco, Uher, Nagra, Tandberg, and Wollensak. A reporter ranging far from his station can record program elements that can be incorporated into a newscast or edited and re-recorded for a documentary or actuality program.

Station personnel at work within the community may use telephone lines leased from the telephone company. The lines vary in quality from Class E and D lines for short-distance voice signals to long-line music feeds of 50 to 15,000 cycles per second (herz). Costs vary from Class AAA for continuous use to Class BBB for occasional line utilization.

Citizen band or FM two-way radio is absolutely necessary for transmitting information from news mobile units and trafficopters. In addition, some sophisticated news departments may even monitor short-wave international broadcasts for incorporation into news programs or for reference material for the news writers.

Many stations develop mobile studios to take advantage of the community interest in air personalities. Such studios often are located in trailers or minibuses and consist of a remote amplifier, microphones, and two or more turntables for music. Even when it is feasible to play the music from the studios, stations often will play music "on remote" so that listeners at the remote spot can get some idea of what occurs during the broadcast schedule. Sometimes, tape cartridge machines are provided in the unit so that commercial messages may originate on location. A reel-to-reel tape recorder also can be useful. Remote units that fold like a card table can be bought for easy transportation and be set up in remote locations. At locations where remotes are scheduled on a regular basis, a microphone, a one-channel amplifier (preferably with fixed volume), and a telephone intercom should be installed on a permanent basis.

Remote lines may have a separate PL (private line) intercom. However, most stations use a single line for both broadcast and "cue-back" to conserve expense. The remote key on the control console at the studio ordinarily has three positions: (1) *override*—to allow the remote operator or announcer to call in and be heard over the station's monitor system; (2) *cue and talk*—to feed the intercom at the console to the remote so that cue signals and cue information can be discussed between operators; and (3) *broadcast*—to feed the remote line into the program bus and thus through the console in the manner of regular broadcasts.

ENG (Electronic News Gathering) is very much a part of the latest technical capabilities of television broadcasting, allowing the television

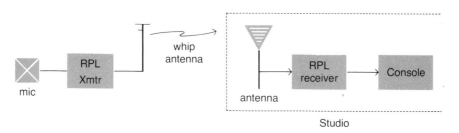

Figure 4.6 Route that an RPL signal can follow.

newscaster to broadcast from remote locations instantly and immediately with lightweight, miniaturized, portable equipment. Radio ENG has been around for a long while without being recognized for its full versatility. Such equipment as high-powered wireless microphones, tone control systems, and mobile repeaters are hardly revolutionary, but putting these items together to make up a highly versatile remote system is a recent innovation. The Comrex Corporation has developed a system which allows reporters and other air talent to broadcast studio quality sound while remaining completely mobile, transforming the reporter into "a walking radio station" able to broadcast the remote event with quality sound. The audio cassette unit allows recorded sound to be mixed on-air with the live signal from the microphone.

RPL's (Remote Pickup Links) are small, easily portable, personnel remote transmitters and antennas which can send a remote signal back to either the studio or to the station transmitter directly. These RPL's can be used in a variety of configurations in conjunction with the normal program route from studio to transmitter via the STL (studio/transmitter link) and via a TSL (transmitter/studio link) which enables a signal to travel from the station transmitter back to the studio. Figures 4.6 and 4.7 show the various set-ups and routes that an RPL signal can follow.

The remote broadcaster can either pack the RPL with the antenna on his person or place the antenna at a point where it has line of sight to

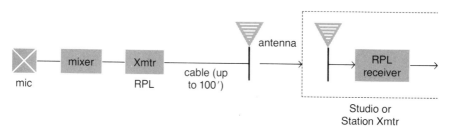

Figure 4.7 Route that an RPL signal can follow.

the studio or to the transmitter. The latter setup is used when the transmitter pack is too bulky for the situation or where line of sight between transmitting and receiving antennas cannot be maintained for quality sound. Figure 4.8 shows the flow of the remote signal from the RPL unit to either the studio or the station transmitter in either direction. The remote signal can go to either the studio or to the station transmitter first, depending upon which site offers the better signal route, and then back to the studio (if to the transmitter first) for mix with other program elements.

RPL units operate in the VHF frequency range of 152–170 MHz and in the UHF spectrum of 450–470 MHz. They are relatively lightweight at 20 to 26 pounds, are approximately 6¼" × 15" × 12" in size, and are modest in price.

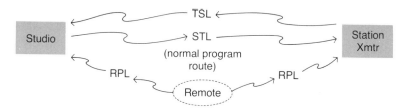

Figure 4.8   Flow of the remote signal from the RPL unit.

Broadcast Sequence

The student needs as much practice handling program elements in sequence as he can possibly get, working either alone or with an engineer. The following example from a major-market station's morning shift may be of value as a guide. This sequence contains records, phone calls both outgoing and incoming, two-way radio reports, recorded reports on semiautomated systems (such as a Sigalert[1] from state highway patrol headquarters), news filed by a newsman on remote, a UPI audio report prerecorded on reel-to-reel tape transports, and a live studio guest. The 40-minute sequence might be arranged as follows:

1. Engineer plays station-ID cartridge (10 sec.) leading into:

2. Cartridge—standard format introduction of news program

---

[1] Sigalert is a term used to indicate an official highway patrol information bulletin of traffic information, so-named because it was developed by Lloyd Sigman, one-time station manager of KMPC in Hollywood.

3. News announcer—separate studio

4. Commercial insert—on cartridge

5. News—news announcer

6. Traffic report (three remotes in sequence) from two-way radio
   a. Traffic car
   b. Trafficopter
   c. Sigalert recorded from highway department

7. News—news announcer

8. UPI audio report—recorded reel-to-reel tape

9. News—news announcer

10. Closing news format read by newsman

11. 5-second ID—cartridge

12. Commercial cartridge

13. 10-second music intro of air personality—from announcing booth

14. 1st record—turntable in control room

15. Patter by air personality and live commercial

16. 2nd record—control room

17. Patter by air personality

18. Commercial—cartridge control room

19. Air personality makes telephone call (phone in announcing booth) to a woman whose name was sent in for "sexy voice" contest—beeper phone

20. 3rd record—control room

21. Guest live in studio—kidding air personality about the contest

22. Spot on cartridge with 30-second live insert in middle by announcer

23. 4th record—from studio

24. 30-second live spot with cartridge tag

25. 30-second commercial—cartridge in control room

26. 5th record—control room turntable

27. Commercial—read live by air personality

28. Station promo and ID—cartridge in control room

29. Patter by air personality, introduces news headlines

30. News heads—from news studio—60 seconds

31. 60-second commercial—cartridge in control room

32. 60-second feature story on White House—recorded from network lines by group Washington correspondent—story featuring wife of government official—recorded only a few minutes before ac-

tual airing along with two other features to be used in later news broadcasts

33. Air personality gives weather and intros

34. 6th record—control room

35. Commercial—live by air personality

36. Patter by air personality—gives phone number for those who wish to phone in to "Radio's Beloved Answer Man"—studio

37. Incoming phone calls—aired from studio as air personality jokes and talks with persons phoning in questions—four phone calls answered in approximately two minutes

38. 7th record

39. Et cetera—et cetera

In this example, the station uses an engineer and an announcer. Most announcers work "combo," in which the air personality is his own engineer. An air personality must work well with his engineer, if he has one, and, if not, must be doubly talented to combine all of the elements of his program from different pieces of equipment. The program log by and large sets up the order of program elements, yet the air personality and the engineer have freedom for instant judgments. They learn to anticipate each other through constant practice, informing each other by intercom, hand signals, and light and buzzer cues in both the control room and the studio.

Cartridge Tape Equipment

The modern radio station has come to depend upon the use of cartridge tape systems more and more. These systems provide a more convenient method of programing than was previously afforded by the conventional turntables and reel-to-reel tape equipment. In many stations, cartridge tape systems have largely replaced turntables and reel-to-reel machines in the reproduction of spots, themes, station breaks, intros, and other program material of this nature. The engineering department of the National Association of Broadcasters (NAB) has developed a booklet concerning cartridge tapes, entitled "Operation and Maintenance of Cartridge Tape Equipment." The NAB also has published other papers regarding broadcast operations of value to the student of radio.

Cartridge tape units consist of playback-only units or playback and record units. The playback-only units are less expensive and can be used any time that a record unit is not needed. The cartridges are loaded with a continuous loop of recording tape and vary in length. At the start of each spot or other recorded segment, a tone is recorded. This tone is recorded automatically on one of the two tracks when the "record" button is pushed to start the taping of the material to be reproduced on the other track. When the tape plays through to the point where the tone is located, the tone triggers a mechanism that stops the tape; the tape thus is automatically cued up at the segment's beginning. Using the proper length cartridge is important, because if only one minute of material is recorded on a five-minute cartridge, it will take five minutes for the tape to recue itself. Additional tones may be placed on the tape to trigger automation gear or merely to turn on a light that signals the end of the spot, offering a visual cue that aids in tight production.

The cartridge is being improved constantly. Similar progress is being made with cassette tape recorders. Both manual production and automation gear are finding new uses for both types of tape.

A four-track cartridge can provide two tracks of erasable audio, one track of auxiliary tone and data (also erasable), and one track of stop tone and clocking (not erasable). This permits the erasing and re-recording of any single event on the cartridge without disturbing any other event. The auxiliary control tone will cause the cartridge tape to rewind automatically until it "sees" the clear leader, at which time it will stop, play forward, and cue to the first stop tone. The ease of using this kind of equipment will make it very attractive to many modern radio stations.

Stereophonic Broadcasting

Stereo operation of FM radio was approved by the Federal Communications Commission in April 1961. Installing a system that broadcasts high-fidelity stereophonic sound, while preserving compatible reception of monaural sound as well as means to multiplex SCA signals, has provided new interest in FM broadcasting.

The stereo system simulates the natural separation of sound caused by the spacing between people's ears. People hear two distinct sounds, enabling them to localize the directions from which the sounds emanate. The stereo transmission provides this same depth perception by providing separate left and right channels of sound reproduced on left and right speakers. The center sound appears when both left and right signals have equal intensity, giving the effect of monaural sound on two or more speakers. The left and right channels of sound may be provided by separate phased microphones or by stereo record pickups and stereo magnetic-tape heads. A stereo signal is made up of the combination of sum and difference signals between the left and right channels:

$$\text{Sum} = L + R$$
$$\text{Difference} = L - R$$

The L + R signal would produce a compatible aural program in the monophonic receiver.

If the proper control of sound levels is difficult for monaural systems, it is easy to recognize the complexity of stereophonic sound. The stereo control console provides duplicate channels for feeding two output lines—the left and the right channels. Each channel is monitored by its own VU meter and has identical frequency response and phase characteristics. The announcer's microphone can feed either channel or can feed both the left and right channels to provide monophonic sound, depending upon the design of the console. If the announcer is to be heard in stereo, two microphones must be used in the control room.

To record in stereo, each channel must be served by one or more microphones placed so that the center axis of each microphone points along the sides of an equilateral triangle; the placement is correct if a tone sounded at the test point for either microphone is at least 15 to 20 decibels higher than for the microphone away from the tone source. A tone sounded from a center test point theoretically equidistant from the left and right test points should result in equal amplitude from both microphones. Additional microphones assigned to each channel specialize in reproducing sound from a certain pickup area for each channel. Soloists create a problem, since the positioning of microphones for the proper pickup of right and left channels may be so far removed from the soloist as to cause loss of presence. A solo microphone must be placed carefully to prevent loud center sound that might cancel out the natural effects of stereo left-right channel separation. Whenever possible, such as in studio production, the soloist should be isolated in a sound booth and recorded on a separate track for later dubbing. Where isolation is impossible, such as during a live performance, careful blending of the soloist's microphone must be controlled by closing the microphone except when the soloist is actually performing. Recording in stereo requires a great deal of practice.

In the case of stereo voice pickup, microphone placement and movement are all-important. Since the vocal effect depends upon placement throughout the room as well as movement from one part of the room to another, it is impossible to open and close microphones and move people from one channel area to another without considering the problem of maintaining the proper blend of multiple sound sources. Sound presence and the relationship of foreground to background sound are the greatest problems in stereophonic recording and pickup. The illusion of dimension and realism can be provided only if there is an opposite channel sound "leaking" into the dominant "lead" channel.

The use of stereo includes experimental sound combinations as well as simply trying to make sound more real by providing separation and thereby improving presence. Using stereo for its own qualities, thus making possible unusual combinations and effects for their own sake (especially in quad stereo), offers many opportunities for unusual listening experiences. Much experimentation has been done in music recording sessions with the use of 8, 16, 24, or even 32 tracks, unusual mixes, and natural and electronic effects. For some time, the recording industry has been recording nearly everything in multiple tracks that can be mixed interestingly for quad stereo.

Binaural sound is accomplished by using two microphones at the recording source to copy the sound field that two ears would have heard. The microphones are placed on both sides of a dummy head or with a barrier between them, giving the time, phase, and frequency differences similar to in-person listening. At the receiving end, the only requirement is that the person use headphones rather than normal speakers. Binaural is a relatively simple two-channel recording system that requires no new equipment or techniques at the broadcasting station. It can coexist with present or future stereo systems. It has not been widely used, because of the more widely used stereo systems.

AM stereo broadcasting is rapidly developing into a viable broadcasting system. As FM stereo radio stations are providing an increasingly popular program service, many AM stations have found themselves at a competitive disadvantage in their communities. AM stereo may be an ideal way to compete, since AM stereo appears to be readily adaptable to existing AM installations at a moderate cost. The AM station operator welcomes AM stereo as a way of keeping and enlarging the automobile audience, which is essential to AM predominance over FM broadcasting. Pressure from AM broadcasters for a stereo system has been more and more evident as FM stereo stations in many communities have won strong competitive positions with their two-channel operations.

The AM-FM system of generating a compatible stereo signal is fairly simple. An ordinary AM receiver will demodulate the AM sidebands only to produce the $L + R$, or mono signal. To demodulate the $L - R$ sidebands, the receiver must contain an FM detector. A "new" carrier containing all of the FM sidebands of the $L - R$, or difference signal, provides the stereo information. This "new" carrier is amplified and processed to add the AM sidebands to the carrier so that the output of the transmitter contains two information channels—the AM containing the $L + R$ or monaural information, and the FM containing the $L - R$ or stereo information.

The AM-FM system is one example of a compatible stereo system that will not make present-day monaural receivers obsolete. It is clear that the time is right to seriously consider AM stereo as a viable broadcast service.

Quadraphonic (4-channel) Broadcasting (also called quadrasonic)

Recorded sound strives continually to perfectly emulate live sound. Since people exist in three-dimensional space, perfect sound reproduction requires that recorded sound also exist in three dimensions— left-right, front-back, and up-down.

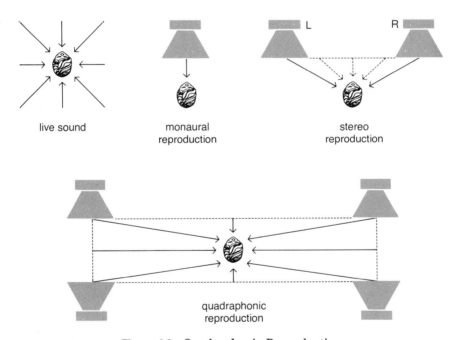

| live sound | monaural reproduction | stereo reproduction |

quadraphonic reproduction

Figure 4.9 Quadraphonic Reproduction

Quadraphonic broadcasting adds front-back information to the existing left-right stereophonic signal in one of two ways. Four-channel FM can be obtained either by a discrete transmission system where four channels of discrete information are used, or by matrixing the four-channel information (LF − LB, RF − RB) onto the present two-channel stereo system. At present, the discrete system is only being tested, while the matrix system has been used by at least one FM radio station in every major market in the country (not always with positive results).

The National Quadraphonic Radio Committee of the Electronic Industries Association has completed extensive research into the feasibility of a discrete system of four-channel FM broadcasting. The NQRC concludes that discrete four-channel FM is thoroughly practical with present FM broadcast technology. In a direct comparison between the discrete and matrix systems, listeners tested in the NQRC research project strongly preferred the discrete four-channel reproduction to the matrixed two-channel reproduction sound. The tests clearly demonstrated the viability of quadraphonic broadcast services both from the practical and the quality aspects. Currently, FM broadcasts are licensed for monophonic and two-channel stereophonic (biphonic) programs, but, following the NQRC report, at least five corporations, including RCA, Zenith, and General Electric, have developed four-channel discrete FM systems.

Quadraphonic broadcasting has the ability to reproduce and broadcast sounds occurring at any point in 360°, and to reproduce each sound from the correct location in playback and broadcast. Thus the discrete system is the ultimate in three-dimensional sound. While the matrix reproduction of sound is a significant improvement over the two-channel stereo sound, the discrete system carries this improvement to a full four-channel sound whose superior quality is immediately apparent to the listener.

Stereo, quad, and multiplex signals (Subsidiary Communication Authorization) are possible in FM broadcasting because the channel bandwidth for FM is 200 KHz, which is a larger range of frequencies than is needed for even the highest fidelity monophonic sound. All of the frequencies necessary to broadcast quadraphonic sound using the discrete system can be accommodated in one FM broadcast channel. Four discrete audio signals 15,000 Hz wide can be broadcast by using the existing main channel, the 38 KHz stereophonic subchannel as defined in the present FCC rules, and two additional subcarriers which carry the amplitude modulation. The four signals are universally designated as follows:

$$M = LF + LB + RB + RF$$
$$X = LF - LB - RB + RF$$
$$Y = LF + LB - RB - RF$$
$$U = LF - LB + RB - RF$$

The main channel (M) carries the sum of all four stereo signals. This assures monophonic capability. The 38 KHz subcarrier of FM stereo carries two of the signals in phase quadrature. The 19 KHz pilot subcarrier is used as a reference for all of the quad signals. By putting the Y signal (LF + LB − RB − RF) on the 38 KHz subcarrier, two-channel stereo compatibility is provided. Stereo receivers will get the L + R on the main carrier and the L − R on the subcarrier, as they do now with two-channel FM. The front-minus-back X signal (LF − LB − RB + RF) or the criss-cross U signal (LF − LB + RB − RF) is placed on the 38 KHz subcarrier, while the fourth signal (either X or U) can be placed either on a subcarrier at 76 KHz or at 95 KHz.

In any case, it is apparent that quadraphonic broadcasting is entirely feasible, giving FM broadcast transmission a unique signal unduplicated by any other transmission system, including AM stereo. Its development has been slow, however, because of a slowness in settling on one system and developing and marketing it.

SCA (subsidiary communications authorization)

FM broadcasting has the ability, as previously mentioned, to broadcast several program signals simultaneously. Because the 200 KHz channel width offers a greater range of frequencies than any one audio signal needs, several signals or programs may be multiplexed on the carrier for simultaneous transmission. These multiplexed programs are referred to as SCA transmissions authorized by the FCC for very specific purposes and for audiences other than the general radio home audience. Many FM radio stations have used SCA broadcasting to provide specialized broadcasting services such as storecasting and background music services for offices and factories. Such services augment FM station revenues and can be the difference between profit and loss for an FM radio station. Companies such as Muzak lease SCA channels from stations to provide a music background service free of commercials for the waiting rooms of professional offices. SCA broadcasts are becoming more and more important as various services recognize how SCA can be used effectively. An entire network of medical information is being provided to doctors who subscribe to the service via SCA, since this is information which has little value for the general public and, in fact, could be potentially dangerous if not interpreted correctly. Public broadcasting stations are using SCA increasingly for public service projects. Several National Public Radio (NPR) stations are using SCA for a continuing radio reading service for the print handicapped. In communities that are bilingual, SCA can be used to translate popular television programs and other fare into the several native languages. SCA is proving to be an effective social tool for high-density Latin-American populations along the Mexican border and throughout the United States.

SCA broadcasting requires a special receiver which is crystal-tuned to the main channel of the FM station transmitting the SCA signal. The SCA is a part of the FM carrier, so it can only transmit when the FM station is on the air. The SCA generator is a part of the FM transmitter limited to the frequency band from 20 to 75 KHz above center for a monophonic FM service and a frequency band from 53 to 75 KHz for biphonic FM broadcasts. This translates into two SCA transmissions for monophonic FM and one SCA channel for FM stations broadcasting in stereo.

A company called Fax Net has even started publication of specialized "newspapers" using SCA. The first systems, in Chicago, Detroit, and Madison, Wisconsin, use FM subcarriers to transmit encoded electronic information activating a high-speed "radioprinter." Subscribers receive only those services they pay for, but time-sharing and signal multiplexing make it possible for one subscriber to receive different services on the same printer, paying for each service separately. In the Chicago area, through facilities of WCLR, retailers have received trade and general news, while stores of a grocery chain have received spot news, agriculture department bulletins, and market reports. In the Detroit area, the Macomb County school board has received an educational edition of Fax Net's news service. A banking edition has been transmitted to subscribing financial institutions in the Madison area through WLVE.

SCA service for specific purposes and for specific audiences is of growing interest for the radio broadcaster. Therefore, the broadcasting student might well consider the kinds of services a community might wish to have provided via SCA broadcasting.

Roadside Radio

A special government funded service to assist highway travelers in getting essential information operates in many areas on the AM frequencies 530 and 1610. The FCC calls this form of radio TIS, or Travelers' Information Station. Most broadcasters refer to it as Roadside Radio. TIS's are operated noncommercially by local and federal governmental agencies in the immediate vicinity of air, train, and bus terminals, public parks and historical sites, interstate highway interchanges, bridges, and tunnels. They provide information on road conditions, directions to parking lots, availability of lodging, and similar information. The stations operate on very low power and cover a limited area. Travelers are alerted to the service by roadside signs such as "For Park Information, 530 on Your AM Radio." Broadcasters have not been particularly happy about such stations because they feel that such services fragment their audiences that much more, and that they discriminate against FM.

Automation

Like the cartridge tape recorder that gave the broadcast operator instant availability and control of the broadcast day without an attendant, operator automation has severely changed the operating procedures of many modern radio stations.

Automation equipment is expensive and often is of such a sophisticated nature that specially trained people are required to operate and maintain it. A recognizable need for automation equipment must be evident before its purchase can be justified. The system must be capable of doing a better job than presently is being done at the same or a lower cost.

Automation has become an attractive way of providing music services for clients over a multiplex system. It also is attractive to the 24-hour station, which weighs the cost of automation against keeping an operator on duty during the nighttime hours.

Before deciding on the exact type of automated equipment, a radio station must analyze carefully its present and future requirements. These are some of the questions that need to be answered:

1. Is the system to be used for full-time programing or only for part-time utilization?
2. Is it compatible with any existing equipment that is to be incorporated into the total system?
3. Is it possible to add to the system in the future?
4. How much and what kind of maintenance will be required for the system?
5. Is it versatile enough to handle present needs and possible format changes in the future?
6. Are proper installation and space requirements satisfied?
7. Will special personnel training be needed?

Basic to all automation systems is the requirement that multiple program sources can be fed into a control unit that will select the right source at the right time. Several general types of systems have been developed that are being refined and upgraded constantly.

Reel-to-reel Music

Reel-to-reel simply refers to the traditional tape machine known as a deck or a transport. One or more tape decks can be mounted in an equipment rack and controlled by a clock mechanism or simple switching device so that the decks can be alternated in any pre-set manner.

Reel-to-reel Music and Cartridge
Tape Voice Tracks

Automated systems make full use of the cartridge tape, which alternates with music transports and uses various kinds of cue tones and switch units. Random selection of cartridges is available in all current systems.

The carousel multiple cartridge player, to use one example, holds twenty-four tape cartridges in a revolving drum. The playback head is stationary. As a cartridge appears in front of the head, it is pulled mechanically into position for play. When the tape has played, it is released from the head and the revolving drum advances to the next head. Another type of multiple-cartridge unit is used by the International Good Music system. In this system, fifty-five cartridges are placed in order of use in a stacking arrangement and remain stationary while the head mechanism moves from one to the next.

Switching Methods in Automation

Without reliable switching, modern automation would be impossible. The most basic method is the clock device. A clock trips a switch that (1) notifies the announcement tape that it is next on the schedule and (2) notifies the music tape to stop at the end of that selection. Since the clock itself cannot sense when the musical selection has ended, some form of electronic sensing must make the program-change decisions. A most widely used system is the subaudible tone. A 25-cycle tone is recorded between musical selections and after each announcement. These are used to cue each tape machine in sequence. Silent sensing can also be used, but, unfortunately, the rests and pauses in some music can cause certain systems, if set too tightly, to switch in the middle of a song. It is impossible to cue tightly with this system. A photoelectric cell may be used for switching by means of transparent windows in the tape. Metal foil strips applied to the recording tape can be used to trip a switching mechanism.

Although the most widely used method uses cue tones, a sophisticated automation system in a radio station could use all of the switching methods described here. Subaudible tones provide the bulk of the switching information between music and voice. The clock trips in special program sequences such as network feeds or time checks. The photoelectric window can cue up announcement tapes, while the metal strip can be used to reverse the direction of the music tape. The silent sensing device stands guard over the whole system, ready to take over if any unit should fail.

Over 500 AM and FM radio stations switched from manual to automated operations during 1974. Currently it is estimated that over 20 percent of all radio stations in the United States are now automated in some form and to some degree. If this present growth rate continues as expected, over one-half of all radio stations licensed in the country will be automated by 1980. Automation systems and program syndication (discussed in detail in another chapter of this text) have grown together, one dependent upon the other. Thus, more sophisti-

Figure 4.10 Traffic control center for WBEN-FM, Buffalo, New York, using Systems Marketing Corporation's DP-2 system. This system, using a microprocessor computer and a digitally controlled audio switcher and processor, can program the station for a full week. The twin monitors show current running program display but permit display of any part of the week's programing and allow for changes or additions to the memory instructions. Common with such systems are automatic logging, automatic network recording and playback, interfacing to other computers, and a master clock system.

cated program formats have developed more sophisticated automation equipment and vice versa, providing greater flexibility in enabling the broadcaster to achieve greater quality for his broadcast service.

Two of the largest manufacturers of automated broadcast systems are Schafer Electronics and SMC (Systems Marketing Corporation). Figures 4.10 and 4.11 show the SMC stereo-mono automation system

Figure 4.11 Control rack for Systems Marketing Corporation's DP-2 automation system in use at WBEN-FM, Buffalo, New York. The system has 40 channel switching, 8,000 programable events.

and the system operated entirely by digital computercasting. Figures 4.12 and 4.13 show the rotary and stacked cart system of organizing the cartridges in sequence for automated play.

Automated systems come in all types and sizes and in degrees of complexity that range from simple sequences to ultra-sophisticated systems with microprocessor control. The latest designs have CRT (cathode ray tube) readouts and disc memories which will store several thousand events at one time. Somehow the broadcaster must determine what kind of automation system will best fit his particular broadcast situation before he begins to sort out the manufacturer and model he desires. Indeed, the state-of-the-art is now at the point where the broadcaster utilizing syndicated programing, computerized business systems (discussed later in this chapter), and automation hard-

Figure 4.12 Systems Marketing Corporation carousel cartridge tape player. Any cartridge can be randomly selected in combination with manual or automated systems.

ware that can run a station for days without human operation, can operate under total automation conditions with almost no in-house effort.

The SMC DP-1 automation system consists of nine ITC reel-to-reel playback decks, four carousels, four single-play cartridge decks, and two time-announce units with drop-in capability. The DP-1's computer is digitally loaded with magnetic tape.

The Schafer/NTI-770, using a Digital Equipment Corporation PDP-8 computer as the controlling element, provides storage capacity for 19,200 program event instructions (eight full days of programing at 2,400 events per day); 9,999 descriptions of music, public service announcements (PSA's), ID's, and commercials; and up to seven days of complete program logs showing material actually broadcast as well as a pre-log based on planned programing. The #770 can sort titles of music, commercials, and PSA's in different ways for music and commercial rotation without fear of competitive products being placed

Figure 4.12 (continued)

Figure 4.13 Cetec Schafer multiple cartridge playback system. This unit allows three cartridges to be played simultaneously, can be used with manual or automated systems. Allows random access, can be programed sequentially.

back to back. The #770 allows three different levels of command entry. One level is by the program department, another is by the traffic department, and the third is by the engineering department for technical routines. Each department has its own password which gives it access to its area of the computer.

The Harris System #90 is run by a microcomputer. This system has a standard input capability of 16 sources and a memory of 1,200 events, which is expandable to 32 sources and 3,700 events. Program entries can be made on either a time or sequence basis. The computer puts them in the right order regardless of entry order in the carousels. Random access to the memory makes last-minute changes available.

These systems, among others, have operational features that make for total radio station automation, such as automatic network join and automatic voice tracking so that a recorded voice can be sequenced with music. They also have time-announce built in and provision for live air-talent to call up any individual item or any sequence he wishes at any time during the operation.

This latter feature describes the essence of station automation. It allows the on-air talent to create the program in the most effective and creative manner of which he is capable, and at the same time affords full program quality and control through the use of the automation system. Automation frees the creative people of the radio station from the time-tyranny of routine jobs so that they can improve the on-air sound of the radio station. Whatever talents the station's creative staff have, automation can multiply those talents and make them effective over a wider range of programing techniques.

In the past, many radio stations, especially those most competitively oriented in the largest markets, have not been able to succeed with automation. Even stations playing wall-to-wall music have dropped their automation systems or modified them to give a less impersonal quality to their programing. Others go live at key periods of the day and automate during fringe periods. Some have automation but bring in live announcers for some breaks to relieve the montony. Still others are trying to get a live sound by allowing the new generation of equipment to give, not an automated canned sound, but freedom from so many of the burdensome chores of cuing tapes and discs and pushing buttons. A lot of good air personalities are not technical geniuses or even slick board operators and would appreciate the freedom from technical chores.

Many are looking toward the day when their entire record libraries can be put on some kind of data retrieval system, even to the point of storing and playing the music by computer.

Two areas in particular have ramifications of special interest in broadcast operations. One is the technology just getting its start in video-disc. Flexible discs the size of phonograph records can store an enormous amount of information that can be "read" by laser sensors (without the physical contact required by the phonograph needle). This has great implications for sound alone, as well as for sound/visual information. These include improved sound quality, discs that don't wear out, and enormous savings of space. Another system, a digital method of storing a large amount of information, reads the information off IBM-size cards by means of scanners which do not physically touch the "card." This system, which can presently store a 30-minute film on a single "card," has enormous possibilities.

Such sophisticated hardware will not replace voices, or writers, or creative artists, or managers, or salesmen, but they will certainly alter the manner in which they work.

Computerized Business
Automation Systems

Several hundred radio and television stations have made the conversion to computerized automated business operations to take full advantage of EDP (electronic data processing) in the handling of sales, traffic, and accounting, as well as for programing and operations. The trend is to total automation based on an interface between the business system and automated switching. Recent surveys indicate great satisfaction with business automation by radio station administrators and owners. Most stations have experienced increases in efficiency of inventory utilization to more than justify the expense of the business automation system start-up costs. However, it is important to note that any station that is poorly organized or managed cannot expect that business automation will bring order out of chaos. The secret of successful business automation is strong and aggressive leadership at the station.

Several kinds of automation systems have been designed to perform complex clerical tasks at high speed. There are time-shared on-line systems, off-line batch systems, in-house minicomputer systems, network distributive systems, and systems that offer a combination of the above approaches. On-line system designs are based on the use of a large central computer, owned and operated by the system supplier and linked to their customers by telephone lines. The subscribers get the computer services on a time-shared basis by paying a monthly charge. The central-computer design is either on-line, where the subscriber is connected to the central computer at all times by dedicated telephone lines that are open twenty-four hours a day, or by distributive processing where a minicomputer is located at the station for immediate on-call attention to current jobs such as sales availabilities, daily logs, etc., which are needed quickly at any minute. Larger jobs requiring more "computer power" than the minicomputer can provide, but which are needed only periodically, are handled on a "batch" basis by the central computer, which can come on-line at stated times during a day or week.

Various firms offer specialized automation services to broadcasters. The choice of which one to use will depend as much upon the nature of the radio station as upon the computer service. Each station has its own way of operating and conducting its business. The computer automation service selected will undoubtedly be the one that most nearly conforms to the operating and management style of that radio or television station. A number of business automation systems are capable of serving the business organization of the radio station from operations to sales.

BCS (Broadcast Computing Service) is a time-shared, off-line broadcast automation service provided by the Kaman Sciences Corporation. BCS has been a leader in interfacing business and technical operations' automated systems. The BCS system using an on-site minicomputer creates the log (including all card numbers, sources, sponsors, etc.). It times the entire log exactly and adds other operational information needed in sequencing program elements. When the final log is completed, it is "dumped" into the minicomputer of the automated switching system, which generates the signals causing the switcher to perform automatically all of its operations called for by the schedule at the proper clock times. In 1976, BCS was serving forty television and ten radio stations.

BIAS (Broadcast Industry Automation System) is an on-line time-shared automation system furnished by the Data Communications Corporation. In 1976, it was the biggest in the business, serving 126 television stations and 26 radio stations. The BIAS host computers are large Burroughs machines at their headquarters connected by 24-hour dedicated telephone lines to their subscribers. Each subscriber has input and output equipment plus an in-station minicomputer which does many of the routine jobs on the spot, as well as speeding the flow of data to and from the central computer. BIAS has been working with a tie-in between data systems of advertising agencies and station representatives serving radio and television stations. Ratings data are analyzed to match up the requests of advertising agencies for spot availabilities with the appropriate station audiences in various markets. In this manner a complete station/representative/agency cycle of business procedures can be accomplished.

Compu/Net is a division of Arbitron, based in Los Angeles. In 1976, it serviced thirty-seven radio stations. Compu/Net utilizes an on-line time-shared system with large host computers at its headquarters. An added service gives its radio station subscribers an on-line research capability for analyzing competitors' schedule proposals and evaluating its own rate card based on each new market survey.

The Cox Data Services, while a large automation service embracing a "stand-alone" in-station computer system, has concentrated its services in television.

Columbine Systems utilizes a very different approach to automating its station subscribers. The Columbine system is a "stand-alone," but the company does not lease or sell hardware. Thus, Columbine offers only the software programs, allowing the particular station to make its own agreements for equipment installation. Columbine, then, designs the station system, specifies or recommends the hardware, helps the customer install it, trains station personnel, and aids in getting the system operating at the station level. Columbine even writes new programs for a station if their (Columbine's) available computer programs will not serve the particular and special needs of that subscriber. This system has become quietly popular, and is presently serving seventy-two radio stations and thirty-six television stations in the United States and Canada.

Another important, though relatively new company in the field is PSI (Paperwork Systems, Inc.). In 1976, PSI was serving 170 radio stations and ten television stations. PSI was the first company to use the minicomputer as the basis for a small, relatively low-cost, stand-alone automation system. PSI specializes in handling all billing, accounting, and traffic processes for a radio station. PSI, like Columbine, is particularly active in developing computer programs that will answer very specific needs of their clients.

From our discussion of automation systems, it is evident that radio stations may use these systems to whatever degree they desire. Nowhere is the use of computer systems more evident than in radio planning and buying. To show the extent of computer radio services in all areas of station support from technical maintenance to program services, it may be of value to discuss the use of computerized systems in the buying and planning phase of radio marketing.

Four major buying programs adopted by advertising agencies, station representatives, and networks are as follows: RADSKED was devised by Telmar/McGavren-Guild for their clients to evaluate reach and frequency data for multi-media schedules and to select out of that media mix that which best meets the user's advertising goals. Blair Radio has developed a program which they call BRAIN (Blair Radio Audience Information). The basic printout provides market, audience, and cost data for each area/demographic/daypart specification. For each ranked radio station, the printout gives number of announcements, gross impressions, net reach in persons, average frequency, gross rating points, and the station's total cumulative audience ("cume") in the area/demographic/daypart specified. The Katz Agency has developed a program called PROBE, which can determine a number of buying goals for their clients. The goals can be: (1) number of spots per station or per market; (2) gross impressions; (3) gross rating points; (4) cume rating points; (5) frequency; and (6) dollars per station or per market to be budgeted for the "buy." CBS Radio has developed RADPLAN to give those advertisers without a previous background in radio advertising answers to the basic questions of, "What can radio do for me? What does it cost?" One of radio's problems, say marketing and sales people, is that there has been too little dialogue between radio and many of the potential advertisers who could benefit from using it. RADPLAN attempts to provide a kind of "instantaneous demographics" service to connect the computers of rating and research services to the stations of the CBS Radio network so that these data are immediately available to them.

In each case, these plans have sought to cope with the vast proliferation of data now available concerning radio audiences, recognizing the basic fact that there are just so many data that without computers it would be virtually impossible to digest and use this information to extract just what is wanted and needed at any given time. The clear contribution that these computerized programs make to radio broadcasting is that it is easier to plan, buy, and analyze radio time as an advertising tool.

Broadcast Transmission Systems

It is obvious from the discussions in this chapter that radio and television broadcasting is undergoing rapid and profound technological change which affects the entire operating procedure of broadcasting as we have known it. The transmission systems of each radio station are no less immune to change. Undoubtedly the future will see radical changes in the way broadcast programs are delivered to a radio and television audience.

Point-to-point satellite television and communications networks are presently in operation. All of the broadcast networks are using, or are planning to use, satellite transmission as a means of interconnecting domestic services. The Public Broadcasting Service is actively developing a nationwide satellite network with downstations located at each member television station. The National Public Radio network will use these facilities to interconnect the radio stations using the NPR service. While these satellite services are not presently considering direct home reception, such a possibility for the future cannot be discounted. It is more likely that a satellite/cable link will be developed by which programs will be distributed nationally via satellite transmission delivered to the head-end of a local cable system for house-to-house interconnect, eliminating entirely the need for over-the-air station broadcast transmissions.

The most exciting possibility for a new transmission system currently under development is a broadband system using fiber optics. Such a transmission system can carry a very large number of TV channels, telephone circuits, and radio frequencies. The Bell Telephone Laboratories are using a laser beam transmitted over a high-purity glass fiber no bigger than a human hair which is capable of carrying 4,000 telephone conversations or six television channels. About one hundred such fibers can be packed into a single cable no larger in diameter than a pencil. Such a cable would be flexible enough to be threaded through existing conduits. Because of the enormity of the task and the cost of "rewiring" the entire nation with fiber optics, undoubtedly a hybrid system using new technologies and present coaxial cable will be developed to replace over-the-air broadcasting where practicable, simply because the broadcast frequencies, especially those used for UHF television, are badly needed for other electronic transmission services. Radio is less susceptible than TV to such changes, but radio is not immune, because changes in consumer behavior alone can have great impact.

Many of the concepts and types of equipment discussed in this chapter are not yet in use in most stations, especially in medium and small markets. A radio station can be a simple business operated by a few skilled persons. However, in these times the winds of change blow exceedingly strong, and space-age technology is causing an impact in communications that is as dramatic as anything in our history.

In all cases, it is wise for the student as well as the broadcasting professional to be familiar with the brochures, manuals, and descriptive articles about the changing systems of broadcast operations.

Suggestions for Further Learning

1. A student cannot learn the special rhythm and timing of the broadcast operator with a "tight fist" by reading about them. Devise a broadcast sequence similar to the one described in this chapter. Practice it as if you are both the announcer and your own engineer, and again with a separate engineer. The "buddy system" can work here. Many of the elements can be prerecorded.

2. Visit different radio stations in your market and compare their studio layouts and control consoles. Note the operational distinctions between different types of stations, such as Top-40 versus classical music.

3. If there is a recording studio in your area, observe the recording and editing techniques used in the production of a commercial announcement or a music number. Produce a radio commercial using all of the production elements available to you.

4. Develop an SCA program that might be of interest to your community and that you might discuss with an FM station in your market.

CHAPTER 5

Production

Audio production is only partly a manipulation of hardware to obtain a desired sound or combination of sounds. It is, first of all, a sharing of ideas and emotions, a sharing of human experience. In radio this is accomplished only through the use of sound; but the creative process, the ordering of ideas and emotions, has much in common with film, television, and the printed word. All demand good writing, with the content shaped to the intended audience, using the characteristics of the medium and its attendant tools, methods, and conventions to transmit human experience.

Surprisingly, the production that takes place in the sound medium, radio, is usually simpler than sound production in the visual media, television and film. Most elaborate sound production is not done at a radio station but in a recording studio. Most radio production involves announcers, recorded music and sound effects, a fairly simple audio console, single-track recording using reel-to-reel tape recorders, turntables, and cartridge tape machines (in some cases, cassettes).

Beginning students often feel that there are some tricks to learn, that if they can just learn the magic formulas they can produce good radio programs or program elements. That is certainly wrong. As in all creative endeavors, the good work is done by those who understand their audience, who have something to say, and who can manipulate the tools of their medium to communicate. While there are principles, this communication is not done effectively over the long term by the use of formulas. Each communication problem requires a logical and creative solution which makes use of the peculiar circumstances, messages, and talents of the moment. There are always many right ways and many wrong ways to communicate something.

The basic equipment needed for sound production includes a console, also called a board or mixer. The console is used to mix and control the sound. With a tape recorder it is possible to record one or many sounds, but it is not possible to effectively mix several sounds from several sources with only a recorder. With a microphone it is possible to pick up one or many sounds, but it is difficult or impossible to get a large number of sounds from different sources and present each in the right perspective unless a mixer is used. By combining the mixer with tape recorders, microphones, and turntables, adding perhaps some processing and electronic effects, it is possible to collect, assemble, and produce virtually as much as can be imagined.

A simple audio console may contain a few inputs, or the capability for handling incoming sound sources, and maybe only a single output, or the capability for passing along mixed sound to some other place. The inputs may be from microphones, tape recorders, other consoles, or remote lines (such as from a network, a stadium, or a concert hall). The outputs may be to a transmitter, to another console, to a tape recorder, or to a remote line. The console may be single-channel, capable of performing only one mix from incoming sound sources at a single time, or multi-channel, capable of performing simultaneous submixes or two or more simultaneous mixes.

An elaborate console may contain the capability for equalizing the sound, filtering out some frequencies, along with other processing. A multi-channel board may be used with 4-, 8-, 16-, or 24-track tape machines. Such systems provide the capability of elaborate sound production involving full orchestrations with sound processing, sound effects, and multi-track stereo.

A production facility may be a small board in a small room where the announcer-producer works combo, or it may be a studio with a separate control room where the producer never touches any controls or performs any talent work.

The Radio Production

Radio productions are often called the "theater of the mind" because the listener's imagination is stimulated to visualize physical action through aural sensory perception. A radio story is perceived by the listener in much the same way the reader perceives the dramatic action of a novel. The listener translates the aural cues provided by the radio story and visualizes the persons and actions and environments of the story in his own very personal terms as he "sees" the story unfold in his mind's eye.

Whether the story evolves around two people extolling the virtues of the latest detergent in a 60-second commercial, or whether it is a radio adaptation of a novel or short story, the radio producer writes the story with sound. The producer has three main sources of sound plus the ability to change and distort sound elements through electronic effects to provide new meanings, psychological and real, for the listener. These elements are: (1) the spoken word (dialogue/narration); (2) sound effects; (3) music; and (4) electronic effects such as filters, echoes, sound compression, etc., where the original sound is changed through the use of signal-processing equipment.

Since the radio story has no physical encumbrances, sound can transport the listener instantly to wherever the action of the story occurs. Like the intercutting of film, the producer can present the story elements in any sequence he desires for dramatic impact so long as the juxtaposition of sequence is understandable and dramatically logical to the audience.

Production Elements: The Voice

Dialogue, or the dramatic present, takes the audience in time to the moment when the action occurs. The agents of the story are not aware of the audience's presence. As with a visual story, the audience "views" the dramatic action of the story through the fourth wall of the proscenium or the lens by listening in on the dramatic action as it occurs.

Narration, on the other hand, occurs in real time; the narrators of the story are very aware of the audience and are consciously speaking directly to each listener. When narration and dialogue are used in sequence, the effect is an annotation to the dramatic action of the story as the characters live it—a kind of commentary, annotation, or explanation of the meaning of the story solely for the purpose of enlightening the audience into its subtleties and ramifications.

In plays like *Our Town* and *The Glass Menagerie*, a narrator who is totally conscious of and who speaks directly to the audience further illuminates the story. The same technique is used in the radio commercial in which the announcer speaks directly to the audience about the virtues of the product advertised while the dialogue or "story" of the commercial demonstrates the use of the product.

The constant interchange between real time and the dramatic present creates an interesting ambivalence for the radio audience. This interplay between narration and dialogue makes for a "string-of-pearls" technique by which the narration providing the exposition of the story line is the string while the pearl is that vignette of an emotional or dramatic high point which, when dramatized, transports the listener back to the moment when the event or action occurs. Thus, in sequence, the audience is told what has happened in the listener's time frame and then is thrust back into the time frame when the dramatic event took place. The listener, then, is effectively there at the point of the action.

This string-of-pearls technique is particularly effective in documentary actualities in which the real events and the real persons of the story, recorded at the actual time the event took place, are intercut with explanatory narration recorded at a later time. This sequencing of actual voices at the scene of the action and a reporter's later comments creates an effect within the listener of at once being there witnessing the event and simultaneously having the weight and import of the event brought into focus by the commentator's remarks.

Since the radio audience is effectively blind and must respond to the story through aural stimulation, nuances of sound must, in the case of the dialogue, give clues to the character and personality traits of the agents of the story. Tonal quality and changes in rate, pitch, and volume differentiate one voice from another. The nonverbal communications so essential to the actor/interpreter/communicator, visually perceived by the television, film, or theater audience as facial expressions, body movements, and pieces of business further indicating character and meaning, are denied the radio communicator expect as he or she is able to use the voice to indicate nonverbal meanings. Consequently, vocal characteristics such as accents and dialects, vocal aberrations, coughs, sniffles, clearing the throat, giggles, etc., are used to replace visual nonverbal reactions. A cold, chilling voice quality can be at least as frighteningly malevolent as a menacing countenance. The interpreter can create vocal variety by changing the pitch or the tempo at which he speaks. The effect of the slow-speaking Southerner or the twangy Texan can be attained partly through sustaining the vowel sounds. The trained radio announcer or actor can vary pitch through a range of at least an octave. Pitch and tempo variety create melody. Vocal quality delineates character, an emotional condition, physical activity, and a mental attitude. The radio communicator must have complete control of his voice to project character and advance the conflicts and dramatic interest of the story. This voice control must be comparable to the body control the film and television actor must have to convey nuances of meaning and emotions. It is no easy thing to imagine how one's voice sounds when he is physically exhausted, and then realistically emulating this condition while standing stationary before a microphone. It should be noted that one does not achieve this effect purely by a mechanical act of vocal manipulation. It is more an act of total emotional control. The voice is a part of the whole which must be controlled, but it is the part relied on for demonstration in radio.

The radio communicator can utilize spatial relations by positioning himself at the microphone in relationship to other actors. By physically moving into and away from the microphone, one can change vocal quality as well as volume. The board fade, created by engineering changes in sound level at the control console, cannot capture variations in vocal quality caused by the changing reflection pattern of a moving sound. While the engineer can vary volume, the board fade cannot capture the subtle tone variations created when the distance between sound source and listener changes.

The vocal varieties can also be changed by electronic effects. Reverberation can be added to the voice to create echo effects or to add sound presence and substance to the voice. Sound compression equipment can vary the rate of speech only slightly causing a subliminal impression, or it can vary the rate more sharply causing a noticeable distortion in rate and pitch. Filters, such as the Urei "Little Dipper," can clip off frequencies on both the high and low end to provide vocal effects like speaking on a telephone or from down a well. Filters and phase shifter equipment can provide ethereal, impressionistic, and surrealistic sound effects which can heighten the mood of the story and intensify the emotions evoked in the listener. Variable filters, compressors, wah-wah pedals, and Leslie speakers (to add tremolo) are among other exotic electronic effects which intensify the dramatic impact upon the listener. Electronic instruments such as the Moog Synthesizer can be used to provide special sound effects either as music or as a representational sound.

Recording techniques can be used which utilize multiple tracks to overdub or sweeten sound where the sound is recorded simultaneously on separate tracks and then mixed down, so that one drum repeated many times can sound like an entire drum corps. Another example of this effect might be to record a violin passage using three violins. This passage might be recorded on three tracks so that when these tracks are mixed down we have a total of nine violins playing the particular passage to obtain the sound required. Many such recording effects can be obtained using 4-, 8-, 16-, and 24-track equipment. Audio processing and mixdown techniques will be discussed in greater detail later in this chapter.

Being an effective communicator on radio requires several things. Perhaps more than anything else it requires the ability to read aloud. Good reading involves taking words from the printed page, thinking them, and speaking them as if they were your own. Unfortunately, most people read poorly. They are too mechanical, or they give every word in the sentence equal emphasis, or they pronounce things differently, like saying "ay" for "a," and sometimes "thee for "the," even when the next word begins with a consonant. Secondly, good radio communication is usually enhanced by a pleasing voice and clean enunciation, free from regionalisms, although these are less important than having something to say and then telling it to the audience. one or two persons at a time. Further, just as Hollywood does not require all actors to be leading men, radio does not require all speakers to be leading men vocally. There is room for character voices, just as there are character faces in the movies. It is not always a matter of being bad or good, but of using the right voice in the right place. Also, radio uses more communicators than actors. Most radio communication involves direct communication of the face-to-face kind, which requires the communicator to be himself (maybe his better self). A minority of radio work requires the communicator to be somebody else. Being a personality (yourself) requires feeling comfortable with yourself and feeling at ease with the audience, at least while on the air. Acting requires the ability to become another person, at least for the moment, although it is easier to play the part of someone like yourself than to play someone totally different. Finally, while good communicating involves considerable learned technique, more than anything else it involves control over our thought processes and thereby our emotions. It is a process of taking thoughts which may or may not be our own and speaking them in a seemingly natural manner.

Production Elements:
Sound Effects

Sound effects, often referred to as the sound bed, are another tool for the program producer to use in communicating with his audience. Sound effects can serve as a kind of aural scenery implying the visual action and environment of the story, which we would physically see in the television or film production, but which we see in our "mind's eye" as we listen to the radio program. Sound can cue the physical action and reinforce the quality of the dramatic action taking place within the story. Sound can clarify and point the interpretation of a scene within the story or a particular action of the radio program to affect the emotional quality of the action portrayed.

Sound effects may be either realistic or impressionistic. A realistic sound effect evokes the memory of a known, recognized sound from real life. A man walking up to his car, opening the door, getting in, and driving away; the sound of a barroom brawl; the roar of a jet engine as the plane prepares to take off, are all examples of realistic sound. This kind of sound needs no dialogue to make its meaning clear. The majority of sound effects used in radio are realistic in order to set the scene for real action.

An impressionistic sound is subjective and may be unreal in comparison to the actual sound which it represents. Thus, the impressionistic sound suggests what a sound means to a specific person. For example, a sound is needed to give meaning to a state of affairs which cannot be indicated effectively by real sound. Two feathers are stroked across the strings of a piano while the sustaining pedal is held down. This can represent to the listener frightful and mysterious emptiness of outer space, the unreality of a dream sequence, or the ethereal quality of a spirit world. Impressionistic sound, then, makes us recognize the meaning of a sound as another person hears it, though it usually needs the addition of dialogue to cue the listener to the environment of the sound and its precise meaning. Impressionistic sounds may be used both in realistic situations and in fantasy.

Music is often used impressionistically as a sound effect to represent an emotional quality. An example might be the use of music to represent rain or a storm. The beating of a drum may represent the gradually increasing pulse beat of a nervous person. For fantasy, a slide whistle might symbolize the appearance or disappearance of a gremlin or a genie. It might be noted here that all bridge, mood, and transition music is impressionistic. Besides merely tying separate scenes together, bridge and transition music also symbolize changes in time, place, and mood from one scene to the next. Mood music behind a narrator's voice heightens the action of the scene. Thus, impressionistic sound not only delineates the sound of the story's action, but creates an attitude toward it.

There are four main purposes and uses for sound effects in radio productions: (1) to indicate action; (2) to establish locale; (3) to indicate a passage of time or of action; and (4) to establish and reinforce character. Both realistic and impressionistic sounds may be used to accomplish the above purposes.

Action sound tells the audience *what* is happening at any given moment, supplementing the spoken word. Echoing in an empty corridor, the opening and closing of doors, or the firing of a gun are all examples of action sound. Action sound paints pictures of specific incidents.

The type of sound establishing locale tells the listener *where* the action is taking place. The sound of rolling surf to suggest the seashore, the sound of dishes amid the low buzz of conversation to suggest a restaurant scene, the noise of typewriters to suggest an office scene— all effectively establish the locale of the story. A pitfall of connecting sound with scenic background is that the sound may fight the action. Sound need not tell every minute detail of the setting. Only enough sound to recall the locale to the listener's imagination is necessary, allowing him to enrich the scene in his own unique and personal manner, depending on the individual experiences the scene recalls.

Sound indicating time or transition can cue dramatic action. The striking of a clock to indicate the hour is perhaps the most obvious example of a sound effect that indicates *when* a particular event is happening. The ticking of a clock has become a conventional device to show the passage of time. The howling of the wind suggests wintertime. Crickets denote a night scene. Similarly, the click-click of train wheels can denote a transition from one locale to another.

Sound effects are sometimes used to help establish the *who* of a program. Sound can amplify character. The jingle of a cowboy's spurs as he walks not only establishes his character, but also heightens suspense in a western drama. The telephone in *Sorry, Wrong Number* becomes a character in itself through the skillful use of dialing, on-line ring, busy signal, etc. Other examples of character sound are the clumping of a peg leg or the tapping of a blind man's cane. Character in sound is twofold: (1) sound identifies and amplifies the character, as explained above; and (2) sound gives meaning to character by how it is performed—e.g., the slamming of a door by an irate character. The cold, insistent, and malevolent ringing of the telephone in *Sorry, Wrong Number* adds to the horror of the action.

While these categories of action, locale, time, and character are the four main functions of dramatic sound, they are not mutually exclusive. A particular sound effect may serve more than one function. For instance, the crowing of a rooster may suggest not only time but also locale. Footsteps on gravel suggest both the action of a man walking and something about the place in which he is walking.

The effects of sound and music as used within radio production may be classified in the following manner: (1) realistic confirmatory effects; (2) realistic evocative effects; (3) symbolic evocative effects; (4) conventionalized effects; (5) impressionistic effects; and (6) music used as a sound effect.[1] Realistic confirmatory effects are those which amplify without adding to the narration or dialogue of the program. Realistic evocative effects are used to create realism and add mood and atmosphere to the action described or portrayed. Symbolic evocative effects are used to explain something of an abstract nature; perhaps to express the confusion in a character's mind. A conventionalized effect is similar to the cliché in speech. It immediately connotes a certain action and serves as the sound equivalent of the theater curtain in the stage play or the conventional transitional device such as the fade-out or fade-in in film and television production. This can indicate a passage of time omitted between two sequences. The impressionistic effect is unrealistic in nature and can be used to create an attitude in the mind of the listener. Impressionistic sound works on the subliminal perceptions of the audience. For example, an artificial echo superimposed on the voice, or the use of choral chanting behind the ranting and raving of the protagonist in the expressionistic drama *From Morn*

---

[1] Lance Sieveking, *The Stuff of Radio* (London: Casell Co., Ltd., 1934), pp. 65–66.

To Midnight, creates an attitude (impression) of the character and his agony which is personal and subjective for each member of the audience. Music used as a sound effect substitutes for real sound to provide an impressionistic quality and meaning to the sound, becoming a flexible and intensely personal sound that adds a dimension to the statement of the radio production which a realistic sound could not provide. Thus, music used as a sound effect can become an emotional expression of what happens as the result of the sound and the action that it portrays.

Too many sound effects only serve to confuse the listener. How many otherwise effective commercials with a strong copy platform have been ineffectual because sound effects have been poorly used or because so many sounds have been crowded into a 60-second sequence that the listener has not known what to concentrate on and the message has been lost in a welter of sound? Sound should be used only if: (1) it clarifies what is taking place in the scene or clarifies the meaning of the spoken message or dialogue; (2) it adds realism or authenticity to the action described or portrayed in the sequence; (3) it adds dramatic and emotional impact to the sequence; or (4) the listener expects to hear the sound effect in connection with the scene.

But remember, unless there is a definite and recognizable contribution that the sound effect or sound sequence can make to the program —leave it out!

Many sound effects used in radio are unidentifiable if they are heard by themselves outside the context of a script. For instance, the rustling of cellophane is often used for the sound of fire. However, it is also used for the sound of frying bacon. Heard by itself, without any means of identification, the rustling of cellophane is unintelligible. The reason for this, once again, is that radio lacks the visual element. In real life we can identify the sound of frying bacon because we can actually see and smell the bacon as it fries. Other sensory perceptions come into play to help us identify the sound. In radio we have to make up for this lack of sight by other means.

Fortunately, there are some sound effects that are self-identifying. These include the opening and closing of doors, footsteps, sirens, howling wind, crying babies, and horses' hoofs. But, for the most part, other sound effects are largely unidentifiable without further identifying and representative cues. Thus, some means has to be devised to identify these sounds so that they will be meaningful. This is done in any of three ways: (1) Dialogue and narration often give cues as to what a sound effect is. To indicate the climbing of stairs, a character might admonish his companion to "Watch out for that third step, it's loose." (2) A self-identifying sound is used to introduce one that might be misunderstood. For example, a howling wind may introduce the sound of rain, or horses' hoofs may accompany and identify the rattle of a stagecoach. (3) As a situation develops, one sound will lead logically to the next. In a street duel, the sound of gunshots leads us to expect the fall of one or more bodies. The objective, of course, is to make use of these cues as subtly as possible.

In most real-life situations, the average person is surrounded by a multitude of sounds. A person crossing a busy street may encounter a diverse number of sounds: tires on the street, horns honking, bells clanging, the babble of conversation, pedestrian footsteps, etc. If all of these sounds were heard in full consciousness, we would soon become babbling idiots. However, we are mercifully protected from the daily onslaught of sound because we psychologically block out most noise to concentrate on those sounds which are important to us. The human mind has the ability to focus on immediately important sounds while other sounds are subdued or entirely eliminated from the conscious mind. Thus, a person crossing a street in the company of a friend would be concentrating on what his friend is saying, and only the most prominent traffic noises would be vaguely apparent to him.

The microphone, however, picks up all sounds and does not distinguish among them psychologically. Consequently, a traffic scene emulated in a radio production, if it utilizes all of the street sounds indiscriminately, would produce a confused roar which would make it difficult for the listener to picture in his mind exactly what is going on. In radio production we must focus the attention of the audience on sounds that are important to the story being advanced or to the message being enhanced. Other sounds must be kept in the background relative to their importance, or must be eliminated entirely. Yet, at the same time, while background sounds must not detract from the focus of attention, they cannot be totally eliminated if they are necessary to establish locale and action. This is accomplished by using various sound levels, as discussed later in this chapter.

Production Elements: Music

Music is still another sound source available to the radio producer in making his point effectively. Music is subjective and evocative in nature. Music is intensely personal, setting up varying emotional reactions in each listener. Music is particularly able to reinforce mood and to provide an atmosphere surrounding a scene, be it a physical action, a character conflict, the environment for a message, or the emotional content of the dialogue. The emotion of a dramatic scene may be highlighted by music underlining the dialogue, thus helping to describe the dramatic action. Music, like other sound, may be used to amplify character. It can also be used to identify a character. For example, in a radio adaptation of the play *Death Takes a Holiday*, the agent of Death can be identified and an attitude can be created about him in the minds of the audience through, say, a rush of celestial strings sounding whenever he is present in the scene.

Music is used in a dramatic setting primarily for the purpose of augmenting the dialogue and/or narration. It may convey emotion, implying evocatively what the dialogue cannot state. It can express expository meaning underlying descriptive narrative passages. Like sound effects, music can set the place or scene; it can suggest and heighten the mood or atmosphere; and it can suggest and/or heighten a particular action described in the dialogue of the scene. Music, then, is a very useful dramatic aid for extending the emotional meaning of the story or message to effect a positive response in the listener.

The intimate and immediate qualities inherent in the medium of radio allow the producer to exploit the "theater of the mind." Because the action and scenery of the story occur in the mind of each listener, the location of the action may change in an instant. The "string-of-pearls" technique, switching between narration which speaks directly to the listening audience and dialogue which carries the listener back to the dramatic present, makes for instant transitions between scenes. Montage effects, whereby action is compressed into a series of one-line speeches or into a series of sound sequences similar to the cinematic montage of dissimilar picture sequences, are used to compress a large amount of activity into the shortest possible time frame. The montage allows the audience to flesh out the details occurring during the passage of time. Music can be used effectively to bridge the parts of the montage, relating and building each part of the montage dramatically in suspense and emotion.

Music, then, is used as a transitional device. In this way it can "bridge" the action of one scene to the next, making an emotional statement about each scene—capping the preceding scene and indicating the emotion of the entering scene. Music played in the background of the dialogue or narration helps convey the emotional impact of the scene, while bridging or cuing music triggers a new direction in the dramatic action of the story and expresses an expository meaning.

The musical instrumentation of the background music for a specific scene can play an important role in the evocative effect of the music. The gemütlichkeit of a guitar, the lonesome wail of a harmonica, the sophisticated chord progressions of a cocktail lounge piano, arpeggios played on a harp—each kind of music distinctly contributes to the exact mood and emotion of the scene it is designed to heighten.

Perhaps it is necessary to differentiate between the words "mood" and "atmosphere" as they are used in connection with sound effects and music used in radio production. The mood of a piece of music is the emotionally evocative effect that the music has on an individual.

The atmosphere of the music suggests an environment or a location in time and place. For example, music can suggest the locale of the court of King Louis XIV as well as a primitive homestead cabin in the old west. Mood music is more subjective and intensely personal than atmospheric music. Mood music indicates and creates moods of violence, love, sentiment, joy, hysteria, foreboding, terror, sorrow, brutality, and many more kinds and degrees of emotional reaction. As with all emotional indicators, discretion must be employed in choosing mood music so that it does not clash with the dramatic action it is designed to support.

Sound and Music Plots

Sound and music are elements supportive of the action of the radio production regardless of the kind of narrative program in which they are used. The sound and music routine must agree completely with the producer's concept of his program. The producer must consider whether music is to be used or not; what kind of music to use and what instrumentation if there is a choice, and if it is important to the mood of the program; how sound and music are to be used within the program; in what manner and how long they are to be played in context with the emotion or meaning they are supporting.

The producer should consider the following questions when developing a sound and music plot:

1. What is the period and/or the locale?
2. What is the dominant mood or theme?
3. What can sound and music contribute to the production?
4. What type of sound and music is appropriate?
5. What instrumentation is necessary to evoke the proper mood?

Both music and sound must be consistent with the producer's intent.

Music and Sound Libraries

Background music can enhance and give added dimension to the mood and atmosphere of a radio production. Because of its intense subjectivity, music can respond to the emotional values of the scene. Music behind a narration or the exposition of a radio commercial can expand an attitude and give a cue to the listener as to how he or she is expected to respond to the message. Music behind a narration can often reveal more clearly than words the inner thoughts of the narrator—how he feels about the action or situation that he is describing.

Because music is at once so eclectic and so personal, it is difficult at best to find the perfect music passage for the scene you are producing. This is why so many radio commercial producers insist on using original music which is designed, composed, arranged, and performed to elicit exactly the right values for that precise commercial message he is producing.

Original music can be used only when budgets are large. Mostly it is a luxury. For the person wanting a contemporary sound, the only way is to use currently available recordings. Also, a number of effects and appropriate musical stingers, bridges, and background pieces can be lifted quickly from any station's library. Probably the most widely used news intro in the country is from an old Percy Faith album, "Viva." Classical music, motion picture sound tracks, jazz, and experimental albums are a rich source. Music can be found which fits an existing script, or, as is often the case in commercials, the music is selected first, and then the commercial is written to fit the musical punctuations. Generally, well-known themes and currently popular songs should be avoided because the music can distract more than it can help—but not always. Incidental music from movies is often the place to find what you need most quickly. Albums by Jerry Goldsmith, Quincy Jones, Henry Mancini, Chuck Mangione, Lalo Schifrin, Marvin Hamlisch, Michel Legrand, or Blood, Sweat, and Tears are rich sources. For graphic examples of how effective readily available classical music can be, see the films *Elvira Madigan* and *2001, A Space Odyssey.* Prominent themes from both films were used shortly after they appeared, for literally hundreds of radio and TV commercials.

For the radio producer who wishes to search out music cues from the vast library of recorded concert music, there is an excellent resource book which is unfortunately out of print, but by no means out of date because virtually all of the music is still available. *Recorded Bridges, Moods, and Interludes* was painstakingly compiled and edited by Henry Katzman and published by Broadcast Music, Incorporated (New York, 1953). This catalogue, found in most public libraries, allows the radio producer to locate music from recorded classics. Later recordings and new album numbers can be substituted for the listings in *Recorded Bridges, Moods, and Interludes,* but the titles and timings remain viable for the most part as listed. This work is a categorical index of timed segments culled from recorded symphonic performances. Part I, entitled *Moods and Categories,* lists in alphabetical order the composer of the symphonic passages that call up the particular mood indicated in each mood category. Part II, entitled *Cue Compilations,* lists each symphony, broken down into its component moods. Each symphony is listed alphabetically by composer, and the list also includes a description of each mood segment, where it is located within the recording by time, and length in time of each mood segment within the symphony. Figure 5.1 shows a random sample of each part of this catalogue of moods.

The selection and collection of sound and music routines that make up the sound bed of radio production can be both an arduous and a time-consuming task. The producer can spend countless hours searching music albums and single records for the exact musical interlude or background passage to fit the desired effect he requires. In the interest of time and efficiency, the radio producer may use Sound Effects and

PART I MOODS AND CATEGORIES

ORIENTAL (Continued)

PROKOFIEV—Symphony No. 5—
(:31) (:38)

PROKOFIEV—Symphony No. 5—
(1:43)

RESPIGHI—Feste Romane— (1:28)

RESPIGHI—The Pines Of Rome—
(1:15)

SHOSTAKOVITCH—Symphony No.
6— (2:06) (3:24)

SHOSTAKOVITCH—Symphony No.
6— (2:13) (5:34)

SHOSTAKOVITCH—Symphony No.
9—DANCE— (:45) (1:41)

SHOSTAKOVITCH—Symphony No.
9— (:48) (:57)

SIBELIUS—En Saga, Etc.—DANCE
— (1:53) (3:15)

SIBELIUS—Symphony No. 1— (:47)
(1:00)

SIBELIUS—Symphony No. 1— (:22)
(1:09)

STRAVINSKY—Suite From
Petrouchka— (:37)

STRAVINSKY—Petrouchka Suite—
(:25)

PAIN

GLIERE—Symphony No. 3— (:54)

PANIC

HINDEMITH—Mathias The
Painter— (:41)

SCHUBERT—Symphony No. 9—
(1:37) (2:40) (4:48)

SCHUBERT—Symphony No. 9—
(1:30) (5:01)

SHOSTAKOVITCH—Symphony
No. 1—472 (1:00) (1:30)

STRAUSS, R—Ein Heldenleben—
(:22) (:57)

STRAUSS, R—Ein Heldenleben—
(:45) (1:22)

TCHAIKOVSKY—Francesca da
Rimini— (1:10) (2:54) (3:07)

TCHAIKOVSKY—Francesca da
Rimini— (1:01) (1:42) (1:56)

TCHAIKOVSKY—Symphony No. 4
— (1:11) (1:18)

TCHAIKOVSKY—Symphony No. 4
— (1:03) (1:09)

OUTDOOR

KHACHATURIAN—Masquerade
Suite— (2:25)

KHACHATURIAN—Masquerade
—1166 (2:32)

Figure 5.1 Information found in *Recorded Bridges, Moods, and Interludes.*

Mood Music Libraries. These libraries provide music catalogued in terms of the emotion each selection evokes and sound effects of various types and lengths recorded from various perspectives.

Such organizations as Major, Standard, Speed Q, Elektra, CBS, E-Z Cue, DeWolfe, and Galaxie, to name only a few sound and music libraries, provide albums and tapes which may be purchased and/or leased for commercial radio production. Often these music cues are recorded in stereo, and all of them are properly indexed for an easy search for the appropriate cue to fit the exact kind, type, and length of sound and/or music need. Figures 5.1 to 5.3 show excerpts from the catalogues of the Major Records Mood Music Library, distributed by Thomas J. Valentino, New York; the DeWolfe Recorded Music Catalogue, distributed by Corelli-Jacobs Film Music, Inc., New York; and the Galaxie Music Library Catalogue, distributed by Galaxie Music Services, Los Angeles.

Since the choice of music to fill the sound bed as the producer

GALAXIE MUSIC SERVICES, INC.

9100 Sunset Boulevard
Los Angeles, California 90069
Phones 274-4198 – 274-6586

LIBRARY CATEGORIES

		Page
A	NEUTRAL, MELODIC, DRAMATIC OPENERS—MAIN TITLES	1
B	NEUTRAL, MELODIC DRAMATIC PLAYOFFS, CURTAINS, END TITLES	9
C	DRAMATIC BRIDGES, STINGERS	17
D	COMEDY & JAZZ OPENERS AND CLOSERS	21
E	NEUTRAL & COMEDY BRIDGES & STINGERS	25
V	OUTER SPACE	94
W	SPOT COMMERCIALS	95

Figure 5.2 A catalogue sample from one sound library.

"hears" it is totally subjective, producers may prefer to develop their own music compendiums. The mood of the music elicits an emotionally evocative effect upon each particular listener; therefore mood is quite impossible to categorize except in very broad terms or in the very personal terms of the person developing a compendium of music. It is much easier, and safer, to develop a catalogue of atmospheric music which suggests the location of the music in time and place.

Atmospheric music can be broken down into seven categories:

1. Period......... the age and dates of the civilization or society the music seems to suggest.

2. Locale......... the setting (imaginative scenery) evoked by the music.

3. Ethnic......... the racial qualities of the music.

4. Social.......... the class mores suggested by the music.

5. Supernatural... the unreal, or supra-real, connotation of the music.

6. Psychological...inner reality (here atmospheric music is closely allied to mood music).

7. Remarks....... other elements and comments which do not fit in the above categories.

T.V. SPECIALS	I. Slaney	244	——	various
20 light dramatic bridges and links—full orchestra				
UNCHARTED VOYAGE	P. Arvay	491	DW/LP 2823	4.34
Light dramatic impression with decorative woodwind and hard runs				
UNDERCURRENT No. 1	I. Slaney	152	DW 2687	1.18
Suspense sequences—tension				
UNDERCURRENT No. 2	I. Slaney	152	DW 2687	1.10
Suspense sequences—tension				
URANIUM 236	P. Arvay	366	DW 2898	2.54
Modernistic industrial movement—title				
VENDETTA	J. Trombey	594	DW/LP 2969	1.56
Semi-dramatic incidental				
VICE CLASH No. 1	I. Slaney	289	DW 2689	1.49
VICE CLASH No. 2	I. Slaney	289	DW 2690	1.16
VICE CLASH No. 3	I. Slaney	289	DW 2690	1.13
Three semi-dramatic incidentals				
VICE PROBE	I. Slaney	150	DW 2599	1.55
Mysterioso				
VILLE SANS VIE	P. Sciortino	680	DW/LP 3030	2.30
Devastation—bass and flute				

Figure 5.3 Sample page from DeWolfe Ltd., Music Publishers Catalogue.

An example of how the producer may use the above categories to analyze a musical selection for its atmospheric evocative effect might be as follows:

The Planets, Op. #32...Gustav Holst
Mars: The Bringer of War.

 1. Period......... eleventh century on.
 2. Locale......... preparation for war (not a battle scene itself).
 3. Ethnic......... not Oriental.
 4. Social.........either civilian or military people doing physical work.
 5. Supernatural... ———
 6. Psychological...unrelenting.
 7. Remarks....... none.

Or Ravel's *Bolero*, if it is not too recognizable, calling attention to the music itself rather than to the intent for which it is used in the production, might break down like this:

 1. Period......... twentieth century.
 2. Locale.........cabaret, tense dance sequence, Spain, Morocco, Mediterranean coast.
 3. Ethnic......... Spanish, Arabian, Moorish.
 4. Social.........fiery working class.
 5. Supernatural... ———
 6. Psychological...heavy tension, danger.
 7. Remarks....... music implies relentless motion.

The imaginative, inventive radio producer can use such a compendium for many diverse effects.

Before we examine a scene from a radio production for its sound and music potential, and before we visualize the scene for its sound perspectives in relationship to the action, it might be of value to understand the terminology used in the sound plot from which the production team can work:

FADE IN.............. as a sound cue, the term refers to perspective; any sound that appears to approach the audience from a distance.

FADE UP.............usually refers to a volume increase, bridge music, etc.; perspective is not involved.

CROSSFADE (X-fade)...where one sound fades up simultaneously with the fade-out of the previous sound.

SEGUE................extremely fast crossfade where one sound replaces another without any appreciable loss of volume—the new sound seems to grow out of the original sound.

ESTAB(lish)...........to hold a sound at a full or prominent level (volume) until that particular sound registers in the listener's consciousness. (This usually takes from five to ten seconds.)

SNEAK IN OR OUT.....to bring in or take out music and sound so gradually that the listener is unaware of what is happening until the moment when the sound is important to the scene.

FADE TO BG...........to bring down the level of the music or sound under the dialogue and to hold at a background level. (The term, BEHIND, is sometimes used instead of BACKGROUND.)

UNDER & HOLD........same as FADE to BG.

UP to CAP & OUT.......sound and music quickly swell to full volume, hold to establish, then fade out abruptly. To CAP a scene means that the sound gives a sense of finality and climax to that scene.

STAB.................an abrupt powerful musical chord used to climax or accentuate an intense dramatic situation.

STING................same as above, except that the chord is higher pitched and more shrill.

In order to develop a sound and music plot, the action of the scene or the situation must be visualized in terms of sound perspective and relationship to the agents of the story. The radio audience must form in their mind's eye a picture of the scene as it might be if it were actually taking place.

Scene Visualization

The following scene presents several problems in scene visualization and sound perspective. It is an elaborate production of the kind done by the CBS Mystery Theater, more apt to be done in a recording studio than in a modern radio station. While most current production involves shorter forms, simpler production techniques involving assembly of prerecorded elements, and much smaller budgets, this scene demonstrates how voice, music, and effects combine to produce the desired effect on the listener. How will the physical action of the scene be carried out and the relationships of the various characters be developed clearly for the listener? Our analysis of the problems is as follows:

SOUND:	CITY STREET NOISES—BUSY INTERSECTION—PEOPLE WAITING TO CROSS
JIM:	I wish that signal would change. We're not going to make that appointment if we don't hurry.
HANK:	Keep your hat on, it's changing now. Let's go.
JIM:	(PAUSE) What did Mrs. Burton have to say when she phoned?
HANK:	All she said was to meet her in the lobby of the Savoy Hotel in fifteen minutes. She sounded kind of frightened. Said she had important information for us, then hung up.
JIM:	We never figured on getting anything out of her. Wonder how come she's decided to blab now?
HANK:	My guess is she saw that story in the papers about the recovery of the Windsor diamonds by the cops, and this frightens her. Probably thinks the Syndicate's on her tail now, and figures she can bargain for protection from us if she tells all. At least we'll find out pretty quick.
JACK:	(OFF MIKE) Get a move on, you guys. I'm all set to go.
JIM:	There's Jack with the car. C'mon. By the way, think she knows anything about Tony and that missing ten grand?
HANK:	Don't know. Frankly, I hope she's still alive when we get there. H'lo Jack.
JACK:	'Bout time you got here. Where to?
SOUND:	CAR DOOR OPENS AND CLOSES. CAR PULLS AWAY FROM CURB.
HANK:	Savoy Hotel. Know where that is?
JACK:	Couldn't miss it.
MUSIC:	SEGUE TO TRANSITION MUSIC.

The producer must visualize the physical action taking place in the scene before he can set up the sound perspective in the studio. In bare form, the scene visualization amounts to this:

> Two men in a crowd of people are waiting to cross the street at a busy intersection. Traffic changes—they cross. Upon reaching the other side, the men quicken their pace as their friend calls from the car. Traffic again changes direction. They reach the car, get in, and drive away.

The microphone remains with the two men all through the scene. Since the listening audience is always at the point of the microphone, the listener in effect crosses the street with these men, gets into the car, and drives away. The scene then dissolves (segues) into the transitional music which sets the mood or atmosphere for the next scene.

As producer, we want to focus our attention on the conversation between the two men crossing the street. To do this, we must create the illusion that the audience is moving along with the two men throughout the scene. Since the microphone emphasizes those sounds which are closest to it, the microphone must be at the point of attention: the conversation between the two men.

If we were to diagram the action of the scene in the manner a cinematographer would lay out the scene for the sequence of camera shots photographing the action, it might look like this:

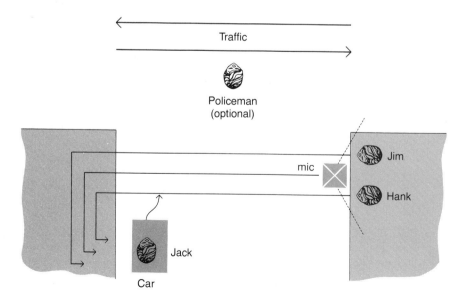

Figure 5.4 Diagram of a Scene

Note that the imaginary microphone is included in the diagram to show the perspective and sound balance during the action of the scene. The sound of a policeman's whistle to indicate the traffic change (just before and after the men cross the intersection) would make an excellent device to aurally orient the listener to the physical action, but it is not absolutely necessary to the scene.

Studio Setup

To capture the sound perspectives and balance in the studio to emulate the cinematographer's camera sequence plot, the two characters of the scene will remain "on mike" while they seem to cross the street by varying background sounds. Thus, all other sounds than dialogue will appear to be "off mike" and lower in volume relative to their importance to the action of the scene. While a distance perspective can be achieved partially by lowering the volume of the sound, it is important to record the sound effect from the spatial perspective in which it will be used, in order to obtain perfect verisimilitude.

Figure 5.5 is a diagram of the studio setup, showing mike placements in relation to the actors and sound effects.

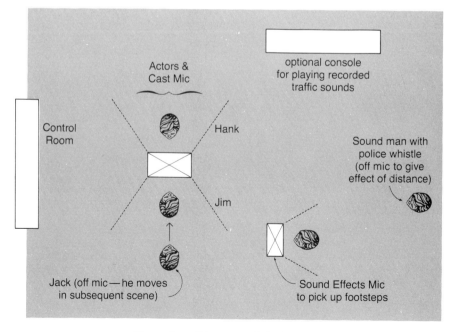

Figure 5.5 Diagram of the Studio Setup

The Production Script

The next step is to develop a production script of the scene so that the production personnel, be they a full crew or one person, can bring all of the sound elements of dialogue, sound effects, and music into the proper artistic blend through variations of volume, timing, and sound perspective. It is the responsibility of the producer/director to develop the production script, which is the "blueprint" of the program, in the manner in which the production will ultimately be achieved.

The production script of the scene we have been working with might look like this:

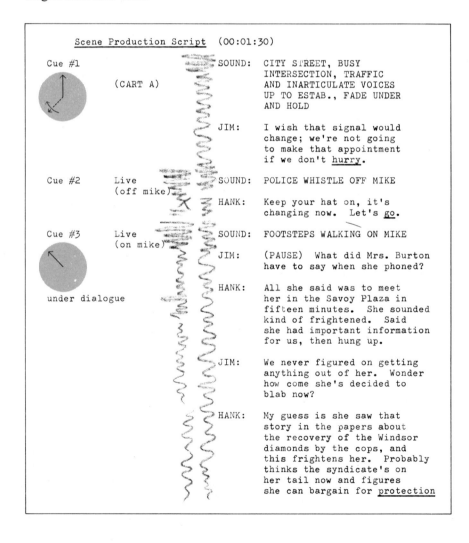

```
          Scene Production Script   (00:01:30)

Cue #1                       SOUND:   CITY STREET, BUSY
                                      INTERSECTION, TRAFFIC
              (CART A)                AND INARTICULATE VOICES
                                      UP TO ESTAB., FADE UNDER
                                      AND HOLD

                             JIM:     I wish that signal would
                                      change; we're not going
                                      to make that appointment
                                      if we don't hurry.

Cue #2      Live             SOUND:   POLICE WHISTLE OFF MIKE
            (off mike)
                             HANK:    Keep your hat on, it's
                                      changing now. Let's go.

Cue #3      Live             SOUND:   FOOTSTEPS WALKING ON MIKE
            (on mike)
                             JIM:     (PAUSE) What did Mrs. Burton
                                      have to say when she phoned?

under dialogue               HANK:    All she said was to meet
                                      her in the Savoy Plaza in
                                      fifteen minutes. She sounded
                                      kind of frightened. Said
                                      she had important information
                                      for us, then hung up.

                             JIM:     We never figured on getting
                                      anything out of her. Wonder
                                      how come she's decided to
                                      blab now?

                             HANK:    My guess is she saw that
                                      story in the papers about
                                      the recovery of the Windsor
                                      diamonds by the cops, and
                                      this frightens her. Probably
                                      thinks the syndicate's on
                                      her tail now and figures
                                      she can bargain for protection
```

Explanatory notes:

A. Sound and music cues are numbered in the order they will
appear in the scene. The action or dialogue cuing the sound is
underlined to indicate the cue description. Cuts and fades of
sounds lasting more than a brief period are indicated by the
end of the relative-volume line noted immediately to the left
of the dialogue.

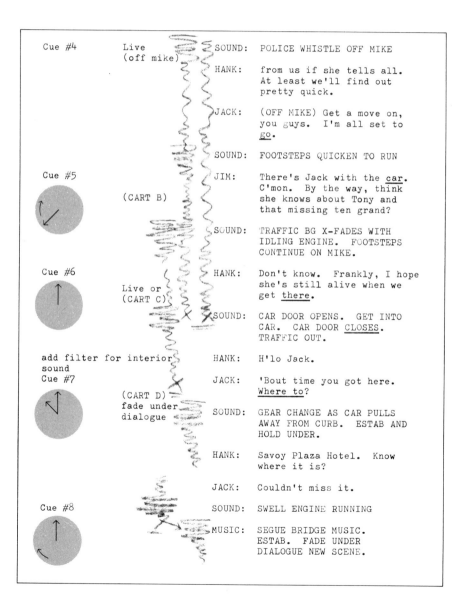

Cue #4	Live (off mike)	SOUND:	POLICE WHISTLE OFF MIKE
		HANK:	from us if she tells all. At least we'll find out pretty quick.
		JACK:	(OFF MIKE) Get a move on, you guys. I'm all set to go.
		SOUND:	FOOTSTEPS QUICKEN TO RUN
Cue #5	(CART B)	JIM:	There's Jack with the car. C'mon. By the way, think she knows about Tony and that missing ten grand?
		SOUND:	TRAFFIC BG X-FADES WITH IDLING ENGINE. FOOTSTEPS CONTINUE ON MIKE.
Cue #6	Live or (CART C)	HANK:	Don't know. Frankly, I hope she's still alive when we get there.
		SOUND:	CAR DOOR OPENS. GET INTO CAR. CAR DOOR CLOSES. TRAFFIC OUT.
add filter for interior sound		HANK:	H'lo Jack.
Cue #7	(CART D) fade under dialogue	JACK:	'Bout time you got here. Where to?
		SOUND:	GEAR CHANGE AS CAR PULLS AWAY FROM CURB. ESTAB AND HOLD UNDER.
		HANK:	Savoy Plaza Hotel. Know where it is?
		JACK:	Couldn't miss it.
Cue #8		SOUND:	SWELL ENGINE RUNNING
		MUSIC:	SEGUE BRIDGE MUSIC. ESTAB. FADE UNDER DIALOGUE NEW SCENE.

B. The cue description indicates the type of sound or music and the control technique to be used.

C. The circle (knob potentiometers) or slider (linear potentiometers) for each cue indicates:

    1. Volume settings for each cue relative to program level:

        a) 12 o'clock setting is voice level
        b) 8 o'clock setting is low volume
        c) 5 o'clock setting is maximum volume before distortion

    2. Sound source is indicated by TAPE or MIKE if sound is live. Recorded cues are usually dubbed to cartridge for ease of cuing, and where multisounds need sequencing into a complex sound routine each sound is assigned a lettered (A,B,C,) cartridge player unit. Live sounds are assigned a microphone (numbered) and are spatially placed at the microphone by the notation ON or OFF MIKE.

    3. If the post-production will use multitrack mixdown techniques, each sound will be assigned a track number by the recording engineer.

D. The relative volume line immediately to the left of the dialogue indicates the length of the sound cue and/or the music passage, showing exactly where the cue begins and ends. The volume of the sound is indicated by the width of the line.

An experienced sound production crew (director, sound technician, recording engineer, and talent) can read this script and visualize in their minds exactly how the scene will "play" as a finished product.

Production Analysis

A sound routine of traffic noises on a busy intersection is needed to establish the locale of the scene. A number of companies provide recorded sound effects which are available to rent or purchase. If the effect must be unique to the scene it describes, the producer can record the sound effect on location under the conditions required by the action of the story.

The traffic sounds in this scene are held at a lower volume level than the actor's voices so as not to detract from the conversation, yet are loud enough to set the aural scenery for the listener.

We must next determine what action sounds are necessary. Do we decide to use footsteps for the men crossing the street? Are they necessary to the physical action of the scene? Would footsteps normally be lost in the din of other traffic sounds so that retaining them in the sound plot might distort the reality of the scene for the listener?

Or might it be that there is simply too much sound happening at once for the listener to assimilate it all?

If we do use the footsteps, these are action sounds. It is quite difficult to prerecord and simulate action sounds in a mixdown with various kinds of audio processing. Sound effects which the actor or narrator needs to time himself on, or which serve as cues for dialogue, need to be performed in the studio. These effects can be recorded and mixed with the dialogue at the time of recording, or they can be recorded simultaneously on separate tracks for a more careful mixdown later.

Action sound also implies a quality. A door slammed in anger, running steps after a skirmish, and many other situations requiring that the dialogue and the sound interact to obtain precise timing and quality, suggest the need for the sound man and the actors to work together in studio real time. Having the sound effects operation right in the studio at some distance from the actors and the cast microphone not only allows the actors to hear the sound effects for direct timing, but also to improve the naturalness and punch of the sound as it is recorded. The combination of main pickup with a microphone at the sound truck plus a low leakage of sound effects into the cast microphone some distance away creates an enhanced naturalness far superior to that of prerecorded sounds.

Action sound effects are more effective and believable when the action is really performed. When a character says, "Put those groceries on the kitchen table," the sound of a heavily loaded paper bag on a formica table top picked up by the studio microphone is totally convincing. When the sound man is measuring the stealthy footsteps of the rapist on a deserted street late at night, the terror of the victim becomes even more eloquent.

In our scene, how are we going to denote the change of traffic direction? Since it is not unusual for a policeman to be controlling traffic at a busy intersection, the use of the police whistle gives us a "cutaway" from which to reverse the flow of traffic by controlling the volume of the recorded sound.

Another visualization problem concerns the handling of the car. Are the characters approaching a parked car, requiring the routine of entering, starting, and driving away, or is it an idling car, suggesting that a colleague has been waiting for them? In this case, the dialogue suggests the latter. Does the audience get into the car with them? Once again, the dialogue directs this action. When the car door closes, the background sounds recede into a muffled background or are eliminated altogether, and the microphone stays within the car as it drives off.

A final production question concerning our scene is how to cap the scene into the bridge music leading to the next scene. It might be done like this: Following the last word of dialogue, bring up the sound of the revving motor as the car pulls away from the curb (recorded from the perspective of inside the car). As the car pulls away, X-fade the transition music into the car sounds and swell this to program level until fading it under the dialogue or narration of the new scene.

> Note: This kind of detailed attention to scene visualization is especially critical in stereo production. The effect of direction reversal becomes very apparent when using the pan pot to move the sound from left to right and from right to left. Very few commercials are recorded in stereo because the bulk of radio advertising is broadcast on monaural AM radio stations. However, as FM broadcasting continues to expand at a very rapid pace, and as more and more stations are broadcasting in stereo sound, it is reasonable to expect that a larger percentage of commercial production will be recorded in stereo. Therefore, it is important to be cognizant of stereo production techniques.

Production Techniques

An important consideration in the production of sound is how far away a particular sound effect is supposed to be from the listener. An explosion that is supposed to be taking place a half-mile from the listener should not sound as if it were right on top of the microphone. Similarly, if an actor on mike shoots a gun, the shot must not sound as if it were two blocks away. Sound effects must always be kept in proper perspective.

Proper perspective can be obtained in three ways: (1) by controlling volume or loudness; (2) by placing sound effects close to or far away from the mike; and (3) by frequency control, i.e., the muffling of sounds through the clipping of high frequencies using audio processing equipment. Each method has its advantages and each has its limitations. Footsteps can be made to sound close or far away by raising or lowering the volume of the footsteps. The recorded sound of a car may be made to appear as if it were approaching the microphone, passing it, and fading off into the distance through proper volume control. The volume is started low, then gradually increased to full level as the car passes by, and finally slowly reduced until the car fades into the distance.

This effect can be obtained in stereo production using the pan pot control to move the sound. However, in other cases the position of the microphones in regard to the sound effect must be considered (the audience is always with the microphone). A car engine will sound quite a bit different from the inside of the car than it does from the outside. This means that care must be exercised in either picking re-corded sound effects or recording them especially for the sequence desired. An explosion that is recorded from a distance of a half-mile will always sound distant, no matter how high the playback volume. Similarly, many manual sound effects that are worked in the studio by the sound man must be positioned in relation to the microphone depending upon how far away they are supposed to be.

To "fade" a sound means simply to raise or lower the volume level of one or more program elements (e.g., with the sound effect of a passing car, the sound must be faded up to full program level, then slowly faded down until it is completely gone). Technically, fades are accomplished either by talent as they move into or away from the microphone, or by the engineer at the audio control console.

There are three ways of fading sound: fade up–fade down, cross-fade, and segue. The fade up–fade down simply means to bring up the volume level, hold it briefly, then bring it down again and under or out behind the dialogue. The passing car, mentioned above, is one example of this. Its use here is to establish perspective. Another use for this fade is to set the scene. Refer to the beginning of our script where the two men are crossing the street. The first thing we hear is the traffic and crowd noises at full volume level (i.e., at normal listening level). This is sustained for five or ten seconds to establish it, then faded under to allow us to hear the dialogue. The diagram below illustrates this.

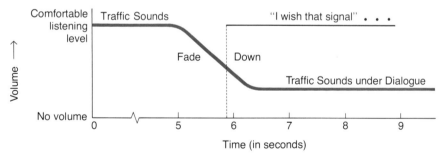

Figure 5.6 Fade up–Fade down

The above fade in reverse, fade down–fade up, is useful to indicate a transition in time and/or place. As an illustration of this, instead of ending the scene we are analyzing with transition music, we could fade out the car completely, allow three to five seconds of dead air, then fade in the car as it comes to a stop outside the hotel and start a new scene. This is a simple but effective transition device. See Figure 5.7.

The fade down–fade up is also useful as a means of editing unneces-

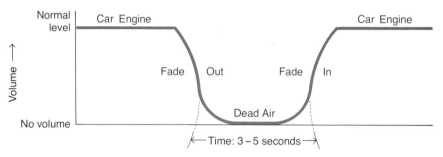

Figure 5.7   Fade down–Fade up

sary or inconsequential dialogue. In a sequence in which a political speech occurs, it might be impractical and unnecessary to present the whole speech. Instead, you could fade down after the first few remarks by the orator, pause, and fade up as the speaker finishes his diatribe. Thus, you have cut out unnecessary dialogue and at the same time a time transition has been accomplished. This is particularly important in the production of radio commercials where you are working within strict time limits in which to tell the story of the product.

The cross-fade is like the fade down–fade up, but without the dead air space between. While one element (sound, voice, etc.) fades in, another element seems to grow out of the first, giving a fluid sense of continuity between the sound elements.

The segue is similar to a cross-fade except that the overall level is not dropped appreciably during the change. Segues are used when you want to create the illusion of identity between several sound elements in a drama. A classic use of the segue occurred in radio drama, in *Sorry Wrong Number*, when a murdered woman's scream was covered by the screech of an elevated train. Pitch and volume remained the same, as only the quality of the sound was changed.

We might bridge our scene into another scene that might possibly follow, opening with the conversation of the three men (including the driver of the car) just after they have entered the hotel lobby. We cross-fade between the bridge music and the conversation because we have a natural break. The car trip is over and a new scene is beginning in different surroundings. Our complete transition would then be as follows: Segue from the car engine to the bridge music, then cross-fade from the bridge music to the conversation in the hotel lobby. Figure 5.9 illustrates a segue. The significant difference between a X-fade and a segue is the length of time that both sounds are simultaneously audible. The X-fade and segue in radio production accomplish the same effect as the dissolve and matched dissolve in television and film production.

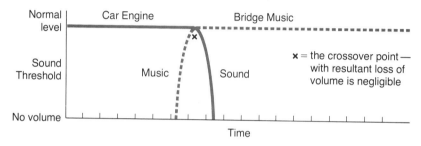

Figure 5.9 Segue

In our analysis of this scene, we have moved from a visualization of how the scene might physically occur to a consideration of how this sound routine can be accomplished in its final form recorded in the studio and edited by a multitrack mixdown in post-production to produce the sound story with complete verisimilitude.

Transitions

Transitions are extremely important in radio production, since the audience is instantly transported from one place to another, one thought or emotion to another. Consequently, the techniques used to make transitions must be precise and clear, since otherwise the audience will become easily confused as they attempt to follow the action of the story and the sequence of events in their minds. Particular care must be taken in regard to transitions within radio commercials. All but the simplest and most straightforward of narrative commercials are replete with transitions between the story, its several locales, and the time lapse between the actors trying the product and voicing satisfaction with it. There are as many other reasons to bridge between one sequence and another as you can creatively devise.

The means available to the radio producer to make transitions are:

(1) music; (2) sound effects; (3) silence; (4) voice (narrator or announcer); or (5) any combination of the above.

Music is the most often used transitional device because of its highly evocative and subjective effect upon the listener. It is particularly useful in making transitions from one mood to another. Sound effects, since they are the scenery of the radio production, are an excellent device for changing locale. A transition from a busy airport to the cabin of an airborne plane can easily be accomplished with the bridging sound of the plane's take-off. Since sound also depicts the physical action of the scene, sound can be used, as in the scene analyzed above, to transport our characters from a busy street corner to a hotel lobby which is the setting for the following scene. The appropriate music can emotionally bridge one scene into the next, foreshadowing the confrontation that is about to occur.

The use of silence as a transitional device can be very effective. It is probably most useful when a time lapse is used to signify the passage of time, indicating to the listener that what has occurred during the lapse is not very important; just more of the same from which the listener is spared. Silence at the end of a sequence can pack a strong feeling of finality. The listener instinctively knows that a following sequence will have no relationship to the action or thought just concluded.

The spoken word is used when the above nonverbal transitions will not suffice. Perhaps a bridge between two scenes is too complicated for the audience to follow without a verbal explanation. Radio commercials are especially produced to make absolutely sure that the listener can easily follow the rapid interchange between the dramatic action of the scene and the commercial message addressed directly to the listener. It is the message that evokes the necessary action to induce the purchase of the product.

Audio Processing Techniques

Sophisticated audio processing equipment is available, and modern recording techniques have been developed for the radio producer to use to the limits of his creativity. The shaping and altering of program sound elements by clipping frequencies, adding reverberation, speeding up and slowing sound rate, and over-dubbing and sweetening sound through various mixdown techniques—all these allow the radio producer to obtain effects which further influence the listener intellectually and emotionally about the sound sequence perceived.

A number of excellent textbooks describe the use of sound production equipment. The latest editions of *The Technique of the Sound*

Studio, by Alec Nisbett, and *Modern Recording Techniques,* by Robert Runstein, published by the H. W. Sams Company for the Recording Institute of America, Inc., are two absolutely necessary technical references. Though both texts are written from an engineering focus, they are suprisingly clear reading for the non-engineer. In any case, a thorough knowledge of recording techniques makes for the greatest skill in radio production.

A filter set such as the Urei "Little Dipper" is an effective tool for creating innovative special sound effects. It contains: (1) a low cutoff filter, tunable from 20 Hz to 200 Hz; (2) band pass filters tunable from 20 Hz to 20 kHz; and (3) a high cutoff filter, tunable from 2 kHz to 20 kHz. What in fact happens to the sound is that the filter passes all of the signal on one side of the frequency on which it is set and cuts out more and more of the signal on the other side of the point on which it is set.

Filters can be used for impressionistic dramatic effect. Filters can distort and clip sound to simulate telephone conversations, public address systems, intercoms, and other social uses of communication which we identify by how the sound is characterized as well as by the message carried.

The frequency range of most telephone systems is approximately 3,000 Hz with a lower limit cutoff at around 300 Hz. A variable filter such as the Little Dipper can be set to pass frequencies between top and bottom cutoffs providing the subjective effect satisfying to the radio audience.

Equalization is a means of restoring level frequency responses to achieve a pleasing balance, such as the proper subjective balance of treble and bass tone control to provide a sound response selection.

Notch filters can be used to produce phasing of "flanging" effects similar to the effect produced when two tape machines play the same material at slightly different speeds. Combinations of high cutoff, low cutoff, band-pass, and notch filters with variable frequency can be used, limited only by the producer's or engineer's imagination.

Thus, the filter can be used to: (1) eliminate coherent noise from the program material; (2) eliminate semicoherent or incoherent noise such as hum from fluorescent fixtures and air conditioning when recording on location; (3) eliminate microphone ringing and feedback; (4) create special effects such as have been described above; (5) enhance frequencies within a sound; and (6) create harmonic distortion.

When the producer "shapes" a sound by equalization, he is able to match sounds which have been recorded under varying conditions. This technique is useful in matching sound when dubbing film. While voices recorded under different conditions cannot be entirely matched, differences in quality and intelligibility can be made less noticeable and obtrusive. Thus, by equalizing the sound, the producer/engineer has control over the harmonic balance or timbre of the sound by altering the frequency response of an amplifier so that certain frequencies are more or less pronounced than others.

Reverberation, or "echo," is important in shaping the program signal for artistic effect. There are three main types of devices which can provide artificial reverberation: (1) echo plates; (2) spring reverberation units; and (3) acoustic echo chambers. Reverberation colors sound by increasing the distance the sounds must travel before they are heard by the listener. Shaping sound by "echo" recalls for the listener situations from life where the presence of the sound dictates the location and the activity of the persons involved at the time the sound occurs. The ricochet of a bullet can describe the circumstances of its firing. Sound reverberation can describe where the person is, locating the sound source spatially in relation to the listener. Speaking in an empty room will sound far different from speaking in that same room fully appointed with furniture, carpets, and drapes. The sound of a person speaking from a closet or from down a well can be emulated and recreated by the amount of reverberation added to the sound. The absence of reverberation also can indicate the environment surrounding the sound. The reverberation plate such as the EMT 140 TS is a rectangular steel sheet $\frac{1}{64}$ inch thick, approximately 3 feet high by 6 feet wide, enclosed in a frame 8 feet by 4 feet by 1 foot thick. Reverberation is created by inducing wave motion in the plate. While the reverberation effect of a plate is two-dimensional, unlike the more realistic three-dimensional acoustic chamber, the difference perceived by the listener is quite negligible. The reverberation plate can control the amount of reverberation, mechanically varying the reverberation time to obtain the echo effect required in the sound sequence. The decay time of the EMT 140 TS is variable from one to four seconds. The decay time is changed mechanically by moving a plate which is covered with an acoustic absorbing material closer to the steel plate to shorten decay time and farther away from the steel plate to lengthen it.

The BX 20E is an example of a spring reverberation unit. This unit is approximately 1½ feet by 1½ feet by 4 feet in size, weighing around 100 pounds. While this type of reverberation unit is small in size and relatively inexpensive, the sound is often tinny, giving an unnatural quality to the echo. This type of unit works better with voice than it does with music in adding "presence" to the sound.

The acoustic echo chamber consists of a room with highly reflective surfaces in which a speaker and a microphone are placed. The sound, broadcast from the speaker, is bounced from the multisurfaces of the room and is picked up by a microphone at the other end of the room. Movable partitions can be set up in the chamber to vary the decay time of the reverberation. Acoustic echo chambers have the most pleasing and realistic quality of echo sounds, emulating the three-dimensional effect of natural echo.

Artificial reverberation is an integral part of the balance and control of the sound signal. When each sound source has a separately controlled echo feed, differential amounts of echo can be added and mixed during mixdown, depending upon the amount of resonance and/or presence required for the effect. The use of echo is a matter for the radio producer to decide in his interpretation of the scene he is portraying in drama, or the music he is interpreting in the recording of a composition. The main problem with using echo in dramatic scenes is one of perspective: moving closer to the microphone produces more feed to the echo chamber. In some cases it may be necessary to use a separate microphone for the echo feed in order to obtain proper sound separation between the several sound sources.

In the scene we have been developing for production, we could enhance room presence by suspending a second bi-directional microphone above the dialogue microphone. This stronger echo presence would help to create perspective in the crowd scenes, separating dialogue from the background sounds. The amount of echo is automatically reduced as the actors move in on the dialogue microphone.

Recently developed audio processing equipment such as the Kepex and the Omnipressor are flexible and have multiple uses. These devices can be used for limiting and compressing in a straightforward manner as well as for eliminating undesirable acoustics and other sound leakage. A good production sense can enhance the radio production immeasurably.

Microphone Placement

There are two basic philosophies of recording a complex sound sequence. One is the old-fashioned method of using as few microphones or line inputs as possible, recording the elements of sound and music in conjunction with the narration or dialogue in real time. That is, sound effects are cued and timed not only to the dialogue of the scene, but to the nuances of the actor's interpretation of the scene, and are recorded with the dialogue. Most producers prefer this method for in-studio production, where all of the elements can be tightly controlled. The other method is the modern technique of close-miking, where each actor has a separate microphone feed. Each microphone, in addition to the line inputs for sound effects and music, is recorded on a separate track so that the entire production can be "assembled" in a post-production mixdown. While theoretically with close-miking there is better control of the quality of the sound of each input, for dramatic work where voices must interact this isolated sound prevents the nuances of intercommunication and that extra "something" that actors get from keying on each other. The old-fashioned method supports their characterization and portrayal of the scene.

Many producers prefer to simultaneously record as many elements of the production as is technically feasible, even though they might record each element on a separate, synchronized track as well as record an overall scene master track. The producer can come close to "having his cake and eating it," since he has the overall track for timing and interpretation nuances and each individual track for post-production mix-down, so that he can obtain optimum sound quality.

The CBS Radio Mystery Theatre uses one cast microphone where possible. A Neumann U67 microphone with a figure-eight pattern is used as the cast microphone. The actors work within the two lobes of the figure eight. Another omnidirectional microphone hangs directly above the cast microphone in order to add room presence around the actors. Because of its placement, this microphone is able to pick up a much higher proportion of reflected sound. It can be mixed with the cast microphone in varying amounts to add more or less room presence surrounding the voices. Another microphone, placed next to the cast microphone at 90 degrees to it and with filter/reverberation added, can be used for "ghost voices." Placed in this manner, this microphone will have a minimum leakage of the ghost voice into the main cast microphone. Whatever number of sound sources are used, the CBS Radio Mystery Theatre production technique is to mix all microphones before the program goes on tape. Where feasible, sound effects and music beds are also mixed into the program before taping, so that a minimum of post-production is necessary. Many commercial producers operate under this philosophy where practicable to save post-production time. Others record individual elements separately to save on studio time.

Final editing and assembling consists of piecing together a number of segments of tape which represent various starts and stops of the production which were necessary to retake sections of the production where some error occurred or something was technically imperfect.

Stereo Production Technique

An increasing amount of radio production is recorded in stereo as more and more FM stations are broadcasting a stereo signal. In many ways reproduction of the scene visualization is easier in stereo production because the pan pot, by varying the amount of signal between the two stereo volume controls and the addition of artificial reverberation, can create an imaginary room about the scene. The pan pot can seem to move the sound source from left-to-right and right-to-left in stereo, and by using a joy-stick device the sound source can be moved in a full circle in quad-channel reproduction.

Current state-of-the-art stereo production must take into account the monaural listener by panning at least twenty percent of the isolated channel toward the opposite channel. If the left channel is receiving the signal, one should bleed approximately twenty percent of the volume into the right channel, in essence moving the sound source more to the center between the two stereo channels, creating a monaural sound without much detriment to the stereo effect. By using this technique, the stereo production can be broadcast satisfactorily on non-stereo FM stations.

There are two ways to set up stereo miking in the studio to obtain the cast microphone arrangement and the close-miking technique for dramatic production already described. One method places microphones in the studio so that each microphone represents an area; that is, microphone outputs fed into the left and right stereo channels are determined by the pan pots. A production which uses a narrator or an announcer who must speak directly to the audience needs to place him in a mono position with the output of his microphone fed to both channels equally so that he seems to be speaking straight on to the listening audience. The stereo effect is achieved at the mixer by rotating the pan pot, which is in effect a variable channel positioner, placing the voice in relation to the listener from left to right and positions in between.

Close-miking places the burden of stereo perspective and the illusion of physical movement entirely upon the mixer, while the actor/narrator almost never changes his or her position relative to the microphone (see Figure 5.10). Right and left is determined from the perspective of the mixer at the recording console (see Figure 5.11).

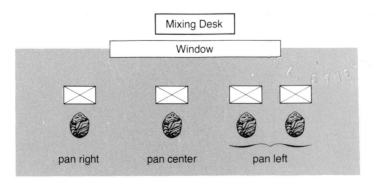

Figure 5.10 Voices on individual microphones controlled by volume and panoramic potentiometers.

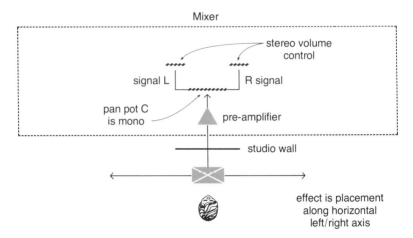

Figure 5.11 Simplified Schematic of Pan Pot

Another method of microphone placement for the stereo production follows the theory that as few microphones as possible are used, positioning the actors on and off microphone to achieve spatial relationships. Two cast microphones placed together in the center of the studio angled in toward each other so that the lobes overlap each other (see Figure 5.12) allow the producer to position the actors and narrator in the studio in relation to each other and at the same time in relation to the stereo channels. By means of the pan pots, the voices can be moved along the left/right axis. The pan pot moves each microphone perspective from far right to center (mono) and far left

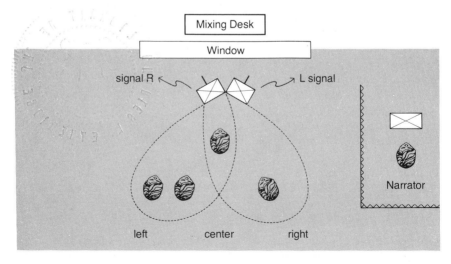

Figure 5.12 Talent placed in microphone patterns for stereo pickup.

to center (mono). When the pan pots of each microphone input are used together, the effect is of flopping the voices from left to right and right to left so that each sound seems to switch sides of the room in relation to the listening audience. The narrator can work directly on both microphones so that he is picked up equally on both lobes of the microphone pattern, creating a balance between both microphones so that he is heard in mono. If sound isolation is needed between the actors and the narrator, the narrator can be placed on his own microphone separated from the other voices and sound effects by a sound-baffled partition.

An excellent discussion concerning miking techniques for each instrument in a musical recording appears in the chapter on microphones, in Runstein's *Modern Recording Techniques*.

Post-Production Mixdown

The artistry of the radio producer becomes evident in the post-production, or mixdown, stage of the radio production. The production may be a one-person affair where all of the skills of writing, announcing, and engineering, as well as the production elements of sound and music are performed by the producer, or it may be a full-scale, high-budget show utilizing the full resources of a production studio with a full crew of technical specialists. In any case, the producer is the final authority, and all of his creativity, discrimination, and technical skills are called into play.

Post-production editing and mixdown are terms used interchangeably, although technically they are not the same thing. Editing is undertaken to shape the program, tightening it for its greatest listener interest. Editing cuts out fluffs and mistakes and properly times both the ultimate length of the program and the internal pace of the production. The mixdown is the process of taking the various elements of the production which have been recorded on separate recording tracks and re-recording them in proper sequence and balance onto a master tape.

This may be a relatively simple process if the producer includes the many elements of the production combined for proper balance during production, recording the output on a single tape. The process becomes relatively more difficult and time-consuming when the dialogue has been recorded separately on one track, music on a second track, with sound effects recorded on several bits of tape which must be first edited into the proper order in which they are to be inserted into the production.

A good recording and mixdown control console and a four-channel recorder are necessary for a quality final production tape. There are a number of very good four-channel mixers and recorders, such as the Neve line of consoles, Quantum's QM-8A, Teac's TASCAM, portable mixers such as the Allen & Heath Quasi series, and the Tapco 6000R series. There are many good four-channel recorders available within a reasonable price range, such as the Revox A700, the Audiotronics/ Stellavox, the Grandson, Nagra S, MCI-JH110, and the new Ampex ATR-100. The ATR-100 can serve as a production recorder as well as a playback for radio station automation systems handling 14-inch reels

StudioWest
CUSTOM SOUND RECORDERS

DATE 3/77
CLIENT GARY SEEGER PRODUCTIONS.
SUBJECT
ID # REEL #
STUDIO A TRACKS 16
ENGINEER L.O. SPEED 30
PAGE 1 of 3

TITLE: HOLLYWOOD PARK — MASTER No. — NOTES: — SEARCH NUMBERS — TIME:

1 KICK	2 BASS	3 DMS	4 GUIT	5 PIANO	6 CONGAS
7 ← VOC	8 ALS	9 →	10 ALL ① BRASS	11 ALL ② BRASS	12 SAX ③ 4 TMPTS
13 B SAX & TMPTS	14	15 AD LIB FLUTE	16 MET	17	18
19	20	21	22	23	24

TITLE: FIRST FEDERAL SAVINGS — MASTER No. — NOTES: — SEARCH NUMBERS — TIME:

1 KICK	2 BASS	3 DMS	4 GUIT	5 PIANO	6 A GUIT
7 BELLS	8 BRASS &	9 REEDS	10 STRING BASS	11 ← VOC	12 ALS
13 →	14	15 STNGS	16 MET	17	18
19	20	21	22	23	24

TITLE: NOODLE MAGIC — MASTER No. — NOTES: — SEARCH NUMBERS — TIME:

1 BLOCKS	2 GONG	3 BELL TREE	4 BELLS	5 PIANO	6 HARP
7 FLUTE	8 OBOE	9 BASS CLAR	10 STRING BASS	11 1 CLAR	12 2 CLAR
13 EXTRA PERC & PIANO	14 F HORN	15 STRGS	16 MET	17	18
19	20	21	22	23	24

TITLE: — MASTER No. — NOTES: — SEARCH NUMBERS — TIME:

1	2	3	4	5	6
7	8	9	10	11	12
13	14	15	16	17	18
19	20	21	22	23	24

TITLE: — MASTER No. — NOTES: — SEARCH NUMBERS — TIME:

1	2	3	4	5	6
7	8	9	10	11	12
13	14	15	16	17	18
19	20	21	22	23	24

TITLE: — MASTER No. — NOTES: — SEARCH NUMBERS — TIME:

1	2	3	4	5	6
7	8	9	10	11	12
13	14	15	16	17	18
19	20	21	22	23	24

Figure 5.13 Post-production Records

for six hours of playing time at 3¾ ips (inches per second tape speed). The ATR-100 is a very new recorder incorporating radical advances in tape handling and electronic design. In addition to playback ips, it can be set for 15 or 30 ips for ease and precision of tape editing.

Let us assume for mixdown purposes that we have recorded our scene on four separate tape tracks. Track #1 contains all of the dialogue and such live sound as the actors need to time and cue on. Tracks #2 and #3 contain the various sound effect routines in order

Figure 5.14 Post-production Records (Log Sheet)

Studio West
CUSTOM SOUND RECORDERS

5042 RUFFNER STREET, SAN DIEGO
CALIFORNIA 92111 PHONE:(714) 277-4714

VOICE PRODUCTION

CLIENT		DATE
TALENT		ENG.
DESCRIPTION	MODE	

FS – false start • LFS – long false start • NG – no good • INT – intercut • C– complete • H – hold • M - master

SUBJECT	TAKE	CODE	TIME	TAKE	CODE	TIME	TAKE	CODE	TIME	TAKE	CODE	TIME	TAKE	CODE	TIME

Figure 5.15 Post-production Records (Voice Production)

that they may be finally mixed for precise timing. Track #4 contains the cue and bridge music as well as additional sound placed on this track for ease of mixing. The four-track tape has been properly synchronized to follow the mixdown legend. If each element is recorded on a separate tape necessitating four playback units, each machine must be securely interlocked for precise entry onto the master dub.

In our production, each track has been edited into its **final** form. Actors' mistakes have either been edited out or re-recorded. The signal quality has been enhanced and boosted where necessary to provide clarity and presence. The timing of the sound routines in relation to the dialogue has been set. Each production element is ready for the final mixdown.

The production script of our scene (pp. 88–89) needs to be translated into a mixdown legend for the producer/engineer to follow in dubbing the tracks or tapes onto a master tape. Figure 5.19 is an example of a legend showing how our scene might be mixed in accordance with the production script. If we use a computer such as the Compumix or any other automated mixdown system to command the

Figure 5.16 A front view of the Quantum Radio Labs QM-8A audio console, a versatile but compact mixer.

Figure 5.17 A front view of the QM-8A audio console.

final mix, the precise time of entry of each cue must be noted in the legend. In our case, since our production is a drama, we may wish to use cue times as a guideline depending upon the "feel" and rhythm of the scene itself to cue the exact mix. Nevertheless, all of the information in precise order for the mixdown is available on the mixdown legend.

Many producers, recognizing the reality of the circumstances under

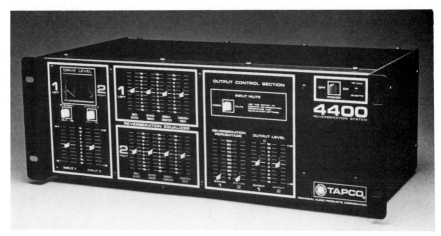

Figure 5.18 Technical Audio Products Corporation's 4400 reverberation system.

Mixdown Legend

00:01:30

Time	Track #1	Track #2	Track #3	Track #4
	Dialogue	Sound	Sound	Music
:00		Traffic routine		
:03			Intermittent voices under	Bridge Out
:08	Q: I wish that signal.....	Fade under		
:10	Q: .....if we don't hurry		Police whistle	
:12	Q: ....let's go		Footsteps (on mike)	
:32	Q: ..bargain for protection		Police whistle	
:36	Q: ....I'm all set to go		Steps quicken to run	
:40	Q: ....missing ten grand	X-Fade to		Idling engine
:55	Q: ....when we get there	car door-opens shuffle-closes-		
:01:06	Q: ...Where to?	gear changes- car pulls		X-Fade
:01:16	Q: ...couldn't miss it.	away-up to ESTAB-fade under & hold		
:01:19		Swell car running - segue to		
				Bridge music- ESTAB & fade under dialogue
:01:30				

Figure 5.19 Mixdown Legend

which most listeners will hear the program or the commercial, prefer to make the final mixdown using cheap car radio speakers from which to hear how the production will ultimately sound, rather than using the high-fidelity monitors usually found in the recording studio.

Conclusion

Radio is a mobile medium consisting of very few long form programs such as dramas and documentaries, although some will always be a part of the medium. The staple of production is the one minute commercial or message packaged using the same techniques as the commercial. Many of these short program features are gems of radio production, using imagination and cleverness as well as the discipline necessary for packaging messages in bundles no shorter than 58 seconds or longer than 60 seconds.

It is ironic that the most elaborate uses of sound usually occur in the recording studio and in film and TV productions. Nevertheless, radio's basic need is people capable of quality sound production.

Suggestions for Further Learning

1. Produce a one minute story in sound using no dialogue and only incidental music. Use either library sound effects or ones you record yourself.

2. Produce a one minute spot using a piece of existing music. Write a script that fits the musical phrasing and works as well as if original music had been written for the script. Edit the music as needed.

3. Produce a short dramatic scene using (1) close miking and recording of elements separately, and (2) the same scene using a technique similar to the one described for the *CBS Mystery Theater*. Which one plays better for you?

CHAPTER 6

Programs

Radio programing is an imprecise art. It is not surprising that many differences of opinion exist regarding the best and most effective ways of programing. This chapter presents some of the significant dichotomies of thought and practice.

What the Public Wants/
What's Good Radio

One basic philosophy of running a station is that you must find out what the public wants and give it to them. Another says that you provide what management thinks is good radio (or what management is capable of doing well) and you let the material seek its audience—in other words, all programing will eventually find its audience. The former idea has in its favor the effectiveness of serving existing wants, of dealing with "proven" practices, and of being responsive to the public. This approach is similar to that of a politician who tries to find out where the people are going because he is their leader. But how does station management know what the people want? Which people—the whole audience or some section of it? A station must either have extremely sensitive decision-makers or very good and frequent research. Even then it may not always accurately read the available clues. Also, because it is difficult to know what an audience will like among the new and untried program ideas, there is a tendency to stick with proven programs and to allow others to set the trends. Stations that operate in this way tend to play "follow the leader." It is possible to get strategically boxed in by others who take the initiative.

The second idea, "to thine own self be true," tends to make leaders rather than followers, for it is often the fresh and unique rather than the familiar that arouses interest. Many listeners are impressed by the integrity of this approach. On the negative side, it is possible to be a leader without followers. Station management may have unrealistic goals. If management is very different from the public they must serve, if they are overly esoteric or abrasive, they may end up talking to themselves. They may fail, for lack of an audience, to sell the advertiser's product, which pays the bills and allows more programing.

Formats/Programs

The term *format* as used in radio has two meanings. First, it is the type of programing done by a station, such as Top-40 or all-news. It also refers to the routine, or the list of specific ingredients, found in a program hour. This includes specific phrases to be spoken, program content, and the order and manner of placement. The format in the latter sense includes specific comments to be used to open and close a newscast, certain catch phrases or slogans to be used with station identifications, and other ingredients.

Most radio stations today deal in formats, in the sense that they produce patterns of continuous programs. That is, most stations have one continuous program. It may be a deejay program or even a magazine program, but it has only a middle, no beginning or end. Radio stations don't like to give listeners a place to tune out. One such likely place is the end of a program. If programs don't end, one tune-out factor is eliminated. If people know that whenever they tune in a particular station it will have a certain kind of program, one source of confusion is eliminated. This is a way of making it easier to listen to a station. However, individual programs have their advantages. They may sell more easily than a segment of a format, and they may give uniqueness to a station. Not all program matter lends itself to lengthy presentations or fits within a formatted program day.

Free Form/Format

Here, the other meaning of format is used. The opposing views are: do you allow each program segment to be organized and produced as its own unique segment, or do you provide a guideline which all programs must follow, with prescriptions regarding sequencing of key elements? Free form is more creative. Formatting is more controlled and safe. Free form is generally more fun and challenging, a vote of confidence in the person producing the program. Formatting is more routine, a way of minimizing mistakes. Free form requires better talent, or at least a different kind of talent. In a free form environment the individual producer is more important, in the format the super programer is the more important. The format method is used in small stations and small markets and in those situations where management has something specific in mind and desires great consistency. Also, the payola problems that some stations have faced have caused some managements to want to centralize control.

The Committee/The Great Man

A technique of decision-making and prediction-making called the Delphi Method involves getting consensus from a group of experts. It has been found to be an effective way of minimizing risk and maximizing accuracy in uncertain situations. Its basic assumption is that "n heads are better than one."

On the other hand, many businesses believe in the strong leader who scientifically and intuitively guides his organization. Great art usually depends upon the vision of the single artist. Even group activities like filmmaking depend upon the vision of a single person. The auteur theory is widely held, seemingly a view that genius resides in individuals and not committees.

On the newspaper sports pages where the individual sports writers make their predictions about football games, the consensus nearly always ranks higher than an individual's predictions. Yet there is a widely held belief in that old line about a zebra (or camel) being an animal put together by a committee. The collectivization of things is sneered at by the rugged individualists. In short, both views have their adherents, and hard data do not support one or the other position in all instances. Certainly, creative employees are happier in those situations where they can participate in decision-making, opposed to being handed out orders already decided upon.

Attract Listeners/
Not Drive Them Away

The one approach holds that you must do things to get attention. You must command audience attention. The other accents the non-irritant approach. You need not be great, but you must not provide reasons to tune out: keep irritant factors to a minimum, play safe.

Generation/Life Cycle

The generation theory holds that each generation is unique, with its own lifestyle and its own music tastes. The life-cycle theory accents the changing tastes and values of individuals as they go through life. This is applied to music especially. Some say that if one grows up liking one form of music, he will like it when he is adult. Others point out that the driving habits of teenage boys differ considerably from those of their fathers. A lot of behavior is transitional. The life-cycle theory holds that if you want to reach youth you play youth music, but to reach adults you play a different kind of music; that adults from two generations are more alike than adults and youth from the same generation.

Automated/Live

In the future this may be a less important question than in the past, since new-generation automation may allow us all to be cake eaters. We can have the flexibility of live broadcasting and the freedom from fighting hardware in the sequencing and playing of recorded and live elements, if we can afford it.

Automation historically has given the advantages of control of format (often linked with syndication packages), elimination of mechanical errors (although when the automation gear breaks down the errors can be horrendous), and perhaps cost savings. Disadvantages have included a canned sound and a general lack of flexibility. Not all formats lend themselves to automation. Automation can certainly eliminate headaches for the manager who does not have good human relations skills. It has allowed small markets to have large market sounds through syndication. In the past it also has usually meant a kind of sterile approach that turns off many listeners. If this latter continues to be true in the future, it may indicate a lack of imagination and effective use of automation capability on the part of management.

Automation can trade personnel problems for engineering problems, for as operation of sophisticated gear becomes easier the knowledge and general engineering competence required becomes greater. Stations in smaller markets may have as much difficulty getting and keeping the engineering help as they have had getting the star announcer or newsman. It is true that servicing and maintenance service are possible on a contract basis. Such services usually are done on a regional basis, with headquarters in larger cities; therefore larger stations in metropolitan areas find it easier to get immediate help than the smaller stations in outlying areas.

Automation can be costly, especially the most sophisticated types. It can be used primarily for control and smooth operation, with increased costs not of major concern (as long as these costs are not exorbitant). It can be used to replace unskilled people and compensate for lack of big-league quality personnel. It can also be used, and probably this is most often the case, to cut costs. Used properly, it can do this. The tax structure in the United States has encouraged this. Forty thousand dollars in automation costs and $40,000 in employee salaries are not equal. Employees also require social security, workman's compensation, sick pay, holiday pay, etc. Automation gear does wear out, but its costs can be depreciated and it doesn't get a job in a larger market. The tax savings can mean the difference between profit and loss for many operations.

Profits or Service

Some kinds of services are not profitable. Some enterprises which seem to provide no useful function to society *are* profitable. Useful public service and profitability can, however, be positively linked in radio as much as in any other kind of enterprise. The terms are in no way mutually exclusive. Some of the very best radio stations, which provide the most useful services to their community, are among the most profitable.

Society exists only through its communications. Radio is one of the most efficient and far-reaching of our communications tools. It can very much be a positive force in society.

Long-Term/Short-Term Success

Some formats lend themselves to longevity. Others are flashes in the pan. Some build audiences slowly and retain them for a long time, while others build audiences rapidly but perhaps do not hold them. Some operators want repeat listeners and repeat advertisers. Others try for the new and fresh, milking it for what it is worth and soon passing along to a new fad. Popular culture is very fad-oriented, but attention to basics of communication and human understanding can build audience loyalty, sometimes in combination with the current fads. Generally, honesty in business dealings and integrity in programing are ingredients every bit as important as brilliance.

Counterprogram/Do What
You Do Best

Counterprograming consists of finding the gap, the unmet need, or the weak spot, and acting accordingly. If a station can fill an unmet need, it very likely can be successful. If it can do something well that a competitor is doing poorly, it can likely be successful. Counterprograming is a valid idea which has some limits, however. It just may not be possible to accommodate available resources or talent to the counterprograming task. Not all comedians can be tragedians.

All-time great basketball coach Johnny Wooden used to say that it didn't matter too much what the competition did if his team did well what they were capable of doing. He did much less scouting of the competition than many other coaches do, preferring to concentrate on preparing his own team to do what they were capable of doing well. Many station managements use this approach, preferring to be pacesetters by using essentially an offensive strategy and forcing others to use a defensive strategy.

In this and other dichotomies above, it is not always a matter of either one or the other containing all the truth. Often it is a matter of emphasis. Just as our language is incapable of describing all of our thoughts and feelings, our theories are most often ways of describing for purposes of aiding understanding, of approximating reality rather than totally capturing it. Most stations combine counterprograming techniques with their own particular strengths. Any station that totally ignores the competition either is not competing effectively or it has much richer resources than anyone else in the market. Any station that only counterprograms is allowing everyone else in the market to decide what kind of station theirs is to be. They will get yo-yoed right out of the profit column.

AM/FM

Many people still feel that there are inherent differences between AM and FM with regard to programing philosophy and requirements. The fact is that both are radio and both have the same basic appeals and requirements. The only difference is a technical one—FM carries a higher-quality signal, one which does not carry as far as AM's. FM's signal does not go behind mountains or to places out of the line of sight from the transmitter. Car radios have always been mostly AM because AM picks up better in cars and the equipment manufacturers have overpriced their FM car receivers. Because FM's signal is higher-quality, it is more pleasing for music reproduction. Other than signal quality, FM and AM are not different. Programing that is successful on AM will work on FM.

In the past, FM stations tended to serve as background-music outlets. Historically, FM has programed more fine arts stations, less talk, less news, and fewer commercials than AM. A larger share of FM listening is done in living rooms, where people have expensive stereo speaker systems. Less FM listening is done in cars. FM listening tends to be proportionately higher during the afternoon and evening hours, while AM listening is proportionately stronger during drive times.

These listening patterns occur primarily for two reasons. One is the set location. Another is the programing. AM has emphasized news, information, and popular music, which attract the large drive-time audiences. FM has tended to provide background music or music which requires more concentration than people give while driving. The trend is changing, however, as FM provides more personalities, more popular music, and more information, and AM picks up some of the successful formats pioneered by FM.

The most important consideration is programing. That FM has historically been a money-losing medium is due at least as much to its programing as its set penetration. Many FM stations have been low-budget, low-quality program operations. People do not listen to poor-quality programs even if they are technically superior. The smaller number of commercials on FM hasn't all been because of good planning. They weren't generally planned to be nonprofit organizations.

For twenty years, people have been predicting FM's rise. They've been saying that AM would become all talk and FM would take over the music programing. AM is dying, FM is the future, was the saying. And for twenty years, FM's success was in the future. But one of the most dramatic success stories of the 1970s has been FM. Between 1970 and 1976, FM's audience share in major cities doubled. In New York, FM's 1970 share was 23.4 percent. By 1976 it was 39.7 percent. Chicago FM shares in 1970 were 13.3 percent; in 1976, 35.1. Boston went from 19 to 39 percent, Dallas/Fort Worth from 20.5 to 48.5, and Washington from 27.5 to 46.2. That growth continues.

FM still has some catching up to do, although in recent years FM revenues have been growing by 25 percent per year. Still, in the mid-'70s, total FM expenses exceed revenues nationally. Advertising rates have lagged behind AM's, as have employee salaries. The 1975 figures for one of the twenty largest markets showed that FM's penetration was at 90 percent, that there were twice as many FM as AM stations, and that FM listening constituted roughly 40 percent of the total listening. That market's FM stations, however, got only 17 percent of total ad revenue. As a group they lost money. In the future they will fare better, but it has been slow coming.

Because of format changes, set penetration increases, the increased number of professionals in FM, and recent audience acceptance, FM should achieve parity soon. FM revenues should increase at 20 percent per year for the next several years.

Local or Syndicated

Some broadcasters say that if a broadcaster needs the help of a consultant or syndicator he should not be in the business. Others are very happy to bring in outside help. Radio is very much a local medium. But networking and syndicating have always been a method of giving greater exposure to the few at the top of the talent pyramid. Also, by pooling resources a number of stations can present material that no single station could afford. In fact, no local station really originates all of its programing material. Phonograph records are nationally distributed, as is the news from wire services. Most ideas are borrowed, not originated. The question becomes: to what degree are available services utilized? Radio is a local and specialized medium. It may be possible for a television station to plug into a network and be assured of success regardless of the local effort; such is much less likely for radio. But a local radio effort does not necessarily preclude syndication or network aids. Networking and syndication will be discussed in great detail later in this chapter.

Small Market/Large Market

Certain variations are found between the small and large markets. Some of the same variations occur between the haves and the have-nots in the same markets. Generally, the larger the market the more specialized the station becomes, but there are exceptions to that. Some of the stations that offer the most diverse services are large-market, full-service stations, affluent and usually clear-channel, that can afford the high costs of their diverse services and broadcast them to a regional audience.

In a large market, competition is more diverse, usually more skilled, and more specialized. A small market requires more diversity in programing and perhaps a broader range of programing abilities, since fewer competitors may fill the total community's needs. A small market requires greater breadth of understanding, tolerance, and communication with the diverse people of the community; although, certainly, a small market has less diversity, fewer groups to deal with, and fewer places to go to keep aware of events than does a large market. A small market requires more legwork and original reporting to obtain news, since wire services and newspapers are less apt to do some of the small-town station's work for it. At the same time, there is less news.

It should be remembered throughout this book that some of the most advanced technologies and practices filter down to the small stations in small markets very slowly. There are probably more have-nots than haves. Eighty-eight percent of all stations have revenues of under $500,000 per year. More than 50 percent of radio stations are in cities of 50,000 persons or less. Thirty-six percent of stations are in towns of fewer than 15,000 people. While many major-market radio stations have more than 100 employees, it is common to have fewer than ten. Radio stations are small by business standards. Some large corporations have more employees than the entire radio industry.

Types of Stations

Today's radio stations can be categorized into several types. The following categorization is not for purposes of prescribing, but rather *de*scribing existing practices. Great diversity exists. The categories are not hard and fast. Stations may combine elements of more than one of the types listed below. Such pigeonholing and labeling always does some injustice. Still, it is useful in revealing the major types of stations found on the air and their essential practices.

Adult Popular Music Stations

These stations are frequently called "easy listening" stations, "middle of the road" (MOR), "adult contemporary," or even "all over the road." More stations of this type exist in America today than of any other category. Eight of the ten highest-rated stations (by audience share) in the top fifty markets were adult pop stations or variety stations whose daytime programing was of the adult pop variety, according to 1976 Arbitron figures. This is a trend which has held for twenty years, although specialization has recently caused this to be less true in the very largest cities. In most markets in the country, the station with the highest ad rate uses this approach. Because this type of station is potentially so profitable, competition is especially tough.

The reason for the high advertising rates and the great number of stations is that this type of station has been successful in attracting large audiences, but particularly audiences in the adult and young adult sector that so many advertisers want to reach. Because of this audience composition, a station with lower ratings than a competitor may still be able to get more advertising revenue if the composition of the audience is more in line with the advertiser's goals.

Adult pop stations have frequently been less specialized than many competitors. They usually combine air personalities, strong news, other information, and frequently sports coverage.

Personalities are important to virtually all adult pop stations. These personalities may have much more freedom to produce their shows and operate a relatively free-form program than some other formats. They are expected to be personable, human, frequently humorous. They offer the listener warmth, intelligence, and involvement, and the advertiser a personal approach to air selling. The personality will frequently spend more time preparing the program than airing it. The best personalities are in great demand for freelance commercial work, public appearances, or television programs, in addition to their radio programs. Such appearances can enhance their visibility as well as stimulating their professional development and bank accounts.

Most successful stations of this type have strong news departments and mature, personable news voices. The news may be network but is more often independent. The news is usually given on the hour for five, seven, or even ten minutes, sometimes with half-hour headlines. It is usually *exactly* on the hour or half-hour, rather than at some unusual time such as 17 minutes after the hour. It is placed there so that it can be easily found rather than easily avoided. During morning and afternoon drive times, news blocks are frequently longer than the usual five to ten minutes. News specials are not unusual.

The music emphasis is on currently popular artists and selections. While current fads are acknowledged and followed, there is at the same time a heavy reliance on standard performers and selections. Albums and singles are both used. Hard rock is usually avoided. Selections are usually upbeat, with more vocals than instrumentals and considerable reliance on Broadway and Hollywood music, although both are becoming scarcer. These stations try to select music with a broad appeal, maintaining a balance between old and new. Many stations have floundered because they have had difficulty sorting out the right music to reach their intended audience. These stations are the ones with the greatest dilemma, because they want to retain a broad-based adult audience balanced between young and old. The specialized music stations have split many of their audiences, and the changes in music record industry practices have left many of the programers bewildered.

Sports coverage is often extensive, including play-by-play coverage of major events and teams. This generally helps their ratings among males and limits the female audience. Also, the ratings go up during sports seasons and drop when the season ends, because there is usually a drastic format change. By the time a deejay show's audience is built up, the baseball season begins again.

Station examples include KDKA in Pittsburgh, KSFO in San Francisco (see profile 11 in the Station Profile section of this book), WGN in Chicago, WNEW in New York, WSB in Atlanta, and KOMO in Seattle. Most have been on the AM band, especially high-power stations with established operations. Until recently, this type of operation was considered too costly for FM.

Conservative Music Stations

These stations are also called "middle of the road" by some people. Others call them "beautiful music" or "good music," "familiar music," or even "wall-to-wall music" stations. This book uses the label "conservative music" because this type of station, while frequently playing many of the same selections as adult pop stations, is usually much less quick to accept the new, relies more heavily on lush instrumental versions of songs, and plays a higher ratio of older music than do adult pop stations. In addition, the conservative stations play more full orchestrations and slow pieces, and they often cluster the music, playing three or more selections without interruption and without announcing the names of the selections. They seldom employ identifiable air personalities, preferring anonymous voices, although a few of the most successful stations do have limited personality approaches. These stations lend themselves especially well to automation. Music is emphasized over all other aspects of programing, with talk at a minimum. Some have no news at all, while others have large news departments with hourly news and extensive morning and afternoon drive-time news blocks.

Commercials as well as music are clustered. Commercials are often limited in number to give maximum time to music and minimum time to talk. Commercials rarely are given the personality approach that some of the other types of stations offer. Many conservative music stations are on FM. A great number are programed using syndicated music services. Some of the largest growth in audience in the past ten years has occurred in this radio segment. There is a conservative station in the top five stations, total audience, in virtually every major market. Even though this type of station does well, music can be a problem because the record companies do not record enough of their kind of music. Some syndicators have resorted to recording some of their own.

Examples include WRFM in New York (see profile 2), KBIG and

KJOI in Los Angeles, WJIB in Boston, WLOO in Chicago, and KABL in San Francisco.

Approximately half of all radio stations airing music play conservative or adult pop music. Eighty percent of conservative music stations are on FM.

Top-40 Stations

These are so-named because they use a very restricted play list for the music, airing only the top 30 or 40 (in some cases as few as 20) bestselling records and repeating them throughout the day. A few (perhaps five) projected hits and some oldies (seldom older than five years) may be included, but the bulk of programing is from the tightly controlled play list. These stations, like some other types, work on the assumption of the changing audience. Most people listen to radio for short periods of time, variously estimated from twenty to forty minutes. Top-40 stations assume that the records which are selling the most copies are those which are most desired by the radio audience. By continually playing only the bestselling records, they provide a listener the opportunity of hearing his favorite selections any time he tunes in the station. It is an assumption that works, for Top-40 stations have been successful in every large market and many smaller ones.

The Top-40 format is credited to Todd Storz, who was in a club with a juke box late one night. Although the juke box contained numerous selections, only a few were played, over and over. And Storz noted that, late in the evening, when few were left in the club and the juke box was quiet, a waitress put some money in the machine. Rather than play a selection nobody had played all evening, she selected one of the heavily played numbers. It made Storz wonder if the programing strategy at his radio station was correct. They had been playing a great variety of music, making sure that songs were not repeated often. He tried the limited play list and it worked. His ratings went up. Today, an axiom for many programers is, when the ratings go down, shorten the play list.

Top-40 stations are usually characterized by a fast, even frantic pace, youthful-sounding disc jockeys, headline news in short rapid bursts and frequently at odd times so as not to disturb the audience flow, much on-air promotion, and singing station identifications. These trappings need not necessarily go with a restricted play list, but they have become part of the usual Top-40 package.

Since the music is selected primarily on record sales, and the people who buy records are the young, such stations have great youth appeal. The trappings that go with the music are usually youth-oriented, too. It is not unusual, even in a large market, for a Top-40 station to reach 75 percent or more of all teenagers every week. These stations also do well with young adults and with housewives who have teenage children. For advertisers who want to sell youth appeal products, these stations are a must buy, but many of the advertisers want to reach heads of households and are less interested in kids or adults who think like kids. While teenagers spend considerable sums of money, it is comparatively small, and the average teenager's discretionary income is spent in good part on snack foods, records, and entertainment. Youth listening behavior is much more homogeneous than adult behavior, with most young people listening to a small cluster of stations. For that reason, it is easy for an advertiser to reach this audience with a concentrated advertising campaign. Radio is a particularly effective medium to use in this instance.

Top-40 stations tend to be relatively stronger in the afternoon and evening ratings than they are in the morning. As much as 50 percent of many stations' revenue is made in the morning drive-time period, but the figure is lower for most Top-40 outlets. Top-40 stations' summertime ratings are usually higher than their winter ratings when school is in session. They generally do better among females than males. Their audience seems to be drawn to television less than audiences for some other types of stations, so evening ratings tend to be proportionately higher.

Overall ratings tend to be better than adult ratings, so ad rates may be lower than for other stations with equal numbers of listeners. Listeners tend to listen for shorter periods of time than listeners to some other types of stations. Listeners to conservative music stations will tend to listen for longer periods of time. Listeners to all-news stations tend to behave more like Top-40 listeners, staying tuned for shorter periods at a time. So all-news and Top-40 stations generally need more total listeners to achieve the same quarter-hour rating as a conservative station. In ratings terms, they have a higher ratio of "cumes" to "shares."

In spite of the fact that less than 15 percent of record volume is in singles, Top-40 stations still rely heavily on singles, with some individual cuts from albums. Multiple cuts from an album are seldom played. Further, many of these stations will play any type of music if it sells enough copies. Though much of the music that is played is rock, that is not because the stations have consciously tried to become rock stations. They play whatever gets enough public acceptance to make the sales charts. Most will play the Mormon Tabernacle Choir followed by the Singing Nun followed by The Rolling Stones if all three records are big sellers. Some are more restrictive as to type of music played.

A large number of Top-40 stations exist. Some of the most successful stations of any type in the country, with total audiences among the very largest, are WABC in New York and WLS in Chicago. A number of others, however, have been hurt significantly by the emerging FM rock stations with their more laid-back and doctrinaire approach. Some Top-40 operations have dropped the high-energy effort, added more mature program hosts, included more news and information, and tried to broaden their adult appeal. While Top-40 has traditionally been found on the AM band, a number of recent successes have occurred on the FM band. Though it is quite common for Top-40 stations to have the largest total audience, it is less common for them to have the largest adult audience or the highest ad rate. Top-40 is probably overrepresented in the American radio spectrum for two reasons. First, it is likely that an unsuccessful station can attract a large audience more rapidly by changing to a Top-40 format than by using any other format. Young people are more experimental, less locked in, and less loyal than more mature audiences. A new Top-40 station can pick up an audience practically overnight. It just does not happen with other formats, except in unusual circumstances. Second is the widely held assumption, not necessarily a valid one, that whatever music sells is what the public wants. Therefore, a great many stations try to present the most "popular" music. The phonograph record industry, from whom radio stations get most of their programing product, tries very hard to reinforce this belief. On the other hand, a large number of broadcast operators with respectable ratings have not been able to sustain Top-40 operations, because they have not been able to sustain adequate advertiser support.

Top-40 stations are sometimes labeled contemporary stations. They are that. But so are jazz stations, adult pop stations, country stations, rock stations, and others. There are also many kinds of contemporary music not played on popular music radio. Successful stations, in addition to those mentioned, include KILT in Houston (see profile 3), stations programed by Bill Drake, and the Storz stations.

Conversation Stations

The conversation format started with night-owl programs which took telephone calls from listeners and allowed them to talk on the air. A number of programs brought guests to answer questions from the audiences. Other programs allowed listeners merely to visit with other members of the audience, with the audience itself choosing the subject and providing the content. Programers soon began to fill their schedules with twenty-four hours of talk from the listening audience. It was a cheap source of material, assured audience involvement, and eliminated those tough music decisions. Much of the talk is nothing but trivia, but some is issue-oriented. Guests are still frequent on some programs.

Telephone talk was the fad of 1967. A large number of unsuccessful stations adopted the format. A number of them prospered. Others remained unsuccessful. A good share of them have since dropped talk programing for newer fads. Many stations which do not base an entire format around telephone talk still use it occasionally.

The format has two built-in problems. One is the difficulty in sustaining audience interest over a long period of time. You can talk about euthanasia, fluoridation of water, and abortion only so many times. The other is that the format tends to attract older listeners than any other format. The greatest segment of listeners is often in the over-fifty group. The programing appeals also to those in the less educated and lower socioeconomic groups more than the affluent and educated. Successful stations of this type usually combine the talk with strong news departments. Many are network affiliates.

Program hosts must be articulate, knowledgeable, and able to converse personably. It helps if they are compassionate. Hosts with these abilities are often expensive.

Example of successful telephone talk stations are KABC in Los Angeles (see station profile 1), KMOX in St. Louis, and WMCA in New York. Other stations program extensive conversation without using telephones, such as WOR, New York.

All-News Stations

Until recently, the all-news stations were limited to the very largest markets, where the potential audience and advertising rates and amount of news could sustain the large staff and facilities needed for this type of operation. The most successful all-news operations have been network owned, or owned by a large group, such as Westinghouse. NBC's News and Information Network (now defunct) and expanded services from Associated Press and UPI made it possible for medium and even small market stations to follow this format. It has been most successful in the larger, more fragmented markets, however.

The all-news approach, like the Top-40 stations and others, works on the assumption of the changing audience. A listener knows that whenever he wants news he can tune to his all-news station and get the headlines immediately. Consequently, rather than providing more in-depth reporting than stations with occasional news programs, an all-news station spends most of its time repeating the important headline stories of the moment. Repetition is needed to attract the listener who will rely on the station as an instant news source, but that same repetition also may cause the listener to switch stations or turn the station off after he has heard the summary.

This type of station has high overhead. In a large metropolitan area, the difference in programing costs between stations with all news and those with conservative music can easily be a million dollars a year. The frequent cost-squeezes that occur in all-news operations make the choice between quality and quantity of news personnel a difficult one.

Because of its necessarily large staff, the station has a ready capability for serving the community in times of disaster or when a particularly big news story arouses high interest. These stations' audiences increase in times of disaster, turmoil, and strife.

In addition to news repeated at intervals, an all-news station may provide specialized kinds of information: traffic information, weather, stock market reports, sports, entertainment news, and features.

Since the primary reason that most people first turn on their radios each day is to get the news, and since people are accustomed to turning to radio first for information, this format fulfills a need in areas where the station can generate enough revenue to cover the costs.

Examples are WINS (see profile 4) and WCBS in New York, WBBM in Chicago, and KCBS in San Francisco. Less than two percent of stations are all-news, but because of their success in major markets their importance is greater than mere numbers would indicate.

Rock Radio

The elements of successful rock radio are both new and very old. Today's rock radio did not exist until the social changes of the 1960s, at least ten years after rock music came on the music scene. It was a mutation: a marriage of progressive rock, Top-40, adult-pop, and unsuccessful FM stations floundering to find something marketable to remain on the air. The 1950s rock music was widely played by popular music radio stations, but stations wanting to appeal to adults began to avoid it, except for some of the more commercial pieces. Top-40 became heavily rock, with repetition, high energy, contests, and gimmicks. Progressive rock then came on the scene, first as an extreme reaction to a lot of things, among them Top-40, and later mellowing to become more broadbased but still in many ways elitist radio for the hippest audience and with the newest and most experimental sounds. Many of the early progressive stations and individuals backed off into a middle ground, incorporating a number of successful elements into a new kind of radio, called by many *MOR*, meaning in this case "middle of the rock," or AOR—album oriented rock. The WABC's and WLS's remained successful with their tight play lists, 45 RPM records, and high energy. They were not about to change.

A great number of young people liked much of the music played by progressive stations, and they liked the low-key approach, the emphasis on the music, the limited commercials, the high-quality FM sound, the awareness of youthful ideas and standards, and the real people of their own age and persuasion talking to them. They grew up on rock but had outgrown much of that music and were contemptuous of the new hits not made by them but by their younger siblings now occupying life space they had passed by. A new kind of radio evolved, not new in any bold or earthshaking manner but only in refinement of existing elements, to serve an audience that could be split off from existing stations. And rock music had changed. Instrumentation changed. Lyrics became more poetic. A greater variety of themes were used. Musicians of stature crossed over to make money in rock music. The term *rock* became more broadly defined and the word became applied to a variety of music in order to sell it to the record-buying public. In short order, *rock* became an all-purpose word almost synonymous with popular music.

The young generation has been variously described, but most social observers have called present-day youth the brightest and most knowledgeable generation in history. They certainly have more—if not better—education. At the same time adolescence for a large share of our young has been extended several years. In the 1930s, Americans became adult at a young age. In mid-teens many were forced to quit school, get a job, and support the family. These people considered themselves adults. The behavior of those in their late teens more closely resembled the behavior of their elders than is the case today. Today's young are more knowledgeable about the world, but they seem less likely to accept the roles and responsibilities our society has considered characteristic of adult behavior. More of them are continuing their education, but in some ways the new college is the old high school. There appears to be less acceptance of the work ethic, or at least later acceptance of it. Partly this is because of extended periods of training required by many professions. There is less eagerness to accept permanent marriage commitments than with other generations in this century. Fewer people are having children. Fewer are buying homes. Fewer call themselves adult. They are in a post-adolescent pre-adult transition period, unwilling and unable to remain children while wary of the responsibilities and behavior they see in the adult world.

Much of this group's radio-listening behavior centers around rock radio, which is, in a sense, a summation of their lifestyle. Rock radio's audience is a college audience primarily, along with large numbers of people of the same age and of those who have similar identifications. In marketing terms, this audience is important, but their consumer-spendable income per capita is still less than many other audiences'. This audience is characterized by high unemployment, low home ownership, high mobility, and high education. The audience is less likely to vote than an older audience, doesn't seem to be interested in radio news as much as its music, is among the largest consumers of snack foods and beer and wine, sees a lot of films, and buys a lot of records and personal appearance products. These people feel as intensely about their music as the younger teenagers do, and their music tastes are much more congruent than among their 35-year-old counterparts. Stations that appeal most successfully to this audience in recent years have been the new generation of rock stations.

Rock stations generally use play lists, but longer ones than Top-40 stations. Music is almost exclusively album, with multiple cuts per album. Heavy emphasis is on current bestsellers, a good indicator since this audience is the one that makes the albums hits. Much of the music is still dance music, and music themes are heavy with boy-girl relationships. Music is usually played in groups or sets, with the announcers low-key personality types. The announcers are told to be real people, but to play the music and shut up. Most of the talk is about the music itself. Commercial content is always limited below the NAB code limit, and commercials are grouped so the music can be played uninterrupted. Few of these stations have long newscasts, although some do a highly professional and creditable job. None have large news staffs, however, and many do only obligatory rip-and-read news. Many try to do an alternative news, either subscribing to an Earth News service or something similar, or by extensive editing and rewriting. Such stations are flourishing in most college towns and virtually all major cities.

While the first progressive stations encountered much advertiser resistance, rock stations are now much more accepted. Partly it is because advertiser attitudes have changed, but also the stations themselves are now generally run in a more businesslike way, and their broadening audiences have become most attractive to a range of advertisers from Levi's to automobile manufacturers to personal care products, to go along with the heaviest early supporters: the record companies, concert promoters, stereo shops, and waterbed companies. Commercials produced by agencies are not always easy to integrate with the format.

On-air staff changes are frequent. Audience loyalty is less dependent upon the familiar than upon constant refreshment. While a progressive station may be free-form, rock stations usually have more restrictive music policies, often with all or nearly all music decision-making made by a program director or music director. The staff is usually the same age or nearly the same age as the audience. Many stations do special programs such as occasional live concerts and many pick up programs like the *King Biscuit Flower Hour* or other syndicated programs.

While no major-market stations of this type have yet become number one in ad rate or in largest total weekly audience, where the competitive mix has been right a number have broken into the upper ranks of Arbitron and Pulse ratings and have especially hurt the Top-40 and adult pop stations. Their growth in number and in advertiser acceptance has been dramatic. These stations have been riding the demographic and cultural waves during the 1970s. The baby boom of the 1950s has resulted in a large percentage of the population being in the 18-to-24 group, a percentage that will not be this large again in the foreseeable future. In ten years this audience will be 28 to 34. Their listening habits will have changed. Stations that appeal to them will have to decide whether they want to keep the same people or the same age group.

Rock and progressive rock stations usually appeal to more males than females. Progressive rock stations have often had male to female ratios of ten to twelve to one. The playing of more familiar pieces and more "mellow" selections seems to have increased the female audience. Some of the most effective rock stations have been the ABC-owned FM stations, which originally were more progressive, tried a network version called "Love Radio," and evolved into the more commercially effective version that has been so successful in Los Angeles, New York, and elsewhere. The CBS-owned FM stations have had some success with their automated "soft rock" approach.

Country Music Stations

This is frequently called "country and western," but people west of the Rocky Mountains might disagree, for the roots are really in the Southeastern states, going west only as far as Texas and Oklahoma. Its capital is Nashville.

Although approaches to country music vary, the music remains the primary identifying factor and the focus of programing efforts. Some country stations use a Top-40 approach, playing only the bestselling country records and limiting the disc jockey to brief introductions, time checks, station breaks, promos, and commercials. Others use a more personality-oriented approach, with heavy news and public service commitments. Some are network affiliates. All play a similar brand of music, but some accent traditional country music and others prefer a modern country or "town and country" approach.

Country music is not new on the American popular music scene, although its acceptance has become relatively more widespread at the same time that America has computerized and urbanized itself. During World War II, a widespread poll of American GIs revealed their favorite musical performer to be Roy Acuff. Even the cross-fertilization between city and country so discussed in country music circles in recent years is not as new as might be supposed. Bing Crosby and Perry Como were recording country songs in the 1940s, and Eddie Arnold (nicknamed the Tennessee Plowboy) was recording with a full orchestra conducted by Hugo Winterhalter in the early '50s. Further, one of the first big hit rock-and-roll songs was "Rock Around the Clock" by Bill Haley and the Comets, a group that had shortly before worn ten-gallon hats and called itself Bill Haley and the Buckaroos. Elvis Presley, Buddy Holly, Jerry Lee Lewis, and a great many others who became known as rock stars were essentially country music performers. Certainly in the '60s and '70s the borrowing of ideas and styles among rock, country, and general popular music was widespread.

Where once all country stations were extremely folksy, with every deejay seemingly named Tex or Dude, today's station is very often very "uptown." Virtually every metropolitan area is served by country stations, with several among the best advertising buys in their markets. These stations are relatively stronger in the South than in the North, and they are stronger in the area from Texas eastward than in the West, but country stations rate highly in Chicago and Seattle, and one is in the top ten even in New York. Although in most parts of the country they appeal to a minority audience, that minority is large enough to support a station in the typical medium to large market.

Audiences tend to be slightly below the general public in education and socioeconomic indicators, but country stations have a good dispersion among age groups. Although most adult pop stations have few teenagers, Top-40 stations tend to be low in adults, and telephone-talk stations do not usually appeal to younger groups, country stations tend to gain a cross section of all ages. There are no generation gap problems with their audience, at least from a marketing standpoint.

Since the mid-1960s, country stations have increased in number more than any other. Examples include KLAC in Los Angeles, WMAQ in Chicago, KRAK in Sacramento, WBAP in Dallas/Forth Worth, and WHN in New York.

Progressive Music Stations

Progressive music stations can be subcategorized into two types: progressive rock and jazz. Some stations play elements of both. Although the music and approach can be similar, they can also be very different, and, while some elements of the two are not very compatible, there are enough similarities to consider them as one basic type of station.

Both jazz and rock stations play music aimed at minority tastes— music that is generally more complex, experimental, and esoteric than other forms of music. Much of the music is improvised. Both progressive jazz and rock stations deal with music that has roots in the blues and may range from very earthy and elemental to intellectual and sophisticated. Both lean toward music which demands relatively more effort on the part of the listener and more acceptance of the avant garde in music. They naturally, then, appeal to a smaller potential audience than most other types of stations.

Both use a low-key approach. Announcers usually speak informally, softly, and intimately. Both avoid the hard sell and have limited commercials, not always by choice. They are more often found on FM than AM, and audiences and advertising rates tend to be low.

Most emphasize the music, to the exclusion of other program elements, and have little or no news. Music selections are frequently much longer than the two to two and a half minutes preferred by Top-40 and adult pop stations. The formats are usually free-form or very loosely structured.

There are few jazz stations. To a great degree, the progressive or "underground" rock station is serving the role the jazz station used to serve. Jazz is not moribund, however, for it has always been appreciated by a small, select segment of the public. Some of what once would have been called jazz has more recently been in the repertoire of the rock musician, and the two have had considerable interaction. There is at the same time some incompatibility between jazz and some of the country-dominated rock elements. In recent years, progressive rock has been a more marketable product than jazz.

Progressive music stations include KBCA-FM in Los Angeles (jazz), WBCN in Boston, and the Metromedia FM stations (see station profile 13). About half of all progressive rock stations are college stations.

Classical Music Stations

Classical stations concentrate mostly on music, although some include other fine arts programing. Most do little news, but a few have distinguished news programing. Classical stations, on the whole, feel that the characteristic that sets them apart is their music and their approach to it, not their news, and that they should put their money and manpower into what makes them unique rather than into competition with others who specialize in news. Also, their audiences tend to be highly print-oriented in their news habits.

Music may range from "switched-on Bach" to baroque, from madrigals to opera, from light concert to experimental music. Many stations broadcast concerts live, often from the Metropolitan Opera in New York as well as local chamber groups, symphonies, and the major metropolian orchestra concerts. Tape delay broadcasts of these events are frequent.

Some classical stations play from a broad spectrum of "serious" music, even including lush string arrangements of pops concert selections and sound tracks from Broadway and Hollywood shows. Some use a serious, no nonsense approach, relying heavily on musical scholarship and emphasizing music not frequently heard. Others use a Top-40 approach to classical music, playing only the best known and most popular pieces. These stations will play Tschaikovsky's *Piano Concert No. 1*, Beethoven's *Fifth Symphony*, and the better known works of Mozart and Brahms with great frequency.

Announcers are usually mature, frequently distinguished-sounding, and sometimes multilingual. Some stations approach the music with reverence, often giving the impression that the announcers wear tuxedos to work. Others are less formal but usually restrained and, soft sell.

Commercials are usually few in number—sometimes by design, sometimes not. Ad rates are often higher than numbers would warrant, because the audiences tend to be in higher income and education levels. Classical stations are found almost exclusively in the largest markets, where their audiences and sponsors are generally affluent.

Classical is not an entirely satisfactory name for this type of station, but this book will use it rather than such other descriptive terms as "serious," "concert," or "fine arts."

Stations include WQXR in New York, WFMT in Chicago (see profile 12), and KFAC in Los Angeles. More than one hundred stations exist nationwide.

Ethnic Stations

Numerous stations around the country direct themselves to a minority segment of the community, such as the Spanish-language stations in California, Texas, Florida, and New York City, the black stations found in many areas of the country, and the polka stations in the upper Midwest. Some specialize in a particular type of music, while others achieve their specialization by airing news, information, and concerns of the intended audience. They hire air personalities who know and understand and have the sound of the audience. There are stations in the United States which broadcast extensively in the following languages: French, Greek, Filipino, Eskimo, Hawaiian, Italian, Japanese, and Polish. Several stations carry more than one language. Others do not broadcast in foreign languages but cater to the concerns of a particular ethnic group.

The ethnic approach can succeed where there is a feeling of community within the intended audience, and where other stations do not serve that community's needs or concerns. Sometimes ethnic stations find it easy to meet such needs. At other times and in other situations it is very difficult, because listeners are basically alike. There are universal patterns and appeals among all human beings. The basics of radio music, news, information, and weather reports are nationally acceptable in this country. On the other hand, one of radio's basic appeals is its ability to be local. Appealing to an ethnic group is much the same kind of thing as appealing to any local audience. It is important to understand their aspirations and to show concern for them and what they are interested in. The attitude should be like the newspaper in Oneonta, Alabama, with the masthead "The Only Newspaper in the World That Gives a Damn About Oneonta, Alabama." That kind of attitude can appeal to an audience.

The nation has become increasingly urban, and communications technologies have made instant communications possible, so people ought to be more homogeneous. But just as radio has fragmented and specialized in recent years, our society seems to have become less homogeneous. Mass, general appeal magazines have declined, and the specialized publications have prospered. The increased media competition has consolidated newspaper readership to a few superpapers in major cities, with a lot of specialized local and regional papers. Most of the audience do not go to films at all; only an occasional film is really a general audience, mass appeal vehicle. Only television remains a truly mass medium, and it is feeling the inroads of cable and specialized independent stations. New York and Los Angeles both have Spanish-language television stations, and Los Angeles also has a Japanese-language station. Nearly everyone likes music, but if you were to go to consecutive Elton John, Tony Bennett, Johnny Cash, Leonard Bernstein, and Chuck Mangione concerts you would not see very many of the same people in the audience. All of these examples are indicative of the differences, at least superficial ones, that have an impact on society and make it possible for ethnic and other specialized radio stations to successfully attract an audience large enough to sustain operations.

Stations with decided ethnic appeals can be among the highest rated stations in their markets. Some of our largest cities have black population majorities that well-run stations should appeal to. Studies show that radio gets a very high priority among black media, although FM has lagged behind AM. Twenty-five black stations in the top one hundred markets were among the top five best-rated stations per market, according to 1975 Arbitron figures. One network serves black stations, the Mutual Black Network.

There has been a sharp rise in immigration to this country from all areas of Latin America, and from Cuba, Mexico, and Puerto Rico in particular. Since 1970, the Spanish-speaking population has expanded at an average of 400,000 a year. More than five percent of the U.S. population is Latin. The posture of the Latin media is that you can't effectively reach the big city market without advertising in Spanish-language media. A number of ethnic radio stations have success stories, especially in Miami, El Paso, and Los Angeles.

To place all ethnic stations in one category may not correctly indicate the diversity among these media. Even all-black or all-Spanish stations show great diversity. All-black stations may be oriented toward gospel music, or rhythm and blues, or very nearly jazz or Top-40, or an amalgam of types. A Spanish-speaking station trying to appeal to a Cuban audience in Florida will vary greatly from one trying to reach Puerto Ricans in New York or Mexicans in California or Texas.

Examples of the ethnic station include WBLS and WLIB in New York, WVON in Chicago (see profile 5), KWKW in Los Angeles, and KAMA in El Paso.

Variety Stations

Variety stations exist mostly in small markets where station management feels a need to appeal to a broad range of the public and in large markets where a station has been able to retain many of the characteristics of the format used by network affiliates prior to television. Many stations use limited variety, such as sports play-by-play, or specialized programs at night, or farm programs in the early morning. Only a few make wide swings in the program spectrum. The variety station in the sense of the old network affiliate which changed programs every quarter hour or half hour no longer exists.

Many variety stations are educational stations, run by governments or institutions for service and not for profit.

The elements used in variety stations are the same elements mentioned in the previous station types, plus some additional kinds of programing. A few quiz programs still exist, as well as dramas, documentaries, "story hours" featuring dramatizations or selections read from books, swap-and-shop programs, entertainment and book reviews, calendars of events, recipes and household hints, poetry, and others. A variety station would include these as programs rather than elements of other programs.

WJR in Detroit, the noncommercial Pacifica stations (see profile 10), and such university-owned stations as WHA in Madison and WKAR in East Lansing (see profile 7) could be considered variety stations.

Educational Stations

This category includes both the "public" stations and instructional stations. As in other categories, differences subdivide this category. Some are noncommercial, nonprofit stations run by independent groups and foundations whose aim is to provide an alternate programing service to what is found on the commercial side. Others are controlled by school systems and universities, and function as an extension of the educational institution, usually as a source for cultural enrichment. Still others are for instructional purposes, playing radio programs which can be used with other audio-visual aids to augment a curriculum. Some serve as a training ground for potential broadcasters, although if that is the primary goal of the station a strong case can be made for using a closed circuit carrier-current station and freeing the radio channel for a primarily communication purpose. Other stations combine functions, such as providing instructional programs during school hours and cultural programs at other times, giving operational and program experience to students who serve in various staff positions. Some of the educational stations, especially those in isolated college towns which have little outside radio service, are quite commercial in their approach even though they do not sell time. (A few commercial stations are licensed to educational institutions, and a number of carrier-current stations operate commercially in much the same way as over-the-air stations. Some of the carrier-current stations are also carried on cable television circuits.)

Most, but not all, educational stations have very small budgets and small audience shares. They perform some of the most creative and provocative programs on the air, but also some of the stuffiest, most boring, and most unprofessional ones. As a group, educational stations have had the most success in presenting serious music, while the least successful aspect has been their failure to extend the knowledge available in our educational institutions to the public. Stations are funded in a variety of ways, depending upon their licenses: university, school district, community organization, etc. They are frequently assisted by listener donations, corporation and foundation contributions, local and state government educational institutions, and Corporation for Public Broadcasting grants.

Federal aid to public broadcasting and National Public Radio have done a great deal to upgrade facilities and programing. The network service has not only added a great deal of fresh programing but has set a standard for local stations to follow and has filled some of the broadcast day so that station staffs could spend more effort filling less time, and consequently doing better programs. Ratings remain comparatively low. (Most ratings are taken only for commercial stations, this being one reason noncommercial stations do not show up.)

Noncommercial stations, like others, need to be concerned with attracting audiences because they need the support of satisfied listeners. If nobody is listening, a station has no reason to be on the air. Educational stations are frequently more interested in a large cumulative audience than in large quarter-hour shares.

Many educational stations are also variety stations. They are given separate mention because of their different funding and posture.

Religious Stations

These are stations run by religious groups to spread their versions of the gospel, and also stations run by private operators who sell time to religious organizations as a means of earning revenue. Religious stations are less concerned with ratings and revenue than they are with using the airwaves as a means of spreading their messages. Many prefer a soft-sell approach, using standard programing fare with religious messages where commercials would be in another station. These stations feel that it is necessary to attract an audience before you can sell an idea. Others use the fire-and-brimstone approach. Some stations use programs prepared and paid for by various religious groups. The religious bodies use the programs as missionary tools. Ratings are generally not very important, because religious groups do not figure souls on a cost-per-thousand basis.

Other radio stations are owned by religious bodies which use the stations as financial investments and operate them as typical commercial stations.

International Broadcasting

Most Americans would be surprised to learn that the most famous disc jockey in the world is not Wolfman Jack or William B. Williams or Gary Owens. It is more likely Willis Conover. Willis Conover plays jazz and American popular music on the Voice of America and is famous almost everywhere in the world but America itself.

AM and FM listening predominate in the United States. However, most of the people of the world think in terms of the short-wave receiver each person aspires to own. World listening by Americans has been more of a hobbyist activity than it is in other countries. International short-wave radio has a lot of interesting listening in multiple languages. The most active countries in international broadcasting are the Soviet Union, the United Arab Republic, Red China, Great Britain, and the United States. Listening to the Wimbledon tennis results on a sports bulletin from the BBC, Japanese lessons from NHK, a blooper on Italy's RAI, Pacific Sunrise from Australia, or rock music from Canada can be fascinating listening.

Radio is an obvious but very effective propaganda weapon. The broadcasts range from programs of cultural content aimed at bridging social differences to blatant political programs aimed at fomenting political insurrection. It is interesting to merely compare the interpretation of an international event. Almost all international radio is government operated and controlled and serves as a valuable listening post for world opinion. Exceptions to government control are a few religious stations.

While it is not at all illegal for an American citizen to listen to the Voice of America, no attempt is made to woo the American listener to the VOA, since the purpose of the service is to explain the American position concerning world events and to make the "American way of life" familiar to all of the people of the world. Obviously, the VOA must reflect U.S. state policy and position, and since this policy is dictated by the party in office, if the VOA programs were readily made available to U.S. citizens over regular domestic channels, programs could be construed as coercive in terms of political power.

When Edward R. Murrow was head of the U.S. Information Agency, the parent body of the VOA, he said that if the VOA was to be believable it must be credible, and to be credible it must be truthful. One of the most effective propaganda tools available to the VOA is its ability to tell the citizens of another country some information their own government has withheld from them and have them later find out for certain that the account was truthful. Many of the Iron Curtain countries do not get free news services, so they rely heavily on the VOA and the British Broadcasting Corporation. Certainly, both are in the propaganda business every bit as much as other nations are. But their tactics are different.

Radio Free Europe, Radio Liberty, and to a lesser extent Radio Free Asia are supported by government funds as well as from private sources with the specific mission of reaching the people of the Communist bloc nations. RFE and RL were previously funded by the government covertly through the CIA, with the impression that all funds were private. That was changed to up-front government funding for these broadcasting systems which are more propagandistic in tone than the VOA, which is only interested in exporting the American position, an open presentation of the news, and an explanation of American life to the foreign radio listener.

The VOA broadcasts in 37 languages as well as English over a network of 113 transmitters, of which 41 are located in the continental United States, for a total of nearly 800 hours a week. These are short- and medium-wave stations ranging in power from 35 kw to 1,000 kw.

Radio Free Europe and Radio Liberty have administrative offices in Washington, D.C., and Munich, West Germany. Both stations are responsible to the Board for International Broadcasting, which was established by Congress in 1973 to evaluate and make financial grants to them and to assure that such funds are applied consistently with U.S. foreign policy. Broadcasts to Eastern Europe are in all of the Balkan languages. Broadcasts to the Soviet Union are in nineteen languages. How many Americans realize that all of the following languages are spoken in the Soviet Union?: Russian, Ukrainian,

Belorussian, Armenian, Azerbaijani, Georgian, Lithuanian, Estonian, Latvian, Tartar-Bashkit, Kazak, Kirghiz, Tadjik, Turkmen, Uzbek, Adygei, Avat, Chechen-Ingush, and Ossetic.

An excellent summary of short-wave broadcasting efforts can be found in the *Broadcasting Yearbook. How to Listen to the World* and the annual *Radio TV Handbook* are important guides to the person interested in listening to the various worldwide services. It may take the inexperienced person some time before finding the great diversity available.

Unlike the U.S., which operates radio broadcasting from a commercial base allowing listener preference to dictate the kind and type of programing, most nations are directly or indirectly involved in the programing fare of their domestic service. Some countries like China and the Soviet Union totally command the airwaves for internal propagandistic purposes. No information or entertainment is heard except that which is acceptable to the government. Radio is supported entirely by government funds.

Many countries develop special agencies answerable to government policy to fund and operate radio and television service. License fees of varying amounts for radio, black and white television, and color TV are charged for each receiver. The British Broadcasting Corporation, operating through the British Post Office, is funded in this manner. The countries of Europe in particular have considered radio and television as a societal force whose main functions are to provide information and cultural content for their listeners. The premise of radio as an audience delivery system for the advertiser has not been a popular concept. However, commercial broadcasting is a growing means of financially supporting foreign broadcast services. In part, this has been because of the successful pirate stations off the coast that were able to attract large audiences and sell advertising. Also, increased cost pressures on governments are probably a factor. Many countries now have both commercial and noncommercial services. One might be considered a public service and the other a service in the public interest.

Additional Program Materials

In discussing station types we have dealt with the main programing materials of different types of stations. Other program materials include such important basics as time, temperature, and features mentioned in Chapter 2. News-related segments are common, either straight news special reports or features such as "First Line Report," "Dimension," "Spectrum," or "Emphasis," or interviews with prominent people. Personality segments feature philosophers, poets, and entre-preneurs. Modern programing also includes dramas, historic vignettes, household hints, consumer information, farm news, special sports features and programs, and teen features. Many program materials can be successfully integrated into a program schedule. Some may become successful formats in the future. Recently, a number of stations have noted response to older records and have decided to play nothing but old records, in some cases only oldies of the rock era, in other cases mostly hits of the '40s. Two of the more interesting efforts at programing include Gordon McLendon's unsuccessful attempt on KADS in Los Angeles to use only classified advertising as program fare, and Dan McKinnon's attempt to operate an all-gospel music station in San Diego.

A salesman is apt to want to clutter up a station format with things he can sell, including specialized program segments of five minutes, fifteen minutes, or longer. Usually he wants to drop them in at 7:30 in the morning. Mostly what is available for advertisers is spot availabilities (in which only the time for the commercial is purchased and there is no program sponsorship involved), and the thousands of spot availabilities open at any time look remarkably alike. The advertiser's commercials had better be awfully good if they are to stand out. On the other hand, if an advertiser can attach his name to a special segment, it may be easier for the salesman to get his contract. Frequently the result is something that will make the advertiser's commercial stand out but will also hurt the station's audience flow. It has been said that if you want to sell advertising to goldfish dealers, get them to sponsor a program about goldfish. Gimmicks are easier to sell than the standard spot package. Salesmen have come in with some strange packages. In trying to please the customer, they have also initiated many good ideas that self-satisfied program directors would not have considered. However, management must be careful that advertising does not get the station to make unwise programing decisions with easily sold program segments that bring short-term gains but hurt chances for long-term success. Many easily sold segments are audience killers. All a radio station has to sell is the audience attracted by careful programing. Specialized segments must be right for the total sound and consistent with overall goals. Some stations do compromise their formats in fringe times, such as late at night or early Sunday morning, either because the programs are easy to sell or because they offer a unique service.

The Information Capsule

Because of the need to retain consistency and maintain audience flow, radio has made great use of the information capsule. The audience is relatively ready to accept commercials of various types as long as they are not too numerous or obnoxious. The same sort of thing has been done with all sorts of other information. Where once it was felt that a program was the way to cover such information, today the information is most often packaged much like the commercials. In that way religious messages, political opinions, beauty hints, historical vignettes, health messages, and virtually every other kind of information and opinion can be presented. Most music selections are short. Most news is presented in capsule form. The networks have become services that provide capsules of information. Many documentaries are divided into "vertical documentaries": pieces that are spread out over a day or a week, usually with considerable repetition. The final effect is to have all of the information presented in bits and pieces, to be put together by the listener. Radio has, in short, taken the "scatter plan" used for presenting commercial messages and made it the basis for all program material. This technique makes sense. People usually do not listen to radio for long periods of time; they do not begin listening to catch the start of a program and stay with it until conclusion. Since radio is available whenever listeners want it, they can tune in and out at their convenience. During a week's time, they are exposed to a great deal of radio, even though they may get it in short bursts. People are conditioned to hearing short interruptions and, even though they may not prefer to hear them, will continue to listen if the surrounding program elements are to their liking. As long as there is not too much clutter, even unpopular messages can be presented.

Listening Tendencies

While there are variations among markets, stations, and individual audience segments, the following discussion outlines basic audience habits.

6–9 A.M. People are getting up, dressing, preparing for work or school, and are in transit. They have a desire for news and information. They want to know that no major disasters have occurred and what generally is happening in the world and the community. This information serves personal needs and social functions—they have something to talk about with acquaintances and fellow workers. They want to know what the weather will be so they can know how to dress. The radio helps them to be punctual by giving time checks, thus helping them to synchronize with the rest of society. They may use traffic information to decide which route to take and whether to leave five minutes early. People also like to hear light entertainment. Adult pop stations and stations which have strong news and information tend to rate relatively high. Most advertising dollars are spent in this period, and the highest sets-in-use figures occur here.

9 A.M.–3 P.M.   Children are mostly in school, and many people are at work. Fewer men are available to listen. News tends to be less important, especially sports news. Radio is used more for entertainment or companionship while people do other things, such as housework. An exception is the noon hour, when many have an opportunity to catch up on the news again. The audience is predominantly female, although, as work weeks shorten and more women enter the work force, the ratio of women to men has fallen.

3–6 P.M.   Children get out of school, and people drive home from work, shopping, and other activities. Stations and programs that do well in morning drive time again do well, although stations that appeal to the young do proportionately better than earlier in the day. Top-40 stations usually show their best audience shares of the day in this period. In areas where there is much auto commuting the audiences are especially large.

6 P.M.–midnight.   From 6 A.M. to 6 P.M. the audience for radio is relatively large. After 6 P.M. the audience fades and shifts to television. Ratings go way down, but some kinds of stations do proportionately better. FM stations pick up higher audience shares because much FM listening is done in stereo and because some of the formats found mostly on FM attract audiences less likely to watch television. Classical stations, conversation stations, progressive music stations, and youth-oriented stations in general pick up. Adult pop stations lose audience.

Some listening patterns are noticeable among various age groupings. Teenagers are probably the most experimental listeners and are generally less resistant to change than older people. Older people have habits and patterns that teenagers have not developed to as great a degree. Older people have made a lot of their decisions and do not want to rethink these decisions on a daily or weekly basis. It is also true that adult listening is more fragmented than teen listening. Adult listening is less a group experience. While teens experiment, most teen listening is to teen music stations—especially Top-40 radio. Boys are attracted by sports programing, but most teen listening is concentrated in a small number of "in" stations. The music is very much a group experience, based as much on conforming to social norms as on personal taste.

A transition group consists of older teenagers and young adults. Their identifications are changing from teen culture and habits toward adult society with increased responsibilities for earning a living and for decision-making. Their listening habits lean to progressive stations and rock radio. Partly this is a process of maturation and greater sophistication, and partly it is a matter of being "included out" by the new crop of teens interested in making their own music an expression of their own individuality. This group's listening is more concentrated among a few stations concentrating on their music than is true of older adults, whose listening habits are more individualistic and less concentrated among a few stations or types. It is possible to reach most teenagers in a week with the single highest-rated Top-40 station, and most college students with a couple of stations, but it is difficult to reach even a fourth of adult listeners with any one station in most markets. Adult listening is also a group experience, with goals and aspirations and self-image important in the selection of radio programs, but adult identifications (and radio listening habits) are more widely dispersed than those of younger audiences. Each individual adult concentrates his listening on a small cluster of stations, generally two or three.

Formats and Sound Hours

Many stations rely on the sensitivity of the programer or on-air personalities as producers to present artistically what is right for the program and station. Many program decisions are made on the basis of what feels right. One program manager put it this way:

> Look, I've only got to deal with six people. Why go in and write out a big elaborate policy book with a checklist of things that make the person feel boxed in and uncomfortable. We hire intelligent people. They are creative and they want to make their shows and the station the best around. If I want them to do something different, I go to them and tell them in a nice way and we discuss it. I tell them why. If they understand what we are trying to do and why, you do not need all that formula stuff. I don't insult their intelligence and I don't treat them like little kids. And you can hear the results on the air. Oh, we might hire somebody and make a mistake, get somebody who's not right for our station. If so, we get rid of him and get somebody else who can do the job.

Another program director said that he brainwashed all his on-air people. In other words, he trains people to do things the way he wants the station to sound. He also deals with air people as individuals and avoids formularizing the sound.

Other programers operate in a different fashion, preferring to tightly control all of the ingredients of a program hour. Some of these are expressed in elaborate policy books. Many use a clock face to prescribe the sequence of events. Following is a run-down of typical sequences of music from Top-40 and adult pop stations. The sequences may be accompanied by strict or loose guidelines. The music may be entirely preselected by the music director or wholly by the deejay, or some selections may be prescribed and others selected by free choice.

Top-40

#1 One of the top ten records.
#2 Segue to another from top ten.
#3 Golden (big seller in the past 5 years).
#4 Record from second ten (11–20).
#5 Top ten selection.
#6 Record from third ten (21–30).
#7 Second ten.
#8 Top ten.
#9 Golden.
#10 Pick for future stardom (one of five).
#11 Record from second ten.
#12 Double play top ten and third ten.
#13 Fourth ten.
#14 One from second ten if time. News at 55.

Adult Pop

Five minutes of news.
#1 Brief establishing announcement and intro opener, bright, up-tempo, current-sounding piece.
#2 Vocal selection from popular album in bin of approved music.
#3 Standard selection, current arrangement.
#4 Currently popular selection, 45 or LP.
#5 Memory tune, something popular in the past, original recording.
#6 Currently popular selection, 45 or LP.
Half-hour news headline.
#7 Currently popular album.
#8 Novelty piece.
#9 New featured artist.
#10 Current 45 or LP.
#11 Standard from LP.
#12 Instrumental to news.

Most of the Top-40 selections above will be 45's, although many may also appear in an LP. All introductions and closing instrumental segments are pretimed and marked on the records. Disc jockeys have instructions to talk over the instrumental part of the open and close whenever possible. The adult pop deejay may be cautioned not to talk over the records. The Top-40 deejay probably will be required to play a musical signature at prescribed places, to give the time and station slogans at prescribed places, to run his board very "tight" with a split-second overlap preferred, and to give the call letters as often as possible so that someone asked by a rating service will remember them. Contests often center around remembering the station call letters and slogans.

The adult pop deejay is likely to have more latitude. He can take as long as he thinks reasonable between records but is reminded to keep the pace moving, to mention the time, temperature, and call letters frequently, to talk between every record, to keep a balance in his music, and to be an entertainer.

Figures 6.1 through 6.5 are examples of some sound hours for live and automated stations.

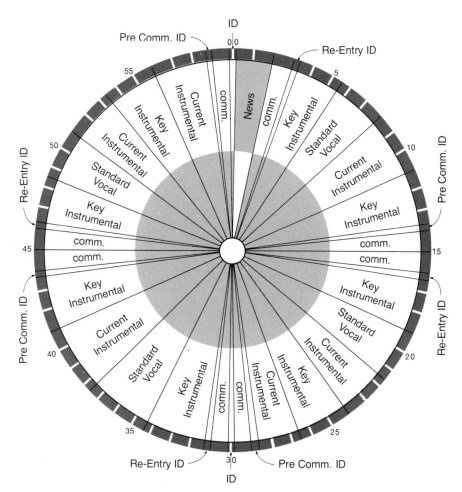

Figure 6.1 Peters Productions—"Music . . . Just for the Two of Us" (Formats B and C).

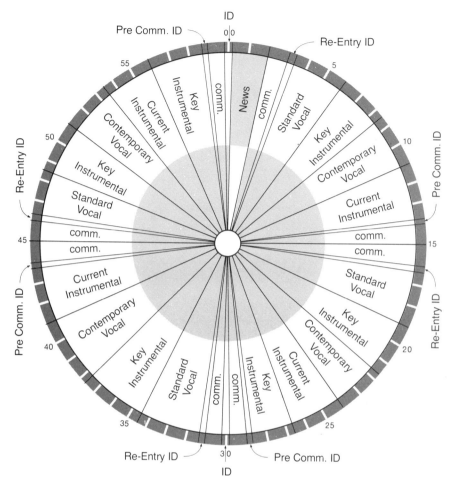

Figure 6.2 Peters Productions—"Music . . . Just for the Two of Us" (Format D).

Music Sweeps

Rating services credit a station with a listener in a quarter-hour period if that person has listened for five or more minutes in the quarter-hour. If an individual listens from five minutes before the hour to five minutes after the hour, he listened for only ten minutes but can be counted as having listened in two quarter-hour periods. For this reason some stations play music uninterrupted (a music sweep) on the hour, half-hour, and quarter-hour clock positions. This is a reason that some Top-40 stations put their news at twenty minutes after the

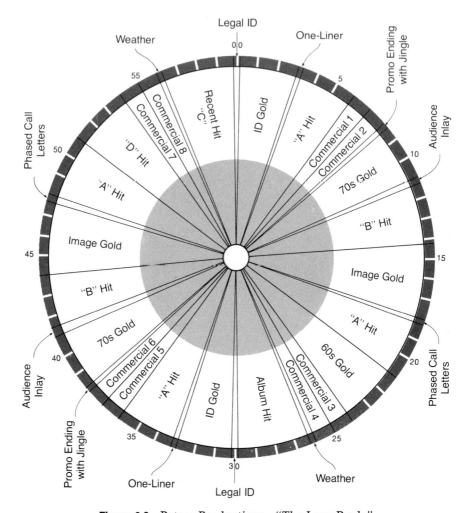

Figure 6.3 Peters Productions—"The Love Rock."

hour or at some other similar time, a kind of acknowledgment that for their audience news is a tune-out. On youth appeal stations, commercials are often clustered in the middle of quarter-hours, and the music clustered to bridge the quarter-hours.

The ratio of goldens may be higher than shown. The play list may also be smaller than forty records. Some stations color-code each record with a tab on the record jacket or with colored tape on the label —different classifications have different colors. Colored tapes placed on the clock in the control room show which times certain categories of music should be played. Such color-coding can make it easier to follow the format.

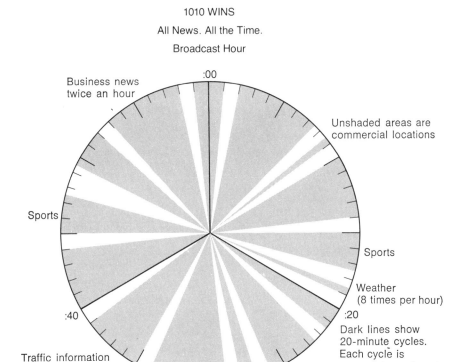

Figure 6.4 The WINS Broadcast Hour.

Networks and Syndications

In the 1950s the networks declined. More and more network services were dropped as they became less marketable and independent stations became more successful. While a network news affiliation remained important for many stations, only a few isolated services of other kinds were provided. NBC and CBS dropped their soap operas and dramas. CBS dropped Arthur Godfrey, and then NBC also dropped its weekend magazine "Monitor." NBC even began to have trouble clearing its morning newscasts, with stations preferring to do their own and use only the network actuality inserts in their local casts. The networks as a group began to lose money. Occasional sports networks provided specialized programs.

In the 1970s a reversal of the trend occurred. Its thrust was different, and it was modest in comparison with the great network days of the 1940s, but it was still significant. This reversal centered around syndi-

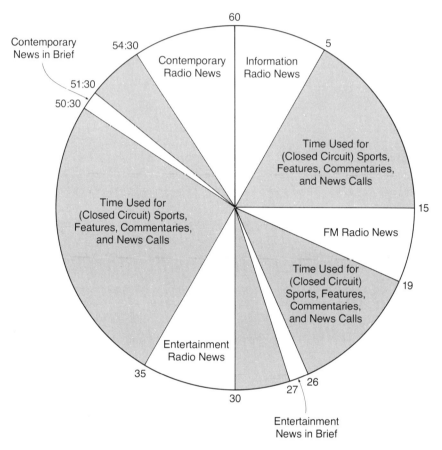

Figure 6.5 ABC Four Network Services Daily Feed Pattern.

cation more than direct network hookup, but networking itself also increased in importance on several fronts. The 1940 radio networks were gigantic, diversified organizations. The 1970s networks and syndications are more specialized and modest. These services exist because they are unique in type or quality or because they provide a service too expensive for a single station to provide. Even with this resurgence, less than five percent of radio revenues are from network sales, and the networks themselves are marginal financial enterprises. Less than one percent of total station revenues are from network compensation. Truly, the networks are more important for their services to stations and listeners than for their revenues.

Radio's talent still follows the dollar flow upstream. Talent funnels into New York, Chicago, and Los Angeles, and ideas return from these major centers back to smaller markets. What works in those cities is instantly copied elsewhere. Some of these big-city successes found it was possible to go to other big cities and to smaller cities and sell their successful ideas and programing in packaged form. If a skilled programer could be successful in New York, it was assumed he could also be successful in Philadelphia and Boston and Denver. Companies like Jim Schulke's SRP Productions, Bonneville Broadcast Consultants, Drake-Chenault, Peters Productions, and many others grew up.

The networks also came up with variations. ABC, finding that it was leasing network lines for sixty minutes each hour and sending less than ten minutes of programing down those lines, diversified services and got many more stations to install those same lines into their stations. Each station was allowed to use only one of the four ABC network services, but it was now possible to have four network affiliates in the same market and use the lines for the full hour. Before, a country station, a Top-40, and a soft conservative sound all might have had dissatisfaction with a single ABC service. Now, each could be served with its own specialized approach. NBC followed ABC's lead and attempted a new news and information service to complement its older news-on-the-hour service.

The major radio networks are:

American Broadcasting Company
   The Contemporary Network
   The Information Network
   The Entertainment Network
   The FM Network

CBS Radio

Mutual Broadcasting System
   The Mutual Black Radio Network

NBC Radio

Associated Press Radio

United Press International Audio

National Public Radio

Syndicators offer stations a great variety of services, from entire formats to taped complete programs to program segments. In addition, production aids, humorous one-liners, station jingles, and other such services can be purchased. Payment is usually according to market size, but it may be linked directly to the station's advertising rate. Associated Press and United Press International news services are increasingly competitive. While a complete run-down of syndication and network packages available would not be feasible or desirable in this book, the following will give a good indication of what is available, as well as the history of the origins of some of the services. This should be especially useful to anyone who may be contemplating establishing his own services.

CBS Radio Network

The basic service is news on the hour, a quality service that gets additional prestige from CBS efforts in television news. Comment, features, opinion, and *The CBS Mystery Theater* are part of the service. It is significant that the *Mystery Theater* airs at night, fringe time, despite its aura of prestige, and that some CBS-owned stations do not break format to carry the program. CBS also offers weekend special coverage of sports, weekend *Adventure Theater*, significant news extras, public service programs, and special sporting events.

NBC Radio Network

This is primarily a news-on-the-hour service, with some additional features and specials, including sports coverage. From 1975 to 1977, NBC offered a second network, NIS, the News and Information Service. Stations subscribing to this service presented local and regional news at the top and bottom of the hour, while NBC Radio was using the lines for their service.

Peters Productions

In the 1960s, Ed Peters, then manager of KFMB AM-FM in San Diego, developed an FM sound he labeled and promoted as "Music Only For A Woman," a lush, melodic sound which could work well with automation. When the station became the top-rated FM station in its market, Peters left the station to form his own company based initially on that programing service. When that became successful in syndication, he added services and formats in a rapid but orderly fashion according to a timetable of projections and expectations for the company. Along with music tapes and announcing services, he offered a promotion package including artwork that could be used in numerous ways to visualize an appropriate station image: print advertising, billboards, and letterheads. As more stations used his service, he was able to offer more services and formats and provide to a client the services of a whole creative group: help in choosing automation equipment, sales training workshops, and ascertainment and public service ideas. Through use of his services, someone knowing very little about radio could present a polished, professional sound on the air and effectively market it. "Music Only For A Woman" became "Music Just For The Two Of Us" in three versions, one gentle and quiet, another soft but contemporary, and a third more up-tempo. An adult pop music service to be used with live air personalities or with automation was added, soon followed by country and rock formats. Commercial production services were offered. A poet, a songwriter, and a jingle service were added. By 1976, Peters Productions was programing one hundred stations in the United States and Mexico City.

Sports Network

One such is the St. Louis Cardinals' network. This is a network originating at KMOX, St. Louis, with more than one hundred stations during the baseball season. Stations are interconnected by one-way lines leased from the telephone company. It should be noted that different quality lines can be used, with the cost related to the line quality. Generally, major league teams use quality broadcast lines, but a minor league team whose games are broadcast on only one station may use a simple telephone line with a telephone coupler. If the phone call results in a noisy line, the sportscaster hangs up and dials again until he gets a good line.

Sports coverage may be complicated by different types of contractual arrangements. For minor events, only permission may be required. In other cases, broadcast rights may be expensive. Some cases require bidding for exclusive station or network rights, with the highest bidder awarded the contract. The station or network pays for the rights and then sells advertising to defray the costs of the broadcasts with hopes of making a profit. In other cases, the ball club or its subsidiary company may package the broadcasts itself, pay the stations for the time, and make its own advertising arrangements with hopes of making a profit.

The Herb Jepko Show

Herb Jepko was a staff announcer in the early 1960s at KSL in Salt Lake City. Even though the station's nighttime signal on 50,000 watts with its transmitter in the Great Salt Lake could generate listeners responses from as far away as Hawaii, the South Pacific, Canada, and much of the United States, the station had not been particularly successful at marketing its all-night programing. Jepko asked to have a try at it with a telephone talk show. This was certainly not the first night owl show or the first telephone talk show during nighttime hours, nor was it an overnight success. Station management had misgivings about the program because by most professional standards it was not very good radio and the audience demographics seemed to skew old.

Jepko does not tell jokes. He isn't glib or cute. The show contained less controversy than almost any other talk show on the air. Jepko's talent seemed confined to genuinely liking people, tolerating their idiosyncrasies, and being able to recognize the voice of somebody in outstate New Mexico who had called once before, three and a half months earlier, and who was now on the telephone at 3:15 A.M. asking, "Herb, do you know who this is?" Long-time listeners to the program knew he seldom missed. After a period of struggle, business picked up. The show is the kind that generates mail. Management knew that other programs had more listeners, but the Jepko show got more mail than all the other programs put together. Partly this was because the program became a kind of club, with Nitecap membership cards sent out to people who wrote in. (Jepko once noted that his name had been misspelled eighty-seven different ways—Jethro, Jefco, Jethcoate, Japco, Chepto, Shaftoe, etc.)

A magazine was added, published by Herb's brother-in-law, with much of the content provided by the listeners—poems, snapshots, recipes, and stories. He began to do remote broadcasts: from airplanes flying over the city; from Carmel and Palm Springs, California; from Ruidoso, New Mexico; from Las Vegas and Tahoe; and later from Memphis and Louisville and the District of Columbia. Stations in Seattle, Los Angeles, San Francisco, and Louisville showed an interest in picking up the show. In 1975 it was added to the Mutual Radio Network, where it ran for about two years.

Even before the program went on the network it had a group insurance plan for Nitecaps. They took group tours to Hawaii and other locations. They filled two cruise ships to the Caribbean. The show is really something of a phenomenon. As a rival station manager stated in the early days of the program, "Nobody loves 'em but the people." During the time Jepko has been on the air, hundreds of other talk shows have started and died, many of them more cleanly produced and with hosts having better deliveries, snappier lines, and more glib phrasing. Jepko tolerates incredible things, like people setting the telephone down (clunk, bang) on top of an organ or an out-of-tune piano and playing some old song. Herb thanks them for contributing to *their* show. He does not insult people, no matter how inept they seem. He is very slow to hang up on someone who has nothing to say. He sometimes has celebrities on the program, but usually not. It is the show of the common people who call and visit with other people who care about them at three o'clock in the morning. In modern society, isolated, cold, busy, youth-oriented, Jepko's show seems to be an anachronism. But his following is incredibly loyal. Even in the early days when Jepko got off the air at 6 A.M., people would be waiting outside the studios with cakes, pies, and flowers. He has numerous advertiser success stories.

Some critics think he is providing a cheap source of nondirective therapy. In an era when many people pay psychiatrists to listen to them, Jepko provides friendliness and acceptance where people feel free to call in and share personal things. (". . . My daughter had twins . . . ," ". . . Oh, I was so worried, I got up this morning and there was blood in my urine . . . ," ". . . It is sure cold here tonight. I just checked my thermometer and it's 37 below right now . . . ," ". . . I just felt so bad when Grace called in. . . .")

National Public Radio

NPR came about with the formation of the Corporation for Public Broadcasting (CPB) to allocate and organize federal and foundation monies to provide nationwide services in both radio and television. National Public Radio serves as the national connecting link for public radio, providing a full network service. It is at present the network offering the most diverse and sophisticated programing, both in content and production quality. Of more than forty hours of cultural and informational programing each week, approximately sixty percent originates with NPR, with twenty percent supplied by affiliates and the remaining twenty percent coming from other domestic and international sources. Affiliates have been greatly aided by this programing, as well as by CPB financial aid to upgrade staff and facilities. In addition, the example set by NPR in its programing and its experimentation with stereo, satellite network linkup, and production techniques has caused public radio to make great strides recently. Public radio has been slow to promote its product as commercial stations have done, although recent strides have also been made there. Many NPR stations continue having difficulty knowing how many people they are reaching, since audience ratings have not included stations that advertisers are not interested in, and of course NPR stations are not funded by advertising but by schools and universities, foundations, listener donations, etc.

O'Connor Creative Services

O'Connor offers short programs, as do Alcare Communications and Nightingale-Conant. The services gross more than a million dollars a year from such programs as the following: *Kids Say the Darndest Things*, 260 five-minute features (which can also be used as two-minute features) hosted by Art Linkletter; *Viewpoint*, a three-minute commentary by Ronald Reagan; *Profiles in Greatness*, five-minute capsules of people who achieved public notice, narrated by Efrem Zimbalist, Jr.; *You and Your Money*, 90-second tips from Eliot Janeway; and *Superfun*, more than 700 features covering everything from one-liners to sound effects.

Sales Networks

Radio time is not easy to buy, because of the large number of stations, their diverse nature, and market-by-market differences. An actual network enables a time buyer to place commercials on many stations in many markets at a favorable cost per thousand. The sales network is not really a network, because no programing is shared (although it could be, through syndications). Stations participating in the sales network may have similar formats and similar market postures and goals, or they may merely share the same rep firm, but they can be bought as a group for a group rate, for advertising purposes.

Consultants

Consultants may offer syndication packages, research and analysis services, or merely expertise at programing certain kinds of stations. Consultants are paid a fee for their expertise and/or services. They are usually people with some proven track record in a major market who are desired for their special perspectives.

FCC Revised Rules
on Networking

In 1977, the FCC issued a new set of rules governing networking, replacing rules in effect since 1941. The new policy reinforced the individual licensees' obligations to serve the programing needs of their communities. Specifically: affiliates always have the option not to broadcast network offerings; networks must not interfere with licensee programing discretion, insist on excessive option time, or try to influence non-network station rates; and affiliation agreements should not be excessively long.

The FCC stated that a network should attempt to have programing not cleared by a primary affiliate aired by other stations in that market. Under the 1977 policy it also became possible for more than one station in a given market to carry the same network program.

The Commission also changed the definition of networking. The FCC now defines a network as a programing source capable of providing simultaneous programing entirely or chiefly by interconnection. Under that definition, Associated Press Radio and United Press International Audio are networks.

Affiliates using network programing five days a week, eight months of the year or more, must file network agreements with the FCC. Educational stations are excepted.

Suggestions for Further Learning

1. Listen to each station in your market (if it is a very large market, choose only the major stations) and analyze its programing and appeals. In which of the categories discussed in this chapter would you place each? Using *Spot Radio Rates and Data,* compare the advertising rates of those stations analyzed. If you can obtain one, a recent audience-rating book can assist you in your comparisons.

2. By listening to a station, try to determine its music format—ratio of vocals to instrumentals, tempo, type of songs, size of play list, DJ policies. If you can, speak to the station's program director or manager or have him speak to your class. If he will (many regard this material as very secret), have him detail the mechanics and policies involved in his station's format.

3. Using a stop watch, note how much time a music program host spends talking in a given hour. Compare that with the amount of time spent on commercials and the amount of time spent playing music. Note which kinds of features and materials are used to provide the "mortar" in a music program.

4. In what ways do the stations in your market use the networks? What percentage of the revenue in your market is from network sales? Are their regional networks serving your market? Special networks? What other sources of programing materials do you find being used?

5. Using a short-wave radio, listen to as many broadcasts from other nations as you have time for. What differences in attitudes do you note? Production techniques? Is there something that you could adapt effectively to programing for an American audience?

For number 3, the authors listened to two different programs on different stations for an hour each. One program had 5 minutes and 20 seconds of talk by the program host, 12 minutes of news, one minute and 40 seconds of traffic reports, 14 minutes of commercials, and 27 minutes of music. Ten and one-half records were played. Included in the news was a stock market report and a sports report. The disc jockey referred to the music very little except for introductions by name and artist. About half of the records were announced before play, the others back-announced. About 40 seconds of the talk was introduction of the various news and traffic segments and chatting with the traffic reporter; approximately 40 seconds was given to reporting the weather; and about a minute was given to record introductions. Of the remainder, most was humorous banter. One piece centered around a couple of news items, one on a feature item that was funny in itself, and the other on a straight news item to which the announcer gave a funny twist. Approximately half of all commercials during the hour were read live; the others were recorded. The program host was an important ingredient to this segment, had a definite identity, and used his name often.

Program number two featured 4 minutes of news, 11½ minutes of commercials, 1½ minutes of promotional material centered around a station contest, and a total of one minute and 50 seconds of DJ talk. All of the talk involved time, weather, and record introductions. Only 40 seconds of the talk were not done over musical introductions. Music was given 42 minutes; 19 selections were played. The DJ gave his name and the call letters of the station 7 times in the hour but did not add other features. Most of his talk was in the form of slogans and the naming of artists and songs and where they were on the popularity charts. The program host, while an important ingredient in the hour, was essentially anonymous and could be replaced by another DJ with almost no change in the station's sound.

CHAPTER 7

Music
on Radio

A vital aspect of programing with which most managements spend a great deal of time and concern is the kind of music their stations play. Music is the staple of radio because it is one of the program elements radio can present best and most cheaply. People want music on radio. What kind of music and how to program that music are basically simple questions but have no simple answers.

Radio does very little live music. There is so much music on record and tape that only an exceptional live effort can compete. In fact, the availability of cheap quality music is the biggest single reason that there are so many radio stations on the air in America today. If phonograph records were banned, or for some other reason were unavailable, very little radio would be left. No other medium has a source of programing material that is as cheap, as readily acquired, and as desirable to the public as recorded music on radio. Radio stations receive records either free or at very low rates. For the use of this product, the station pays a small licensing fee, which goes to the songwriter and publisher. Approximately ten percent of all program costs is for music (including licensing fees and acquisition of music); yet three-fourths of all radio programing is music.

For this reason, much of radio follows the lead of the phonograph record industry, sometimes acting as a subsidiary sales arm of it.

Music Selection

Music is emotional and personal, and its enjoyment is dependent upon the taste and state of mind of the listener. It is no wonder that music programers also get involved emotionally and personally in the selection of music for their audiences. How to choose, how to program, and how to please the listeners are matters of constant debate and diverse opinion. Each programer knows what he likes, and he relies on introspection and experience to tell him what his listeners will like. As soon as he decides, he clashes head-on with someone else who feels differently and thinks the audience prefers something else. Arguing about what is good or liked in music is as conclusive as arguing about politics or religion.

Personal Judgment

A number of methods are used by programers to select the music they play on their stations. Foremost of these is personal judgment, a subjective method that can be given either to brilliant perception or brain flukes, depending upon the decision-maker and his environment. In organizations, confusion may arise from too many opinions. The president, manager, program director, and individual program hosts may each have different perceptions of the audience's wants, in addition to their own different styles and tastes. (They may not even agree on the intended audience.) Their points of view often are unsubstantiated opinions without reference point or common ground on which to meet. Each blind man describes the piece of the elephant he touches.

A case may arise where none of the decision-makers is representative of the listening public or aware of what it wants. For instance, a corporation president is most likely middle-aged, has many associates who are above average on the educational and socioeconomic levels, is likely a member of a country club and service clubs, and has an unusual number of contacts on those levels. If his radio station is programed to appeal to top-level, middle-aged businessmen, the president may be a very good decision-maker. But what if the intended audience is another group?

To use another example, a program director is usually younger than a manager or president. He works with music day after day and probably becomes more musically sophisticated than his audience. He becomes something of an expert on the recording business, is aware of performers, and tires of hackneyed musical and verbal phrases and gimmicks. He tends to reach for more personally rewarding music— music that is more innovative, newer, and fresher than what many nonexperts would like. He begins to think like a musician and to appreciate forms of music such as jazz and classics, and artists who have not yet become widely known. Unlike the musician, he does not face a live audience and cannot see, hear, or feel his audience's reactions.

A programer can become tuned in to a different part of music than the general audience, which is rather casual about radio music and wants to be entertained rather than to be pursuers of art pieces. A programer often thinks that his audience is just as aware of what is going on in musical circles as he is. They may not be, just as he may not be aware of what is happening in the construction industry, or what additives are in his gasoline.

In like manner, other people on the staff may or may not be representative of their audience. Everyone has his own opinion, making it difficult to rely on judgment alone.

The Skewed Sample

No good music programer relies strictly on his personal tastes. Very few will program music just because they like it. They realize that they are programing for audiences, so they look for other clues. They ask their wives, friends, parents, and children. They observe people and habits.

They watch television to see what music is being used on popular programs. They note the movies that are big at the box office. If music is an integral part of a picture, it may prove successful on radio as well. Telephone and mail responses are also noted.

Each of these inputs is useful, but in each case the findings are not representative samples. Too many comments from friends and acquaintances tell him what he wants to hear. Mail and telephone calls are very seldom representative of the feelings of the audience. The motion-picture industry serves primarily a young audience that may or may not be the audience the station is seeking. If a million people see a movie, it has done fairly well. If ten million people have seen it, the movie has been a smash. But there are more than 200 million people in the nation; the movie-going public is not a cross section of the total population.

None of this information should be ignored, for each bit of feedback is an indicator of something. These are clues, but not solutions.

Record Sales

Similar to the skewed sample as a source of information are record sales. Virtually all radio stations pay some attention to record sales. Many stations play only those records which are selling in large quantity, the rationale being that the records which are selling the most copies are the ones which audiences will most like to hear. As we have stated earlier, that is not necessarily the case.

The people who buy records are seldom in the 25-to-55 age group—the audience that radio stations are most interested in reaching. The record industry's market is dominated by the under-20 age group; radio audiences are dominated by people over 20. It is fallacious to assume that the records which are selling well are the ones that a station should play, unless, of course, the intended radio audience is the group that buys records. To check the listings of nightclubs to see which performers are playing Las Vegas, Miami, New York, Chicago, and Hollywood would be as rational as to check record sales. The audience that gets to nightclubs, in fact, is probably a more accurate gauge for music selection than the audience that buys records. A quick check in *Variety* will show that the performers at the top of the record charts are not, for the most part, the same ones singing in Las Vegas. However, the nightclub audience is not closely representative either.

A look at television ratings for prime-time shows reveals that the performers who sell best on record have done miserably in television ratings. Television music shows have been on a steady decline for years, mostly because of the fragmenting of the audience for music. Only a handful of musical performers appeal to a varied audience, and they don't usually sell records. Even the Grammy Awards, the music industry equivalent of the Academy Awards, do not get high ratings comparable to the Academy Awards or the Emmy Awards. And the Rock Music Awards, when presented on television, rank in the lower third of all prime-time shows for the year. More than twenty years into the rock music era there has never been a successful prime-time TV show based on rock music, the music which accounts for more than half of all record sales. It should be pointed out that record sales charts do not take into account record club sales or direct mail from private record labels, both of which sell a different brand of music than the local record store. Also, a number of radio stations which are rated number one play *no* current bestselling records.

Record sales are not to be ignored, but, for most stations, simply following the sales charts is not an effective way to choose music.

A station that plays the bestselling records can obtain a certain halo effect, in that telling people they are hearing the most popular music has an impact on those who want to be "with it." Americans are prone to follow what is "popular." We tend to be true democrats—we believe that if a lot of other people like something it must be good. Also, the station serves the audience's social function of being knowledgeable and being able to talk to others about the most popular records.

Another aspect of the record industry is not consistent with broadcasting's needs: the recording industry is a fad industry. Broadcasting is also, but to a lesser degree. Since the phonograph industry survives only on record sales, it needs planned obsolescence of the product. The ideal record is one which sells at a fantastic rate but is out of date in a few months, giving way to a new fad which also sells at a fantastic pace and then dies quickly.

Most listeners do not turn off a favorite piece of music simply because it is no longer selling. Familiar music is a staple of programing in nightclubs, on television, and in public performances. People invariably appreciate a piece of music more once they have become familiar with it than on the first hearing. The anticipation of the melody is part of the fun of music. The adult audience tends less toward fads than the younger, record-buying audience. Adults who buy records keep them and play their favorites often. The "better" songs become standards and are re-recorded for decades. Many radio stations will no longer play a record when it has stopped selling. Depending upon the record and the intended audience, that may not be the best policy.

Copying

It is common, not only in radio but in most of life, for people to copy something that is successful. Music formats are widely and, for the most part, easily copied because of the availability of the records. If a station in a major market is successful with a particular format or idea, others quickly copy it but often are not as successful. A music format may be successful because of unique competitive situations. Success may come because an outstanding program host is playing music that is readily available but is injecting something unique— himself. Strong news around the music could be the major attraction. Other factors than music cause success, and copiers should analyze and proceed carefully, being sure that the music itself is the ingredient responsible for the particular success and that the copied music will be successful in a different situation. Frequently, stations are successful because they fit their markets particularly well in a unique manner. Copying ingredients and using them in another market is no guarantee for success.

Market Research

Many of the successful stations hire research firms to perform market-research studies for the confidential use of management. More research is done than is publicized, although many stations do not hire any research firms. A number of managers feel they know all the answers, or they are distrustful of the ability of researchers to help them with their problems. Some feel the research is too costly or decide that they already pay enough money for research since they buy audience-rating services. When station managers are asked if they have had any research done, they almost invariably will answer, "Sure, we buy Pulse" (or Arbitron, or some other rating service). The audience-rating services are sales-oriented research. What the managers need is management research—in-depth surveys that determine more objectively the station's image, the image of its competitors, and the preferences of its listeners, broken down by age, income, and education. Knowing the type of music the listeners want to hear can be most helpful in planning strategy.

Market research does not perform miracles. It does give management some additional input to help it make more rational decisions. If the research does nothing else in the area of music programing, it will focus a station's personnel on certain goals. It will give them common assumptions around which to concentrate efforts. If the research can bring the station manager, president, program director, and program host to a common ground where each has somewhat the same vision of the task, the research will probably pay for itself.

In addition to specially commissioned research, other available data must be continually scrutinized. Many types of materials are available, including census reports, federal and state government publications, association and trade-press articles and publications, scholarly publications and university research, and research done by associates, advertising agencies, national sales representatives, and others. Added to the feedback mentioned earlier—phone calls, letters, record sales, and all of the others—and combined with good judgment by capable people, market research can provide much wisdom in the selection of music.

Systems of Selection

A number of systems are used by stations for preparing and programing music. Each one mentioned here is being used successfully by some station.

In a few stations, the manager personally screens every record that comes into the station and approves it for play or rejects it. Most managers are too busy to do this adequately.

Often the program director, music director, or a board composed of each of them plus one or more disc jockeys will perform the music-clearing task. Once the records are cleared for play, the DJs may select from them, sometimes without further restriction, sometimes with stipulations about the ratio of albums to 45s, old to new, standards to current hits, and other such limitations.

In some stations, the program directors or music directors personally select and schedule every record the station plays. The DJ has no discretion in the process but plays what is selected for him. These stations work on the assumption that there are many good entertainers and announcers who are not capable of programing music or who should be concerned with other aspects of the programs and should not have the burden of selecting the music.

Many stations hire on-air personnel who they feel are capable of programing their own shows. The stations establish broad policy guidelines and give the program host freedom to program his own show. If he cannot do it well, they get someone who can.

Some stations pick their music strictly by what is selling best according to *Billboard* or *Cashbox* magazines or local surveys of their own. They play only the bestselling records, frequently the forty bestsellers. No discretion may be used by the disc jockeys except to repeatedly play those which are selling. Others choose partly by sales and partly by sound. They will play anything which sells *and* has a certain kind of sound.

Some stations choose by sound alone. If a record has what they feel is their sound, they play it.

For a fee, programing consultants provide stations with music services on tape. Others send music lists that recommend which records to play and give tips on how best to program. Some of these consultants operate by intuition and experience, others by performing a market survey. At least one firm, after doing market research, employs a person to select music from his interpretation of the study, and then the firm uses a computer to randomize the approved selections or to randomize some and include others at more frequent intervals, to take advantage of greater popularity of certain artists, songs, or types of music.

Tip sheets, such as *The Gavin Report, The Walrus,* and *The Friday Morning Quarterback,* are used as an aid by some programers.

Some music programers feel that basically all approved selections are equal and that repeating selections frequently is undesirable. Others say that not all records are equal, that many songs are better or more popular and should be played more frequently.

Selection Characteristics
of Station Types

As has been noted, Top-40 stations rely most heavily on record sales in choosing music. Adult pop stations are frequently "schizophrenic." They do not ignore sales of records, but they also give importance to quality control and try to select music that they think their audiences will like. The popular music charts change rapidly and adult pop stations are frequently unsure which trends to follow and which to ignore. These stations also consider the many excellent artists and songs which do not sell particularly well but have artistic merit. Many songs appear destined to become standards. Probably more adult pop stations have been remarkably successful than any other type, but twice as many of them have failed as any other type of station. Because selection criteria are unclear, the programers are unsure of decisions and vacillate a great deal.

Conservative stations tend to be more certain. They select more on sound. They also are slower to pick up on new trends, usually waiting until something is proven, then following. They emphasize melodic pieces, keeping one foot firmly on familiar ground while venturing gently into newer areas when it fits their image. Many conservative stations are automated and use a music syndication service.

Rock stations depend more on sales. Jazz and progressive rock stations lean more to sound and artistic merit for selection.

Classical stations worry very little about whether something is commercial; they choose primarily by taste.

Country stations lean heavily on sales charts, which seem to reflect a more accurate cross section of that segment of the listening public than any other.

To generalize about tastes, teenagers lean toward fad music. Also, if a record is not liked by adults, it may consequently be liked by teenagers, in the same manner that teenagers frequently change their own slang when older people begin to adopt or understand it.

Adult tastes are varied, ranging from fad music to standards to classics, jazz, country, and so on. But, generally, people prefer certain elements over others. The American adult seems not to mind a beat, but prefers music that is melodic rather than dissonant, opts for ballads over other forms, and does not mind a slight amount of improvisation. Adults, as a group, seem to show no strong preference between instrumentals or vocals, or for particular tempos, except that late at night the majority of people prefer slower and more gentle music. Overall, adults seem to prefer natural but soothing voices, balladeers over other types of vocalists, and lyrics that have the quality of poetry. Adults arc not quitc as aware of trends, or as quick to pick up on them, as younger people are. The type of music that will attract adults more than any other is popular music in its various forms—primarily the melodic mainstream music that is a simplified amalgamation of all the forms of music. Rock, jazz, classics, and country music generally will reach a smaller segment of the adult audience. This does not mean that exceptions are never found, that the top-rated station in a given market will always play one brand of music, or that situations will always be as they are. Tastes do change. But popular music is that which borrows, ameliorates, or assimilates from all other types of music. It is dynamic and evolutionary. Popular music is that which is popular—by definition.

Music Distribution

Availability of records varies greatly by size of station. Major stations receive multiple copies of every record made. Small stations in a small market get almost nothing free and cannot always get what they want even when they pay.

Approximately three-fourths of all stations have to pay for their records. The others are large enough stations or are in large enough markets that they get special service from the record companies and others who wish to get the exposure on the air that can generate record sales. The record companies find it economically unfeasible to distribute records to all stations. By placing records in the largest quarter of the radio stations, the record companies get coverage over a large percentage of the population. Also, very often, hit records are "made" by key stations in key markets. The smaller stations and smaller markets are presented with established hits and are unable to affect the national charts in the way that larger stations can. The record companies find it unlucrative to distribute nationally when one-fourth of the stations can suffice.

The record companies have a subscription plan for the smaller stations which allows the stations to subscribe to services for a small cost. Many stations get their records in this way.

Other stations arrange to purchase records at low cost from record stores, or exchange advertising for records. Some records are obtained from public relations men who promote certain records, artists, or products of publishers. The stations that get the most service from these persons are not usually the small stations. Obtaining records for the small station is a key problem, at least for those who want to stay with the latest trends and latest hits. Some small stations get around the problem by subscribing to a music service which provides all of the music on tape.

Even with all these problems, music is a bargain for a radio station. Only about three percent of all station costs are for the licensing fees and purchase of music.

Suggestions for Further Learning

1. Using the music glossary in Appendix E, determine which of the types of music are not found on radio in your area.

2. Program three different radio-station sound hours. List all music by title, artist, and playing time. Determine how much music you need and how much time will go for commercials, news, and other program content. In which time period would your programs go? On what bases have you made your program decisions? To whom are you appealing?

3. Why does music appeal to people? What do people enjoy? Why do people especially enjoy songs they already know? Research and discuss.

4. You might base a class discussion around these four statements:

   a. Give me the making of the songs of a nation, and I care not who makes its laws.—*Andrew Fletcher, 18th-century English political writer. (A similar phrase has been credited to Plato.)*

   b. The popular tunes of each epoch have a particular value in translating and crystallizing the dreams of the time to their appropriate rhythm.—*Sir Osbert Sitwell*

   c. Instead of striving for leadership through moral initiative, modern man has developed a kind of Gallup Poll mentality, a mechanistic conception of relying on quantity instead of quality and yielding to expediency instead of building a new faith. We're stigmatized by an irrelevant slip-cover civilization, and our sense of duty turns into a timid and insipid attitude which often accepts imitative cosmetic treatment as a substitute for creativity.—*Walter Gropius*

   d. (A letter to the editor) For some months now our office has been taken over by transistor radios. Some employees believe that listening to big-beat music for eight hours a day makes work easier. These music lovers ceaselessly manipulate their sets, forcing all other employees to listen to most unusual noises. The office "musicians" disregard our pleas. Since the fight against noise has been taken up often by TV, radio, and the press, perhaps you could, dear editor, speak to the "musicians" on our behalf and persuade them that they are acting incorrectly. Please explain to them that one does not come to the office to bother others and ruin their nerves by forcing them to listen to the "big beat" during working hours.—*Daily reader, Tribuna Robotnicza, Katowice, Poland*

CHAPTER 8

News

Earlier, it was mentioned that news is the foremost reason that people turn on the radio, even though they do not spend the most time listening to news. News is the most important service that radio dispenses.

In the news area, approaches range from no news to all news. Stations that broadcast news range from those that rely on the news wire services to stations with on-the-spot coverage or those that at least rewrite every story.

The basic approach to radio news is no different from that of other news operations, in that good reporting is the key to good news in all media. Accuracy, fairness, good writing and presentation, significance, timeliness, and appeal to the intended audience are as important in radio as in the other media. The difference is that radio news, since it is nonvisual, is done quickly, requires brevity, and is simpler than in other media.

The News Story

No substitute has been found for getting the facts and reporting them accurately. Believability is based upon a past record of having reported thousands of occurrences with accuracy. Believability is built up slowly. A few cases of bad reporting can ruin a reputation quickly.

Fairness also is necessary for credibility. Reporters who see events through a set of blinders and report it that way alienate segments of the audience. Even newsmakers who wish a station would report about them only in the most favorable light will trust a station's reports about others if they think they and their affairs have been dealt with fairly. People respect integrity even though they find frustration in their own unsuccessful attempts to manipulate news to their advantage.

Timeliness is important to the radio news story. Radio can perform better than any other medium, including television, in bringing information to an audience quickly. Radio is usually faster than television and is far more timely than the print media. Timeliness also includes the judgmental matter of rebroadcasting an important story long enough to get the information to the people; timeliness is not simply airing a story one time early in the life of the story and then forgetting it, feeling that only the newest story is worth airing.

Some news stories are more significant than others because of the effect they have on the listeners, or because they are of high interest. Significance, like so many other factors, is judgmental, and different editors will have varied opinions (although studies have shown a remarkably high agreement among news editors in judging what constitutes an important news story).

Appeal and interest to the intended audience are important, especially in using the local angle. If a station appeals to the black community, it must select from all of the occurrences of the day and present those which have most interest to that audience. New developments in war are of interest to all audiences. But if the mayor of a city has been indicted for fraud, he is news for stations in that market but not necessarily news in a city fifty miles away. If plans for a park have just been announced in the section of a city where a large share of a station's listeners live, the news is of greater interest on that station than on some others. Some names are more important to people in the black community than in other segments of society. Stories concerning specific groups may have a higher place in the news on some stations than on others. Sports news may be more important on some stations than others because of their perceived roles or because of their varied audiences. Generally, the closer the story is geographically, the greater the impact on local residents will be; and more time and effort should be given to it.

A tendency in some areas is to slant the news toward what is believed to be prevailing opinion among the largest segment of the audience served. That approach is not reporting. Broadcast news has a tradition of fair reporting, partly because the networks established a tradition with excellent reporters and remarkable fairness that others tried to follow and partly because of the Federal Communications Commission's *Fairness Doctrine*, which has required radio stations to attempt to present various sides of issues. When "news sources" pander to segments of the audience by telling them what they think the audience wants to hear rather than what is fact, the American system is weakened. The system is dependent upon the public's being able to get factual information which it may use to make decisions. If the public is uninformed, it cannot make rational decisions. If the public is misinformed, it cannot make accurate decisions. The public may wish the world were flat, but the news media cannot reflect that wish. The media must report that "the war is continuing." Fairness is also good business. A favorable news image is the biggest single factor behind a strong public service image, the image that convinces the audience of a station that it cares about them.

Good radio writing demands *spoken* language, the kind of language that is understood clearly on first hearing. Radio has no place for florid, complex, or ostentatious verbiage. Radio writing must be simple (but not simple-minded). Sentences must be clear, short, and concise. Words must be appropriate, easily understood, and of conversational quality. The writing should be informal. Complex structure and headline clichés should be avoided. The writing should be precise, the meaning understood. It cannot be reread and contemplated.

A number of excellent books are available to help the writer and the news writer. Two of the best are Strunk and White's *The Elements of Style*, and United Press International's broadcast news style book. Along with their tips, you might enjoy the following.

1. Don't use no double negatives.
2. Make each pronoun agree with their antecedent.
3. Join clauses good, like a conjunction should.
4. About them sentence fragments.
5. When dangling, watch your participles.
6. Verbs has to agree with their subjects.
7. Just between you and I, case is important.
8. Don't write run-on sentences they are hard to read.
9. Don't use commas, which aren't necessary.
10. Try to not ever split infinitives.
11. Its important to use apostrophe's correctly.
12. Correct spelling is esential.
13. Proofread to see if any words left out.

News Approaches

News approaches vary. Many stations approach news as seriously as the *New York Times*. Others air news only because they have promised the FCC that they will spend a certain percentage of the broadcast day presenting news. Radio news approaches and quality are so varied that it is hard to generalize about radio as a medium. Some radio news teams are extraordinary; other "newsmen" really do no news at all—they simply read black marks from a sheet of wire paper. Too many "newsmen" are disc jockeys who run into the newsroom thirty seconds before air time and rip off a summary from a wire service. If there are typographical errors in the copy, the disc jockey will stumble over the air. Quite a few stations consider news as part of entertainment, and much news truly is entertaining. But the stations that emphasize the most sensational stories and leave out more important news probably would be as well off not doing any news at all. Yet, news must be interesting. Radio has no captive audience. One way to make news interesting is by presenting important facts that people want to know. Presenting factual information accurately and clearly is often interesting. The news must serve existing interests.

Different approaches are taken as to the organization of a newscast. One philosophy dictates that nothing but the barest of headlines should be presented, with fifteen to twenty stories covered in a predigested, terse, and simple manner during a five-minute newscast. Others believe that, in a short newscast, the top one or two stories should be presented in considerable depth (comparatively), and the others should be skimmed. Some organize the newscast entirely by type of news, leading with the national and international, then covering the local. Others emphasize the local first, filling in with national later. Others integrate the news, putting the top story first whatever its source and emphasizing local angles on national or international stories wherever possible. Whatever style is used, the newscast must be paced; a station should not use all of the top stories in the first minutes and leave the less interesting ones for the rest of the newscast. The number of actuality reports and correspondent reports, the importance of the news, the geography, other natural groupings, technical considerations (such as needing time to recue a tape or even, in emergencies, having to wait for final editing on a late-breaking story), and the length of the newscast all dictate to some degree how the newscast will be organized.

The time and length of the newscast are dependent upon the type of format. Generally, however, listeners have come to expect news on the hour more than at any other time; on the half-hour is the next most preferred, or expected, time. Also, people want more than just five-minute newscasts from most stations. A significant majority of the audience expects and wants newscasts fifteen minutes or longer in length. Obviously, many others want nothing more than headlines, or want no news at all.

Specialized Types of News

Many stations compartmentalize their news by having separate voices for different types of news, making news types into separate programs such as sports news or business news. The success of these methods depends on how well and in what manner they are done. Sports news can gain credibility if broadcast by someone who is recognized as having special knowledge of and expertise in sports. The weather can be more believable if a meteorologist presents it (but a poor presentation by an expert is still a poor presentation). Sometimes the mere change of voice can improve the pace of the news program. There is one danger in this approach. A station may be giving the people more information than they really want to know. If reading a newspaper, a person interested in the financial news can turn to that page and pore over it, while a person who is not interested can bypass it. On radio, the only way a person can bypass a five-minute business program is to change the dial or turn it off. A fairly small percentage of people are interested enough in business news or farm news to listen to five minutes at a time. Fewer than half of the listeners are seriously interested in sports news. In some stations, only the highlights of these specialized news types should be covered, and they should be incorporated into the general summaries. On the other hand, because of the specialized nature of radio, this specialization may be needed for a specific station if it fits with the other program elements. Certainly, sports is a big item for many of the most successful stations. For others it antagonizes the female listeners.

Desired Characteristics
of Newsmen

A radio newsman first needs to be knowledgeable about people and about society. He needs to be curious and interested. He needs to be able to write and to deliver his story on the air. In large news operations, he may be able to specialize—to be a reporter, a rewrite man, or an announcer. In most radio stations, he must be able to do it all. Also, because most radio staffs are relatively small, he must have a wide range of interests; he usually is not able to specialize as much as newsmen in other media. He needs to be a skilled interviewer—to pull stories out of people.

A personalized presentation of the newscast is highly important.

The newscaster is someone who talks *to* listeners, not *at* them. Listeners like a soothing, pleasant voice with a smooth delivery free from distracting accents and mannerisms. They like a presentation that is not self-conscious, one that does not call attention to itself. They are interested in the information, so the newsman's emphasis should be upon communicating rather than displaying vocal virtuosity. They like someone with a sense of grace and an easy, friendly, intelligent manner with a sense of humor that is controlled yet evident. They like newsmen who sound informed. They dislike overloud, strident, and pompous types, and resent condescension. They like a presentation by someone who shows an attitude of being one of them. They do not like extremes in pace, either excessively fast talking or excessively slow. Listeners do not like monotone voices. They dislike the excessively emotional, repetitious, biased, hostile, sarcastic, and sharp-tongued types, or the person who is too syrupy or too folksy in a phony sort of way. They do like sincere, honest, enthusiastic, informal, warm, friendly, and well-informed types. They like a newsman who will take a stand on an issue but who does so with the appearance of fairness. They do not want a hard-sell advocacy. They want him to be factual and always accurate.

Other than the all-news stations, conversation and adult pop stations broadcast the most news. Certain Top-40 stations have strong news programing efforts, but more frequently Top-40 stations have minimal news efforts. Some conservative music stations have extensive news programing, while others have no news at all. Few country stations have anything other than "rip-and-read" news. Most classical music and fine arts stations emphasize non-news programing, and very few progressive music stations place much emphasis on news.

Report, Analysis, and Commentary

A report is a description of what happened. When that report is expanded in the context of why it happened and what didn't happen, it becomes an analysis. When opinion is added, it becomes a commentary. When that commentary is the official position of a station's management, it is an editorial.

A lot of time can be spent in discussion of news objectivity. David Brinkley has often been quoted as saying that nobody is objective and that he isn't, but you can be fair and he is. Certainly each person has a unique perspective on things, has prior experiences which limit his ability to analyze a situation objectively, and has a set of values which he wishes the world shared. If you take a Republican and a Democrat, ask them to listen to a political debate between the two presidential candidates representing their parties, and later ask them who won, if the candidates have both done a good job the Republican will most likely tell you the Republican won the debate and the Democrat will tell you the Democrat won. But the question might also be asked— what will the reporter tell you? For one thing, he will not likely give such a simple answer as which candidate won. He will describe the setting, describe the positions each took, and perhaps get comments from a Republican and a Democratic observer to get their opinions. Four reporters may tell the story in slightly different ways, highlighting things that each saw as being important. But it is important that anyone called a reporter try to report, and that he learn the difference between a report and the other forms. There certainly are gray areas where the colors intermingle on the continuum between report, analysis, and commentary. A trained newsperson should be aware of the differences. Perhaps it is not humanly possible to be objective, for that may be a kind of perfection man is not capable of. But it is a goal, an ideal toward which a reporter strives. The reporter should report as if both Republicans and Democrats will hear what he has to say about those debates.

Sports

Sports programing in some cases is a specialized kind of news. In other cases it is primarily a form of entertainment programing. As mentioned, the majority of the audience is not highly involved with sports, although with males and especially young males it is of special importance. Many radio stations give about as much sports coverage as the Walter Cronkite News, meaning World Series and Super Bowl scores and occasional one-liners about other major events. Other stations focus significant shares of their broadcast days around baseball, football, basketball, or hockey. Both approaches are successful.

All-news radio stations invariably have time set aside regularly for sports news, often one or two slots hourly. At the same time, these stations realize that, like stock market reports, this is a specialized kind of news, so they limit its length to little longer than a commercial or two. Most locally originated five-minute newscasts spend no more than a half minute on sports news. A few full-service stations and a number which especially try to reach males may do five- or even fifteen-minute sport summaries. Many of these same stations also carry play-by-play events. The sports news sustains interest in the play-by-play and the game coverage lends credibility to the sports news. Also, these play-by-play events are nearly always exclusives. It is very possible such an exclusive may interest only fifteen percent of the total audience, but if you are in Los Angeles or New York it is unusual for anything else to generate that kind of audience share. Sports coverage usually attracts a minority audience except for a few super events, a hot baseball pennant race, a football game against a key rival in a college town, etc. Because sports broadcasts are exclusives they are easier to sell to advertisers, who not only will buy them more quickly but may even pay a premium price. Also, many of these events are scheduled out of radio's prime time. Television kills radio in the evenings, but the station broadcasting an exclusive of a sports event can more effectively compete against TV for audience and advertisers. Another factor is that the sports audience is relatively homogeneous, appealing to some advertisers who want to reach that particular audience without spillover into the mass audience.

Some sportscasters are journalists and others are cheerleaders, house shills, "honks." In most journalistic efforts reporting is separated from comment. In sports it is often intermixed. In most newscasting the language is relatively objective. Sportscasters frequently say things like "Let's hope the Anteaters can pull this one out. . . ." The sportscaster tells you what to think. We accept that from sportscasters. We are offended if a newscaster tries to do the same. In play-by-play events, the sportscasters often are hired by the ball clubs whose games they announce. If not, they are virtually always approved by the ball club. Because of this, it is rare that any searching criticism of the ball club finds its way on the air. Even for those not employed by the ball clubs, many want to be employed to do play-by-play in the future. They do not go out of their way to offend a potential employer.

Football has become television's biggest sports draw (except for specials like the Olympics). It is important to radio also, but not nearly as important as professional baseball. Football may take up ten or fifteen Saturday or Sunday afternoons. Baseball takes up half a year of afternoons or evenings. There is no comparison in terms of economic impact. The construction of the games makes both good radio programing. Football is perhaps more dramatic, but baseball allows more personality involvement, more anecdotes, and more long-term identification. It is interesting to note that football and baseball have been around roughly the same amount of time on the American sports scene, both starting in the last century. As long as there was only newspaper and radio coverage, baseball was the bigger draw. But football is constructed for television. The players are focused in a central area for good camera coverage, there is appropriate pacing for dramatic involvement, and it is violent. Baseball is spread out, more unpredictable, less evenly paced, and more of a finesse game. On radio you can tune it in and out. If you miss a couple of days it is like missing a soap opera. It is strongly dependent upon the skill of the sportscasters. On a given night there are more listeners than actual spectators.

Baseball, from high school to pro, is highly effective in some geographic areas. Hockey is even more a minority programing effort than the sports already mentioned, but in selected areas is highly effective programing. In this era of heightened interest in a variety of sporting activities, perhaps others can also work for a station.

News Sources

The answer to the question, "Who uncovers the news?" is not a reassuring one, for the most part, for either radio or television. For the electronic media are much better at relaying the news to people than finding the news. The person who originates the facts as presented by radio news is usually not a reporter from the electronic media. He is most often a newspaper reporter. In most markets, the major daily newspaper has more reporters than all the broadcast media put together. It is constantly amazing how many news stories that happened midday Tuesday are not reported until after the morning paper comes out Wednesday. It is then that these stories make the broadcast news wires and radio stations call or send some reporter out to get some sound to embellish the basic story.

A newspaper is usually willing to send a reporter to cover a city council meeting, stay for the entire meeting, and do follow-up research to fill out the details of a story. Virtually all radio stations, if they send anybody to cover that story at all, will try to find out in advance when the most significant action is to occur, have their person on hand to record significant statements as they are delivered, and rush out to another story. They will rely on the wire service to fill in the details. The wire service will likely get many of its facts from the newspaper reporter's account. The radio station may not send anybody to the actual council meeting but later may try to get one of the key participants to summarize what happened and to make a statement evaluating such action. Also, a radio station is unlikely to send anybody to the city council meeting unless it knows for certain in advance that an important story is in the making.

Radio is generally better at covering first-hand news stories that are known about in advance. Those that have no advance notice or those that take considerable research are covered first-hand by few radio stations.

Stating that this is the case is not to say that it should be the case. Nor is it saying that individual broadcast reporters and stations do not do a good reporting job. But as a medium, radio covers a very small percentage of the news it relays to the public.

A common place for the wire services to be housed is with the major daily newspaper.

The network is a prime news source for many stations. The network offers excellent reporters, good writing, in-depth analyses, and actuality reports, and frees the local news people from spending so much time with the national and international news. The networks have set a high standard of quality, although the difficulties of integrating important local news with network news and airing longer newscasts to include the local news are frustrating to some operators. In addition to programs, the networks provide closed-circuit feeds that include actuality reports to be recorded and used in locally originated news programs.

The news wire services are the backbone of the coverage even for the networks. Associated Press, United Press International, and other local and specialized services such as city news services in major cities, sports wires, and weather wires gather a large share of the news. Many stations subscribe to only one wire service—either the AP or UPI *broadcast wires*. Larger stations subscribe to both. In larger cities, a station may also use the city news service. A sports-accented station can subscribe to the Western Union sports wire. In areas where weather is fast-changing or in major farming areas, stations frequently subscribe to a weather wire, or they may even have their own weather station and meteorologist. Large stations may also subscribe to the *newspaper wires* of both the AP and UPI to get more in-depth coverage of stories and for use in rewriting.

Larger stations or chains may also operate state capital or even Washington or overseas news bureaus. Frequently these bureaus are small, often only one man.

A station may establish a system of stringers instead of using staff reporters to cover certain beats. Stringers are frequent in areas where only occasional stories are important enough to be included in the news. A stringer gets paid only per story. Since he is not really an employee of a station, he may report at his own convenience, and he is less apt to operate at the station's convenience than a staff reporter; but he is paid much less too.

Radio stations frequently trade stories with other stations. Stations under common ownership usually will make their top stories available to each other, usually by telephone reports, sometimes by using a special line installed for the purpose. Other stations under informal agreements simply call friendly stations in other markets for reports on particular stories.

Stations also get a number of stories from competitors in their own markets. This is not to say that they borrow a whole story and air it without change. Stations use their competitors for leads on stories they may not have uncovered otherwise. Sometimes an attitude exists among competitors that if one medium uncovers a story, especially an item uncovered by investigative techniques, the others will not touch it, feeling that it is the first medium's story. The authors of this book feel that if a story is good it should be reported by other media, using the competitor's story for leads for new angles and information. Other radio stations, TV, newspapers, journals, periodicals, and research reports are all useful for source material.

Radio stations seldom have enough newsmen. Whenever possible, stations prefer to have reporters who can cover particular areas or subjects and who can come up with original stories—people who actually report rather than read material written by others. In small stations and small markets, this breed of reporter is rare. Even in large markets, more time is spent in editing than in writing and true reporting. Good news operations, however, always have people who are capable of at least supplementing and improving upon the basic wire service stories. On big local stories a station always should have a representative on hand to report from the scene and to get actuality recordings. The telephone, used for digging out information as well as for "beeper" reports of the voice of persons making news, is the biggest time and money saver.

A number of stations have offered money for the best news tip of the week or for each story used on the air. Opinion is mixed about the usefulness of such techniques. Seldom can a news story be aired using only the information obtained from such sources. Such tips are most effective as leads to be checked out. Even in situations where no money is offered, a good news organization will get a lot of leads from tips phoned in by listeners, and even from listeners who call up to ask for information, thereby tipping off the newsmen that something is happening that should be checked out.

A good share of news can be anticipated because meetings, hearings, and news conferences are announced in advance. The courts and the legislatures and many business functions take a great deal of time to complete their work, and advance planning is necessary.

A rich source of news, but one that must be handled carefully, is the public relations handout. Many important people and groups employ a public relations specialist, or information director, to operate as an intermediary between the newsmaker and the news gatherer. These intermediaries often make news-gathering easier by doing some of the reporting. They also can also make it more difficult by preventing aspects of a story unfavorable to the source from being obtained easily. Much of this information is self-serving and one-sided, or is given solely for the good of the employer. The public relations man can be a rich source of news and very helpful. But, again, his information must be used carefully.

The most important source, however, is the newsmaker himself. Interviewing newsmakers is the key to providing accurate, vivid reporting.

The Interview

The interview is the basic tool for obtaining much of the news. Much news comes from printed reports, but a good share comes from interviews with newsmakers. Statements, opinions, and answers to questions make up the body of many news stories.

The interview can be used to gather information that can then be written and delivered like any other news story, or it can be recorded and excerpts used in the body of a newscast. The interview, if important or interesting enough, and depending upon the station format, can also be a program or program segment in itself. The interview can be useful in providing vividness and a change of voice, and is more believable because of the person saying it himself, adding a vital and immediate dimension to the news broadcast. It can also be a crutch, a time waster, or a tool for covering the inadequacies of the writer and reporter. Simply adding a change of voice to the broadcast is not justified if it does not add impact to the news. A recorded segment should be left out if the source is inarticulate or overly verbose with words that can be shortened and clarified by the reporter in his own summarization, or if it is merely self-serving publicity for the speaker. Although it is true that interviews are sometimes revealing glimpses of a person or an issue, often they merely fill time and get in the way of good reporting. Judgment is needed; segments of statements or interviews that are well used add much, but, poorly used, they get in the way.

The technique of interviewing is best practiced by newsmen who are knowledgeable and sensitive and who react well to people. A good interview results from thorough preparation, rapport with the interviewee, careful listening and follow-up questions, helping the person to express himself, and representing the listener who cannot question the interviewee himself. Ways of making the most of an interview opportunity are discussed on the following pages.

Good interviews are basically good conversation. Younger, less experienced people, especially, tend to be intimidated by someone they have allowed to become "bigger than life"—a prominent politician, corporation executive, famous performer, or super sports figure. An interviewer must be aware of and concerned about people's personal and physical needs, and treat them as people, not as products, adversaries, or heroes.

The interviewer is not the expert. The focus is on the interviewee, not the reporter, and it is not the reporter's role to show how bright he is or that he knows more than the interviewee. A reporter, however, must not be ignorant of the interviewee's expertise and should prepare as much as he can before doing an interview. Sometimes, news events and knowledge of their context will adequately prepare a reporter for specific interviews, and little additional preparation will be necessary. On other occasions, a newsman may have to do additional homework before the interview.

The reporter should refrain from arguing with the interviewee. If the interviewee gives answers that are not forthright, the reporter should use follow-up questions that draw information from him and cause him to expand upon his points. Offering varied points of view often can elicit precise responses.

Preparation for an interview may include drawing up a list of possible questions. These can be used as a starting point, or used to fall back on during an interview. However, under no circumstances should the interviewer proceed dogmatically through his prepared list regardless of what the interviewee is saying. A good interview requires that points be followed up, that the interviewee be drawn out or cut off or channeled, and that evasive replies be clarified. The response of the interviewer must be appropriate to the occasion, content, style, and meaning of the interview. Many politicians or starlets are very adept at giving partial or evasive replies and focus on giving a sales pitch for their programs or shows. The interviewer must not be intimidated, must politely and gently keep the interview on the track, and yet must be flexible and adaptable to the occasion. The most interesting talk is often unforeseen by the interviewer. The interviewee's best ideas may require stimulation from another person, in this case the interviewer, before they surface.

The interviewer chooses the questions. The general subject area may be agreed upon in advance, but not the questions. The person being interviewed may have suggestions, but the interviewer must control the interview. The audience and its interests must be kept in mind so that the station does not talk only to itself when it broadcasts an interview.

The questions should be appropriate to the person being interviewed. Too many interviewers ask questions outside the guest's interests or expertise. Although the type of program, the hour, and the station varies, radio does go into the home, and questions, therefore, must be in good taste.

An interviewer should be conversational, yet precise and understandable. He should not be too cute, sloppy, or overly formal. He must be careful of patterns that distract—either vocal patterns, pet phrases (*I see, Isn't it true that . . . ?, Wonderful!*), or just dropping in *umm hmm* at every "dead" place.

An interviewer must show interest. To do this he must *be* interested, at least during the time he is doing the interview. Expressing interest requires discipline more than anything else. A reporter must convince himself that each story is important and worth doing, for if he can, he will sound interested, and listeners are also more apt to be interested.

Interviewers should ask one question at a time and avoid the multiple-question attack; the interviewee will not know where to start. Avoid questions that call for a *yes* or *no* answer unless they have follow-up questions built in. Certainly there are exceptions: "Are you going to be a candidate for the presidency?" The answer to that question is a big story in itself, and the follow-up answers will be less dramatic than the answer to the "yes or no" question.

If controversy is inherent in a subject, an interviewer should not avoid it. He should deal with the controversy objectively and gently, but as tenaciously as is necessary to get the story—getting the information without offending. Some reporters can ask the tough questions without arousing ire. Others can irk an interviewee with very bland material. Skilled interviewers lead off with the easier questions, warming up the person before using the controversial questions. Interviewers should be friendly, considerate, and objective, with questions carefully constructed to sound unbiased. A reporter should not appear devious or seem like an adversary. He should listen to his subject's comments, being sympathetic to the interviewee personally if not to his ideas, and find some common ground with him, while retaining his objectivity toward the subject matter.

Consideration of an interviewee's time deadlines is important. The interviewer should not waste a second of the guest's time, and should check on proper names, titles, dates, and any other necessary information beforehand.

An interviewer should be himself and develop his own style—not simply to be self-consciously different but because the interviewer, like the interviewee, should have personality.

Since tape editing is not difficult, taping more material than will be needed is a practical idea. This technique is useful unless the editing process distorts the interviewee's comments or is used as a crutch that makes preparation unnecessary since mistakes can be edited out. It allows the interviewer to gamble a little more, and allows him to pick the good material from a long, wordier segment. Since most people are apt to repeat themselves and stammer somewhat, an interviewer who tapes more than he needs has a greater chance of eliminating the worst and airing the best.

Interviews are used in more than news programs. The techniques are basically the same for either news or non-news, except that too much levity about a serious issue in a news report is inappropriate. A personality interview or feature material lends itself more to the humorous, anecdotal, informal approach, since it more nearly resembles a casual conversation than does the formal press conference.

The Documentary

One specialized type of news is the documentary. Few documentary programs are scheduled on a regular basis, although many stations schedule them on occasion when a particularly important issue presents itself. Some stations do not produce documentaries at all; others program their documentaries in pieces, taking information bits, producing them not unlike commercials, and scattering them throughout the program day to urge the listener to piece the bits together into the whole form.

A documentary is a program which integrates narration, comments, or statements with music or sound effects into program form for the purpose of exploring an issue, synthesizing a body of material, or structuring material about an event or issue. The documentary can be a commentary, an editorial, a report, or simply entertainment.

Two basic approaches are taken in producing documentaries. One is to gather available documents as an issue unfolds and structure them into a program. The other approach is to focus on an existing issue and then gather the necessary materials which present the point of view chosen. These are basically deductive and inductive approaches. Major disasters or important public events such as the assassination of an important figure or the moon exploration successes lend themselves to the one approach. Concerns over the environment or the quality of life would be examined using the other approach.

The documentary requires considerable time for gathering material, writing, and production, and is therefore an expensive program form. Also, since it is in the nature of a special program which interrupts the normal programing, its use is selective and relatively uncommon. Most radio stations that broadcast documentaries repeat them in different time blocks so they will attain the exposure necessary to justify the effort.

The Editorial

Not long ago, only a few radio stations editorialized. More recently, many, if not most, broadcasters have felt it their duty to speak out as advocates. But because the Federal Communications Commission licenses and regulates all radio stations, this right of free speech is different from the rights of the print media. Radio stations can editorialize, but they must give equal time to spokesmen from "responsible" groups who disagree with the position taken (see Fairness Doctrine, Chapter 12). In practice, most newspapers demonstrate their sense of fairness by printing a letters-to-the-editor column, although they are not required to give equal access the way broadcasters are. No accepted standard of broadcast editorializing exists, with the exception that editorials are generally separated from the news reports and labeled as editorials, with an announcement that opposing viewpoints will be aired.

Not all stations are enamored of the editorial, for several reasons. One is that good editorials require a lot of work, manpower, and research. A large percentage of stations are not very profitable and constantly are seeking ways to cut costs. Another reason is that listeners and sponsors can be offended by points of view that are courageous or provocative. Important issues are marked by differences of opinion. The easy route is not to offend anyone by not saying anything. A third reason is that the credibility of the news effort can be hurt if a station is doctrinaire in its editorials, especially if the news department has a hand in their preparation or if the news or public affairs director voices them.

On the plus side, an editorial policy which commits a station to advocating action that will benefit the community, even though the editorial may offend some, shows a concern for caring as well as for earning money. It tells the community that the station is interested in the quality of life and in the people. Listeners probably will not be offended greatly by viewpoints with which they disagree if the station gives opposing points of view (which it must), and if the editorials are presented thoughtfully and carefully with an air of restraint. The simplest way to avoid the credibility problem is to separate the news department from the editorials, having management voice them and prepare them.

The procedure that is frequently used for preparing editorials is to establish an editorial board composed of executives of the station and a writer-researcher. The news director may or may not sit on the committee, depending upon the station. It might be argued that he should, since he is the person in the organization most closely allied with the issues. It might also be argued that he should *not* participate, because his area is reporting, and separating him from the editorial board leaves him untainted by the partisanship required for editorials. Most managers are too busy to spend time writing the editorials, but many use fact sheets prepared for them by an editorial writer and rephrase the writing so that they will feel comfortable with it. Whichever procedure is used, the process is expensive because of the man-hours needed. The expense can be justified if the product and the results are good, but not if the editorials merely waste time, mouth platitudes, or antagonize people.

Some stations editorialize regularly—daily, three times a week, or less frequently. Others editorialize only when they feel the need to take a stand on a particular issue. Most air their editorials several times during a day, since audiences tune in and out and several airings may be necessary to reach an audience cross section.

An editorial is a station's official position on an issue, and is not to be confused with a commentary, an anlysis, or a report.

The Well-Equipped Newsroom

The equipment needed for radio news is simple and relatively inexpensive. However, good newsmen do not come cheap. People are always more important for turning out a good product than equipment. People use equipment to facilitate their jobs, but nobody turns out a good news product without good announcers, writers, and reporters—newsmen. A staff need not be large, but it must be professional.

The foremost tool the newsman uses is the telephone—for leads and for stories. The beeper phone can save much time and money if well used. If a station can get to a newsmaker quickly on the telephone and get a statement, it will frequently beat television to a story and perhaps get more honest and dramatic reactions than if the newsmaker has had time to prepare for an in-person appearance. It should be noted that to record a person's statement on the telephone and use it on the air without his approval is illegal.

Another valuable aid is the portable tape recorder. No radio reporter should ever be without a good-quality, battery-operated tape recorder. The tape recorder is now so mobile, unobtrusive, cheap, and easily used that the radio reporter readily can get information at the source of an event to make reporting more effective and interesting.

A newsman should be careful in editing taped comments to accurately reflect the substance of the remarks made. Radio has a tendency to shorten and condense most statements. People frequently are wordy and rambling. A good editor can tighten up most spontaneous statements, but he should do so in a manner that will reflect the truth of what was said.

Using the voices of people making the news is very important; the voice of a reporter in the field or an expert in a given subject area added to the newsman's voice can make a newscast more interesting and give it more impact. However, sometimes these are used as a crutch—as the lazy man's way of getting a story on the air. Many actuality reports add nothing and can be condensed and told by the newscaster better and in a fraction of the time. Good judgment must dictate the use of voices.

The mobile unit equipped with telephone or radio control and a portable tape recorder that can play back directly from mobile unit to studio is useful for covering many kinds of stories. A mobile unit can be an automobile, a truck, a helicopter, or an airplane. For obvious cost reasons, most stations have only autos so equipped.

Many stations overlook basic reporting aids such as having printed aids and research material in the newsroom. A set of encyclopedias, an almanac or two, lists of government officials with their addresses and phone numbers, phone numbers of possible news sources, good dictionaries, and other material can help immensely in reporting and research. At least one station has a computerized list of phone numbers of potential news sources so that information can be obtained quickly and accurately.

Suggestions for Further Learning

1. Compare the news approaches of the major stations in your market. Is each approach compatible with the station's other programing? Note the schedules, quality of writing and presentation, significance of news covered, and amount of specialized kinds of news.

2. Compare the news approach on a major afternoon or early evening radio summary (fifteen minutes or longer in length) with the news in an afternoon newspaper and the early evening TV news on the local ABC, CBS, or NBC affiliate. Are news judgments similar? Where is radio weak and strong compared with the competition?

3. What problems in your area could be dealt with by radio news in a constructive manner? What kind of programing and approaches would you use?

4. On a given news day, with the aid of the morning paper, prepare an assignment list of stories that ideally could be covered in your market during that day. How and to what degree should each be covered? How many radio newsmen would it take to cover those stories?

5. Over a period of several newscasts, analyze the news efforts of any local station. Is the emphasis more on significance or sensation? To whom are they appealing? Do they care about the news?

6. What use is made of mobile units and other "remote" news aids in your market? Does the use of these aids add substance or merely flair to the news?

7. Investigate the editorial policies of stations in your market. How often does each editorialize? Who writes and voices editorials? How are topics chosen and researched?

CHAPTER 9

Promotion

The term *promotion* as used in a radio station differs in meaning from its use in most businesses. Broadcast promotion includes advertising and publicity, including the contests and merchandising tools that other businesses consider to be promotion. In this chapter, the term is used to refer to those efforts that seek to build audience and revenue for the radio station.

Radio employs two kinds of promotion: *audience* promotion and *sales* promotion. Audience promotion is aimed at the station's listeners or potential listeners, and sales promotion is directed at the station's advertisers or potential advertisers.

Audience promotion is further broken down into two categories: *on-air* promotion and promotion that uses methods other than radio— *off-air*. On-air promotion includes such things as station identification, musical signatures, slogans, announcements, and contests that are presented during the broadcast day. Off-air promotion includes the use of newspapers, television, billboards, and other ways of reaching people in an attempt to attract them to listen to the radio station.

Any promotion plan must be a part of a station's overall goals. The type of station, its intended audience, and its public posture must be reflected in the promotional activities in which it engages. A promotional plan, therefore, must be conceived with delicacy and carefully coordinated between the program and the promotion departments.

Audience Promotion

The product that radio stations sell is programing. The strongest vehicle any promotion campaign has going for it is a good product.

A campaign also is easier if the product is different from the other products available to the consumer. If differences exist between the products, advertising and promotion can exploit those differences. If no real differences exist, the *method of presentation* becomes more crucial. The manner in which messages are presented is always important, but with the absence of real product differences, qualitative or stylistic, the promotion itself must initiate a difference. In recent years, business in general has seen a decline in qualitative differences between products, at least differences that can be detected by the public which uses the product. Most products are produced by alert, aggressive large companies that are skilled in market research and that quickly copy any successful competitor. Many products are difficult to evaluate without expert knowledge. If cigarettes are longer, or if they have packages that are bright and new, do they taste different? Cooking oil comes in many shapes of bottles, but is that the only difference between oils? Differences in advertising and promotion techniques substitute for the lack of product differences.

A similar approach has been used in radio also, especially in the large metropolitan centers. For example, seventy or more radio stations are heard in the city of Los Angeles. At least ten of those stations are trying to reach one large segment of the market by playing approximately the same kind of music, all with a similar format approach. A group of at least ten other stations is trying to reach a different but similarly large segment of the market using similar programing styles. Not all of these stations do an equally good job; some spend a great deal more money than others. Situations like this challenge promotion departments and lean heavily on promotion for the success of the station. In many cases, the promotion department simply responds by bribing listeners with contests that give away large sums of money; but that can be an expensive game.

A promotion department must also consider long-term success versus short-term success. Most stations consider long-term success to be the more important, believing in the utility of developing a faithful audience that will stick with the station over time, as opposed to overnight success followed by overnight failure. Promotion plans must be made with this goal in mind.

Advertising is linked to market research, in that the messages presented must be relevant to something the consumers want or can be persuaded to want. Market research is not only valuable in pointing out directions for advertising but is also useful in the earlier stages of planning the program type and content and the subsequent promotion of them.

Advertising does three things: it *informs*, *persuades*, and *reminds*. Sometimes advertising succeeds in all three at the same time, sometimes in only one. Advertising may also *entertain*, but unless it does one of the other three at the same time, it is not successful. Entertaining may make one of the three goals easier, but not necessarily.

Advertising a station must be done thoughtfully, carefully, and imaginatively if it is to have a favorable effect, because Americans are inundated daily with advertising. The average American adult is aware of seventy-six advertisements per day in the major media. One survey noted that, even though a large majority of the public—three out of every four—had a favorable attitude toward advertising generally, more than half of the public felt that "most advertising" insulted the intelligence of the American consumer. Similarly, more than half believed that advertising did not present a true picture of the product advertised.[1]

Conception of the Campaign

Who conceives a promotion campaign? Ideally, it should be a cooperative effort between the programing department, which conceives or at least administers the strategy upon which all else succeeds or fails, and the promotion department, which articulates the station's goals and qualities to the public. Occasionally, promotion managers, like others in the station, initiate excellent program ideas and concepts. However, the promotion department, sales department, or engineering department may tend to recommend excessive input into the program area. Each employee has a natural tendency to want his tastes reflected in his station. On the other hand, the program department can be hypersensitive to outside suggestions and can put up a negative barrier to anything that does not originate within its own area. The station manager must make sure that the promotion efforts are kept in perspective. Once the goals are formulated, the promotion department administers the campaign.

Advertising Agency

The off-air aspects of promotion frequently are coordinated by an advertising agency. This makes sense for most stations since it costs the station no more than it would if the station were to buy adver-

---

[1] American Association of Advertising Agencies' *Study on Consumer Judgment of Advertising*, 1965. For attitude surveys, see Raymond A. Bauer and Stephen A. Greyser, *Advertising in America: The Consumer View* (Boston, 1968).

tising space on its own. (The agencies are paid a commission, usually fifteen percent, by the advertiser. Fees are sometimes charged the client, in this case the radio station, for unusual production work.) Since radio stations are small businesses that seldom have more than a hundred employees and usually have far fewer, a good advertising agency is usually a welcome asset. A station usually will not have the breadth of expertise that an agency will have, and having an agency coordinate the advertising campaign will free station personnel to concentrate on other work, such as on-air promotion.

An additional reason for having an advertising agency assist a station with its promotion is the goodwill generated from giving one of the agencies the station's own business. A good share of a station's revenue in any medium or large market comes through the business handled by the agencies. Hiring an agency to do its advertising rather than using station personnel is a vote of confidence in advertising agencies that hopefully will help overall agency-station relations. However, the station itself should conceive the campaign, set its goals, and establish guidelines.

Budget

How much money should be spent on promoting a station is a difficult question. The amount spent depends on the resources of the station. Many wealthy stations will promote heavily even in financially hard times. Poorer stations cannot afford to. The budget is also dependent upon the type of station and its relative success at reaching what it feels to be its share of the market. If a station has many listeners, on-air promotion can make up for what stations with fewer listeners would have to go to other media for. A key factor is the competition; a promotion budget must be geared to meet the competition. Also, the market and station size determine the promotion budget in large part. A large share of most promotion budgets is marked "contingency," to allow maximum flexibility.

Theme

Some of the most effective campaigns have revolved around a central idea, theme, or slogan. If a station can find a theme upon which to base a concerted and coordinated campaign, results can be most effective. This method is often seen in the advertising of products: "Ford has a better idea." "The greatest show on earth." The CBS corporate eye. "The friendly skies of United." "Boss radio." "Two-way radio." The coordination of visual identification, a sound, and good ad copy can be particularly effective.

An ad campaign often centers on an identity that starts with the call letters of the station. Many stations have gone to great lengths for such an identity; stations have even bought from other licensees call letters that can be said in a word, or that have a connection with a city, or that project an image. Examples of such call letters include KOOL in Phoenix; KFOG, KABL (cable car), and K-101 (actually KIOI) in San Francisco; KDIG, KHIP, and KJAZ, all chosen for jazz stations; the network flagship stations WCBS, WNBC, and WABC; and KPOP and WILD. (You can imagine the fictitious ones that are created in the announcers' lounges.)

Off-Air Promotion

All of the standard advertising techniques can be used in off-air promotion: newspaper ads, billboards, television, and specialty advertising such as bus and taxi cards, bumper stickers, and even skywriting. Radio uses the same methods of attracting attention that a toothpaste or detergent manufacturer might use. The only limit is the budget. On the following pages are examples of off-air promotion that can be used in addition to major ads in newspapers and on television.

Sister Media

It is especially helpful for radio if "sister" media are in the same market. Many stations with common ownership give plugs to one another. Having AM, FM, and TV stations all with the same call letters is a definite advantage, for each can run promotional announcements for the others. If print media are also in a complex, they increase cross-plugging even more. This advantage of conglomerates is one reason the Federal Communications Commission for years has tried to encourage more diversity of media ownership in the various markets. Stations have been forced to use sister media with discretion.

Entertainment Booking

An off-air promotional technique frequently used is the booking of entertainment acts. This technique may require considerable on-air promotion, but it also may include advertising in the other media. A station's call letters are always associated with a show, gaining attention and hopefully goodwill from the fans of the entertainers. Country stations frequently book *The Grand Ole Opry* into their cities. Top-40 stations and progressive music operations book rock and jazz performers. Stations often broadcast live performances, with a station personality introducing the performance and getting exposure before the live audience. Frequently, a station will also make a percentage of the concert gate receipts.

Personal Appearances

Personal appearances and involvement in community organizations by station personalities, newsmen, and management personnel often are used as soft-sell promotional tools. Many stations encourage, even require, such participation and frequently pay the organizational dues for the employee. If a station has good people representing it, such contacts can be very useful. Disc jockeys appear at record hops. Other personalities are in demand as masters of ceremonies. Many work in the Kiwanis or Rotary clubs, or in other service organizations. Many are active in the Boy Scouts, Chamber of Commerce, and other groups. Such involvement not only helps a station's image, but is useful in making sales contacts.

Some air personalities and newsmen have become well known "off mike," and in so doing have added prestige to their programs. Some have written books or articles. Others have made hit records, and still others have performed on local or national television shows, all while keeping their radio programs.

Free Publicity

A great deal of free publicity can be obtained if a station keeps the local newspaper, TV, and radio editors informed about events at the station. Informing does not mean bombarding them with constant promotional releases, but rather making their jobs easier by letting them know when the station has legitimate news. Also, through enterprise and leg work, a number of feature stories that come out of a station can find their way into the paper, even if they are only one line. The newspaper editor is trying to do a job too; a station should find out what he needs or will use. If a station can help him fill his columns with interesting material or make his job a little easier, the goodwill and rapport built up over time can be of benefit to the station. The TV/radio section of a newspaper contains material with a high readership and has great potential for informing listeners of station efforts. Unfortunately, a few papers are still biased against the electronic media and will print almost nothing about broadcasting. Cooperation with them is difficult, but fortunately they are in the minority.

Feeding the media's trade publications information can accrue benefits, but mostly within the broadcasting fraternity, since the general
public does not read them.

Graphics and Design

Many stations put great emphasis on their graphics and design, involving visuals ranging from their stationery to the logos appearing
on station cars and other equipment. Such emphasis can include com--
missioning an artist to design a Christmas card or to create mailers for
the national sales representative. Graphics and design can be used as a
visual focus for both audience and sales promotion.

Record Sheets

Many stations put out their own lists of bestselling records, taken
either from *Billboard* or from local surveys. These sheets are made
available to music stores as guides for people who want to buy currently popular records, and as promotion pieces that give the impression that a station is up-to-date on music. Top-40 stations especially
emphasize record sheets.

Unusual Ideas

A number of stations have had charity baseball games between their
air personalities and girls from the Playboy Club, airline stewardesses,
or professional athletes. The fun, good humor, and worthy cause can
reflect positively on a station.

One unusual idea was dreamed up by an engineer who owns a San
Francisco radio station. The transmitter is located on a mountaintop
and can be seen for a long distance. The engineer wired the tower to
operate as a kind of VU meter which lit up brightly when music or
other sound was loud and went off with complete silence. People could
watch the tower while listening to the station and be treated with an
electronic light show.

Stations have created events, such as frog jumping contests. One
station has sponsored a snake race on St. Patrick's Day for fifteen
years.

Some stations have used mascots. One has had great success in
getting publicity through having a person dress up in a chicken suit
and appear just about anywhere the public goes in large numbers. It
started as a kind of fluke when a competitor was giving away houses
and Rolls Royces and lots of cash. This station countered by giving
away Kentucky Fried Chicken and dressing a guy in a chicken suit to
help promote it. Soon he was going to ball games, concerts, getting

noticed in the papers and on television, and creating a lot of word-of-mouth by his antics. But it's not all fun; on a hot day the person in the KGB chicken suit can lose several pounds.

On-Air Promotion

Call Letters

The most obvious on-air promotion technique is the constant reminder to the listeners of what station they are listening to. All station operators, in addition to fulfilling the FCC regulation of mentioning station call letters once an hour, feel it important to have their call letters in the foreground. The reasoning is that: (1) the listener should be able to determine readily which station he is tuned to; (2) repetition makes a person more likely to recall the station's call letters if contacted by a rating service; and (3) repetition builds up a more definite image in the mind of the listener, building brand-name familiarity and confidence. Station call letters often are accompanied by a slogan or are built into a slogan intended to make the call letters easier to remember and impressive to the listener. Slogans such as "hits of now and then" and "the music station," or such modest bits as "the world's greatest radio station" are plentiful. Some stations insist that the time, temperature, and weather always include station call letters with the announcement. Others insist that the station call letters be given at least once between every record, plus during newscasts and at every other available opportunity. The frequency also must be repeated often so it will be remembered. It often accompanies the call letters, as in KLUB 570 or 76 KFMB.

Musical Signatures

Jingles, or musical signatures, often are used to help sell the call letters and build the proper identity. An abundance of jingles is available to a station operator. Some are fairly expensive and quality is variable. They can add to a station's sound, or they can irritate and detract. Generally, the best ones are short, simple, professionally performed, and will endure repetition over time. The best ones usually are also quite expensive, although some stations have had good luck with packages done by local groups at a nominal charge. The cost of a custom-tailored package done by professionals can quickly soar into five figures. Many of the best jingle packages are done by some of the best musicians and writers in the music business. KSFO in San Francisco claims that its listeners request the station signature, "Sounds of The City," more than any other record they have ever played. Some stations have had jingles done by talented local college students who often were more interested in the exposure and experience than the money; such efforts, however, are very risky. A number of jingle packages are offered on a syndication basis. The jingle producers record the instrumental part of a jingle separately for permanent use, since lyrics are changed and re-recorded according to the needs of a station. A station receives exclusive rights to a package in its market, but stations in other markets may have the same package. Syndicated packages are usually considerably cheaper than custom-made ones, since the cost of creating the idea is divided up among many stations.

Contests

Some managers think of only one word when promotion is mentioned—contests. Contests are more effective with certain types of stations and audiences than with others. The audience generally most receptive to this type of promotion is young, but, of course, it depends upon the contest. Top-40 stations rely heavily on contests; other types of stations use them to varying degrees. One contest approach is to give away a large sum of money in the midst of resounding publicity. In several markets in recent years, individual stations have given away several hundred thousand dollars in continuing giveaways with prizes of ten or twelve thousand dollars at a time. In many contests, a program host announces an amount of money to be given away or mentions a secret word, then changes it frequently; the only way to know the current amount of money or the latest word is to listen constantly to the station. Once an hour or so, the program host telephones someone selected at random from the telephone book. If the person knows how much money is in the jackpot or what the secret word is, he wins the prize.

A longtime favorite of many stations is to ask the listeners to answer their phones mentioning the station call letters, or repeating a station slogan. The station telephones someone once an hour, and if the person who answers the phone responds with the proper words he wins the money in the jackpot. Others have used a "mystery man" walking in the city streets dressed in a particular way. If a listener walks up to the mystery man and repeats the required slogan, such as "Are you the WXXX mystery man?," he wins the money. Of course, the mystery man is dressed like a thousand other people. Numerous wrinkles and variations have been tried on the contests mentioned. Contest ideas are limited only by imagination and the budget. Merchandise from sponsors frequently is given away in exchange for free advertising.

Another approach to contests is to give away smaller prizes but increase the fun of playing. Contest letters that are sent in by the listeners and read on the air give the listeners some personal attention and exposure on the air and generate a feeling that the station belongs to the people. They are participating in the station's programing, and participation can create audience loyalty. Even when they do not win anything, the listeners have had the fun of playing the game and comparing their efforts with those of the other listeners. Many stations do not even give away prizes; they merely have funny "put-on" type contests in which the grand prize is something that nobody could conceivably want.

An honor for unusual gifts for a station contest probably should go to the Houston station that made an unusual arrangement with the Ringling Brothers' Barnum and Bailey Circus. To winners in their contest they gave "pachyderm poo for your petunias, zebra zung for your zinnias, and camel chips for your corn." Winners were to bring pickups and shovels and do the work themselves. They actually did.

Awards

Many stations constantly seek awards and keep a master list of awards available, criteria for winning, and dates when entries are due. Any program or series which might qualify is entered. Programs are occasionally produced with an award in mind. When awards are won, a station may compliment itself publicly and attempt to get outside exposure from the print media. Stations are happy to be able to display trophies and citations in their lobbies and to run trade-magazine ads regarding the awards won, but this promotional tool is less important than most others.

Tours

Some stations schedule chartered air trips for listeners, having one of the station personalities promote the tour on his program and then act as tour guide on the trip. Trips to Europe, Hawaii, the Caribbean, and other places have proved successful for many stations. In addition to reaping publicity and goodwill from a successful tour, stations may also make money by taking a percentage of each ticket sold. The tours are welcomed by the people taking them, because tour rates are cheaper than regular commercial rates. The listeners on tour also may find they get special treatment because the hotels and entertainment spots try extra hard to get special publicity from the tour through on-air mentions and even remote broadcasts from location. A poorly planned trip with unpleasant experiences can, of course, cause ill will and will backfire on a station.

Remote Broadcasts

Many stations air remote broadcasts from various places. One large, clear-channel station, interested in promoting its regional image, originated its morning show from small towns in its coverage area for a month. Another station broadcast a program from a good fishing hole on the opening day of one fishing season. Broadcasts have been done from airplanes, resorts, hotels, fairs, and beaches, as well as from used-car dealers and supermarket openings. Remote broadcasts can be effective, but care must be used to assure the desired positive response. If the personnel who go to remote locations make favorable in-person appearances, and if the situations are carefully chosen, "remotes" can be beneficial. However, the mystique surrounding the radio voice may be shattered. A sloppy disc jockey in a run-down shack or a used-car parking lot can do more harm than good. Blatant misuse of the remote, such as long commercial pitches about how good a car wash is or interviews with the sales manager of a business, detracts from the programing and the station's image.

A station should determine what it wants to accomplish by such broadcasts. Remotes can provide goodwill for the station that goes to meet its listeners. Remotes sometimes provide interesting program material (also sometimes not so interesting and a waste of time and manpower). The remote can be a sales gimmick to encourage advertisers to buy schedules on the station, but it should not be used in this manner if it could hurt the station in other ways. The audience is interested mostly in interesting programs, and remotes should not detract from them. Another consideration is the amount of effort, money, and manpower needed to do remotes. In some cases, the efforts might be better placed somewhere else; on the other hand, remotes can be worth much more than the effort.

Program Information

One of the standard aspects of on-air promotion is giving listeners information about regular or special programs and conveying other information that builds awareness and a favorable image among listeners. Such service is directed mainly at a station's listeners.

Public Service

The last on-air promotion technique, and one of the most important, is performing a legitimate public service. Doing so with grace and without excessive "ballyhoo" can be one of the most effective forms of promotion. Performing worthwhile service helps a station's local image, promotes goodwill, is good business, and fulfills a station's desire for a place of service in the community. Every station has the power to perform some service for the community through its efforts, and needs always can be found to be provided for if the station personnel will look for them. One California station took a strong stand against a watered-down automobile smog-control bill, using on-air appeals and newspaper ads containing petitions to be sent to Washington in support of a stronger bill. More than a million signatures were sent to Washington. A stronger bill was passed. Another station made a personal campaign of aiding schools in raising money for music and athletic programs after a local budget shortage was compounded by a gubernatorial veto of state funds. The station influenced many prominent local people to appeal to the community for financial aid in funding these activities. Another station asked people to send in trading stamps to buy a school bus for retarded children. Still another station had listeners send in trading stamps to buy an enclosure for a pair of apes that had been given to the local zoo. One station raised funds to build a new day-care center for children with cerebral palsy. A number of stations, with varying success, designate a member of the staff an "ombudsman," or "action reporter," to assist people with virtually any problem they have not been able to solve. Stations constantly get pleas for assistance and must use extreme care in the projects they choose to get involved with. But legitimate concern for the community and efforts to better it are always appreciated.

Sales Promotion

Much of sales promotion is carried on at a more personal level than is audience promotion, because the group of people in broadcasting and advertising is relatively small, and over time they get to know each other. Promotion efforts can include expense-account entertaining, a Christmas gift, a personal presentation, or less personal mail pieces and trade-press advertising. Such mailers are often very elaborate and expensive brochures, since they reflect the quality of the station advertised and are made for a select group. Stations vary as to the size of their promotion departments. Often, both sales promotion and audience promotion are combined into a single promotion department. In some stations, sales promotion is a separate department, and in small stations one person may handle all promotion. Promotion departments are seldom large.

Research

Ratings sometimes are used in program decision-making, but their primary use is for sales purposes. Most stations, especially in larger markets, must subscribe to rating services because the advertisers demand information about audiences to help them make buying decisions. Some stations sponsor research other than ratings—research done in greater depth and often involving image studies. Buyers of advertising time can be influenced by such special research studies, although they are often skeptical of self-serving research efforts. Stations often prepare a number of printed mail sheets or handouts which summarize research or rating data but which emphasize information that shows the station to best advantage. A station can pull obscure data from ratings that might not be noticeable immediately from a cursory look at the reports, such as data showing strength among 25-to-35-year-old housewives between 10 A.M. and 2 P.M., or noting that the last three rating books have shown an ascending share of audience. Some stations rely heavily on ratings as a sales tool (especially those with high ratings), while others lean more to selling the advertiser on success stories, creative ad campaigns, or other techniques. Ratings are used often by national advertisers, because their agencies' time buyers usually know little about an individual market or station.

Presentations

Some stations sponsor parties and make presentations to groups of advertisers, agency representatives, or specific clients. It is common for television stations to hold one or more gatherings prior to the new fall season of shows each year. Radio stations, although seldom having a new season of shows, may have similar gatherings when announcing a new program or concept, or sometimes for no specific reason at all. Some of these functions are more social occasions than sales, with low-key efforts. Others contain elaborately prepared speeches with displays, film, or slide-audio presentations. One radio station has a policy of inviting key personnel of different local advertising agencies to an elegantly catered breakfast each month. The station's air personnel thus meet the agency people, get acquainted, and maintain goodwill.

Barter

Barter can be helpful for sales promotion purposes but can work in the opposite manner intended if a station misuses the technique. In barter, or "trading-out," a station exchanges advertising time for other advertising or merchandise. Many stations discount their own product by unwisely giving more advertising time than their payment is worth. This instills in the advertiser the feeling that the time is not worth as much as a station has been asking. Barter is also used to trade for something a station does not need in order to get an advertiser to use the medium in hopes that his use will be successful and that he will want to buy more advertising. Some stations trade for automobiles or other station needs, often from advertisers who will not buy regular time on the station. Many stations will not barter at all.

Merchandising

Merchandising is offered by some stations as a bonus for buying advertising, but it is not uniform throughout the industry. Most strong stations do not practice it except in special instances, such as for an advertiser that spends an extremely large amount of money with a station, or as a joint effort with the sponsor of a big program or program segment in which joint promotion is carried on. Merchandising includes such bonuses as window or floor displays to aid in the point-of-purchase sales of a product and direct-mail pieces to dealers carrying a product. Merchandising is a rather nebulous area, actually amounting in many cases to a discount of the advertising rate, since a station may spend its own money for displays or mail pieces and not charge the advertiser anything other than the regular rate. Advertisers used to demand merchandising more often than they do today. Most stations consider it a headache and would rather not bother with it.

Trade-Press Advertising

Trade-press advertising is highly thought of by some, lightly regarded by others. The trade press is read mostly by people in broadcasting and by advertising agency personnel. Such advertising may have little impact upon the local advertiser. A side benefit is that it aids in the recruiting of top talent by making a station well known in the industry.

Success Stories and Premiums

Advertisers frequently want an indication from an audience that the commercials a station broadcasts for them are being heard and are generating response. Stations, too, relish advertising results that they can show advertisers. For this reason, stations prize the testimonials they get from advertisers who have used the station successfully. If an advertiser notes that soon after he advertised on a station about a specially priced item great numbers of people came to his store and he had to order additional supplies from his distributor, the station is delighted. If an advertiser writes a station a fan letter which the station can show to other potential advertisers, the station's sales staff will be helped greatly.

Sometimes a special offer is mentioned in commercials for the purpose of evaluating the listeners' response to a station's advertising. A listener may obtain a small gift or a free sample by writing to the station or visiting the sponsor's store and mentioning that he heard about the offer on the radio station. If the listener response is high, the advertiser and station are pleased; but if little response is shown, the sponsor is apt to take his advertising dollars to another station.

Evaluation of Promotion

Evaluating promotional campaigns is difficult due to the lack of sufficient objective data with which to analyze the results. Management can gather gut reactions and some informed opinions, but not much in the way of cause and effect observation. Promotion is never done in a vacuum; the program, competition, and other variables affect the results. Promotion offers little that is tangible enough to measure. Ratings and the boss's opinion are about all that most promotion directors rely on. More objective information can be obtained through public opinion research, but most stations do little of that, in part because such evaluations are expensive.

Suggestions for Further Learning

1. Assume that one of the real radio stations in your market has just hired you as audience-promotion manager to help it create a new image. Choose any station other than a Top-40 station. Your assignment for now is to lay out the theme and broad working principles for this new promotion campaign. Obviously, you must first familiarize yourself with the station's programing and objectives. This can be done by extensive listening to the station, visiting it, and talking with the station's promotion director. Try to invent a realistic innovative proposal that will project the desired image to your market.

2. You are the promotion director of a Top-40 station. Your strongest competitor has been running a very successful money giveaway. His contest is very simple. The disc jockeys mention four times each hour how much money is in the station jackpot. Once each hour they make a call to a phone number selected at random. If the person who answers the phone knows how much money is in the jackpot, he wins it. Your station manager does not want to give away as much money as your competitor is giving. What is your solution to meet this competitor's promotion?

3. Analyze the audience-promotion efforts of your market's major radio stations. Do they each have a theme? Are they truthful? Are they interesting? What use is made of other media? What on-air techniques are utilized? Does the on-air promotion interfere with the programing? Are the efforts effective? Compare with Profile 14, p. 299.

4. Build a scrapbook of sales-promotion brochures and ideas obtained from your favorite radio station.

5. Pinpoint five potential public service campaigns that a station might help with in your community. Lay out plans for a station to provide a service to the community and in so doing build goodwill. These campaigns should be local (at least a local angle on a national concern), feasible, and legitimate. Do not use traffic safety.

Approaches to meeting problem 2: Your manager may be wise in refusing to battle the competing station with matching money. In several markets where stations are battling, the stations have forced each other to give away larger and larger sums until the prizes have escalated to such a high level that the stations cannot afford the giveaways but are reluctant to back down and stop the contest. Such bidding for listeners can cut into station profits and can also cut into budgets that might better be spent offering the listeners some services. One station manager, faced with such a situation, told one of the authors of this book that he could not afford to pay the $240,000 a year that such a contest was costing his station, but that, until his competitor stopped, he did not feel he could. He even had tried to reach an agreement with the competing manager to stop the contests altogether, but without success.

It is possible for your station to minimize the opposition's advantage by meeting them directly but in another way. Your station can have someone monitor the opposition to find out how much money is in the jackpot, then have your station also announce how much money is in the opposition jackpot so that people can listen to your station and still win the money. Your station can also publicize the odds of winning such a contest. (In a medium-large metropolitan area, the odds of a person winning the money on a given phone call would be approximately eight million to one.) An announcement might read, "If anyone should ask, the Cash Call Jackpot this hour is worth $12,553. Of course, the odds of your winning that jackpot are eight million to one. So, for good music instead of bad odds, keep listening right here to fun lovin' XXXX."

A second alternative is to come up with a tongue-in-cheek contest of your own that is a parody or to invent a contest that is fun to play in itself. An announcement for the first type would read something like this:

> Have you heard about fun lovin' XXXX's great new contest? It's so easy to enter. All you have to do is memorize the last 47 numbers of the Hometown phone book, the chemical formula for lizard sweat, and tell us the middle name of John Smith. And the prizes you'll win! An all-expenses paid camel ride from Ishpeming to Walla Walla, accompanied by Phyllis Diller, *plus* a year's subscription to *Collier's* magazine. Keep listening, because if we call you, and you can give us the answer within three seconds, you'll win the grand prize. Of course the odds are only eight million to one that we'll call. If you have an unlisted phone, move in with a friend. For more contest details, keep listening to XXXX!

The second contest might be to have the listeners call in to see if they can repeat a tongue twister the DJ says to them, with the prize being something small such as a current record album or tickets to a concert or movie. The contest can be run for an hour or more with the first three people to call the station getting a chance to play. If the listener can repeat "Are you copper-bottoming 'em, my man? No, I'm aluminiumin' 'em, mum," or some other of the hundreds of tongue twisters that can be found or made up, he wins the prize.

The disadvantage of the above approaches is that each can call attention to the opposition. Two of the approaches might make people feel the station had committed a breach of ethics or taste. Another disadvantage is that the Top-40 station often relies heavily on playing lots of music and keeping talk short and crisp. People probably listen most because of the station's sound. Additional announcements and contests tend to clutter up the music sound.

Perhaps ignoring the competitor completely, avoiding additional clutter in the on-air sound, and spending promotion monies in other directions would be most effective. This approach might go even so far as reducing the number of commercials allowed to run on the station per hour, thereby

increasing music time. Added to this could be the elimination of all unnecessary talk and ballyhoo (DJs can be personalities and still be brief).

In addition, your station might put forth a strong effort to sponsor local
concerts by rock performers and other popular performers. Such performers have a special appeal to the listeners of Top-40 stations. The possibility
of profit exists in booking such acts, and carefully presented shows can
give the station effective publicity. However, booking such acts is not without its headaches—exorbitant salaries demanded by some groups, possibilities of violence and legal infractions, and negative feelings that some
adults get from rock concerts. Good shows can promote a positive image
for the station; bad shows can create a bad reputation.

Another possible addition to the above approaches is the hiring of one or
more writers to create comedy material for the DJs to use in their shows
or for special station bits. Comedy writers are not common in radio, except
in a few large stations. Radio uses so much material so fast that it is difficult to sound fresh. Good humor is a commodity that audiences enjoy and
is not usually plentiful enough or local enough in radio. If the station can
find or develop some writing talent and can afford to keep it on the staff, it
might be money better spent than in an expensive contest.

This is a difficult problem to give one right answer for because of the
dynamics of the individual market, and because not only *what* but *how well*
the steps are taken is important. This book's authors would, however, recommend a strategy that does not try to match money with the competition's
contest, but instead spends additional funds to give the best quality programing, minimizes extraneous clutter, and retains a crisp personality approach. Booking of concert acts might be a helpful adjunct.

CHAPTER 10

Sales

Most broadcast students and others interested in a career in broadcasting think of working in the programing department. Only a minority are interested, at least initially, in working in sales, even though the sales department is generally the quickest route to management. A salesman's chances of good pay, meeting interesting people, and getting a creative outlet are good.

A station's sales efforts are handled by the local sales staff, which may sell directly to clients or through local advertising agencies, and by the national sales manager who primarily coordinates the sales effort with the selling done by the national sales representative. In some cases, one sales manager has responsibility for both local and national sales. The station manager often is the national sales manager. The size of a sales staff varies from one to seven or eight, generally. In small stations, most of the selling is local; in very large stations, most of the advertising dollars may be national or regional. Highly rated stations in the twenty largest markets get a high percentage of national spot business.

Advertisers may purchase program sponsorships or spot announcements. In radio today, most of the business is spot, but some special programs are sponsored, such as newscasts, baseball play-by-play or other sports coverage, and, occasionally, music segments.

A 1976 study by Torbet-Lasker, a New York rep firm, showed that approximately three-fourths of all radio commercials are one minute in length (in TV, 30-second spots predominate, and forecasters expect increasing use of "30s" in radio). Advertisers most want to buy drive time. And if you wonder why so many radio programers, when asked which audience they are trying to reach, answer that they are going after the 18-to-49 audience (hardly a meaningful statement), it is because more than half of *national* spot-radio campaign flights specify the target audience as the 18-to-49 age group. Another twenty percent specify the 25-to-49 age group. Ten percent say they want to reach those 18 to 34. If you are under 18 or over 49, you are not in highly desired audience segments. Overwhelmingly, the national advertisers want justification for their advertising buys by the use of Arbitron ratings.

Local Sales

Local sales provide most of the revenue for most stations. Salesmen usually are paid a base salary with an additional percentage of the revenue they bring in above their established quota. The quota incentive is used to share the profits with the most productive salesmen while forcing them to produce if they want to make a good wage. A salesman has two main factors to consider when he tries to make a sale. He must have a good product to sell. If he does, he may enjoy the rare luxury of being able to take sales orders without having to do very much real selling. The other factor is his own selling ability. Much of selling consists of preparation—knowing the needs of the client and knowing how the station can help fill those needs. Vital to selling is the salesman's personality—his ability to relate to other people and to say what he needs to say to make the sale.

A good salesman needs to know everybody else's business, at least to the extent that he can understand their product and their marketing goals. He needs to demonstrate how his services can help accomplish those goals. Except in small markets, radio is not the only or even primary advertising medium for most advertisers. The radio-station salesman also needs to be able to show how his station can complement other media and other stations and to make a "pitch" for an appropriate share of the advertising dollars.

Once he has analyzed his prospective client's needs, he must have tangible support to sell the client with. His support may be a dummy campaign with sample commercials produced and recorded. If the rating reports are good, he can use the data to help build his case. If other advertisers have used the station successfully, letters of appreciation from them along with brochures that tell the success stories can be impressive. Extolling the type of programing may be helpful, especially if the programing is the type the client himself listens to. He tends to think that if he listens everybody else does. A map showing the station's coverage area with statistical data about the potential listeners to his message can be impressive. The client is especially interested in the cost, so rates must be competitive.

A salesman may find it necessary to sell a client on radio as an advertising medium before he can sell him on his specific station. One of the strongest points that can be made to a client is the relatively low cost of radio advertising. Generally, radio's *cost per thousand persons reached* (a commonly used yardstick) is lower than the other media except billboards. Radio rates are so low in some markets that a potential client can get the impression that it cannot be worth much or the stations would not be selling so cheaply. Many stations charge too little for advertising and need to re-evaluate their worth. Many are fighting rate patterns that have built up over many years, and advertisers are getting the benefit of the low rates.

A job is not finished once a client is sold. On a direct sale, the station's continuity and programing people must present advertising that effectively tells the story for the client. Also, the traffic department must schedule properly, and the salesman must follow up to keep the client informed and satisfied.

A sale handled through an advertising agency is simpler in some ways. Agency people are more knowledgeable about the medium than are businessmen. (Their knowledge often makes them tougher to sell unless they are predisposed toward the station.) The agency sale is simpler in another way, in that the agency writes the copy and does the production necessary for the client. For this, the station pays the agency a commission of fifteen percent of the client's time charges. Some larger business firms evade the agency commission by hiring their own people to act as an advertising agency within the business firm. These are called house agencies. Some house agencies do save their companies money; other companies would be better off using the professionals in the agency. Since the number of people working in radio and in advertising is not large, the various sales people get to know each other quite well. Much of the business is carried on at a very personal and informal level. Repeat business is dependent upon the success of the first contract. Reputations, both positive and negative, are established quickly and firmly.

The local sales manager should divide the accounts, both direct and agency, equitably among his salesmen. The star salesman or the one that has been employed the longest usually gets the choice accounts. Newer and younger salesmen generally have to prove themselves before getting the better accounts.

The National Rep

A station's national sales representative is a separate company that serves as an additional sales force for the station. Sales "reps" are used because stations usually cannot afford to have a local sales staff plus staff salesmen stationed in New York, Chicago, or other cities where the large national advertisers are located. The rep firm represents several stations, giving greater efficiency to each of them. A station pays the rep firm a percentage of the sale as a commission. The rep firm does not handle competing stations in the same market. Its client list may contain only a few select stations that get personalized attention, or the list may be long with minimal attention to each station. Some of the rep firms are part of broadcast groups. Westinghouse and Metromedia, among others, have established their own rep firms which represent company-owned stations as well as other clients. Many of the reps offer services that go beyond sales. Some of the reps are very sophisticated in programing strategy, are knowledgeable about the total broadcast picture, and serve as research, promotion, program, or sales consultants along with their function of selling to national advertisers.

The most effective rep firm is generally one that becomes totally familiar with a station and its goals. A station and its rep must have good communication if the rep is to tell the station's story accurately and positively. A station's national sales manager serves as a coordinator between the rep and the station and also participates in some of the sales presentations.

Small- and medium-market stations frequently have two rates—a national rate and a rate for the smaller local advertiser that is lower and competitive with local market conditions. For that reason, national spots usually get priority over local spots in getting the best time slots. Also, large advertisers that spend more money or sign long-term contracts generally get a lower rate than the short-term buyer, just as in other businesses where buying in bulk gets bulk rates.

Because radio time buying is only partly scientific, a salesman must possess the ability to be flexible and sell in a personal way. While station success stories, quantitative and qualitative audience research, the halo effect of a good reputation, and services such as merchandising are all important, the sales presentation and sensitivity to interpersonal relationships still play a special sales role. Considerable judgment is needed by the time buyer to make the most effective "buys" for an individual client. Audience ratings are important to a station trying to attract business, but ratings alone are not enough. A rep firm of effective salesmen can make a great difference to a station. (The same thing is, of course, true of local salesmen.)

Attempts are increasing to computerize time buying through more sophisticated research on demographics, standardized forms and practices, and computer-linked stations and agencies. Expert judgment has not been eliminated, however. In audience-rating reports, it is not uncommon to find ten stations that have no significant difference in audience size; a judgment thus must be made as to which is the best advertising buy for a given product. Also, since few radio markets can be covered by buying spots on only one station, the best combination of stations and times among those available must be decided upon with a fine touch to get the most effective coverage at the lowest cost per thousand listeners. Time buying definitely can be influenced by effective salesmen.

Sales Policies

Sales policies, written and unwritten, vary according to the station and type. The most common policies are those which are in accordance with the *NAB Code,* much of which is concerned with advertising.

Sales below Rate Card

When business is slow, stations tend to sell their time at less than the published rates on their rate cards, a common practice in other businesses as well. Some businesses sell products under the list price even when business is thriving. In some businesses, a customer feels cheated if he has to pay the "window-sticker price." Most businesses have sales or specials. Responsible radio station managers generally frown on the practice, however. They do not believe in the practice of conditioning the client to believe that he can negotiate a lower rate or more spots for the same rate. Radio stations too often have sold their product for less than its worth. Sticking to the rate-card price is believed to show integrity and stability in the product. Cut-rate stations often are looked down upon.

Trade-out, or Barter

Many stations exchange advertising for merchandise or services. This practice can be abused if a station gets lower value in goods than the advertising is worth. It also can be used legitimately if a station needs the goods (cars for station use, airline tickets, office equipment) and if it gets full value for the advertising. Occasionally, a salesman will use barter to persuade an advertiser to use radio advertising for the first time, then switch over to a cash contract after the initial contract has expired.

To some the word "barter" connotes a third party in the sales transaction, involving an arrangement like brokerage of time. An outside packager provides a program or series to the station free except that some specified commercials are run in the program while leaving some unsold commercial availabilities in the program. The packager makes his money from sale of the commercials that come with the program. This practice is probably more common to TV than radio because radio deals with formats more than programs.

Per-Inquiry Contracts

A few stations will accept advertising for which they are paid only by the number of responses generated. A coupon may be offered, or the listener may be asked to phone a particular number or write to a particular address. If the advertising brings no response, the station gets no pay. Most stations will not accept such advertising.

Co-op

It seems that at least once a year at some broadcast conference somebody stands up to tell station management that the industry is not doing a good job of bringing in the co-op dollars that are available, and that if they really went after this source of revenue their earnings could increase significantly. And every year it appears that only a few station managements are able to use co-op to great advantage.

A local retailer who sells a nationally distributed product may be able to get the manufacturer of the product to share in local advertising expenditures to advertise the product *and* the retailer. The manufacturer may pay for half of the advertising cost, or in some cases nearly all. The percentage depends upon the specific arrangement that is made between the two parties doing the advertising. In many cases, the manufacturer has a policy of sharing with local retailers but the retailer is not adequately informed about how he can get this assistance. A sharp station salesman can help to put such an advertising package together, get dollars on his air that would not otherwise be there, help the retailer to make his dollars go further, and also get assistance from the manufacturer who may have professionally prepared sales aids that can make the retailer's commercials more like the best of the national advertising. In some cases, one manufacturer's product is advertised for several retailers in rotation. In other cases, the national advertiser gets a local rate rather than a more expensive national rate.

Rate Protection

As ratings go up, or as inflation drives costs up, or as an excess of business prospects warrants, a station may raise its advertising rates. Stations offer a rate protection to advertisers who already have signed contracts—a promise that rates will not be increased for those advertisers for a specified period. *Spot Radio Rates and Data* lists lengths of time for rate protection to continuous advertisers ranging from twenty-eight days to twelve months, depending on the station.

Discounts

Some stations' rates are the same for both small advertisers and those that buy many spots. Most stations, however, offer rates on a sliding scale—the more spots and the longer the contract, the lower the unit price. In order to achieve long-term discounts, some clients that advertise most heavily on a seasonal basis will continue to run the minimum number of spots needed to qualify for long-term discounts. This minimum schedule is called a *rateholder.* Station policy may allow as few as one or two announcements per week for an advertiser to qualify for the low rate. If an advertiser signs a contract for fifty-two weeks, getting a low rate for his spots, then changes his mind after ten weeks and cancels, the station likely will charge him at a higher rate for his ten weeks of spots than the contract stated. This is called a *short rate.*

Production Services and Fees

Policies vary with regard to what the advertiser buys with his time. Rates quoted may be for time only, but they usually include music copyright fees and standard services such as the use of staff announcer and available facilities. Additional fees may be charged for special considerations, such as a talent fee for using a particular announcer to voice a commercial or special production work. Advertisements handled through an agency usually require very little of a station other than to air them at the contracted time. Direct sales accounts in a small station may include elaborate production without additional charge by the station. Remote pickup facilities, production, talent, or any unusual services may be subject to extra charge, depending upon the individual station and its policies.

Commercials as Programing

Commercials are certainly part of programing. In most successful stations, commercials account for about twenty-five percent of each program hour. (The *NAB Code* specifies no more than eighteen minutes per hour.) Some stations program more than thirty percent commercial content. Others deliberately limit the commercial content to twelve, ten, or even four minutes per hour because they feel they are more competitive by doing so. Sheer number is important, but quality and integration with the programing are also important.

When commercials are prepared by ad agencies, a station plays little part except in scheduling and in exercising veto power over commercials thought to be in bad taste or in violation of station policy. Small stations have more control over commercials because they usually have the responsibility for writing and producing each commercial. Too often, unfortunately, a small station has the writing done by the most poorly paid person on the staff whose prime reason for being given the job is that he works cheaply. Sometimes a small station's salesmen have to write the copy and are in charge of producing, too.

Commercials are the biggest single irritant to listeners, the programing they complain about most. But commercials also can be interesting program matter and some of the most creative and entertaining parts of the program day.

A station must decide what kind of role its commercials are going to fill. Some stations will accept virtually any type, as long as it is paid for. Others are very particular as to the type of sponsors and presentations they accept. A station can be so selective and protective that agencies and sponsors find it difficult to do business with. Other stations have only one goal—to make money in any way possible. The proper role is some reasonable middle ground, with the station showing flexibility and desire to work with advertisers and agencies while cognizant of the need for standards. A station, not its advertisers, must decide its own policies. Some advertisers may criticize certain policies, but if the policies are realistic the same advertisers will admire the station for its standards and respect those standards. *Good Housekeeping* and *Sunset* magazines have policies that will allow no product to be advertised in their magazines unless the magazines feel they can endorse the product and the advertising. Most stations cannot afford to go to that extreme, although for some it might not be a bad idea. Other stations do not follow such a policy, because they feel that their role involves a certain amount of "equal time" in products as well as in programing and news. It is not only ethical but it is smart business for a station to establish policies and stick to them.

Station management must decide upon the degree of balance between programing and sales. Sales departments tend not to overlook any potential dollars and to "sell anything that moves." In highly rated stations with favorable demographic figures in large markets, selectivity is easy because stations deal from a position of strength. Salesmen can be more particular. In weak stations in small markets, salesmen cannot be as selective. The salesman is not only the agent of his station working on an incentive plan; he has other obligations. He is pressed by his station manager and his creditors to bring in money.

On the other hand, a program director can be a purist, an idealist interested in providing service to the public and impressing his fellow broadcasters or men's club friends with his creative programing. He is interested in ratings less because they help sell than because they indicate that his efforts are receiving public acceptance. His on-air people may be interested in building themselves up as personalities in the community, in achieving a certain amount of fame or attention because of their popular programs. A programer thinks of advertising as something he has to tolerate in order to put programs on the air. A salesman sees programing as an audience delivery system. On days when programing wants to cut down or eliminate commercials due to a major news event or special public service effort, the commercial department either must give the advertiser "make-goods" or refund his money.

Too many stations have the balance of power on the sales side. This happens because more managers come through sales than through programing, and because sales pays the bills. Stations sometimes do what is expedient, forgetting long-term successes. Also, a great many programers are unaware of the sales point of view and the financial needs of the station. Some programers are not oriented toward money matters and are unaware of overall station needs. A station must have a balance. Salesmen cannnot rely on gimmicks that bring short-term achievement at the expense of long-term success. The program department must provide programing that attracts a large enough audience of the right kind of people for the sales department to do its job. Management must provide the overview and establish the balance.

The number and type of commercials is a factor of programing, since commercial matter provides many interruptions and constitutes a high percentage of the content. If a station allows commercials on the air that are offensive, in poor taste, too numerous, or poorly presented, it is offering bad programing. The commercials must be at least as professional and in as good taste as the programing. They can provide information about new products and businesses. They can raise local awareness and be a legitimate service. Commercials can be entertaining and add variety to the programing.

Many stations limit the number of commercials to well below the

NAB standard in the belief that they will have an advantage over their competitors who program the maximum number allowed. There is, no doubt, some truth in that, but the optimum number of commercials is not known.

A number of stations cluster their commercials to give the appearance of less clutter and fewer interruptions. Many sponsors do not like their commercials surrounded by others, fearing that their own will have less impact if heard with a group. Many stations promise that they will not double-spot (play two commercials back to back). This generally appeals to advertisers, who like their messages to stand out.

Some stations will not carry commercials felt to be foreign to the station image, such as those with music of a type radically different from that the station programs, or those that promote certain personal products.

Stations may allow only spots, or they may allow sponsorship of segments of the program day or special programs. Frequently, a station will allow only participation spots in shows with disc jockeys but will allow sponsorship of a newscast.

Suggestions for Further Learning

1. Ask the sales manager of a local station to let you sit in during a sales presentation with a client. Note the types of material he uses to sell his product.

2. Browse through *Spot Radio Rates and Data.* Try to get a feeling for the policies and comparative rates of the stations in a market with which you are familiar.

3. Read carefully the advertising manual prepared by the Radio Advertising Bureau in Appendix B of this book. Use the tips you find to draw up a specific advertising campaign for a large department store in your area.

4. You have $10,000 to advertise each of four separate products in each of five separate cities. The products are a soft drink, a household appliance, a breakfast cereal, and a major airline. The cities are Buffalo, New York; Spokane, Washington; Pittsburgh, Pennsylvania; Jacksonville, Florida; and Wichita, Kansas. Using the information in *Standard Rate and Data,* make the buys for the appropriate stations in each market. What other information would be helpful?

CHAPTER 11

Research

Research serves two general purposes in the radio industry: (1) research basically is used to help a station's sales effort; and (2) research is used to help management make decisions about the future course of the station. Some research serves both functions. The main reason for audience ratings is to provide information that will help a station's sales department. Management research is usually more secret and used for in-house decision-making. Audience ratings are demanded by advertising agencies and clients because they want to know what their advertising is costing them per thousand persons reached, and they need to compare radio advertising costs with the advertising costs of the other media. Most research done is sales research, and most of it is done by one company —Arbitron. Pulse, Hooper, The Source, and Mediastat also do ratings. These companies also will do more expensive image studies, as will other companies. Such qualitative studies, commissioned by individual stations, are more suspect among advertisers than are ratings because of their lack of standardization, and because of the general suspicion about research that appears to have been purchased by one company to show its best side. A station frequently may find it advisable to keep this type of research secret, because it may have information that competitors do not have. With effective use, this information can give a station a competitive advantage.

Sampling

The basis of survey research is the fact that not everyone must be interviewed to determine the habits and thoughts of the public, just as it is not necessary to taste all of the water in the ocean to find out that it is salty. If part of the public is questioned at random, some generalizations about the habits of the entire market can be made. The accuracy of the generalizations is determined by the way the sample is chosen, the size of the sample, and the manner of questioning.

The first problem in obtaining representative points of view is that of finding a random sampling of the public in a station's coverage area. An interviewer cannot stand on a street corner and ask the people who pass by their opinions. Not everyone goes by that street corner; people who live or work in that area will be over-represented. An announcer cannot ask his listeners to write or phone in, because those who reply would not be a cross section of the public. Those who are busiest will not bother. Neither will those who think it unimportant. And, of course, not everyone listens. Unsolicited letters to a station are seldom representative of opinion. It is not at all unusual for a low-rated program to get much more mail than a highly rated program.

Research companies choose their samples by obtaining lists of phone numbers or housing locations from the total market and selecting, through the use of random numbers or an interval selection procedure, the number of desired contacts to give the number of responses that provide the best sample size for the accuracy demanded and the available budget. One frequently used list is the telephone directory. Another is a map of housing locations, obtainable from governmental agencies. The Post Office, through its zip code, quite accurately pinpoints the location of the population; the number of mailing addresses within each zip code area is known and can be useful in sampling. If every person in the telephone book or each housing unit is numbered, and a table of random numbers is used to select the persons to be contacted, the chances of getting a sample that is representative of the public are better than through the street-corner or mail responses approaches. If the *interval selection* procedure is used, to obtain a sample of 2,000 in a population of 1,000,000, each 500th unit on the list could be used. Interval selection is an effective way to draw a sample. When all other elements of survey procedure are held constant, the bigger the sample, the smaller the statistical error. However, doubling the sample size does not double the accuracy. Costs increase faster than the accuracy improves, because the size of the standard error is approximately inversely proportional to the square root of the sample size. A compromise point exists at which the available funds for research and the allowable statistical error meet. Stations would like the research to be constantly more accurate but are only willing to pay for so much accuracy.

Two sources of error are inherent in a sample. One is the statistical error itself, which can be calculated mathematically. This is a known error, or at least the probable limits of the error are known. The other source of error is in the data used. If telephone books are used, the sample will not be able to use statistical procedures on all of the people in the coverage area because many people are not listed in the telephone book. The very rich who do not want their names in the phone book, the very poor who do not have phones, and people who do not want their creditors to track them down will not be included in the sample. It is not uncommon for twenty-five percent of the public to be left out of the phone book. In Beverly Hills, California, among other places, the percentage of people listed in the phone book is low. Statistically, the accuracy of a sample can be judged. For example, with a sample size of 1,000 and a rating of 6, ninety-five percent of the time that rating will fall between 4.5 and 7.5. However, it is difficult to know if a sample has been biased by excluding some people from the sample because their names were not available for inclusion.

Other kinds of errors are possible. One is a bias that is built in by the way a question is worded. Questions can be worded in a manner that will encourage some responses and discourage others. An interviewer can be a source of bias if he allows his own opinions to influence the responses. Another possible bias is nonresponse; that is, the people who are not at home or do not wish to be interviewed may be different from those who are home or were interviewed. Also, an interviewer can record the responses inaccurately, or the data can be transcribed inaccurately in or out of data processing. Although the errors tend to be random, meaning that they cancel each other out, all of these potential sources of error indicate that ratings are an exacting business in which careful controls are needed. The research firms train interviewers to be as unobtrusive as possible. Questions are carefully worded. People not at home must be checked by follow-up contacts.

Radio ratings are generally less definitive than television ratings, for several reasons. The radio audience is more fragmented, with more stations to be rated. A sample size of 1,000 is more meaningful for five television stations than thirty or forty radio stations. For example, if 1,000 units were sampled at a given time of an evening and twenty percent were listening to radio, only 200 of the people contacted would be listening to the forty radio stations in the market. That leaves only two people per rating point. The percentage of homes using radio at some times of the day can be quite low. The lower the percentage figures, the greater the percentage of variation. For instance, a rating of 20 with a sample of 1,000 will fall between 18 and 22 about ninety-five percent of the time, while a rating of 5 with the same sample size will range between about 3.5 and 6.5 for ninety-five percent of the time.

These examples are not to demean ratings. Ratings are useful and valid. They are much more accurate than asking the boy down the street and your mother-in-law. But, they are a rough indicator. The limits of each rating are stated on the inside front and back covers; the sample size and coverage area are shown. Ratings should not be used to try to differentiate minuscule variations in audience levels.

Methods of Obtaining Responses

Some ratings are obtained by telephone, some by diaries, and some by door-to-door polls. Television ratings also are obtained by attaching a meter to the TV set which records the program watched. Since radio is so mobile, meters are not feasible.

Telephone ratings are obtained by drawing a sample from the phone book and calling the home to find out what the family members are listening to at the time of the phone call. Telephone calls are fast and relatively cheap but do not lend themselves to getting information as detailed as other types of surveys. There is margin for error in using only people who have telephones. Detractors of telephone ratings also add that children are more apt to answer the phone than other family members, perhaps giving children greater weight in the ratings. Hooper's ratings are done by telephone.

Some ratings are obtained by going from door to door, generally using women interviewers who work between about 6 and 8 P.M. Women are used because fewer women at home will respond to male interviewers in some areas of our cities. The early evening time is used because most of the family members are apt to be found at home then. The sample usually is chosen from the phone book, but, because the interviewers are going out to reach the respondents in person, they use the cluster method, starting at the house next door to the address obtained from the phone book. By starting next door, the chances of getting some houses with unlisted phones are improved. The interviewer calls on several homes in the same area—a cluster. The reason for taking a cluster of homes is purely economic. It would be better to get responses from the random names, but a sample size of 1,000 would mean going to 1,000 separate locations. Since that would make costs prohibitive, the interviewers go to fewer locations, but they get more responses. Other things being equal, the statistical error for cluster sampling is greater than simple random sampling, but the difference can be overcome by increasing the sample size. Also, because of the in-person interviews, the cluster method can have advantages which offset this disadvantage. Generally, the in-home interviews find the greatest absentee rate among male heads of household. Pulse uses the clustered in-person interview.

Diaries also are used in research. These are usually placed in homes by telephoning a home and asking if the family will keep a diary of their listening habits. The family usually gets a small gift for doing so. At the end of each week, the diaries are mailed in to the researcher. Because of the use of the telephone, again, some persons are over-looked. Some will not accept a diary, just as some will not talk to you on the telephone or in person if you disturb them during dinner. Some will not fill the diaries out very conscientiously. Arbitron, using the diary method, has been a leader in providing expanded demographic information. The Source also uses diaries but places the diaries in person rather than mailing them.

The telephone rating has the advantage of being fast and relatively cheap. It also asks people what they are listening to at the time of the call. That means they do not forget between the time they listen and the time they are asked.

The interview is more personal. It avoids some of the sampling problems although creating others. Detailed information about the household is easier to obtain in interviews. An interviewer asks only what was listened to in the past twenty-four hours to minimize forgotten data and uses a printed sheet listing stations and programs as a memory aid.

The diary obtains detailed information also, but may be accepted and kept more readily by older people who have the time to follow through with the request. The diary and interview are believed to provide better information on out-of-home listening.

After the raw data are obtained, the companies generally check with zip code data to see if they have the correct geographic dispersion of the respondents. In some cases, they also cross-check to see if they get a balance of other factors, such as the correct proportion of education groupings, ethnic groups, or income groups. If the sample does not match the population, a correction factor may be added to weight the responses of one group more heavily in order to reflect the population most accurately.

Use of Rating Data

The biggest abuse of the ratings is not by the rating companies. These companies provide a useful service. What they provide is too often misunderstood and misused.

One mistake the users frequently make is not reading the fine print —the detailed material that accompanies each rating, spelling out the limits and conditions under which the rating was taken.

The rating is not a fine caliper. It could be made more accurate if stations were willing to spend considerably more money, but they are not. The rating should be used as a rough indicator. It is clear that a station with a rating of ten is doing much better than a station with a rating of one. But a rating of 4.0 is essentially the same as a rating of 3.8. Yet, many managers will panic if their ratings slip one-tenth of a point.

The rating should be correlated with others over time. If a station gets one rating that is out of character with the two before it and the one following it, that one rating book may be merely a vagary. Ratings are most meaningful when looked at over a long term. If a station shows a declining share of audience over a three-year period, that trend is far more significant than a slight shift from one rating book to the next.

Information Provided by Ratings

The prime purpose of the ratings is to find out who is listening and when. Ratings are presented in quarter-hour intervals, 6 A.M. to midnight. The data is given in *ratings* and *shares*. Some surveys use homes and some use people as the unit base. Depending upon which rating service is used, a *rating* is the percentage of either all *homes* or all *persons* (potential listeners) that are tuned to a given station. A *share* is the percentage of all *listeners* (either homes or persons) who are listening to a given station. If thirty percent of all people are listening, and ten percent of all people are listening to one station, the rating is 10 and the share is 33. The homes using radio (HUR) percentage is 30. The share is the rating divided by the HUR.

The rating book usually summarizes the data into different categories. The one most frequently looked at but not necessarily the most significant is the average quarter-hour rating, 6 A.M. to midnight. This shows the stations' relative positions with regard to all persons reached but does not show who is being reached. The ratings are further broken down into time blocks, 6–10 A.M., 10 A.M. to 3 P.M., 3–7 P.M., and 7 P.M. to midnight. Also, according to which rating is taken, the information may be broken down further into other categories, such as the ages of the listeners. The station that reaches the most total persons may reach mostly those under 24, or over 50. If this is the case, most advertisers will not be interested, in spite of the total numbers. Advertisers are much more interested in demographic break-outs that provide the best potential customers. Arbitron ratings have been especially popular because they have given data in terms of persons rather than homes and because of the demographic aids. For an additional fee, Pulse offers the LQR service (local qualitative radio) that breaks down listening in terms of occupation—blue collar, professional, and others; income; education; working women/women at home; which stations' listeners drink the most beer, use the most toothpaste, or use the most household detergent. The Source will also tell you which people have specified credit cards, which stations have the most grocery purchasers, which stations have the most homeowners, and similar information that can be used as a buying aid for advertisers.

Cumulative audiences, or "cumes," are a measure of the circulation or reach of a station. The cumes are the total unduplicated numbers of persons reached in a specified time period. The time period may be a day, a week, or maybe just two or more parts of the day. A station may have a greater average quarter-hour audience than another station but may have smaller cumes. This happens when the audience is loyal and listens for longer periods of time. A news station may have an audience that does not listen for long periods of time, but its total number of listeners—its cumes—may be larger than for many music stations with similar average quarter-hour ratings.

While ratings are primarily a sales tool, they can yield useful programing information. The rating services are happy to assist a station in making full use of the data. Arbitron, for example, allows station representatives to examine the diaries used for a survey at their offices in Beltsville, Maryland. They have pamphlets which help station personnel to understand ratings terminology and the limits of reliability of the ratings, ways for the station to increase its competitive position in the rating books, and ways of learning more about the audience to solve programing problems. Following are some of the things a station manager or programer can do to make maximum use of his ratings.

1. See if the station's audience is on the upswing or downswing or remaining steady. Compare present ratings with the last rating, compare ratings for the same time a year ago, and compare overall ratings for the past three years.

2. Compare the average ratings and cume ratings. If average listening is up and cume listening is the same, it means that the same number of people are listening as in the previous period but they are listening for longer periods of time. If average listening is down but cume listening is up, then people are spending less time listening.

3. Compare your station with other stations aiming at the same audience and see who is most successful.

4. Compare your type of station with other types of stations in your market. Add the percentages for the all-news stations and put them in one category, add the percentages for the conservative music stations and put them in another category, and so on until you have analyzed audience listening by station format.

5. Compare how your station does in away-from-home listening. (Is it proportionately better or worse than your overall shares?)
6. Calculate how long the average person listens to your station.
7. Calculate how often listeners hear the same record.
8. Calculate how many listeners listen only to your station.

Ratings—Who Is "Number 1"?

Who is number one is not always a very meaningful question. No doubt, many an advertiser and broadcaster felt a warm amusement at the little struggling radio station that promoted itself in the following fashion: "We're the number two rated radio station in town. We have to be—everyone else is number one."

Stations often look at the 6 A.M. to midnight summaries for the total week. The station which records the largest number of ears calls itself the winner, number one. But this station may not be pulling the ears the advertisers are interested in. This station with the most total listeners may be number four or five in ad revenue. Others will point out that *The National Enquirer* outsells *Time* and *Newsweek* combined, but that doesn't make it a better use of newsprint. Increasingly advertisers have become interested in whom they are reaching, and many station operators have always felt that things other than raw numbers were important. The most influential station in the community may or may not be the one with the largest total numbers. And the station owner who has other goals and who reaches those goals may find every bit as much satisfaction as the operator who chases the mechanical rabbit of total audience.

A breakdown of audience from Pulse, Source, and Arbitron in one market shows the following. Station A is a high-energy, tight playlist Top-40 station. Station B is a low-key adult pop station with personalities, sports, and news. Station C is modern country. Station D is an innovative rock station. Station E is a conservative station. These are actual data from one of the top twenty markets.

In total audience for the rating period, Station A leads. Examining the previous four rating books (fall and spring rating periods), we find that it averages out to be number one, also. Station B ranks fifth in this rating period, a fall book. In looking back over the previous four books, we find that its record is better, an overall number two. Also, we note that every spring its ratings are stronger than its fall ratings. In analyzing the current book, we note that the baseball season has just ended. Where Station B had baseball, it is trying to establish a deejay program, and afternoon ratings are low. In the spring its baseball ratings were strong enough to make it number one in that time slot.

Station C ranks number six in this book overall. Over the previous four rating periods it has usually been number four.

Station D ranks third in this overall, about where it has been the previous two rating periods. Before that it ranked much lower.

Station E ranks second in this rating period, approximately where it has placed over the past four rating periods.

Let's look at audience subsections and note the great variations. In morning drive time, 6–10 A.M., Station B (which we noted was fifth overall) has the largest audience. Station B has an audience twenty percent larger than A's. Station E, second overall, is third in this time period. Station C is number six, and Station D is number seven.

The station which attracts the most teenagers each week is A, leading any other station three to one.

Among male homeowners, Station B (again, fifth overall in this book) is far ahead of everybody else. No other station comes close. Among males earning $25,000 or more per year, Station B leads any other station by more than two to one.

Among total men, 18 years and older, Station B has the most listeners, slightly ahead of Station D. But if you take employed men, B leads D by more than two to one. According to the rating figures, more than thirty percent of D's audience is unemployed (many are students).

Among males with department store charge accounts, Station B leads any other station by more than two to one. Station D ranks eleventh. However, among those who eat at fast food restaurants several times a month, Station D ranks first. And Station D has more male beer drinkers than any other station.

We see that Station B, which ranks number five in overall ratings, does much better in the subcategories. It does especially well among the male listeners with money to spend. It also ranks number one among women who earn $8,000 or more per year. Its audience is weak among teens and college-age males, but for those in their late twenties and in middle age the station is very popular. For many advertisers it is by far the best buy.

Station A, while not doing so well among males, also has its story to tell. Among 25- to 34-year-old males it ranks very low, but among women it does much better. Among women who buy groceries it is the most listened to station. Among women from households with $25,000 or more a year income it ranks number two. Among teens it is far and away dominant. And among the mothers of those teens there is considerable listening, maybe not all voluntary.

Station E (second overall) is the most listened to station of professional and executive women, and ranks high with total women. Slightly fewer total women listen to E than A, but those who do listen, listen for longer periods of time.

Station C, the country station, ranks number one in no categories.

However, when you take the 25-to-49 or 18-to-49 adults, it ranks very close to the leaders, and for those listeners it is the best advertising buy in cost per thousand reached in the market.

Station D looks better in total numbers than among the spending audience. But if you want to reach 18-to-24-year-old males it is the most effective station in the market.

So which station is number one?

Image Studies

Many radio stations, at license-renewal time, have gone out into the community to find the needs that can be served by the station and by radio in general. Stations also request a research study of their market to find out what the public thinks of them and their competitors to gain information that might be used to competitive advantage. For instance, a music-preference study might be performed to determine the music favored by the different segments of the audience. A survey might include material about news, features, air personalities, or the likes and dislikes of the listeners. This research is expensive because, unlike the ratings, the cost seldom is shared by other stations. In-depth interviews take more time and therefore more money. The same careful control of sample, interviewer, the wording of questions, and the recording of responses must be exercised. Some of this information might be used in community ascertainment.

Suggestions for Further Learning

1. For a class project, perform a survey of radio listening using three methods. Take a telephone coincidental survey. Also, have people check radio listening and station preferences of motorists at random service stations. Third, do an in-person survey of transistor use at a recreation facility. Compare listening habits and methodologies.

2. Develop a way of researching buying decisions at the point of sale. Set up a survey team at a supermarket and question buyers of specific products to determine motivation for buying. Preferably, use local products that advertise only on a limited number of media.

3. Take a listener survey that will give information about listener reactions to various facets of station image. Separate adult listening from all listening. Find out which station is preferred for local news, which newscaster and DJ are preferred, primary reasons for radio listening, opinions about editorials, station music images, attention to sports news, and reasons why some stations are not listened to as much as others.

CHAPTER 12

Governmental and Nongovernmental Controls

Two people who are indispensable to someone planning to put a new radio station on the air are a consulting engineer and a good attorney. The reason for the attorney will be readily apparent from reading this chapter. Most broadcasters use the services of a Washington law firm as well as local attorneys because the laws are complex and dealing with the courts and regulatory agencies requires much specialized knowledge.

Radio stations operate within a complex of laws and social pressures. This complex undergoes such constant change that only by keeping in close touch with actions of the courts and the Federal Communications Commission through the trade papers, attorneys, and the National Association of Broadcasters can the broadcaster really keep current.

The Federal Communications Commission

The Federal Radio Commission, from 1927 to 1934, and the Federal Communications Commission, from 1934 to the present, have had federal regulatory responsibility for radio. The federal government stepped into regulation only after the need for regulation was demonstrated. Regulation began primarily as a reaction to the confusion of radio signals. Before 1927, no frequencies were assigned and the interference was terrible. Some unethical program practices also needed controlling. Because of the way the Communications Act of 1934 was drawn up, the government always has been more efficient at technical controls than program quality control or even the control of unethical practices. The Act itself is not the reason. Technical standards are clear-cut; ethics and aesthetics are much more debatable. The Act was drawn up to reflect the U.S. Constitution's requirements for free expression. Under the American system, when there are questionable practices, the citizen usually gets the benefit of the doubt. The Act, if frustrating on numerous occasions, generally has given the broadcaster great programing freedom.

The FCC generally has been an overworked governmental agency. It has proceeded slowly and cautiously under the eye of a watchful Congress that has included many persons with broadcast holdings and a general desire not to ruffle the feathers of the media which provide them with the ready means to reach their constituents. The FCC has had power to regulate programing only through the vague phrase in the Act which states that broadcasters must serve in the "public interest, convenience, and necessity." Since 1934, the FCC has tried to form an operational definition of that phrase that is clear to both the commission and the broadcasters. The commission has tried with numerous public pronouncements, guidelines, a blue book, and numerous hearings to communicate to the broadcasters what the government expects of them. The FCC has, on occasion, spoken loudly, but mostly has not carried a very big stick. It generally has not substituted its judgment for that of the licensees.

The basic approach used in obtaining licenses is that a licensee promises what he has to promise to get a license. If the channel he wants is much sought after, he may be forced to make promises of providing considerable public service time and effort in order to get the license. If nobody else wants the channel, he can get it for fewer promises of service. What he promises is what he is judged by when his license comes up for renewal.

Starting in the late 1960s, groups of listeners and potential licensees began to challenge the licenses of stations that came up for renewal. Those stations without good records of service to their communities were vulnerable. Since each station must renew its license every three years, this more active approach by the listeners and a tougher FCC renewal policy have combined to make the broadcaster somewhat nervous. Very few licenses have ever been revoked for bad programing, however, so the conscientious broadcaster has had little problem getting renewals. The aspect that worries the broadcasters is that the FCC requires numerous forms and filings to prove that they are worthy broadcasters.

The following list shows the rule violations most often policed by the FCC. As is evident, most concern engineering. Not one involves a program judgment.

1. *Maintenance log* Failure to enter signed statement of required daily inspection, failure to record required quarterly tower-light

inspections, failure to enter required weekly antenna base current and remote meter calibrations, and failure to enter notation of external frequency checks and monitor correlation.

2. *Transmitter operating log* Failure to make entries of required meter readings at half-hour intervals and log-required daily tower-light observations.

3. *Station identification* Failure to identify the station by the assigned call letters and location at the specified intervals.

4. *Engineering records* Failure to make available for inspection program operating and maintenance logs, equipment performance measurements, and field intensities measurements.

5. *All logs and records* Failure to make required entries and failure to do it legibly and factually.

6. *Indicating instruments* Failure to calibrate remote antenna ammeter within 2 percent of the base meter, failure to label meter function, failure to provide calibration curves for remote meters, and failure to calibrate remote meters once a week.

7. *Equipment performance measurements* Failure to make spurious and harmonic measurements and failure to include all required data and curves.

8. *Program log* Failure to authenticate sponsorship, failure to enter required details of public service announcements, failure to sign log and initial corrections, and failure to show political affiliations of political candidates.

9. *Transmitter* Failure to provide proper fencing and lock around antenna base, failure to attenuate spurious and harmonic radiation, and failure to maintain transmission lines in good condition.

10. *Operators* Failure to have properly licensed operator on duty, failure to verify that Third Class Operator Permits are endorsed for broadcast operation, and failure to make required five-day-per-week transmitting equipment inspection.

11. *Modulation monitor* Failure to provide properly operating modulation monitor, failure to notify the Engineer in Charge of District when operating without monitor, and failure to file informal request with the District Office for additional time when the monitor is out of service more than 60 days.

12. *Station and operator licenses* Failure to post station authorizations and modifications thereunder and operator's licenses at the principal control point of the transmitter.

13. *Operating power* Failure to maintain power within the limits specified in the rules and failure to maintain ratio of antenna

base currents in the directional antenna system within 5 percent of the specified value.

14. *Modulation* Frequent failures to control modulation in excess of 100 percent on negative peaks.

15. *Antenna lighting and painting* Failure to maintain antenna-tower painting and lighting in accordance with the terms of the station authorization.

That list is quite detailed, but a study of the list will reveal where a good share of FCC staff time is spent.

The FCC does not have one programing standard by which all radio stations are judged. Each station is given the obligation of ascertaining the needs of its community through (a) a survey of the public, and (b) a survey of community leaders. Station management must tell the FCC what those needs are and how the station determined the needs. The station then must demonstrate that it fills them (see Appendix D). If the stations feel frustrated because they are not sure what the commission wants of them, certainly the commission feels equal frustration that it cannot establish a formula that will be fair and clear. Each case must be decided on its own merits, which is not the simplest way to decide, but is the fairest. Basically, what the broadcaster has to demonstrate is effort and good faith. More specifics are contained in the FCC's 1960 programing policy statement (Appendix C).

Penalties for violating FCC regulations can be revocation of or refusal to renew a license; issuance of a short-term license which allows the commission to review the station for a specified time and then decide to renew or refuse; or fines.

Any ruling of the FCC or other governmental regulatory agencies may be enforced by the district courts under the direction of the U.S. Attorney General. Likewise, any decision may be appealed to the U.S. Court of Appeals.

Section 315

In most cases of violent revolution, among the first institutions attacked are the communications media. The attackers take over to get their messages disseminated quickly and to convince others that they are in power. The writers of the Communications Act realized that another kind of political power existed—the potential power to persuade a free society if an imbalance to media access were to occur. For this reason, the Act, under Section 315, requires that radio and television, unlike the print media, provide equal access to candidates for political office. Stations are not obligated to let candidates for office use their media, but if they let one candidate have access they must provide equal access to all other legally qualified candidates for the same office, except on (1) bona-fide newscasts, (2) bona-fide news interviews, (3) bona-fide news documentaries, and (4) on-the-spot coverage of bona-fide news events. Furthermore, a station must keep records of all requests for time for a period of two years. A station need not give equal time to Communist candidates. Persons speaking on behalf of a candidate are exempted from the equal-time rule. The licensee may not censor remarks of candidates.

The Fairness Doctrine

The "Fairness Doctrine" has been in existence since 1949, but it has been evolving ever since. Like the phrase "public interest, convenience, and necessity," it is subject to interpretation and provides one of the gray areas about which broadcasters feel uneasy. The National Association of Broadcasters repeatedly has tried to get the doctrine repealed, overturned in court, and otherwise disposed of, because broadcasters feel that they should have as much freedom as do the newspapers. Because the doctrine is broad rather than specific, it sometimes has been troublesome to administer. A good share of broadcasters favor its repeal. The authors of this book believe, however, that, although it is sometimes difficult to live with, the doctrine is in good part responsible for the fair and honest image that broadcast news has had.

Section 315 spells out regulations with regard to political candidates. The "Fairness Doctrine" requires the same kind of fairness on a much broader plane, requiring contrasting viewpoints on all controversial issues of public importance. A licensee is given a charge to provide varied viewpoints and is given wide discretion to make decisions. In an attempt to clarify for broadcasters the FCC's stand on the fairness issue, the Commission issued the following statement:

> The fairness doctrine deals with the broader question of affording reasonable opportunity for the presentation of contrasting viewpoints on controversial issues of public importance. Generally speaking, it does not apply with the precision of the "equal opportunities" requirement. Rather, the licensee, in applying the fairness doctrine, is called upon to make reasonable judgments in good faith on the facts of each situation—as to whether a controversial issue of public importance is involved, as to what viewpoints have been or should be presented, as to the format and spokesmen to present the viewpoints, and all the other facets of such programing. In passing on any com-

plaint in this area, the Commission's role is not to substitute its judgment for that of the licensee as to any of the above programing decisions, but rather to determine whether the licensee can be said to have acted reasonably and in good faith. There is thus room for considerably more discretion on the part of the licensee under the fairness doctrine than under the "equal opportunities" requirement.

The Commission has stated that if the "Fairness Doctrine" has any validity its fulfillment cannot be predicated upon the ability to pay. Therefore, granting free time may be required in some circumstances to answer something said in time for which payment was received. This was the case in the late 1960s when broadcasters were required to carry antismoking messages if they carried cigarette commercials. Also, this requirement did not stipulate that one free antismoking spot be run for every cigarette commercial. In this case, it was judged that a 3 to 1 ratio was sufficient.

The policy of not refusing opposing viewpoints is not adequate, for the Commission requires that a broadcaster actively seek out opposing points of view. This applies to editorials as well as to other controversial matters.

Paid political announcements that do not feature the candidate himself are covered by the "Fairness Doctrine" rather than Section 315.

Included in the doctrine is a personal-attack rule that requires a broadcaster to take special action whenever the integrity, character, or honesty of an individual or group is questioned by the broadcaster. The Commission requires that the broadcaster forward a copy of the script to the person attacked, either prior to or at the time of the broadcast, and afford the attacked person or group reasonable opportunity to reply. If no tape or transcript of the remarks is available, the broadcaster must send as accurate a summary as possible. The broadcaster cannot bar a reply from the attacked party on the basis of financial consideration. If the attacked party cannot or will not pay for air time, the broadcaster must give time. Personal-attack rules do not apply when a political *candidate* makes an attack. Broadcasters feel somewhat uncomfortable about the rule, since they are afraid that by calling questionable comments to the attention of an attacked party they may be viewed by a court of law as having given some kind of admission that the attacked party has a substantial legal case against them. This book's authors are unaware of any cases, however, in which a court has used such admissions as evidence leading to a legal settlement to the detriment of a broadcaster.

The Federal Trade Commission

Another federal regulatory agency that scrutinizes some of broadcast programing is the FTC. This commission's basic function is to prevent unfair methods of competition and false or misleading advertising. The staff of the FTC regularly scan samples of commercials. A station occasionally, on short notice, gets a request from the FTC for typed scripts representing the text of all advertising originating in the station's studios and disseminated through the station's facilities on given dates. The FTC also has monitoring stations that constantly seek to be aware of advertising, in order to prevent illegal practices.

Copyright

A copyright protects the author of an original work of art or literary composition from having his work used or copied without his permission. A copyright enables him to earn rewards for his labor.

Copyright applies to radio stations especially in using scripts, books, articles, and musical compositions. Copyright law does allow quotation of copyrighted materials for review purposes, although not for other program matters unless permission is received. Permission may require payment of a fee. Copyright infringement is not common in radio today. Most written materials used are from commercials produced by advertising agencies, are written by a station's continuity staff for advertisers, or come from wire services for which stations pay a fee.

Music is also copyrighted. Payments are made to the authors, composers, and publishers through licensing fees paid to one of three licensing firms—ASCAP, BMI, or SESAC. ASCAP, the American Society of Composers, Authors, and Publishers, was the first licensing firm and held a virtual monopoly on music until the broadcasters themselves helped form BMI, Broadcast Music Incorporated, in 1940. Most music played on American radio is licensed by these two firms. SESAC, the Society of European Stage Authors and Composers, originated in Europe but now licenses in the United States. These licensing firms collect money in the form of licensing fees from radio stations as well as dance halls, clubs, theaters, and wherever music is performed. Most of the standard songs are ASCAP, as is a good share of Broadway and Hollywood music. Most country music and most rock music are BMI. Stations generally have "blanket" licenses which enable them to play all licensed music, although a few stations pay per selection used. In the case of a station which is all news and uses very little music for production, the per-use charge may be cheaper, but the station must keep track of each piece of music aired, whether for production effect in a promotional spot or in a commercial provided by an advertising agency. Logging of each piece of music can be bothersome. The licensing fee is a percentage of station revenue, which means that small poor stations do not pay as much as large rich ones.

Libel and Slander

Defamation by print is considered libel; defamation by word of mouth is slander. Because of the wide distribution given to spoken material on radio, the laws of libel, which are more severe, generally are applicable rather than the laws relating to slander, even though the material is spoken. The defamation can be statements of fact, opinion, or merely imputation. Even if statements are not meant to harm, they can be libelous if they do cause harm. Persons, corporations, or groups can be libeled. Material can be libelous if it causes public aversion to any person, deters others from dealing with him, or lowers him in the estimation of others. Radio stations have a stronger voice than the average individual, and thus they have an opportunity to work for the betterment of the community. By careless or inappropriate action, a radio station also can harm innocent persons. Therefore, a station's responsibility for presenting the truth and not harming innocent persons is greater than that of individuals, whose voices are not so strong.

Since radio stations are important links between occurrences and the public, they do have privileges that most people do not have. They get easier access to newsmakers and to the scenes of events. They are the people's representatives at many of the occasions where news is made. In its legal definition, the word "privilege" means that the laws of libel are altered to fit certain circumstances. Participants in judicial and legislative proceedings and public officials engaged in official business have complete protection from accountability for their statements. This protection is called "absolute privilege." Broadcasters and other newsmen do not have this freedom from accountability, but do have what is called "qualified privilege," which protects fair reports of legislative, executive, and judicial proceedings. The idea of qualified privilege arises from the view that it is more important for the public to be informed about matters of official governmental proceedings than it is for the individual to have legal redress. Good faith and absence of malice are the requirements placed upon the broadcaster to avoid libel in reporting such events. This kind of privilege abused is no privilege at all. Details of grand jury actions, off-the-record statements about official actions, and statements by governmental officials that do not pertain to official actions reported by radio are not covered by any kind of privilege and must be made carefully.

Stations should be most cautious at times in presenting opinions or statements. Repeating statements of others does not give immunity to actionable proceedings, unless these statements are given under conditions of absolute privilege and are reported accurately and in good faith. Repeating wild rumors which cause damage to innocent persons may make the station a better target for action than the originator of the rumors, because the station's louder voice enables it to do more damage than the lone originator. Also, since the station is likely to have more resources, it is more likely to be able to pay the kind of damages that would satisfy an injured party. What scares so many radio station managers is not so much losing a lawsuit as having to pay out the expenses to fight the lawsuit, which can mean the difference between profit and loss in an operation with a thin profit margin. Some proceedings can be broadcast with impunity, because, though they may not be "safe" in the strict sense of the law, convention has made it unlikely that any legal problems will occur as the result of reporting them.

These are complicated legal matters that cannot be covered fully in this short amount of space.

Canon 35

The First Amendment to the Constitution provides for free speech and a free press. The Sixth Amendment provides for a fair trial, and the Fourteenth provides for due process of law. In some cases, free speech can infringe upon the right to a fair trial. Conversely, the electronic media feel that fair-trial rules infringe upon their rights under the First Amendment. The kidnap trial of Bruno Hauptmann in the case of the Lindbergh baby and the Billie Sol Estes trial were covered in such a way by the reporters with cameras and electronic equipment that questions were raised regarding the ability of the defendants to get a fair trial if reporters with cameras and microphones were allowed in the court. Reporters undoubtedly can act with restraint and can cover such events with microphones and with movie, television, or still cameras in a way that will not interfere. But, in the past, a few reporters have not acted with restraint. Therefore, the American Bar Association passed a canon of conduct—Canon 35. Enacted in 1937, Canon 35 is not a law. It has no binding effect on the courts but presents the view of the ABA that no broadcasting or photographing of court proceedings should be allowed. Since judges and

trial lawyers are members of the bar, the canon is effective in preventing broadcasting and photography in the court. In 1966, the U.S.
Supreme Court, in a five-to-four decision with six separate opinions
issued, ruled that when the First and Fourteenth Amendments conflict
due process takes procedence over a free press. The basis of the decision is that nothing is more important under the law than justice to
the individual. In its ruling, the Court also decided that a conflict
results whenever pretrial disclosures create notorious publicity and
whenever proceedings in the courtroom are disrupted by broadcast
and photographic equipment and personnel. The flamboyant practices
of reporters resulted in the canon's passage. Broadcasters have continually argued that they are capable of acting responsibly and that
they should have free access to court proceedings along with their
microphones and cameras just as reporters have with their pencils.
There has been a slow, gradual trend toward allowing them greater
access. Some states, such as Texas, allow the judge the discretion of
allowing them in the courtroom. This privilege is due to a state canon
of ethics and, again, is not a law.

Other forces are pressuring for stricter limitations on trial information. In England, permissible news of criminal proceedings is limited
strictly. In France, little news is permitted out of penal proceedings.
Those limitations are not likely here unless the news media themselves,
through extreme sensationalism, were to provoke them. On the other
hand, free access with microphones and cameras is not likely to occur
unless the newsmen, over time, can show they are deserving of the
right and will not disrupt proceedings in the way that some did to
cause the restrictions in the first place.

Canon 35 does not apply to closed meetings in the legislative committee rooms. The U.S. Senate has not allowed broadcast of its sessions, although some senators have thought that allowing broadcasts
might help to provide a countervailing force to the power of the
President, who frequently talks to the public through speeches and
news conferences. At times, access would not be beneficial to the functions of the government, but most of the time better access would be
beneficial to the public and would not interfere with proceedings at
all. The open Watergate hearings are a good case in point.

Other Governmental Controls

The Federal Communications Commission does most of the regulation of radio, but a whole network of additional controls exists.

International treaties affect stations. As an example of the effect of
these treaties, past agreements with Mexico have forced some stations

to change channels, because the governments had negotiated to allow the maximum flexibility and coverage without interference between the two countries. In doing so, the two countries gave up some channels and got others in return. These negotiations generally are oriented to resolving problems of a technical nature.

The President of the United States has considerable authority under the Communications Act to assign authorizations for broadcasting stations that are operated by the federal government. Section 305 of the Act states that these stations are not subject to licensing or to the regulations that apply to stations subject to the FCC. They must not interfere with or restrict the rights of other stations, however. Section 606 gives the President the power to suspend the operation of any broadcast facility in the event of war, a threat of war, or a national disaster or emergency. He also may seize or remove any facility "in the national interest."

The President is assisted and advised by the Office of Telecommunications Policy, an office that took on a new image and emphasis with the Nixon administration. The duties of the office are not clearly defined. Its director acts as an advisor to the President and helps coordinate all telecommunication functions of the various agencies of the government, including the FCC, Civil Defense, and others.

The President also has indirect influence on the direction of broadcasting through his appointments to federal regulatory agencies, most importantly the FCC. He has the power to designate the chairman of each of the agencies, but his appointments are subject to Congressional approval.

Congress carefully watches broadcasting. The Senate Interstate and Foreign Commerce Committee must pass on every presidential appointee. The Appropriations Committees of both houses have influence over budgets of the agencies. And special committees have been set up from time to time to investigate the functions and activities of the various agencies as well as specific broadcasting actions and practices. Considerable "jawboning" is done by Congressmen and other officials hopeful of influencing the behavior of broadcasters in their home states.

Little governmental control of radio is found on the state and local level, primarily because of the supervision done by federal agencies. Certain corporation laws affect broadcasters on a business level. Also, taxation can be assessed by state and municipal governments. The "commerce clause" of the U.S. Constitution forbids states and municipalities from assessing any tax that directly or indirectly places an undue burden on or discriminates against interstate commerce. Broadcasting stations are engaged in interstate commerce. However, many courts have upheld taxes levied against broadcasters, the portion taxed being derived from local commerce and not the interstate variety. Rules are not uniform regarding such taxes.

Local ordinances may have an effect upon the operation of stations through regulations concerning radiation devices, tower heights and placement, and other matters.

Two other federal regulatory agencies that affect broadcasting are the Food and Drug Administration and the Federal Aviation Agency. The FAA is concerned with tower locations and lighting. The Food and Drug Administration's main concern is with the prevention of misbranding and mislabeling of commodities. The FDA has a close working relationship with the Federal Trade Commission.

Stations also cooperate with the government through the Emergency Broadcast System, a system established to operate in time of war or other emergencies. AM radio stations are the primary stations involved. Emergency information is relayed through the Associated Press and United Press International as well as electronic warning systems. National Defense Emergency Authorization stations are authorized to broadcast during emergency periods. Other stations are under instructions to inform their listeners where to tune for information and then to leave the air. The U.S. Weather Bureau uses the system in case of a tornado, hurricane, or other disaster.

Regulation of Competition

The FCC broadcast policy generally has been to promote free competition through the absence of regulation. Economic injury has not been sufficient grounds to enable a radio station to prevent a competitor from coming into the same market, but other rules do attempt to give a diversity to the voices that are heard across the country. The FCC limitation of seven TV stations (of which no more than five can be VHF), seven AM stations, and seven FM stations under one ownership has prevented giant networks or corporations from gaining communications monopolies. Starting in the late 1960s, the FCC also moved to break up concentration of ownership of the mass media in a given city. It is not unheard of for a newspaper in a market (maybe the only newspaper or one with simply a combined sales and printing agreement with a radio or TV station in the same market) to be joined in ownership with a TV station, an AM radio station, an FM station, and cable TV as well. That kind of combination has the potential for limiting the points of view that can gain access to the media. FCC regulations forced several separations. The separations' effect on radio has been either to give radio the identity it never had as a step-sister in a TV-oriented plant (the positive effect) or to force a cutback in some community services that radio could no longer afford because of the loss of the corporate news department, which included such services as the Washington bureau (the negative effect).

Because of these FCC rules, little antitrust activity of other kinds has been initiated by the government. Corporations that are parent companies of radio stations and are involved with business dealings that are unethical are not looked upon favorably by the FCC at license-renewal time.

Changing Laws

The present regulatory climate is one of change. 1976 saw a new copyright law passed. While this new law appears to change the 1909 law's basic intent very little, it acknowledges the impact of new technology. Many court cases will be decided before the full impact can be assessed. In addition, the Congress, under the leadership of Lionel Van Deerlin, is attempting to revise the Communications Act of 1934. Strong pressures to ease regulations on radio and to amend or eliminate the Fairness Doctrine exist, even if no new communications act is passed. Further, FCC policy, without change in the law, has always been evolutionary. Major changes have followed important court cases, changes in administration, and industry lobbying. The changing social climate has caused its own strain on the regulators and broadcasters alike.

The National Association of Broadcasters

The NAB is a trade association and lobby group. With headquarters in Washington, the NAB is close to the action at the FCC and is adept at relaying useful information about dealing with the FCC to its member stations. The NAB is an active partisan, protecting broadcasters' rights with the FCC and Congress and affecting decisions mostly in a protectionist way. It also deals with industry problems through conferences and conventions, through the funding of research that helps broadcasters make decisions and tell their sales story, and through liaison with educators by working through the Broadcast Education Association. One of the most noticed jobs of the NAB is the establishment and administration of the code of broadcast standards. Since television began, radio broadcasters have often felt that too much of NAB time has been spent with TV, but they also realize that one unified trade association gives them more power and influence than two separate ones would. The NAB has a difficult job dealing with the volatile business of broadcasting.

Less than half of all radio stations in the country subscribe to the NAB Radio Code. Stations are not forced to join the NAB, and even if they do, they do not have to subscribe to the code. Many small stations do not participate in NAB, because they feel that a trade association is not important to them. They feel very localized and spend their efforts trying to survive in their marketplace. Some do not subscribe to the code because they do not want to follow code standards. They want to program as many commercials as they can sell and not worry about taste standards that the code might impose upon them. Some do not subscribe as a form of protest, because their standards are higher than the NAB's. Even though it receives only partial participation, the NAB Code is an important document. It comes closer to setting a standard for American radio than any other document. Some criticize it as being a collection of platitudes; others say it is an idealized document, vague in its expressions and so open to interpretation that it is meaningless. Yet, as a general code written for diverse radio broadcasters and interests, it is a document that points a positive and admirable direction for men of good faith and goodwill. Even cynics admit that the code at least sounds good and helps keep the government out of station affairs. (The text of the code is found in Appendix A of this book.)

The NAB is a useful organization. Many of its publications are helpful guides for station managers, especially for the small station owners who have small staffs and little access to private research reports, Washington attorneys, and the counsel of national sales reps. The NAB's lobbying in Washington is done carefully. Its public relations efforts for radio as a medium are energetic. But as a leader of broadcast ethics and standards, the NAB has been only partially successful. The NAB itself is sometimes too strident against suggestions that might improve service if financial risk appears to be involved. The NAB sometimes seems to spend more time worrying about broadcasters' short-term profits than the long-range strength of the medium. (Perhaps fewer stations would belong if NAB were any different.) There are so many maverick radio stations and owners that any attempt to put up a united front on issues is not easy.

Other Trade Associations

A separate association, for a long time called the National Association of FM Broadcasters, later the National Radio Broadcasters Association, has appealed to a number of broadcasters who feel the NAB spends too much time and effort on TV. In the mid-'70s it has been a strong advocate for radio and has forced the NAB to be more responsive.

The Radio Advertising Bureau tells radio's story to advertisers and encourages research which helps that end as well as providing workshops and sales aids to individual stations.

Citizens' Groups

If a broadcaster has good feedback on his audience's desires, the most effective controls of all are the listeners themselves. Listeners seldom organize into groups to demand action about radio station practices. They usually just turn the dial, which is effective if ratings are accurate and if the listener has reasonable alternatives on the dial. In a few cases, however, and it is occurring with increasing frequency, the listeners have organized to cause changes. Listeners have challenged licenses, and they have gotten changes from managements desirous of serving the public. It can happen when people feel strongly enough about an issue.

Advertiser Influence

No radio station operator is completely immune from advertiser influence, and should not be. Advertiser influence is healthy if a station uses an advertiser's wishes as one indicator of public wants and services. No radio station manager or programer should allow tampering with the station's image through dictating about programing, however. Advertisers do not really expect to dictate, but they do want to be heard. They always respect a manager with integrity, one who has a standard and sticks to it (especially if his station is successful).

Legal Counsel

It should be apparent from reading this chapter that the legal matters have been skimmed rapidly. Attorneys attend school for seven years; even the enlightened layman is incapable of coping with all the potential problems that can be encountered in a few years of radio broadcasting. Many stations, generally the smaller operations, have no regular counsel. The large stations and groups nearly always make recurrent use of a Washington attorney as well as local people. Because a station must renew its license every three years, it has constant need for counsel and representation. Frequent challenges arise under the "Fairness Doctrine" and the equal-time ruling. Copyright law, defamation of character, on-air controversies, and simpler matters (such as "how long do we save these records?") need specialized advice. Short-term costs in the form of legal fees that seem high may be inexpensive in the long run.

Suggestions for Further Learning

1. Using FCC form 301, prepare an application for a radio station license.
   a. Examine FCC programing policies as they might affect your proposed station. Especially familiarize yourself with the blue book and the 1960 programing policy statement.
   b. If you were asked to testify before the FCC regarding Canon 35, what would be your position?
   c. Differentiate between Section 315 and the "Fairness Doctrine" in regard to your station's policies.

2. Compare print and broadcast pressures from the government in light of the issues raised and the restrictions placed on each by the Ellsberg papers/*New York Times* case and "The Selling of the Pentagon" program done by CBS news. What are the long-term ramifications for radio?

3. Examine the NAB code (Appendix A) in the context of America's current social revolution. Should changes be made in the code? Discuss the problems of making changes that will be acceptable to diverse radio broadcasters.

CHAPTER 13

Criticism

The authors of this book believe in radio and feel that radio's positive characteristics outweigh its negative ones. Radio always has something that can make the day of almost everyone a little better. Radio's future is as bright as its past. But all of the endeavors of men are flawed. We would not be realistic if we did not notice that radio, like other appendages of modern society, has problems.

Too many broadcasters are looking for a cheap buck, getting by with the minimum of programing service that they can provide and still sell, and hiring staffs primarily on the basis of who works the cheapest and not who can do the best job. These people seemingly have no sense of pride, no concern for the public, and no sense of responsibility.

Many people with talent, sensitivity, and concern have left radio for other fields that have more stability, greater financial rewards, or maybe just a greater concern for them as individuals. Radio cannot afford to lose any of the really talented people it attracts. Too few managements are sensitive to employee needs to the degree that their employees can make broadcasting their careers. For too many it is a stopping-off place, a part of their education. Many an idealistic or star-struck young person, crusading or on an "ego trip," has become disillusioned with radio and has moved into another line of work. Too many of the brightest and the most competent young people also leave because they see too little future. Not many people use radio's retirement plans. Partly that is because more people are attracted to the field than it can support. Partly it is because much of radio is like other forms of show business. Dancers and football players realize that they can't go on forever; for many radio people the situation is similar. Partly it is because too many managements are short-sighted.

It is ironic, but radio might be a healthier medium if there were not so much radio. Television has been a healthy medium financially because it has had so little competition from itself, forcing more stations to share the available audience. Only in recent years have the specters of cassettes, video-discs, cable TV, and increased competition from independent stations fragmented the audience, and television has a long way to go before it is fragmented to the degree radio or magazines are. Radio's audience has become so dispersed that many stations can exist only on the cheapest kind of programing. In some areas all radio is hurt because the available advertising revenue is not great enough to support the number of licensed stations. Certainly, a number of diverse voices makes radio strong, but too much competition can weaken the medium. Generally, the FCC position has been that economic injury to an existing station is not sufficient reason for denying a license to a new station in a market where there will be no technical interference. An optimum number of stations surely exists for every market, although no person or agency has the power to decide what that optimum number is. We would certainly feel uncomfortable if any agency had the power to decide that question. The bright side for broadcasters is that not many channels are still available to put on the air—at least under the present technology.

We have noted that the American consumer is a tremendous consumer of sound, but to what purpose?

Radio provides entertainment. We all like to be entertained. This entertainment frequently makes commuting and housework and other chores more palatable than would otherwise be the case.

Radio provides information. Some of this information is also entertainment. Some of it helps us in making decisions, from choosing a president to whether to carry an umbrella. Some of this information is more subtle than what is received from a direct announcement of the weather or news. Music also communicates with us, often saying things in nonverbal fashion. Despite the old adage, music is not a universal language, but rather is shaped in terms of the culture of which it is a part. It may not convey much meaning to someone who does not understand the particular musical idiom. The rhythm, the shadings of sound, and the poetry all contribute to passing along this information.

Radio provides emotional expression. Commercials are not just intended to play on our intellect, but on our emotions as well. Many pieces of music are in effect commercials for a particular philosophy or feeling. Emotion may be presented in dramatic form through music, through the sharing of ideas spoken by professional or amateur communicators. Music especially provides opportunities for a variety of emotional expression, whether religious exaltation, romantic passion, or military courage and vigor. We sing to put babies to sleep, to make our enemies look ridiculous, and to get rid of anger or frustration within us.

Radio forces conformity to social norms. *Forces* may be a strong word for some, but radio certainly helps in the socialization process of all who share group feelings, who want to fit in and be part of the crowd. All of us share these needs at some time or another. The various elements on our chosen radio stations assist us in conforming. Even our choice of stations tells something about which people we want to be associated with. Radio can contribute to the integration of society, but also to the maintenance of separate identities for sub-groups of society.

Radio provides aesthetic enjoyment. Whether or not there is a real difference between this and entertainment may be a semantic con-sideration as much as anything else, but some of radio's elements can provide a kind of higher-order experience, one which helps to uplift us, to aid our understanding of ourselves and others, to express the spirit of an age or a people, and to give form and meaning to our lives.

Radio affects the continuity and stability of a culture. Through the music especially, it is possible to glimpse the heart of a culture without the protective mechanisms which surround some social structures. Note the way immigrants to this country use music both to become absorbed into the culture and to preserve old customs and values. Music also functions to validate social institutions and religious rituals, as can be seen in many places but most obviously in revival meetings and political rallies.

Former FCC commissioner Lee Loevinger has said that broadcasting is an electronic mirror that reflects an ambiguous image of society in which each member of the audience sees by projection his own vision of himself and society. Loevinger also has said that much of the dis-satisfaction that is voiced with broadcasting is really an expression of basic dissatisfaction with society. We agree with these statements. But we are not willing to say that we accept things as they are, for we want to see radio improve just as we want to see society improve. While we understand a need to serve existing tastes as they are, we also have the desire to upgrade these tastes and to see man evolve upward.

Certainly radio reflects society. It is imperfect, fragmented, diverse, sometimes light, sometimes pompous, sometimes significant, and sometimes not very ethical. Sometimes radio leads the public; some-times it distorts public taste.

There is in our society a snobbish view that if something is popular it cannot be good. This view holds great belief in the law of raspberry jam—that the wider you spread it the thinner it gets. There is also an opposing view, that if something is popular it must be good. Anybody can cite evidence which supports and contradicts both views. In life, mediocrity is the rule rather than the exception—by definition. Medi-ocrity is that which lies in the large middle area of the bell-shaped curve that results from quantifying human behavior. If, in ten years, our society has achieved a tremendous cultural renaissance which raises competence and awareness tremendously, what we will have achieved is a heightened level of mediocrity, to be sneered at by the artist and the expert, each of whom has still achieved a greater level of skill than the average person. But each of us can be an artist or an expert in our own area of specialty while we remain mediocre in other areas of specialty.

Perhaps the specialization of kinds of radio has allowed more opportunity for the listener to pursue specialized interests, while at the same time becoming less aware and maybe less understanding of society as a whole. Perhaps we know more about ourselves, and less about those not like ourselves, because of it. There is a danger in assuming that the audience that is not like us is more passive, more manipulated, or more vulgar than may be the case. It is easy to forget that what strikes one person as trash may open up new vistas for the unsophisticated. Further, the judgment of what is trash is dependent upon our self-image, our personal insecurities, our vested interests, and our group identities. For certain, radio has allowed us to choose to improve ourselves or to choose chewing gum for our ears, at least if we live in or near a large city. If we can make these choices, how can we be critical of the system? If we really have our free agency functional by having adequate choices, the system works well, even if most of what is on the air does not please us. In reality, this free agency is not absolute, because what is listened to on radio depends upon gatekeepers, upon promoters and their tastes. Before a band can play or a record be made, a middleman has to give consent or risk his capital. We are all somewhat at the mercy of vogue, spontaneous or contrived. We deplore that this taste is not our taste, for we ourselves want to be the gatekeepers.

We can only choose from what is available. This means that we have an obligation to let the gatekeepers know what we want, and they have an obligation, since they are trying to reach us and they are using the public's air, to serve us. Radio managers must keep in constant touch with reality, which may be something other than conventional wisdom or the fads of the time. At the same time, managers must not be afraid to exercise rational judgment or to rely on their own standards of ethics or good taste. Radio is, but is not *only*, an audience delivery system.

It is easy to criticize radio programing services. It is very easy to view them with alarm, to join with thousands of people in pointing out the apparent superficialities of the broadcast media, and to call for more and more government controls as well as other strictures on broadcast programing. Nevertheless, nearly all of the population of the United States is exposed to radio broadcasting. Obviously, radio must be doing something right, fulfilling at least some of the needs of the

American public. What is wrong with radio is a reflection of what is wrong with society. In a sense, radio's style is that of the cocktail party conversation—a background to life as it is lived. To be strongly critical of the medium is to be strongly critical of ourselves, for radio is among the most responsive of all the mass media.

Modern radio wears both its faults and its virtues openly for all to see. Radio is an important medium, an ambiguous mirror playing back to us sounds that we hear and evaluate according to our own visions of ourselves and society.

Station
Profiles

This collection of station profiles attempts to show American radio programing in action through brief descriptions of some of the more successful stations in the nation. Various types of stations are represented, although the primary use of larger markets and larger stations makes this anything but a random sampling of American radio. These stations are more successful than the average. They tend to be larger, more professional, and better run than the average. They are mentioned because they set trends and are leaders with influence that reaches beyond their own signal limitations. These are the stations that are copied by other stations all over the country.

This is not an exhaustive list; other stations could have been used. But these stations comprise one of the best lists that could be made. We do not mean to give the impression that these stations are without flaws, are superhuman, or are invincible. On the other hand, anyone who spends some time with each, as we did, would have to be impressed with their quality and with the capable, articulate, and thoughtful people who serve in responsible positions with these stations. These are people who would probably be successful in any field they entered, but who think their radio stations are important enough to warrant their full commitment.

The order of presentation is not significant. It is essentially random.

Profile 1

Call Letters and Location: KABC–Los Angeles, California
Owner and Affiliation: ABC–American Information Network
Classification and Power: Class IIIA–5kw

In the middle and late '60s, the all-talk station came on the scene, with the telephone usually providing the content. Many of the stations that went all-conversation have since changed format to all-news or country or conservative music. Only a few have survived to remain near the top of the ratings and prestige in their markets. One of the first to go all-talk and one of the most consistently successful is KABC, owned by ABC, which has been particularly successful with its owned and operated radio stations.

People in Los Angeles believe that their market is the toughest, most innovative, and most competitive radio market in the nation. Television and film production are headquartered in Los Angeles, and much of the action in phonograph records is also there. The radio market is highly fractionalized. The average listener can get more than seventy stations. It is common for a dozen stations to have Monday through Sunday listening audiences within a rating point of each other. In a given rating period, half of the stations on the air may not show up in the rating books. Unlike many other cities, Los Angeles has no single dominant radio station. Detroit has long had WJR, St. Louis KMOX, Minneapolis WCCO, Chicago WGN, Atlanta WSB, and Pittsburgh KDKA, all stations with dominant audience shares. In Los Angeles the same station seldom leads the ratings two books in a row. For several years KABC has consistently been at or near the top of the rating books in total audience. At one time the staff of ninety was considerably larger. In the late '60s and early '70s, the station had a four-hour news block in the morning and a four-hour news block in the afternoon, with talk in the less demanding time slots. The news blocks required a large staff. After KNX (CBS) went all-news, with KFWB (Westinghouse) already all-news, management felt that a straight, competitive, hard news effort appeared increasingly difficult and costly. KABC earlier had been successful in going head-to-head talk against KLAC, which changed to country. Another all-talk competitor had been KGBS, but an inferior signal and coming in against an established station made it difficult for them to compete, so they changed format, leaving the talk segment of the market clearer at the time the news competition was becoming more difficult. KABC also lightened up its talk, getting away from hard news and politics and going more in the direction of everyday affairs and concerns. The talk is topical and provocative, with considerable humor. They like to keep calls short and keep the show moving, feeling that more calls make for more chances for people to express different ideas, better programing, and higher ratings. In fact, a red flasher hooked to a timer goes off automatically in the studio every time a call exceeds two minutes.

The station is very much personality-oriented. People who can keep a talk show going and get good ratings at this level are scarce and expensive. The personalities and the format have evolved and are the result of the peculiar characteristics of the station and the market. The station proceeds by feel more than by formula, mixing good planning with circumstance. The sound is constantly evolving.

In addition to the morning news, and conversation most of the time, KABC has extensive sports coverage. They carry Dodgers baseball, USC football and basketball, and the Los Angeles Lakers. A sports talk package surrounds the play-by-play broadcasts.

Let's consider 5 A.M. the start of the broadcast day and follow the programing through twenty-four hours. 5 A.M. to 9 A.M. is Newstalk with three anchormen. This is essentially a rip-and-read news operation, but with several resources, and with bantering, personality-style news. Ken Minyard is co-anchor of the entire four hours. He formerly was a talk show host on the station prior to the changing of the newscasts from their more traditional form to Newstalk. The 5 to 7 portion is co-anchored by Bob Arthur, a former CBS newsman, and the 7 to 9 portion is co-anchored by TV newsman Chuck Ashman. Two writer-editors assist the anchors, who are really the final editors of what airs. The anchors ad lib around many of the stories and collect a number of feature stories on their own. A reporter in the field can also go on live from a phone or mobile unit. Integrated with the KABC-produced material is news from the ABC Information Network, along with news comments and features such as "Drivers Digest" and syndicated pieces such as Ronald Reagan's viewpoint. The station editorializes.

From 9 to 1, Michael Jackson hosts talk. Jackson retains his British accent, which perhaps sounded more at home on the BBC, where he once worked, than on the San Francisco Top-40 station where he also once worked. Jackson is on the air four hours a day and prepares constantly when he is off the air. He has the most intellectual approach of the station's hosts and feels very much at home with world affairs, news, and topical issues. Usually labeled a liberal, he also has a reputation for being fair-minded. He is precise, uses considerable humor, and believes that one in his position may disagree with others but should not insult the listeners during their calls or talk about them after the calls in such a way as to invite ridicule. If he has a guest who is the author of a book, the odds are that Jackson has read the book.

Bill Ballance hosts from 1 to 3. Ballance got a lot of publicity as the originator of "Topless Radio" in the early '70s when he hosted a program called "feminine forum" on KGBS. Though less explicit than some of its imitators, the feminine forum was dropped after FCC pressure and public response made many station owners cautious. At KABC, Ballance retains his mischievous manner and plays the role of dirty old man, gag writer, and provocateur, which he tempers with the expertise of guest experts, frequently from the field of psychology and sociology. In fact, he has regulars with psychology Ph.D.'s and clinical experience who share the program on Monday, Wednesday, and Friday. Some of his typical topics include: What's the most unusual thing that's ever happened to you in a trailer, camper, motorhome, or van? What do you do when you absolutely cannot sleep? How do erotic movies and books affect you? What do you dislike most about a physical exam? Did you get married for all the wrong reasons? What was the niftiest bargain or treasure you picked up at a garage sale or swap meet? What is your favorite maxim, epigram, slogan, or saying? What fears do you have of getting old? What was your wildest Halloween experience? What fears or threats of rape have you had?

From 3 to 7 P.M., KABC runs Sportstalk, for a long time (though no longer) hosted by Superfan. Superfan is Ed Bieler, who owned a bar and one day came in off the street and told Jim Simon, then program director, he wanted to get into radio. KABC tried him out with short air stints which he built into four hours a day. He sounded like a guy who runs a bar, or maybe a truck driver, but he was able to provide interesting calls. When sports events are broadcast, Sportstalk is sandwiched around the play-by-play.

From 7 to 11 P.M. Carol Hemingway hosts a topical show which sometimes wanders off into the occult, astrology, etc.

From 11 P.M. to 5 A.M., Ray Briem plays the role of the station conservative, discusses a wide range of topics, and makes his own calls out to a cast of characters all over the country. He'll call a sheriff in a small Southern town, a person who runs an all-night service station in New England, or a truck stop in the Northwest, and visit with people about what is happening in their areas. Los Angeles listeners suggest places or people to call. Many of them turn out to be unusual and interesting and give a look at some of the regionalism and local color that exists.

Apart from the morning news block, the rest of the day's programming includes ABC Information Network news on the hour, preceded by a 90-second report of Los Angeles headlines.

The maximum eighteen minutes of commercials is frequently sold out.

The overall feeling of the programing is crisp, bright, and upbeat. While the range of conversation is wide and many guests and experts are heard, the overall feeling is not intellectual, but common, everyday, and trendy—more tuned to popular culture than the fine arts. Yet there is frequently a kind of eloquence in the unpretentious, direct, unstudied manner of the nonprofessional communicator who makes up the bulk of KABC talk radio programing.

Since the programs run six days a week, Saturday is similar to the rest of the week, but Sunday varies slightly with some specialized talk show hosts. including a consumer affairs specialist, a segment devoted mostly to phonograph records and artists, a segment featuring a restaurant critic, and talk about religion.

Profile 2

Call Letters and Location: WRFM–New York, New York

Owner and Affiliation: Radio New York Worldwide (Bonneville)–
Independent

Classification and Power: Class B–5.2 kw horizontal, 3.7 kw vertical

WRFM is one of the nation's most successful FM radio stations. It has not always been so. The station began in 1953 and, for a long time, was a modest, low-budget operation playing classical and semiclassical music. Under new ownership in the 1960s, the station experimented and faltered until the format settled down in 1969. The station had tried various versions of conservative and adult pop formats, first with automation, then with personalities. The format that became successful is a very simple one, disciplined and consistent. The programing consists of familiar melodic music in 15-minute segments, a maximum of seven commercials per hour, very little talk but with names of the music selections given along with headline news, traffic reports, editorials, and community affairs capsules. About forty-six or forty-seven minutes of each hour is music.

WRFM's music is programed by former manager Marlin Taylor, who started a whole company based on WRFM's original music format. When he was station manager, Taylor picked every record the station played and scheduled all of the music. (He also talked with most people who called the station to express an opinion on the programing.) The music was programed in 15-minute segments, with each segment comprising a balanced, complete unit. Each of these segments was recorded and made available to other stations as the Bonneville Broadcast Consultants' first beautiful music format, for which stations pay from $400 to $3,000 per month, depending on the size of the market. The music package consists of 200 hours of music, with fifty percent rotation each year. As that became successful, Taylor left WRFM to head the separate company and began to add formats of different types that other stations could use.

A typical thirty minutes of WRFM music would be as follows: "The Sound of Music," Hugo Winterhalter; "Somewhere, My Love," the Gunter Kallman Chorus; "Never on Sunday," the Boston Pops Orchestra; "What Now, My Love," the Tijuana Brass; "Theme from *The Apartment*," Ferrante and Teicher; "Hawaiian Wedding Song," Andy Williams; "Spanish Eyes," Bert Kaempfert; "The Impossible Dream," Mantovani; "Moon River," Henry Mancini; and "Tenderly," Paul Weston. WRFM tries to emphasize the pretty, the melodic, and the familiar or soon-to-be familiar. A maximum of four vocals per hour is played. The station feels that the music is the most important single ingredient in the programing.

In a regular hour, the commercials are placed at approximate times as follows: two at :15, two at :30, two at :45, and one at :55. The news runs about four minutes at :55 hourly from 6 A.M. to 9 A.M., every two hours at other times. In the morning and afternoon commute hours, traffic information is given each half-hour. In the morning, time and weather are given frequently, the time every two records. The idea is to emphasize the music as much as possible, to keep clutter to a minimum, but to provide essential services that the listening audience wants.

Other talk features include editorials, aired four times a day. The editorials are taken from suburban newspapers, of which there are more than forty in the New York City area. The editorials are chosen from those newspapers cooperating, about half of the total.

Another information feature is the "Community Affairs Capsule," a one-minute program that shows the audience the station is concerned with the community. This news and service feature takes two people working full-time to produce.

The format remains the same twenty-four hours a day with a couple of further exceptions. A Sunday-morning religious segment runs from 7:30 to 8:30, consisting of a CBS broadcast of the Mormon Tabernacle Choir lasting twenty-five minutes and a local New York organ recital of sacred music, which comprises the other part. The station carries no paid religion. Five times on Sunday, an information feature, "Topic," explores an issue or presents a newsmaker in a segment that lasts four to five minutes. The station feels that this presentation is more effective than taking up a larger block and presenting one single program. They do not want to invite people to tune the station out and feel that they can present more effective public service if they can keep the people listening.

Also, "bonus hours" are scheduled throughout the week, in which only music is played, without any talk.

The announcers have an identity. They are not disembodied voices, as are sometimes found in stations that emphasize music. They do give the titles of the records played. They sound natural and human, but do not waste words. They are identifiable people, but are not "personalities" that entertain.

On-air promotion pieces are few in number. WRFM's philosophy is to not use air time to tell everyone how wonderful the station is. They feel that a station cannot tell people how good it is; it must show them. By limiting on-air promotion pieces, the station has more time for music.

The station does one remote broadcast daily from noon until 2 P.M. from a remote studio at a permanent high-fidelity trade show and exhibit. The station is careful about the quality of its signal, broadcasts in stereo, and feels that the remote is useful in giving them visibility and helping their image. They do not change format for this remote.

The station uses one brief, singing station-identification per hour. The ID is simple, using station call letters and the words "the sound of beautiful music."

The news is brief, carefully edited, and to the point. Although news reports are brief, the station has more news resources than might be expected. Associated Press and United Press International broadcast wires, the UPI audio service, the services of the corporate (Bonneville) Washington news bureau, a direct stock market wire, and one on-the-street reporter give the station a great amount of news to choose from.

The station has a staff of twenty-five, small but adequate, and well-equipped studios in a good location in Manhattan.

Its philosophy toward off-air promotion is to try to present a Rock of Gibraltar image. The station does not do a tremendous amount of promotion, but it is promotion-minded. WRFM aims at promotion that is done well, that is different and stands out, and that motivates and intrigues. It has bought the full back page of the *New York Times* for ads. It has advertised in buses and trains, and at one time had an ad in every car of the subway system. The station has purchased billboard space and has run ads in some trade-press publications—*Modern Grocer, Supermarket News, ANNY* (Advertising News of New York), *Variety, Radio-TV Daily,* and *Broadcasting.*

A good part of the promotion effort centers around FM dial cards. A number of stations have used this technique, although probably not as extensively. The station has distributed several million 3 x 5-inch FM dial cards. On the front is an FM dial with the call letters and location on the dial of all the FM stations, including a notation of which broadcast in stereo. There is a flag at WRFM's dial location, above which are shown the call letters and location in larger print than for the other stations. At the bottom of the card, it merely says "WRFM stereo–105 Begin to like radio again." The back side of the card has more information about the station, including a short sales pitch and a listing of a typical thirty minutes of WRFM music. The station employs one full-time worker to distribute these cards to locations throughout the coverage area where potential listeners can pick them up. Three versions of the card are distributed in appropriate areas, each showing different stations that can be received in the three different geographical areas.

The manager feels that programs come before sales in importance. He is not unaware of the need to sell, but he feels that sales follow a good product. He feels that program decisions should be made with the audience in mind. He also operates on instinct, although he looks for clues from his audience. He reads every piece of mail written to the station, and he speaks to a good share of the callers who call about programing matters. He thinks of the station as being listener-oriented.

In summary, the station is disciplined and consistent, emphasizes the music, which is pretty, melodic, and familiar, but concentrates enough on information, local awareness, and involvement to make it more than a music station. The station sounds friendly, live, and involved with the community. The format is simple, uncluttered, and human.

Profile 3

Call Letters and Location: KILT–Houston, Texas

Owner and Affiliation: LIN-Texas Broadcasting Company–Independent

Classification and Power: Class III A–5 kw

KILT in Houston is a very successful Top-40 station, with ratings and ad rates among the top in the market. Like other successful stations, it has a halo effect that makes the total impact of the station—the image—greater than the sum of the parts making up the station. KILT does many of the same things that similar stations in other markets are doing, but with greater success. Perhaps the execution is better. Perhaps it is because KILT is very Houston; that is, it understands its market better than other stations understand theirs. KILT has more broad-based appeal than many other Top-40 stations. Its demographic breakdown is better. The music list includes mostly singles but contains some albums and more blues than some other stations of its type. The DJs all are personalities (though brief and crisp in presentation), not human automation as found in some tight formats. The news, presented every twenty minutes, is brief but solid. The station sounds very aware of its city, and participates and shows pride in Houston.

Many radio stations promote successfully, but few have more fun or get more attention from contests and promotions than KILT. Many of the ideas may seem a little zany, but the station carries them out with such flair that they are acceptable. For instance, the station got front-page coverage in the *Houston Chronicle* as well as space in *Sports Illustrated* when it showed awareness of the jogging-for-fitness habits of Americans while getting publicity and funds for the Living Bank, which accepts organs for transplant. The station attracted several thousand people to the Astrodome at 6 A.M. to watch the KILT Jog Corps race, plugging fitness and recruiting donors. Judge Roy Hofheins, who built the Astrodome, and then-Mayor Louie Welch had a foot race, won by the mayor. He donated his purse of $200 to the Living Bank. The starter was heart-transplant surgeon Dr. Denton Cooley, also an avid jogger. A preliminary event was a race between penguins. The final event had the crowd follow the Methodist Hospital transplant team around the track. Bikini-clad girls acted as cheerleaders.

One hot, sticky summer day, KILT gave away a snowstorm on the front lawn of a contest winner. A snow machine did the job while neighbors and friends of the winner built snowmen and threw snowballs. (The snow killed the lawn.)

To publicize and help the fight against pollution on "Earth Day," the station teamed with Gulf Oil Company to give away plastic garbage bags. Gulf donated the bags, KILT the publicity. About 250,000 of the bags, with KILT printed on the side, were given away at Gulf service stations within forty-eight hours. The station offered $6.10 (the station dial position is 610) to a random number of people who used the bags. On garbage day, KILT people roamed the city, giving money to a number of people who had cleaned up their trash and garbage and placed it in the GULF/KILT bags. Hundreds of dollars were given away. A group of college students took some of the bags and cleaned up the Galveston beach. Many citizens joined in to help clean their neighborhoods. City officials and garbagemen wrote letters commending the station for its efforts.

The station invited listeners to Astroworld amusement park on KILT Night. They set an Astroworld attendance record for a Friday evening promotion, even though it rained early in the evening.

In one contest, KILT gave a car to the winner and four other cars for the winner to give to his friends.

The station's disc jockeys attracted a large crowd to the Astrodome to watch them play a preliminary baseball game against the wives of the Houston Astros' baseball players. (The wives won.) On another occasion, the station gave away a million yen and a trip to Japan. On another baseball promotion, the station attracted the largest weeknight crowd to watch the Astros in three years when it played the Astros one night. Each of the KILT personalities was given the chance to bat against major-league pitching. Manager Dickie Rosenfeld promised that if any of his announcers could get a hit they would get a check for $1,000. Nobody did, so he gave each announcer $100, plus $50 to each Astro player. All of the mentioned promotions used only KILT to spread the word.

The station also has a daily contest. A word is given on the air, then phone calls are made to numbers chosen at random from the phone book. If the person who answers knows the word, he wins money. Generally, though, it is the fun of playing the game, the skill of the contest, or the unusual nature of the promotion that interests the station more than big-money giveaways. Strangely, KILT has no promotion director. The manager and program director organize the promotions.

The station has been on the air since 1957 with basically the same format, although the present structure has been used only since 1967. Since 1967, when the station's success began to show most dramatically, staff turnover has been almost nonexistent.

The music is chosen by the program director, who uses surveys of local record stores, trade magazines, and tip sheets—especially, those of Bill Gavin—to aid him. The play list includes the forty records on the survey sheet that the station publishes weekly and distributes to music stores, the "KILT Hit-Bound" and "Star of the Week" new single records picked as future hits, plus as many as six other new records that seem likely possibilities. Also featured are ten to twelve albums, each having usually one to three approved cuts. A stock of about 2,000 past hits also may be used. The "oldies" are only as old as rock music—they do not date far back. The DJ has freedom to choose from those approved for play, but he is restricted by a rigid format. Each record is placed into one of four categories—A, B, C, or D—plus oldies. Each hour must be programed according to the format with an order such as A—oldie—B—oldie—A—oldie—B—A—C, and so on. The DJ may choose records which fit the categories, but he must play a cross section of the list rather than just a few of his favorites.

The music, although basically the same throughout the day, does change character slightly according to the time of the day. There is a formula for 6–10 A.M., another for mid-day and all night, and a third for afternoon and evening. Basically, music in the morning is fairly straight, so that adults will be attracted as much as possible. Mid-day and all-night music is softer in sound, and every other record is an oldie. Late afternoon and evening slots are aimed more at the younger audience and are heavier on teen music, especially with hard-rock sounds. The character of the music also varies slightly according to music trends. The records that are selling are the records that are heard.

In addition to following an order of music selections, each DJ must follow a policy book which establishes "sets." The order and style of programing between records is prescribed. All comments must come immediately after a record. This is the time when the DJ has the opportunity to be a personality. It is his freedom period. After he has made his comments, the rest is prescribed. He can make no more than ten seconds of comments for the rest of the set and until the next record is finished, although he does talk over the open and close of the musical selections. All commercials are categorized and color-coded according to whether they are talk, talk and music, or all-music. The talk spots always must go first, the all-music commercials last in each set. A number of radio stations use such sets, with procedures that vary slightly according to the station. The KILT morning program from 6 to 10 spotlights a two-man team which has more latitude with the format than do others in the schedule. This team makes extensive use of humor, along with reports on the morning traffic, news, weather, and time, making them sound more like the morning show found on adult pop stations than on many Top-40 stations.

Like many other stations, one of the main things that KILT tries to do is to eliminate irritants. The station does not want to sound too shrill or to have too much idle chatter. It does not want the DJs to talk over the vocal parts of the records. DJs, who work "combo," use a foot-operated timer in the control room to aid them to time comments accurately so that they will not miss cues. All record intros and closes are timed carefully, and times are marked on all commercials. At the end of each taped commercial, a subaudible tone is recorded which triggers a light on the console telling the DJ the tape is over and giving him a visual as well as aural cue.

A most important factor is that all air personalities are local. All are from the general Houston area and have lived there most of their lives. They know the people, the mores, and the expectations. This factor shows on the air. The station sounds like it is part of Houston. The local sound is genuine and effective.

The news is broadcast every twenty minutes. The major newscast is at twenty minutes after the hour, with headlines at :40 and on the hour. KILT employs six newsmen, only one of whom is outside the plant. The station has radio wires plus UPI audio service and a newspaper wire. Traffic reports are picked up from the police dispatcher and aired by "Tiger," the traffic girl. The station has carried only Houston Oilers football play-by-play and is not interested in more live sports coverage. A feature from the medical society, "Call the Doctor," gives tips on health. The format shows a variation on Sunday with religious programing from 5:00 to 8:30 A.M. and public affairs and religion from 10 P.M. to 1 A.M. Public-affairs specials are programed on occasion, and experimental documentaries produced at the University of Houston are aired. The station tried a talk show nightly from 10 P.M. to 2 A.M., but dropped it.

KILT presents editorials in a manner different from most radio stations, which simply voice their views unemotionally on a subject. KILT's editorials may use music, production effects, and may be more emotional than intellectual on occasion. Editorials are done by the program director and the public affairs director. On at least one occasion, the station did more than editorialize. It filed a million-dollar suit against a state agency for pollution.

Like some other stations, KILT assigns names to new DJs rather than allowing them to use their own. The name is the property of the station. Should a DJ be hired away by a competitor in the same market, he would have to use a different name, thereby lessening the chances of his taking his audience with him immediately.

KILT plays its own game rather than counterprograming to the strategies of the competition. Program director Bill Young tells his programing people not to even listen to the competition. He feels that if the station does what it can do well, it will be successful regardless of what the competitors do.

KILT is a well-run radio station that always looks for new challenges. It is willing to break format if anything big enough or interesting enough warrants a change. The announcers have fun on the air. They are interested in Houston and they sound like it. Bill Gavin's program conference named KILT "station of the year" in 1970.

Profile 4

Call Letters and Location: WINS–New York, New York
Owner and Affiliation: Westinghouse Broadcasting Company–
                             Independent
Classification and Power: Class II–50 kw

WINS in New York City is an all-news station owned by Westinghouse. In 1965, the station, then playing music, was not doing well
against its competitors. The New York broadcasting spectrum, with
sixty-three receivable signals, was crowded with seemingly every radio
type. At that time, Westinghouse decided to try all-news. The first station to present all-news was XETRA in Tijuana, Mexico, broadcasting
to southern California. XETRA was a rip-and-read news operation with
a small staff. When WINS went to all-news, it did so in a big way with
a big budget. One of its strong competitors in New York, WCBS, also
is all-news. An all-news station is very costly to operate since the
big-city, all-news station budget for programing averages about fifty to
sixty percent of the gross. For other types of formats, the average is
about thirty percent.

WINS has an audience size that is about equal to that of WCBS.
WINS's ad rate is among the highest in the market.

WINS has a news staff of approximately 100, plus stringers in outlying areas who get paid per story. The station uses eighteen anchormen, plus writers, reporters, editors, secretaries, and executives. The
station also has access to the Washington and overseas news bureaus
of Westinghouse and gets stories that break in other areas from other
Westinghouse stations. WINS has six studios, used for on-air presentations, production, and editing.

The station relies more on people than machines or gimmicks to
present the news. The philosophy is that the reporter who makes contacts, knows people, and digs for stories is the best source of news
material. The newsmen spend a lot of their time outside of the station
working beats and gathering information. It definitely is not a rip-and-
read news operation. All material that airs is either written or rewritten from other sources, except for late-breaking bulletins.

WINS feels that the biggest reasons it has been able to compete with
the excellent product produced by WCBS in New York are: (1) that
WINS was first in New York with all-news; (2) that WINS emphasizes
the local news more; and (3) that WINS news copy is very tightly
written, with greater emphasis on hard news and with fewer features.
WINS also feels that it has more flexibility because it does not have

network commitments that compartmentalize the news as CBS does to WCBS.

WINS went to all-news just before the big power blackout of 1965. It was well equipped to cover the emergency and received so many plaudits and column inches of newspaper space for its excellent coverage that it got attention that no promotion campaign could have given it. From then on, WINS had a news image in New York. They were the first station to be "all news all the time" in their market, which gave them an advantage.

The anchormen have a mature, intelligent, and conversational approach. CBS always has had such professional quality news and such excellent voices and presentations that anything less than a thoroughly professional sound on WINS's part would hurt them severely. WINS plays the news straight, but the newscasters are personable and full-voiced, with an easy manner yet crisp pace and production. Voices change frequently, both by switching the anchormen and by including numerous correspondents, specialists, and actuality reports. The station uses no singing jingles and no sirens or sound effects, except for the beeps that introduce a bulletin.

The present format is shown in sound-hour form on p. 147. WINS previously used a variation of that format, as follows. When plotted on a circle, the format looked very symmetrical. At the top of the hour, a five-minute news block used approximately the first minute for headlines of stories to be covered in the next half-hour. At five minutes after the hour, a one-minute commercial, thirty seconds of weather, and another minute commercial brought the time to seven and one-half minutes past the hour. Another five-minute segment of news continued the stories that were headlined at the top of the hour. Following were another commercial, weather again, and another minute commercial. That brought the time to fifteen minutes past the hour, when there were another headline summary, continuation of the news stories headlined, and the continuation of the pattern around the hour. The format had two basic units of time. One was the hour, with no story repeated in depth more often than hourly. All copy was rewritten so that the stories that were repeated in the second hour would not be just a replay of what was broadcast earlier. The other basic unit was the seven and one-half minute segment. The hour contained eight equal segments of five minutes of news, one minute of commercial, thirty seconds of weather, and another minute of commercial. That totals sixteen minutes of commercials, eight 5-minute news segments, and eight weather forecasts per hour. Specialized types of news were and are contained in the 5-minute news segments. Sports is heard at approximately :16 and :46 around the clock. Stock market reports, including hour-by-hour summaries, are heard from 10:25 A.M. to 8:25 P.M. weekdays. Brief summaries of business news are presented at five minutes before the hour and half-hour. At least four traffic reports are given each hour in peak traffic hours, twice an hour at other times. Consumer information is given between 10:00 A.M. and 4:00 P.M. Seasonal reports include twelve weekend fishing reports, eight hunting reports, and nineteen skiing reports.

Another public service is the "community calendar." Frequently throughout the schedule, short periods are used for announcement of events.

The station uses specialists, people who have expertise in given areas whose voices become identified with specialized news types. All reports, however, are written tightly and kept short, usually not more than a minute and one-half, but some last as long as three minutes. WINS has four religion commentators—one Jewish, one Catholic, and two Protestant—who present religious or religion/humanities information and comment not only on Sunday but throughout the week. Four Group W commentators are heard regularly, plus Group W specialists, including a theatre critic and reporter, a motion picture specialist, a social critic, a science/medical specialist, and others.

WINS's parent company, Westinghouse, or Group W, provides considerable resources for covering not only local news but world news, although a 1975 cutback reduced overseas bureaus and forced a change to Associated Press audio feeds. The station also has access to stories that are covered by Group W stations in other cities. On occasion, when the importance and immediacy of a story warrant it, special live news coverage is carried from the Washington bureau or from elsewhere that a major story might be occurring.

The station editorializes, but the editorial functions are separated from the news-gathering and presentation functions. An editorial writer prepares the editorials; he is a specialist, not a staff newsman. The general manager voices the editorials. The manager may rewrite the copy to conform to his style and, on occasion, will even write the editorial himself. The editorials concern mostly local issues within the station's 17-county coverage area.

A half-hour block on Sunday is given to a news conference. A newsmaker is brought into the studio and questioned for thirty minutes by a small panel of WINS newsmen. Such news conferences frequently provide stories for the following morning's newspapers, and excerpts are used on the station's own news programs.

The station promotes heavily both off and on the air. The on-air promos primarily consist of information about features to be presented, but they do contain a certain amount of puffery about the quality of the product presented. Off-air promotion includes newspaper ads, billboards, bus and subway cards, and some trade-press advertising. The station occasionally uses contests as a promotional tool.

Newsmen are told to search for good sounds. Tape recordings of newsmakers' voices are heard frequently. Sound must contribute to the news, however, and not be thrown in for its own sake.

The station relies heavily on its professionals to ferret out and present the news. WINS uses fewer pieces of apparatus than some other stations. It has seven mobile units, each equipped with "handy talkies" so that the reporters can report from places inaccessible to cars. The station does not use helicopters to present traffic reports. It relies on police dispatchers along with the standard broadcast news wires, having both AP and UPI, wires for weather and stocks, a greater New York wire, and a police wire. The reporters rely heavily on contacts and working their beats to get information. The station also has a master contact book of news sources that took three years to compile and contains numbers and locations for all sorts of information. This sort of catalogue is most useful and not compiled easily. It is virtually impossible, for example, just to get the home telephone numbers of the elected congressmen and congresswomen from the New York area.

WINS has been well "in the black" for years. Its national accounts are among the bluest of the blue chips. Like most all-news stations, its appeal is stronger to men than to women. The advertisers consist of the automotive industry, financial institutions, grocery and drug producers, beer and beverage makers, entertainment promoters, retailers, publications, oil and gasoline companies, travel promoters, restaurants, and services, among others.

WINS can provide the listener, in a very few minutes, with a fairly complete breakdown of the news of the world. People can hear the headlines, but they also can get details about the main stories. After a listener gets the main news, he can switch to his favorite music station or turn off the radio. For those who want to listen longer, the station does a better job than most at continually bringing in fresh information. The station provides news in depth by returning to a major story or feature and presenting additional information or points of view. A long interview or feature is frequently broken up in a way that individual segments will be interesting in themselves, in addition to providing a complete story for listeners who stay tuned.

The station hits local news very hard, and does it well. The station's staff is tuned to New York and its suburbs, knows the area well, and sounds like it. Staff turnover is small, enabling the people to learn their jobs, build up contacts, and, in the case of the anchormen and other on-air reporters, allow the audience to get accustomed to them and build up a kind of friendship.

Occasionally, the anchormen mispronounce a name or a place or misread copy. This can happen to anyone who is on the air for an hour at a time. For the most part, however, changes of voice are frequent enough, and sufficient new information is well prepared to make the station sound thoroughly professional. However, it is a little disconcerting to hear the newscaster reading commercials. The credibility of any newscaster is not helped by selling goods part of the time.

At first thought, it would seem almost impossible for a station to bear up under the strain of presenting news twenty-four hours a day, even in New York City. However, because of the pace and format, the impression is given that there is not enough time to get all of the news in. After the commercials, the weather, the traffic, the sports, the stocks, and the other features, not much time is left. The pace is fast. The writing is tight. The program really moves.

In summary, WINS news has a pleasant, intelligent sound. Its first emphasis is local, yet it covers national and international news well. The station has made an effective compromise between presenting the headlines and giving too much repetition. The news is well edited, well reported, and well presented. The news hour, broken into 20-minute components, serves as a good package. WINS is an expensive effort that only a handful of markets and broadcast operations could handle.

Profile 5

Call Letters and Location: WVON–Chicago, Illinois
Owner and Affiliation: Globe Communications–Mutual Black Network
Classification and Power: Class III–5 kw

WVON–Chicago aims its programing to the black audience of the city, a population of one and a half million. It does this by being a local radio station, which is to say that it involves itself in the concerns and cares of that part of the community which is black. WVON's staff is not entirely black and the ownership has never been black, though management is. The station's community awareness, its attitude of service, and its attempt to entertain, inform, and aid its audience segment enable it to be successful.

WVON is basically a Top-40 radio station. It has tight, crisp production, publishes a survey, and runs on-air contests. A lot of the music it plays is also played on other stations. WVON plays more blues and mostly black artists. The playlist is usually about forty selections. Four selections each hour are oldies. All music is selected by program director E. Rodney Jones. Deejays play the records according to a prescribed formula. Disc jockey comments are short, many of them over the opening and closing of the musical selections. The format varies a bit from midnight to dawn as more blues and some gospel music are included. Between 11 P.M. and midnight, a telephone talk program called "Hot Line" airs. Sunday church service remotes have been a regular service.

Throughout the broadcast day a number of service features are aired. Brief segments called "Aware" concern health, hygiene, and public service information. "What's New" includes church, fraternal, social, and club news. Other features have been used periodically, such as "Bouquet of the Day" recognition to people who have made a contribution to the community. In the past, the station has broadcast information from the Better Business Bureau about unethical businesses operating in the area.

Vice President and General Manager Bernadine Washington does program features presenting fashion information, household tips, and feature material, called "On the Scene with Bernadine." She also hosts what is called "The Bern Club," which hosts about 1,000 women twice a month for classes in poise, dress, hygiene, programs on current events, and participation in civic projects. The club has no dues. They have taken group trips to Washington, D.C., Nassau, world's fairs, and other places. Mrs. Washington also voices the station's editorials, which are aired on an "as needed" basis.

Community activity is important to the station. Station personnel are active joiners and participants. The station gives twelve college scholarships yearly, half for academic achievement and half for athletic achievement. They do occasional remotes for special funds, such as the Urban League. At Christmas they raise funds for Christmas baskets for the needy. A summertime program has used professional athletes as coaches of organized activities for children on the South and East sides of Chicago. They have also sponsored programs to encourage young people to stay in school. The list is but a sample.

WVON plays music with a lot of youth appeal to both blacks and whites. Many songs that become popular first on WVON are later picked up by other popular music stations. Chicago has long been a good blues market. Program director Jones consults others, including deejays, record stores, trade press, music tip sheets, and record distributors, but it is he who decides what music the station plays. The commercial policy is a maximum of eighteen minutes per hour. Three commercials are played in a cluster so that music sweeps (in which there are no commercials) can be scheduled during the hour. The format has evolved and the music changes some according to current trends. As Jones says, "We bend a little."

The news is a combination of Mutual Black Network and local origination. News of special interest to the Chicago black community is emphasized, but of course all major stories are included. WVON makes use of wire copy, the network, and their own local coverage. Local coverage seems to have been de-emphasized since the addition of the network. Prior to the addition of the network, each local news-cast started with a produced opening which included an excerpt from a Martin Luther King speech.

WVON gains identity with its community through distribution of *Soul*, a tabloid-sized biweekly magazine. The publication contains a feature article on a person or subject of interest to blacks, plus several by-lined potpourri columns on entertainers and prominent people, a letters-to-the-editor column, and advertising. WVON gets its call letters on the front page in the Chicago area and use of the center page for promotion of the station. The publication is distributed nationally from Los Angeles.

The station, in its present location but with different call letters, and even a different channel, has existed since 1925. It was purchased by the Chess brothers, Leonard and Phil, in 1963. Leonard Chess had become interested in the art of black musicians and had formed a Chicago-based record company that made considerable money from the sale of rhythm and blues and rock-and-roll records. Chess records, formed in 1947, and its subsidiaries, Checker (1953) and Argo (1956), featured such artists as Muddy Waters, Howlin' Wolf, John Lee Hooker, Jimmy Rodgers, Chuck Berry, Bo Diddley, and Clarence "Frogman" Henry. Initially the records were sold locally and then regionally. Artists were from the Mississippi delta, although some were from Chicago. Of course, many Chicago blacks themselves had come from the delta regions. Chess got help with his record company when the music, which had previously been called "race" or "rhythm and blues," became more marketable under the name "rock-and-roll," the nebulous term that soon became applied to many varieties of beat music. Chess was helped by disc jockey Alan Freed, who played many of the Chess records and used the Chess artists in his live stage shows.

With the success of the music, Chess became interested in giving the black Chicago audience a radio station that played their music and cared about them, owned by him but programed by blacks given considerable freedom to appeal to their audience. The station was not the first black-oriented station in Chicago, but in the long run it has been the most successful. This success has in recent years caused even stiffer competition. Not long after the decision to program to black audiences, the station received strong competition from Gordon McLendon's WYNR, which had a similar target audience but which eventually lost the ratings race and switched its format and call letters. WVON has maintained a constant format after the initial shakedown period and has been consistently strong in the ratings. Changes since then have been evolutionary and gradual. The call letters were selected to stand for *Voice of the Negro*. To be sure, the station has not represented all black people. No one radio station can do that, any more than one radio station can represent all people of one skin color, or sex, or political persuasion. As one of the station staff stated, "We don't have too many black Ph.D.'s. We don't program to them." Pulse ratings showed that by 1967 they were reaching ninety percent of Chicago's black households each week. Their success has spawned more competitors for the black audience.

The station is no longer held by the Chess interests. After Leonard Chess died, it was sold to the Harlem Globetrotter interests and in 1974 changed frequency and power while keeping studio location and call letters, in a multimillion dollar deal involving another station. Studios remain out of the high-rent district. They are functional and adequate, although the small physical plant with its bustle gives the impression of containing more than the thirty people on the staff.

WVON, in addition to charging a relatively low rate per thousand listeners reached, woos advertisers with extras. The station does more merchandising than most, including bonus ads on the back of Top-40 sheets, advance mailings, in-store promotional displays, buy-of-the-week features, and help from station personnel in calling on key distributors, buyers, and retailers.

Profile 6

Call Letters and Location: WCCO–Minneapolis, Minnesota
Owner and Affiliation: Midwest Radio/TV, Inc.–CBS Radio Network
Classification and Power: Class I A–50 kw

WCCO may be the most successful radio station in the nation. It claims morning drive-time audiences larger than much of prime-time television. Its share of the audience is fantastic. Program directors and managers from all over the country make pilgrimages to Minneapolis each year to find the magic secret to success so that they can transform their own stations into similar successes. Many of these people go home shaking their heads, saying the same thing that some of WCCO's competitors say: "They aren't really that good. I don't understand it." Some of these people say, "Well, they couldn't do that in our market." That may be true. Maybe they could not do that well in another market. Maybe they are not "that good." WCCO is very human, not superhuman. It does many of the same things that other stations are doing in other markets. But WCCO is a very professional station, with exceptional balance in its strengths—a station that relates to its own market exceptionally well.

WCCO has been a winner for a long time; it has a rich tradition. It has financial ties through common ownership with a leading television station and was also, until recently, a sister to the major newspapers of the city. It has the maximum power available to a radio station— 50,000 watts. It thus has power, coverage, and financial backing. It has a name that is respected in the city. When a listener thinks of radio in that area, he probably thinks of WCCO. WCCO is a case of the rich who continue to get richer. The station is strong and aggressive, and it has the money to move quickly into costly new areas, to bid on contracts, and to mount new efforts.

WCCO puts strong emphasis on its thirty on-air personalities. Its on-air people sound intelligent, have professional deliveries and voices, and sound natural. The station does not have an automated sound, by any means. The individual air personalities have adequate time to prepare for the on-air stints. They have the freedom to choose their own music and to create their own repartee and features. The station is deep in personalities, having enough to cover contingencies and give special coverage. An important element in the programs is humor; the on-air people use considerable humor. The personalities make a large number of personal appearances, are in great demand as speakers and masters of ceremony, and seem to be involved in all aspects of city life. They give the impression of caring about their market, of knowing what is going on, and of being involved. During vacation periods, the station often will hire a "name" entertainer to fill in for the vacationing program host.

The station tries to be contemporary in its music, being watchful of trends and new sounds and trying to play a broad spectrum of popular music without resorting to playing sounds that are too teen-oriented. The WCCO approach is adult popular music. The music director attempts to keep current on the record business, helping to keep the on-air personalities abreast of what is available; but the personalities are their own producers and pick their own records. Overall, the sound of the music is quite consistent, in spite of the freedom that announcers have.

The station carries CBS news, which gives it strong national coverage. Unlike many sister operations, WCCO was always housed in a different location from its sister television station, and the two news departments are not corporate. The radio news department constantly tries to scoop television and the newspapers. WCCO has a large news staff, and the station is very big on news, with an hour at 7 A.M. and thirty minutes at 5 and 10 P.M. Information is an important commodity for WCCO. With CBS news and the strong local news effort, plus weather, sports, farm, community events, and special sports and information programs, the station has a great deal of talk. The station is so informed and current that it gives the impression that listeners do not know what is happening in the twin cities if they are not listening to WCCO. Early in the morning, a farm program presents pertinent information about the major farm region, plays records, and uses humor in its presentation. The farm-program people travel in the coverage area often, give the impression they know what is going on, and convey information with a light-hearted approach. Since Minnesota is very weather-conscious, the station presents a lot of weather information. The station has solid sports news and carries virtually all of the important sports events in the twin cities from major league baseball to major league football, University of Minnesota sports, and even top high school events.

Telephone talk programs are done occasionally, mostly on special issues or with special personalities, although daily from 2:10 to 2:55 P.M. a regular program is broadcast. The station occasionally does a meet-the-press type program, on its own or on a hookup with large stations in other markets, in which the news directors or other news representatives interview government leaders or other prominent persons. Such programs are presented as specials with appropriate promotion buildup.

For a long time, the station has used "On the go with CCO" as its slogan. One reason for this has been that it broadcasts remote from the sites of special events. The state fair is a big event in the twin cities, and WCCO broadcasts from headquarters at the fair. On one opening day of the fishing season, it broadcast from a fishing hole. These remote broadcasts are not of the used-car parking lot variety where the program is one long sales pitch, but are done with a certain amount of flair and reflect well on the station's up-to-date, involved image.

The station promotes heavily with ads in competing media and the trade press, as well as on-air. It also has a number of promotional activities, such as the mentioned personal appearances of its personnel, who are very active in the life of the city. It also charters airplanes to Hawaii, Bermuda, and other places, and a station personality acts as the tour leader. The station takes a percentage of the profits from the tour as well as reaping the advantage of goodwill that a successful and fun tour can bring. Sometimes, short remote broadcasts are done from the tour site, involving the hometowners on the tour.

Because the station programs so much information, and because variety programing is carried in the middle evening hours, the station faces the danger of sounding too cluttered, of having too many starts and stops throughout the day. The management realizes this but believes that heavy information is its strong suit, and it does not want to streamline the programing and thus sound like other stations. To minimize the disruptive effect of the many program features, the station does not end programs—it only begins them. WCCO never gives the listener an invitation to tune out by giving the effect of one program finishing and another beginning. All of the features are part of one program—WCCO radio—and the flow is as smooth as is possible considering the variety in programing. The announcers get in and out of program segments very quickly, with a fast but unhurried sounding pace.

If another station were to copy WCCO in another market, it might have difficulty, because the success is dependent upon the state of the population, which has been conditioned to accept certain things. The station's evolution and its relationship to its market are important parts of the success. For the twin cities, WCCO is a very good radio station. In times past, it has been pressed by other stations, but it has remained strong because its management had conviction in what it was doing and continued to go its chosen way. The station never panicked, and, in time, the competitors weakened, with WCCO remaining as the market's dominant station.

WCCO is unique. It knows its market. It is a station with courage, substance, personality, and power. It is in the middle of the city and the city's issues, and thus the lives of the listening audience. Its success is dependent upon heavy information, humor, personalities, music, and integrity. It is not counterprogramed; WCCO is the standard. It goes its own way, forcing others to do the counterprograming. Everything it does—and that is considerable—it does well.

Profile 7

Call Letters and Location: WKAR and WKAR–FM–East Lansing, Michigan
Owner and Affiliation: Michigan State University–National Public Radio
Classification and Power: Class II–10 kw, Class B–110 kw

WKAR and WKAR–FM in East Lansing, Michigan—the Michigan State University radio stations—are among the most ambitious noncommercial stations in the nation. They concentrate service in four separate areas: AM, FM, subcarrier services, and program services. The AM radio station is 10,000 watts daytime, and focuses on news and public affairs programing. The signal, from the center of Michigan, has a large coverage area. FM, also with a good signal, and with stereo, leans to classical music and fine arts. The subcarrier programing includes such things as blind and handicapped services, including some networking. The program services provide specialized taped programing to commercial and other noncommercial stations—in 1976 this amounted to 6,000 hours of programing. These stations and services are an extension of the university. With a full-time staff of approximately thirty and approximately fifty part-timers (mostly students), plus the further resources of the university such as guest experts for information and opinion, the stations provide a broad range of services to the community and the state. University lectures, concerts, and other presentations supplement National Public Radio and staff-produced programs.

AM and FM programing services are one hundred percent split. A few programs air on both, but generally at different times. AM offers early-morning and noon farm programs. Michigan is, of course, an important agricultural state and WKAR is in the center of the agricultural belt. The university has important departments of food science, agriculture, and veterinary medicine. The farm service department of the station provides market news, extensive weather information, and informative features using some of Michigan's top experts. The morning includes *The Radio Reader*, a half-hour program done by manager Dick Estell, reading from books. In addition to WKAR, the program is heard on seventeen noncommercial stations, including stations in Alaska, Arizona, California, Pennsylvania, Washington, and other states. The rest of the morning is given over to magazine programing, interspersing music and features. Afternoons consist of programing to blacks through a magazine program of blues, jazz, rock music, and features of aid and interest to blacks. Since the state capitol is in Lansing, a few minutes' drive from the station, this program makes extensive use of its ready access to state and other governmental agencies with first-hand information. Most of the features are produced in short segments, mostly one to two minutes with some as long as five minutes.

Variedades en Espanol attempts to do for the Spanish-heritage people what the black program does for its listeners, including some programing aimed at migrant farm workers. Twenty-five percent of all programing on AM and FM is aimed at minority audiences.

The six full-time and twelve part-time people in the news department provide WKAR with more locally-originated news and public affairs programing than most noncommercial stations can afford. For some time the station used Westinghouse's Group W news service until it was reduced. In addition to wire services, the station now uses the Associated Press audio service, which aids the general news coverage and the farm and sports coverage as well. National Public Radio provides important news coverage, including *All Things Considered*. ATC airs on FM starting at 5 P.M. and on AM starting at 6 P.M. Faculty members and state officials are a rich source of additional news information and background.

Sports coverage is significant. Full coverage of university football, hockey, basketball, and baseball includes play-by-play of approximately sixty events a year, heard not only on WKAR but on a network of stations. Play-by-play of the state high school basketball champion-ships is a yearly feature also. Sportscasts are part of the regular news service.

FM emphasizes fine arts programing, including much serious music from recordings and a good number of originations of campus lecture and concert events. Faculty and student concerts and music depart-ment recitals are heard. Metropolitan Opera broadcasts are heard live. Saturday evenings feature a classics-by-request program.

Services to other stations include *The Radio Reader* and literally hundreds of separate programs and features. While some are in the nature of traditional 15- and 30-minute programs, an increasing num-ber are short, under 4½ minutes, so that they can be integrated into existing commercial formats and extend informational coverage. Sta-tions from throughout Michigan and many other states make use of these programs. Individuals, institutions, agencies, and schools fre-quently request copies. Programs have included information on home improvement frauds, the increase of simple goiter in Michigan, a health report, and a summer theater guide. Two hundred stations re-ceived a series on youth smoking.

Subcarrier services are broadcast to those who have special re-ceivers. Initial services were to the blind and otherwise handicapped, but have been expanding. A special series of informational programs on veterinary medicine sparked interest in a statewide network of subchannel services. Since Michigan's law requiring physician re-licensing every three years requires physicians to keep updating, such a network can aid by special information to subscribing physicians. Similar efforts in nursing, veterinary medicine, and other areas are projected.

WKAR has been active on the national scene through its programs and through the efforts of its personnel. Station Manager Estell has been a member of the National Educational Radio board of directors, the NPR board, and was one of the incorporators of the network. As-sistant manager Rob Downey has long been the executive secretary of the Radio and Television News Directors Association.

Because of its location near the state capitol, the station often puts together occasional networks for the governor's state-of-the-state ad-dress and for special legislative sessions. When Michigan was in the process of changing its state constitution, the station did extensive special coverage which it made available to stations all over the state. For such efforts as the latter and for many others, it has won signifi-cant awards, especially in the news and public affairs area.

While WKAR's staff size and efforts make it a large station by radio standards, especially by educational radio standards, it must use its resources carefully. To expand services it has increasingly had to look to outside sources of funding. Government, through the university appropriations, provides a base of financial support. Other support comes through program grants and through direct fund-raising. Special fund-raising weekends have been set aside to generate support from the listenership. The station has hired a full-time development director to aid in getting support for new programs and services.

WKAR is a vigorous and active broadcasting operation. Its program philosophy has been one of presenting matters of consequence without being stuffy or pretentious. It tries to be as slick and polished as any commercial station without resorting to gimmicks. The station makes use of humor and lighter material to balance the heavier material. Because of the programing variety and appeals to disparate groups, most people probably would not prefer to listen all day every day, yet something is offered for most in the audience every day, especially those willing to explore intellectually. The station is not afraid to experiment, nor is it afraid to fail, but a kind of caution is necessary for a station that is the public voice of a major university in the capitol city. The situation is at least as sensitive as dealing with any commercial enterprise.

WKAR is among the strong public radio stations in the nation. Some of the best stations are located in the upper Midwest. WUOM in Ann Arbor, WHA in Madison, and the WKAR stations are all atypical in that they command resources uncommon to educational or public radio. Yet, they are lightly funded compared with educational television and compared with the cost of reaching their audiences and extending the resources of the university in other ways.

Profile 8

Call Letters and Location: KSON–San Diego, California

Owner and Affiliation: Broadmoor Broadcasting Corporation—American Information Radio Network

Classification and Power: Class IV–1,000 w days, 250 w nights

KSON is a small country music station in San Diego that for several years has been one of the best advertising buys in the market. KSON has been so in spite of the fact that its news effort has been minimal; its signal of 250 watts has been one of the weakest signals in the market; its staff size has been small; its manager came into broadcasting with little experience; and relatively few country records have been sold in the market. The single factor that seems to have been the success ingredient for the station has been the type of music. Prior to "going country," the station had tried different formats, but other stations with more power and resources kept beating them in the ratings. KSON went country at a time when no other station in the market was programing that kind of music. It has continued to refine its format, to grow, and to gain in ratings and ad rate.

KSON's success has been followed by an increasing number of stations in other cities. Virtually every market of size in the nation has people who like the type of music and has enough of them to support a station. Even supposedly sophisticated markets such as San Francisco have country music stations that rate highly. KSON's is very much an "uptown country" sound. Boots, spurs, horses, and DJs with thick accents are out. Hee Haw and Grand Ol' Opry style and fiddles are out. Full orchestrations, Glen Campbell, urbanity, and tight production are in. KSON leans toward Top-40 in its music format approach and toward adult pop in its music selection and jingles, although most of the artists and songs are country. About sixty to seventy-five percent of the music is the same as that played on more traditional country stations. The difference is that KSON plays more popular music, both country-flavored rock and ballads with a country flavor. Music that would be liked by only those who like deep country music is avoided. KSON tries very hard to keep its roots in the country but to be very modern and to make its appeal as wide as possible. KSON hopes that its audience will include a good many who would in other markets be listening to adult pop stations.

The music format is very much like that of Top-40 stations. The play list is tight and varies in number according to the records available at a given time; the list contains generally fifty to seventy 45-rpm records. These are placed in five categories. Category I includes about a dozen records, all bright or moderate tempo, as middle-of-the-road as possible. Category II includes about a dozen upcoming or established hits in any tempo. Category III contains "hit-bounds," between ten and fifteen records that are expected to become popular. Category IV includes all other current records on the list. Oldies comprise Category V. Three of these are played each hour, and there are several hundred to choose from. Additionally, some albums are used. These include six to ten LPs, each of which may include three to six selections approved for play. The format specifies four separate sound-hours, all of which are fairly similar, and prescribes the order for play, such as a #1 followed by a "hit-bound," then a #2 followed by an album cut, and so on. The records on the list are not compiled strictly by record sales. As has been mentioned, San Diego is not a big country music record market, so the station considers record requests to be an important indicator. The record sequence includes "sweeps," or periods of uninterrupted music, each hour to give the impression of playing more music. Since the commercial policy is a maximum of eighteen minutes per hour, triple spots are played in heavily commercial time periods. Approximately fifteen to seventeen records are played per hour.

Talk is kept to a minimum. The DJs are told to keep comments brief. No absolute maximum time is set on comment between records, but no more than twenty to thirty seconds is ideal. DJs are limited on talk to one subject at a time.

News is from ABC. The station has little other news and no newsmen. Prior to the ABC news, a one-minute summary of local news is presented; news in depth is covered only as needed. Giving news in depth takes a special effort by the program director or other DJs. Station personnel have mixed feelings about the network news, but it is carried because the news is competently presented, it requires no local staff, and the station gets paid for carrying the news and network advertising. KSON employs a full-time editorial writer. The president of the company chooses the topics and has his writer research and write the editorials, which are aired as needed five times per day.

The format remains the same throughout the week except that from 6:00 A.M. to 12:30 P.M. on Sunday, paid religious programs and public service and public affairs programs are aired.

The station has a custom-made jingle package. The manager and program director created a tape of musical sounds from records that presented the kind of image the station was after. Along with preparing the tape, they wrote lyrics that also presented the image sought. They took both to a company that makes musical identifications, and the company wrote the original music, styled the arrangements, and recorded KSON's jingle package. These signatures are aired three times each hour.

KSON has a staff of fifteen. Its format has evolved into the modern country sound from one that was more traditional country. Its power was increased in 1971 to 1,000 watts. Among the male audience aged 25 to 49, the station is a leader in the market. For a good share of the advertisers who want to reach the people of San Diego, KSON is a wise buy.

Company president Don McKinnon has been active in the NAB and other organizations, and is the first broadcaster to be president of the Country Music Association.

Profile 9

Call Letters and Location: KWIX–Moberly, Missouri
Owner and Affiliation: Moberly Broadcasting Company–Independent
Classification and Power: Class IV–1 kw days, 250 w nights

The following speech[1] was presented to a radio assembly of the 1968 NAB Convention in Chicago. It outlines the approach of a small Midwestern station.

I am delighted to talk to you about how we are billing *$325,000* in a town of *13,000*. I have been asked, "How do you do it?" There is no "one" secret, nor are there any secrets. Even though there are no secrets, there are some key concepts which we operate by, and I can easily name them for you:

1. Our programing is sound. We are a service, news, and information type of operation with much community and area involvement. I will admit this is an expensive type of operation but this format garners the listeners—especially the right type of listeners; the business men. If the advertiser listens, he believes everyone listens. If the advertiser doesn't listen, he believes no one listens.

2. We are more of a sales organization than we are a programing operation. It could be said KWIX is a sales organization with the programing to support it. The sales ability brings us the income to do all the other things we want to do.

3. We most strongly believe we are a basic advertising medium rather than a supplemental advertising medium. By this I mean we believe we can do the whole and complete advertising job. Most of the local merchants in Moberly, Missouri, do their basic advertising job on the radio with no newspaper advertising, or use the newspaper as a supplemental medium.

4. We operate almost exclusively with half-minute spots rather than minute spots. This gives us almost twice the potential income compared to using minute spots.

---

[1] "Billing $325,000 in a Town of 13,000," a speech by Jerrell A. Shepherd, owner and manager of station KWIX. Reprinted by permission of the speaker.

5. We believe in the value of our product. Our rates have been continually raised. Our half-minute spots will average about $4.00 each.

6. We sincerely strive for item and price copy and do everything within our power to discourage and limit institutional copy, even to the point of refusing advertising. We feel we must move goods and services—every day, and in such a way the advertiser can check the results of his advertising, and only item and price copy can do that.

7. We operate on an area concept in both programing and sales. We almost deny we are a Moberly radio station. When we go into all of the surrounding towns to sell advertising we are not coming in as an outside radio station. We are their radio station. Half of our income is from outside Moberly.

8. Last, and certainly not least, we set goals: large overall long-range goals and also short-range or immediate goals. Goals to us are very important. I don't see how anyone can get anywhere if they don't know where they're going and how they're going to get there.

Now, if I may go into some of the details on these points.

On the subject concerning goals: we were not always doing $300,000 per year. In 1960, KWIX was billing an average of about $12,000 per month, which was as much or more than other stations in our size market. In January 1961, a very large long-range goal was established. It was a double goal. We were to establish KWIX as the finest small-market radio station in the nation, and as an intermediate part of that goal we were to increase our billing to $20,000 per month or $240,000 per year. It was believed this amount of billing would start us on our goal by providing the income to do it with. To become the finest small-market radio station in the nation we thought we should:

1. Do the most business.

2. Have the finest physical plant and equipment.

3. Have the best staff.

4. Render the finest and most service to our listeners and advertisers.

Some of these goals we have reached and some we haven't. We're still trying—all of us.

In a minute I will show you some figures. I'm not divulging any information to you today but what every staff member knows. We keep a so-called Manager's Book at the station, and every day we put the gross figures for the day in this book. A running total is there by the day, the week, and the month. Now this book is not hidden in my office. It is out front in the reception area, and everyone on the staff knows how much business we do. We also keep our books right on the program logs, and every spot and every program is priced on the log. This way we can set goals and have everyone on the team and knowledgeable of our goals—all the way from the manager to the custodian.

The increase from $12,000 per month to $20,000 per month was our largest step up the ladder, as this was almost doubling our business. This was done with no change in programing (we were already doing a good job in programing), no change in plant, and no change in equipment. It was done by a pure sales effort. We already had a flat rate card, and I believe it is essential to have either a flat rate card or a frequency discount card with a minimum spread. This keeps the large advertiser from buying out the station at a very cheap price and it also lets the small advertiser on without such a heavy penalty.

This goal of $20,000 per month was not wishful thinking on our part. We laid concrete plans to do it. This was not a private goal that I had. This was a goal in which the whole station as a team was to be involved.

I believed radio advertising was underpriced, especially when compared to newspapers, and newspapers were our main competition, at least in our area. A story was built up by using Starch reports on the readership of newspaper ads. By giving the newspapers everything they claimed and using our listenership figures, we came up with very sound figures that the local newspaper was delivering only twenty percent of what the radio station delivered for the same amount of money spent. Newspaper advertising cost five times as much as our radio advertising cost, by their own Starch reports. This story, with irrefutable proof, was hammered away at our staff, week after week. Not just the sales staff, but the whole staff. With the newspaper comparison we built up value in our advertising. It isn't too hard, you know, to go out and sell something for only twenty percent of what it's worth.

Sales training was given every day. A formal sales meeting was held every Saturday morning. These Saturday morning sessions were full-fledged training sessions with salesmen making dry pitches at almost every session. Training was given in collections. Salesmen were taught there was no neutral ground in collections—either an account was being taught "to" pay or, heaven forbid, the account was being taught "not" to pay. If we did not press for collections, we were actually training the account "not" to pay.

Perhaps the main sales concept we have, the one which has brought KWIX the furthest up the ladder, is the belief we are a basic and primary advertising medium rather than a supplemental advertising medium. Traditionally the newspapers have been the basic advertising medium, with radio taking the role as a supplemental medium. With this in mind, we never ask for half the advertising budget, or seventy-five percent of the budget. Always we ask for 100 percent of the budget, and we have a detailed plan to use 100 percent of the budget. A 100 percent advertiser is one of the best salesmen you can have. He can't admit he is spending his money foolishly.

I felt the greatest problem we and most radio stations had in the selling of advertising was the fact we didn't value it high enough ourselves. We didn't really believe in our own product. We did everything we could to convince the sales staff and the whole staff that radio was underpriced and that our advertising was worth more than we were asking for it. As I mentioned earlier, we used the newspaper comparison very heavily intra-staff. We did not use the newspaper story with the advertisers because the comparison was such we didn't believe the advertiser would believe it anyway and we didn't want to openly knock our competition. We used all the success stories we had to help us build up the value of our advertising.

There was one fly in the ointment. I, as the station manager, was giving away advertising in wholesale quantities as if it had no value, yet asking my salesmen to go out and sell it for hard cash. We were running a lot of public service announcements, non-commercial spot announcements. Nowhere in the FCC Regulations does it say you *have* to give away spot announcements. It just asks how many you *are* going to give away: and if you say you're going to give away some, you've got to do it.

We stopped the big giveaway. The newspapers weren't giving away display space. That's valuable. Spot announcements? Not really worth much, give 'em away.

Out comes the drive chairman for the Red Cross, and he has a packet of tremendous size. He has spot announcements. He has celebrity spots. He's got this and the other. He comes to the radio station and wants to know what we're going to do for him. Now in this packet it's explained to him in a little private slip that the radio station has to give away and is *obligated* to give away a lot of time: so he has come out to claim what rightfully belongs to him!

Well, I think this is an opportunity to be a good Joe, an opportunity to make some points with the FCC. I'm scared he's going to ask me for a hard cash donation; and if I can give him enough spots, maybe he won't ask for cash.

I ask him how long it's going to run. Well, it runs the whole month. How about ten spots a day, every day during the campaign? He thinks that's all right. He never listens to them, and I'm not really "giving" him anything. It's the government that's giving them to him. He's just come out to claim them. Ten spots a day, three hundred spots at $4; that's $1200 worth of advertising. Then he asks me what *else* I'm going to do for him. Well, I'll run his special programs, I'll do most anything. I'm going to be a hero downtown because I'm giving away *my* radio station.

He goes away thinking in his own mind the spots weren't really worth anything—and I actually hadn't given him anything. The government had given him the ads. He'd much rather have $100 cash donation than the $1200 worth of time I gave him. In other words, $1200 worth of spots was not worth $100 in cash.

Down at the newspaper he meets the Editor who says, "Hi, Charlie, we want to help you. We'd like to run a front-page news story on you and your drive, perhaps mention your lieutenants, like to give you a big story. Charlie, we need a picture. Got one?"

Charlie just happens to have one. What is the newspaper going to do for the Red Cross drive chairman? They're not going to GIVE him anything that he could buy. They don't give him display space, but they do give him something he can't buy—a front-page story with pictures.

With all that, we decided that we would operate like a newspaper. We would give them what they couldn't buy; but what they could buy, they'd have to pay for. We decided that, instead of running public service, we'd try being a public service. We'd give them stories, but spots? No, no, those things are *valuable* on our radio station: and they'd have to *pay* for those. It has worked beautifully. Our spot announcements are too valuable to give away.

We have since been relicensed twice, and each time in the box where the FCC asks how many non-commercial spot announcements we propose to run, we have placed a big, fat, round zero. No problems. We do our public service the hard way. We do it with news stories and interviews.

We think advertising copy is one of the real keys to the progress we have made. No strident commercials, no irritating horns, no whistles, and no echoes. Commercials, instead of irritating listeners, had to be informational and acceptable to the listener, because we were going to run a lot of them. These spots had to be good news as to where the new products were, where the best bargains were, and where the sales were going on. We had to move merchandise every day for the retailer. If he wanted institutional copy, this wouldn't move goods.

An advertiser is happy with his newspaper advertising whether it moves goods or not, because he saw it, knew about it, and was proud of it. When he saw it he believed everyone else did. Radio copy? He didn't hear his radio ads; so the radio ads had to produce and make the cash register ring every day. To do it, we had to have copy that had *items and prices* just like the newspaper did.

A great many stations will say, "Inventory type copy? How stupid can you get? You can never have over two or three items in a piece of copy, because no one can remember over two or three things."

They're right. If you're trying to remember a LOT of items, you can't. You can't remember items you're not interested in. If I mention ten items in a piece of copy and you're interested in two of these items, you can remember those two. And if I do mention ten items rather than two, I've created five times the opportunity to be effective.

Newspapers have proven this for about two hundred years. Almost all ads you see in the papers for department stores, grocery stores, drug stores, and so on, have a LOT of items because if they can get a reader on just one or two items, they've created a customer for the store.

People do remember what they're interested in.

Up to now nothing much has been said about programing. At KWIX our programing is no problem. If you've got the money coming in, programing is all set. You can have the mobile news crews; you can have as many telephones as you want; you can have all the equipment, a capable staff—the works.

That's what we've done. We've reversed the process at KWIX. We get the sales, and then we get better programing. If it's not good enough to be sold, it's not good enough to be broadcast. Let me give you a few figures that will show how good our sales-oriented programing turned out to be:

Year	Gross	Increase
1960	$146,697	$ 4,327
1961	172,523	25,826
1962	197,434	24,911
1963	236,199	38,765
1964	268,162	31,963
1965	272,887	4,725
1966	293,797	20,910
1967	325,357	31,560

Our rise up the revenue ladder is due largely to our KWIXLAND area concept. There are two basic reasons: First, the wider the area in which a station operates, the greater the sales base you establish; and secondly, close-in advertisers realize a greater effectiveness from the advertising that reaches the outlying listeners.

What greater psychological effect can you have on a close-in advertiser than for him to hear other businesses perhaps thirty or fifty miles away using the station? Our essential element is that KWIX creates the image of being a basic advertising buy for all of KWIXLAND.

In all of this, you must have a sales staff sufficient in size to get the job done. For operating as an area station, this is a must. At KWIX we have six salesmen.

The thirty-second spot was perhaps one of the most important single moves we ever made. After we reached $20,000 a month in a small market, our logs became a real problem. We were holding to the NAB Code and we still do, but it got a little rough. Salesmen began to squabble over availabilities. Advertisers wanted additional spot packages, and we were sold out. It was a happy feeling to be sold out but a bad spot to be in, for we had no place to go.

We set up a trial period of about two months to see if, in our minds, we could effectively boil down our price and item copy to half-minutes. We found out that we could, because we quickly learned that in the majority of cases the longer copy just repeated and was redundant. The short copy was harder to write, but it turned out doing a better job for the advertiser.

So we decided to go half-minutes only. We didn't change the rate card; we just shortened the spots to thirty seconds. You see, our rate card had said "up *to* one minute," and the majority of our spots weren't a minute anyway. We did have a few, but most of them were about forty seconds. So a lot of advertisers really didn't know the difference when we switched. We just had a little harder job writing copy.

In switching to half-minutes only, we had, in one fell swoop, twice as many availabilities, twice as much business opportunities, and still do as good a job, and usually better, for our advertisers. Now we run our spots in two's. Some people call them "back-to-back." We call it "clusters of two." We thought this might prove wrong, that there might be clutter; but it has worked fine. When the income flows in, many problems disappear. When business is low and money problems arise, the mole hills rise up and become mountains.

To sum up, we are not billing $325,000 *in* a town of 13,000. We are billing $325,000 *from* a town of 13,000, in a market of 80,000 people in what we call KWIXLAND.

The billing was built on a solid belief that radio is the greatest and lowest-cost advertising medium there is and we in the radio business are not second-class citizens but first-class citizens.

It was built on the belief that radio can do the primary and basic advertising job and that no newspaper advertising is needed other than occasionally as a supplementary medium.

It was built on the premise that radio advertising must not be institutional but of the type that will ring the cash register every day in such a way that the advertiser can check his results every day.

It was built around the whole staff knowing of our goals, being on the team, believing in our methods of operation, taking pride in our *station* leadership in the area, and believing solidly that our advertising was far underpriced and that no one in his right mind, who was fully informed, would spend his advertising money elsewhere.

It was built by no magic formula nor because the community was any more progressive than any others. It was built by hard work and a determined effort.

It was built on the development of a fine sales staff and a fine programing staff.

It was built by plowing back much of our earnings into programing after we achieved our earlier sales goals.

The authors of this book do not believe that KWIX is more of a sales organization than a programing operation. If the station did not have good programing, it never would have been able to sell it. It is obvious, though, that Mr. Shepherd knows how to sell as well as program a radio station. By 1970, the station's billing had gone over $400,000 per year. It has continued steadily upward.

Mr. Shepherd believes that most radio stations do not sell their advertising time for what it is worth. By underpricing it, stations are giving the advertisers the impression that what the stations have to offer is not worth much.

One reason for the dramatic increases in advertising revenue at KWIX was that station management realized the product was underpriced and that a positive sales psychology could be established with a more expensive product. Years ago, the station began to program its news on the half-hour, believing that many people went to work on the hour in the morning and that, by placing the news on the half-hour, these people could hear the news just before going to work. For a long time, the station charged six dollars for sponsorship of the 15-minute 7:30 A.M. news. Eventually, another dollar was added to the price of newscasts. KWIX also sold adjacent spot announcements as fixed-position spots. Long-term advertisers got preference for these preferred positions. When the station found out that one of its sponsors of a fixed-position spot next to the news had been offered $1,000 by another business to give up that position, the management of the station decided that it was underpricing its goods. So the price of sponsorship of the news was raised to $15. The sponsor could not accept the price of his sponsorship being doubled, so he canceled, but another sponsor quickly was found. Then, station management did some calculating. It noted that a full-page ad in the local newspaper cost $160. Feeling that the station's time was worth as much as that page in the newspaper, management decided it needed to get more money for time. The station changed the newscast from a 15-minute cast to one 20 minutes in length and told the sponsor that it was not available for sponsorship any longer, but that the station would sell him a 30-second spot in the newscast for eight dollars. He bought it. Nine other half-minute spots were put into the newscast and were all sold. In a fairly short time, the rate on the newscast had been changed from six dollars for full sponsorship to eight dollars per spot. Management realized that the station had been underselling itself and that clients were less interested in extremely cheap advertising than they were in effective advertising. Clients were willing to pay as long as the advertising did the job for them.

KWIX, with a staff size of twenty-five, seven of them salesmen, has an energetic program schedule that is strong on information. It plays adult pop music, mostly vocal. Its music policy is the result of a very extensive music-preference study of listeners in the area. On the station's twentieth anniversary, it played only records made before 1950. The oldies were so well received that the station decided to devote every Monday to old music only.

The station does extensive news programing. Ten-minute summaries are given at 5:30 and 6:00 A.M. Between 6:30 and 9:00 A.M., programing is almost entirely news and information. The news is heavily local and regional. Market summaries include direct hog-market reports from St. Louis, a five-minute obituary roundup, twenty minutes of sports news, features, and syndicated features such as those of Norman Vincent Peale and Earl Nightingale. Weather information is extensive, and, in fact, the station has three meteorologists who specialize in presenting the weather in a way that is knowledgeable and readily understood by the listeners. Other information that is programed throughout the day includes a segment about auction sales, a telephone trading post, a hospital report with telephoned information from the area hospitals, a baby report telling of the births throughout the coverage area, county agent reports, and extensive agricultural information. Occasionally, reports are given by high school coaches throughout the area. The station has a party-line visiting program. KWIX does a tremendous number of live broadcast originations. In 1976, it did 350 live remotes, mostly of sporting events.

Profile 10

Call Letters and Location: WBAI–FM–New York, New York

Owner and Affiliation: WBAI–FM, Inc. (Pacifica)–Independent

Classification and Power: Class B–5.4 kw horizontal, 3.85 kw vertical

WBAI–FM claims to be an unorthodox radio station. It is. WBAI–FM is frequently different just for the sake of being different. Very often, the station is one of the most pseudointellectual, dull, and inconsequential radio stations on the air. At other times, it is simply remarkable. When the station is good, it can be very good. But a listener never knows when he tunes in which it is going to be. Unlike many stations, WBAI–FM is not afraid to gamble.

In late 1970, WBAI–FM aired a special—Leo Tolstoy's *War and Peace* was read from cover to cover. Not long after that, the station played the complete works of Beethoven. Regular listeners to the station also might have heard: "Dinner with the John Birch Society," an hour program detailing current views of the society; a regularly scheduled half-hour of homosexual news; Wagner's *Ring* cycle in its entirety; three lectures by Herbert Marcuse; "Songs of Love and Revolution"; the writings of Edgar Allan Poe; "Your Mother Should Know," one night featuring the songs of Irving Berlin; "Conversations with the Silent Majority"; a tribute to Paul Robeson; "Jazz, Etc."; and "Bill Monroe and the Bluegrass Boys." Other features were "Highlights of the First Dinner of the Black Academy of Arts and Letters"; a commentary on Jewish affairs; "Sunlight on the Snow," a program featuring the voices of American G.I. deserters in Sweden; music from the Mississippi delta; Lawrence Ferlinghetti reading from his published poetry; a two-hour tribute to Billie Holliday; a replay of a 1964 speech by Malcolm X; "The Nude Theatre"; Vietnamese poetry; a dramatic presentation of *The Tragical History of Dr. Faustus;* "The Free Voice of Greece"; children's theater presentations; a half-hour of comedy by Jonathan Winters; and Sex Day, among others. A landmark legal case over the station's airing of George Carlin's routine about seven forbidden words upset FCC obscenity rules, in a 1977 decision.

WBAI–FM considers itself an alternative medium. It is dedicated to presenting, in its own words, "the unusual, the unpopular, the unaccepted, and the unique." It is noncommercial. The station manages to come up with its budget of roughly $500,000 per year from donations from "subscribers" who can receive the station's program guide, the *Folio,* if they give $25 per year ($15 for students and retired people). The station has received foundation money for capital outlay but prefers to get by on the subscriber donations for operating revenue, because that gives them freedom to present anything they want, without strings attached. About sixty percent of the air time is given to public affairs in the form of hard news, discussion programs, and special documentaries. The remaining forty percent is devoted to drama and literature; a wide variety of music, including live concerts; open-mike and interview shows; and children's programing. The station produces original radio dramas and adaptations.

For ten years, WBAI operated out of one studio, one production room, and one announcer's booth in a converted townhouse. The teletypewriters were in the bathroom. In 1971, the station moved to larger facilities in a deconsecrated church. The staff of thirty-five is supplemented by about twenty-five volunteer producers and technical and clerical volunteers. The station personnel more than once have had to wait beyond payday for their paychecks.

The facilities, while not plush, provide an adequate broadcast facility. The station has an auditorium for original dramatic and musical productions or teach-ins, with space for live audiences. It also has two additional studios and four production booths, other booths for listening and editing, and space to house the tape archives, which are used to save programs for resource or rebroadcast or to provide copies to schools, libraries, individuals, and other stations.

The station offers an affiliation program which provides, for a fee, a certain number of hours of programing. WBAI also has black production centers in the planning stages, modeled after a pilot program in Watts, Los Angeles. A modest radio journalism program and consultant service for students operating their own stations also are run by the station.

WBAI is part of the Pacifica Foundation, a nonprofit corporation licensed under the laws of California. The first station, KPFA, was licensed in Berkeley in 1949 and was followed by KPFK in Los Angeles in 1953. WBAI, at the time a commercial station, was donated by its sole stockholder to the Pacifica Foundation in 1960. It is now the Pacifica station that attracts the most money. Another Pacifica station, KPFT, is located in Houston; it was bombed off the air in 1970, but it returned to the air a few weeks later. The foundation was founded by pacifist and poet-journalist Lewis Hill in 1949.

The group frequently has been discussed by the FCC for alleged obscenity, for its liberal politics, and for other provocative programing. The FCC continues to renew the licenses. In its 1964 renewal, the commission stated, "We recognize that provocative programing as here involved may offend some listeners. But this does not mean that those offended have the right, through the Commission's licensing power, to rule such programing off the airwaves. Were this the case, only the wholly inoffensive, the bland could gain access to the radio microphone or TV camera." The U.S. Supreme Court stated, in a 1969 decision upholding the FCC's "Fairness Doctrine," "It is the purpose of the First Amendment to preserve the uninhibited marketplace of ideas in which truth will ultimately prevail, rather than to countenance monopolization of that market whether it be by the government itself or a private licensee. . . . It is the right of the public to receive suitable access to social, political, esthetic, moral and other ideas and experiences which is crucial here. That may not be constitutionally abridged either by Congress or by the FCC."

The station's news consists of a newscast plus shop talk with guest journalists and coverage of the day's events in New York City, which lasts an hour starting at 6:15 A.M. daily. Other newscasts are aired at

9:00 A.M. and 10:45 P.M. The station subscribes to AP, UPI, the British news service, Reuters, and the French Press Agency. The news producer also uses such sources as the *Newark News, Baltimore Sun, Washington Post, St. Louis Post–Dispatch, New York Times, New York Daily News, New York Post, Wall Street Journal,* various college papers, and France's *Le Monde* and *Le Figaro,* which he translates himself.

The station has presented, from its deconsecrated church or from a Shakespeare theatre in Greenwich Village, free concerts that are recorded for broadcast. These are called The Free Music Store. Music ranges from bluegrass to chamber music to jazz rock. As one example, Igor Kipnis played to a packed house with a harpsichord recital that ranged from Bach and Scarlatti to Ned Rorem. The concerts are given on a hit-or-miss basis, depending upon whether any performer is available.

The station programs twenty-one hours a day, if the morning man starts his 7 A.M. program on time. The twenty-one hours are the most varied in American radio as to type and quality. The program schedule is arrived at through negotiation between the program director and the producers. The program director has the ultimate responsibility, but he has a *laissez-faire* attitude uncommon to most organized activities. The people who work there do not do so for the money. Most could do better elsewhere. They keep working there because they have an opportunity for expression, a freedom seldom found, and a feeling that the station belongs to them. The programing is not static. The schedule changes frequently. The station's staff is mostly young (averaging about 25 years), bearded, and in leotards. They work among furniture donated by a local union and sympathetic listeners, among beat-up desks and room dividers that consist of tapes stacked almost randomly, it seems, on shelves of old boards held up by cement blocks. Volunteers and hangers-on come and go, and the sign at the exit reminds all to close the door so that the cat will not get out.

The station does not know for sure the size of its listening audience. It believes it reaches about 600,000 people regularly. Nearly 14,000 people subscribe to the station and receive the *Folio.* The only research the station has done was to include a questionnaire in the *Folio.* About 3,000 replies were received. There is no statistical basis for believing that the subscribers are a good cross section of listeners, or that respondents to the questionnaire are representative either, but the survey results indicated that the listeners were mostly between 12 and 40 years of age, with the most heavy concentration between 17 and 25. The respondents consider themselves mostly apolitical or left of center politically. Few blue-collar workers or executives responded, but a disproportionately large number of artists did.

The station has never taken an editorial stand, but it has provided a platform for the Ku Klux Klan and Black Power advocates, the Nazi-based American Renaissance Party and the Communist-oriented Progressive Labor Party, and William F. Buckley and Herbert Apthecker. It has premiered sonatas written by computers and Arlo Guthrie's "Alice's Restaurant." It has featured unfrocked priests and anti-Zionist rabbis. Regular commentators have included Ayn Rand and black socialist Conrad Lynn.

The station does not present commercials, yet when funds are low it may spend more time asking for donations than the most crass commercial station would use for commercials. Times frequently have looked bleak for the station. It has had to cut back on staff. The staff has taken voluntary salary cuts. Yet, in spite of such temporary setbacks, WBAI keeps building and growing. It continues to attract capable and dedicated people. It continues to do unorthodox, outrageous, and marvelous programs. Some staff members have been known to answer the telephone, "WBAI, the world's worst radio station," and announcers have used the phrase on the air. At times, it well may be just that. On balance, it is a remarkable radio station.

Profile 11

Call Letters and Location: KSFO–San Francisco, California

Owner and Affiliation: Golden West Broadcasters–Independent

Classification and Power: Class III-A–5 kw days, 1 kw nights

For many years leading up into the late '60s, KSFO was very much the dominant radio station in San Francisco, a city with a lot of very good radio stations. It had the best and happiest sounding air personalities, the most sports exclusives, the most fun air promotions, the largest total audience, the best demographics, and the highest ad rates. It seemed that every radio station in town and a good share of radio's brightest and best went against them in head-to-head competition. KSFO always came out on top. It didn't seem to matter that NBC owned KNBR and had 50,000 watts of power, or that CBS owned KCBS and had 50,000 watts of power, or that Metromedia went all out with KNEW, or that others sold AM–FM combinations against them.

J. P. McCarthy, who was Detroit's top-rated deejay, was hired by a competitor. After a few rating books, he went back to Detroit, where he was again that town's top-rated air personality. He could not beat KSFO and Don Sherwood. KCBS finally went all-news. KNBR tried several things. KNEW finally went country. KFRC, owned by RKO–

General, had been a close carbon of KSFO in the early 60's, couldn't win, and eventually went Top-40. KGO, owned by ABC, had tried the KSFO format but couldn't beat them in the ratings and ended up going telephone talk. The KSFO air personalities could actually ride a cable car to work, to studios in the Fairmont Hotel on Nob Hill. From the Fairmont you can look northwest to the Golden Gate bridge, north across the bay toward Sausalito and Tiburon, east to the Transamerica Tower and beyond the Bay Bridge to the Oakland Hills—in all directions the romance of the hills and the lights and the water. The program director could have spent all day every day just talking to the people from San Francisco's other stations and stations all over who would like to work there. Owner Gene Autry's reputation for running a friendly, family business didn't hurt, either. For a few years there was a kind of magical chemistry, a blending of ingredients in such a way that the whole was greater than the sum of the parts. Those who worked at the station understood the town, the times, what radio was about. Of course, not everybody listened. There were too many other good stations for that. But more people listened more often to KSFO than to anything else, and if you were an advertiser wanting to reach an adult audience, the demographics were what you wished every station could offer. Then things began to change.

The station was and is competent in its news coverage. No doubt news has always been important to many who would tune in KSFO. KCBS went all-news, all the time, and did it very well.

The station had sports exclusives. The baseball Giants had moved from New York. They had Willie Mays and a fine team, were constant pennant contenders, and created excitement. KSFO had the Giants. The other stations in town didn't. Then Charlie Finley moved his Athletics from Kansas City. The Giants finished in the second division. They sold Willie Mays (and Marichal and McCovey), and the fans thought that team owner Horace Stoneham wasn't doing enough, and they decided that Candlestick was a lousy ball park, and pretty soon the two teams weren't drawing what the Giants once had. And KSFO broadcasts weren't drawing like they once had, either. KSFO had the football Forty-Niners, exclusive. Then came the Oakland Raiders, and they became winners. Again KSFO had to share audience.

KSFO had the music. They always played from a wide spectrum of popular music, and they couldn't please everybody with each selection, but you felt that each program was carefully selected by the person who was sharing it with you. You felt that there was a sense of taste, that you were current with what was happening, and that there was artistry and substance about much of the music. It was light and fun, there were surprises, and if things weren't just perfect on a given day you knew that in the long run you would not be disappointed. The air personalities actually picked their own music. There was a pattern, a consistency, but nothing like a formula. It was free-form, but controlled. There were current hits, oldies, a lot of pieces from albums (and not always the same cut from the same album). Deejays were chosen because they were capable of programing the music as well as entertaining and reading the commercials. Then the music changed. The record companies greatly de-emphasized standard artists and tunes and those artists that have a broad appeal to adult audiences. While singles had always been dominated by young people, the albums had been more diverse and were bought mostly by adults. In the '60s the record companies realized that not everybody buys records and that those who could be most easily sold were the young. They put their greatest emphasis on those songs and artists who would appeal to teens and college-age people, with incredible financial success. Some radio stations followed suit. The San Francisco rock sound was followed by what is considered the first "underground" (later progressive) radio station, KMPX. In the past, young people, once they got tired of Top-40 KYA, grew into KSFO. Progressive KSAN and others offered them another stop and five more years of radio listening before many of them might be KSFO listeners. Further, the record companies weren't turning out as many records for KSFO to choose from. Music selection became more and more difficult.

Competition became tougher from other directions. San Francisco has always been a good FM town, and the FM musical competition made inroads with more soothing strings and fewer commercials. KLOK in San Jose began to play all oldies. The audience became divided up among more stations.

KSFO had the highest-paid and best air people. They came to KSFO and they stayed. There was stability other stations lacked. Don Sherwood became a morning legend. His success may not have transferred to New York or New Orleans or Detroit, but more San Franciscans woke up to his unpredictable, funny, sarcastic program than to anybody else's. To many he *was* San Francisco radio. A man-child, he quit the station at least every year. He'd go to Hawaii, or live on a boat, or take over the job of hosting a network TV show, or pioneer a deejay show on UHF television, but he always came back in a short time to renew his love affair with the listeners. Never easy for management to deal with, the longer he worked and the greater his success became, the more it became clear that it would have to end some time. The last time he came back he was made program director. The station is still recovering. About this time a combination of events had led to great staff turnover. In the past, Sherwood would come and go, and occasionally some other air personality would leave and be replaced, but the transitions were generally orderly and evolutionary. This time, the station had to try to quickly stabilize, to come up with new staff, new programing policies, and a new program director to restore it to ratings prominence.

What we have today is a station no longer able to dominate the market but one trying to be the top-rated station among its target audience, adults aged 25 to 49. It consistently ranks among the top five stations in total audience and is relatively stronger among adults than in total audience. Air personalities have less control over their own shows, since the music has become more controlled and formularized, even to the point of using computerized data retrieval and sequencing. Personalities are still highly important, as are news and sports.

The air personalities are not time-temperature jocks. They are expected to prepare material for their shows, to communicate and entertain. Humor is a strength of the station. The overall tone is happy and fun, with interesting programing and talk complementing the music. They have done things like the "Amateur Minute." People could call in and perform for sixty seconds—much humor and audience involvement. Morning host Jim Lange has done a number of network and syndicated television shows, flying from San Francisco to Los Angeles to tape the TV shows and back for KSFO mornings.

Nighttime radio breaks format, in that the same music–news–personality approach used in the daytime is not followed. Other stations around the country that appeal primarily, like KSFO, to the broad adult audience have found that they do very well in morning drive time, relatively a little less well in afternoon drive time, and that their daytime audience primarily watches television at night. In order to compete at night when there are no play-by-play sports, something different is needed that is as much an alternative to television as to other radio. Some have gone to telephone talk during the evening. KSFO has a unique package, at least in part. From 7 to midnight, John Gilliland hosts a combination of rare music, comedy, and drama. In San Francisco, CBS's KCBS is all-news and does not want to break format to carry the *CBS Mystery Theater*. KSFO airs it from 8:05 to 9. At 9:05, The Golden Age of Radio features dramas and series of the '30s and '40s. At 10:05, the comedy hour uses recorded humor. Sandwiched around are *The Pop Chronicles*, some of which have been syndicated and made available to other stations.

KSFO usually has some event going that is fun and unique. It may be an individual effort by an air personality or a total station effort. Some involve contests or station promotions, although big money contests are less appealing than something humorous or unusual that involves the audience. Gene Nelson and Rick Cimino had a hot-air balloon race from Sausalito to Berkeley. Newspapers, TV, and even rival radio station KGO covered the race (KGO live by helicopter). That the wind blew the wrong way and they didn't come close to

Berkeley didn't matter. Different air personalities have broadcast from yachts and harbor cruise ships. They held a contest for listeners to write, in twenty-five words or less, "Why I want to go to Los Angeles." First prize was a week in Los Angeles. Second prize was two weeks in Los Angeles (they did it when it was a new joke). Listeners and air personalities had a lot of fun with the San Francisco–LA rivalry. One April Fools' Day, one of the air personalities took a tape recorder with him on a cable car ride, along with figures of famous people borrowed from a wax museum, and recorded reactions of people who were fooled.

One long-running campaign centered around the slogan "KSFO Loves You." The station gave away two million badges that said "KSFO Loves You." Spotters went through the community giving prizes to people wearing the badges. They also had other variations, like bumper stickers. On the station's 50th anniversary, in 1975, they told their listeners that the first 3,500 people who wrote in would get free tickets to celebrate with station personalities and staff at Marine World/Africa USA. Six 60-second announcements were scheduled in twenty-four hours. Ten thousand people wrote for tickets. Air personalities participated in the amusement park shows, and guests shared a giant sundae stacked into a 600-pound dish.

Public service campaigns each year raise funds for charities. KSFO was one of the first to sponsor a charity baseball game, with its air personalities playing the Playboy Bunnies. Other stations followed with bunnies and stewardesses, so KSFO changed to a game between station personnel and San Francisco VIPs. The game, called the PAL game, has filled the Cow Palace, and proceeds go to the Police Athletic League. Since 1960, they have aided the San Francisco Fire Fighters Toy Chest Program at Christmas time. In addition to on-air appeals, KSFO entertainers and others (such as a group from Disneyland) have entertained in Bay area shopping centers to help in the toy donations.

The station has had several jingle packages custom-made for it. One of them may be the best set of musical signatures that any radio station has ever had. It is the "Sounds of the City" package, which has captured the sound and feeling of San Francisco in such a way that listeners can get the impression that it expresses the identity of the whole city. One a cappella song in the series has such a lovely melody and lyrics that station listeners request it, and records of the jingle have sold in music stores. The jingles were syndicated and used in other markets with different lyrics but did not seem to fit anywhere else as well as San Francisco.

The sports play-by-play line-up includes Giants baseball, Forty-Niner and Stanford football, ten-minute sportscasts at 5:45 daily, and extensive coverage of sports news and scores throughout the day.

Regular news on the hour (mostly five minutes) and headlines on the half-hour use both major wire services and the Golden West Washington news bureau. Drive-time newscasts are ten minutes long in the mornings, and an afternoon news block goes from 5:30 to 6:03. Station editorials, documentaries, and special reports are presented as coverage warrants. An airplane and mobile cars are used for traffic reports and news coverage. A minority affairs department prepares comment and information pieces from a black perspective—one-minute drop-ins that work like commercials do, "selling" information about minorities.

The staff of sixty people is large but not excessive, considering all they do, and also considering that sister station KMPC in Hollywood uses more than one hundred with a similar format.

The KSFO music policy, as expressed by program director Vic Ives, follows.

> KSFO has the San Francisco sound! It reaches out and touches people. Our music involves listeners with it and our personalities. KSFO music is up front fun, adult, and entertaining. It provides a showcase for our personalities, our client's messages, and reflects the tempo of the times!
>
> KSFO music is designed for the 25–49 audience with appeal to listeners both above and below that primary target audience.
>
> The key is a carefully calculated and controlled balance of new, recent, and older *familiar* music. This music is blended in prescribed percentages to provide maximum appeal to as large an audience as possible. The music is balanced insofar as possible to bridge the "generation gap" without causing tune-out on either side of the target.
>
> KSFO plays the best of current popular music and artists of the broadest spectrum on the San Francisco radio dial. The older selections are million sellers, standards, and bona fide all-time hits.
>
> The KSFO music criteria screen out records with a high irritation quotient. The basic components of each KSFO music hour (based on up to 14 records per hour, most hours) are:
>
> > Current KSFO hits—5 per hour (every 3rd selection 24 hours a day) PRE SELECTED by title and artist from a list of 40 records which are played in a cross vertical rotation. (Repeated the next day within two hours—example: 6–7 AM Monday, 9–10 Tuesday, etc.)
> >
> > RECENT HITS—3 per hour PRE SELECTED by title from a list of 50–55 KSFO hits of the past 6–8 months.
> >
> > ALL TIME HITS—2 per hour selected from a list of 999 approved oldies (carted) played in a ratio of 1970s–30%, 1960s–30%, 1950s–30% and 1940s–10%.

NEW LP CUTS—2 per hour selected from approximately 30 albums of mostly familiar artists with specific cuts approved for play.

STANDARDS—1 per hour selected from the extensive KSFO library. (Selected for timeless appeal and for the upper end demographic.)

WILD CARD—1 per hour, deejay choice. (Selected for variety.)

KSFO uses the BILLBOARD easy listening top 40 and the GAVIN ROCKLESS list for REFERENCE only, and in return reports to them both weekly at their request. Records are scheduled based on what contribution the record will contribute to the BALANCE of our play list.

KSFO does not use record sales as a criterion for creating our play list, as we don't consider the record-buying public as generally reflective of our target audience. We are more concerned with calls *from* record stores about records we are playing which are causing requests, comments, and inquiries.

KSFO is frequently the first station in the market to program selections which we feel will be enjoyed by our listeners. Nearly all of these eventually make the charts, which is an indication of our sensitivity to the interests and needs of our audience.

Our sound is totally unique to KSFO and is blended to suit the taste of the market and complement the KSFO image and our concept of foreground entertainment-oriented programing.

Program Director Ives believes in a wide spectrum of pop music but avoids hard rock and music that he believes would alienate a general audience. He points to a number of major studies of music taste which show great variation between music tastes and record sales. Also, that medium which is the most "mass" of all mass media, television, has never had a successful prime-time show based on hard rock music. The station tries to be current but emphasizes melody and musicianship where possible.

Few stations have dominated their market the way KSFO once did in San Francisco. That KSFO no longer does so is due to the fact that the competition has become more sophisticated. KSFO has had some internal problems that diluted its strength while the competition was getting tougher, and changing times and the fragmented audience make it difficult to regain such dominance. KSFO does many of the same things that other stations in other markets do, but not many have the quality in news, personalities, humor, and sports that KSFO has. One reason the station has such high-quality personnel is the romance of living and working in San Francisco. In other cities, you can't ride a cable car to work. KSFO air personalities have been

known to say (not more than ten or fifteen times a day), "You're listening to the world's greatest radio station, KSFO in San Francisco." That
may not be true, and they do say it with tongue in cheek, but they also
sound as if believing it is not so far-fetched.

Profile 12

Call Letters and Location: WFMT–Chicago, Illinois
Owner and Affiliation: WFMT, Inc.–Independent
Classification and Power: Class B–45 kw

WFMT does not make compromises and would rather lead public
taste than reflect it. WFMT allows no singing jingles or even recorded
commercials and schedules only four commercials per hour. The
station programs only classical music and other fine arts programing.
The station has only one salesman. Yet, it is considered to be among
the top-rated of all Chicago FM stations. It also has one of the highest
advertising rates. The station has won the Peabody, DuPont, Ohio State,
Edison, Prix Italia, Armstrong, and other top awards. The station also
publishes the city's bestselling local publication. (It is said, perhaps
apocryphally, that the only two Chicago-based magazines not in financial trouble are *Playboy* and the *WFMT Guide.*) Not many stations
have WFMT's integrity, fidelity, or success.

WFMT considers itself an entertainment station primarily. It believes the audience to be intelligent, with high standards, and it tries
to talk *to* the listener, not up to him or down to him. The program
schedule consists of one continuous program—informal, without
themes and elaborate introductions, and not packaged or segmented.
The station tries to present serious music intelligently without being
pompous. It tries to inject humor without being overly cute. The station is flexible about time and tries to integrate the various elements.
It does not play the same kind of music every day at the same time.
The announcers do not work the same shift every day, except that the
all-night program host does not work other shifts. Other features do
run at about the same time every day, such as the news and Studs
Terkel's hour of talk and features. Every Saturday from 10:00 P.M. to
1:00 A.M., a program called "The Midnight Special" is presented, which
is a potpourri of folk music, comedy, and other items. Other programs
include the Boston Symphony Orchestra concerts, chamber music
concerts from the Library of Congress in Washington, D.C., recordings of live performances by Chicago groups, operas from Radio

Italiana, and concerts from the BBC, Holland, France, Germany, Canada, and numerous other countries. All of these are features of one continuous program on WFMT. About seventy percent of the programing is music, chosen from the station's library of 100,000 selections and the aforementioned sources. About fifteen percent of the programing is news. The remaining fifteen percent consists of drama, literature, discussion, folk music, humor, and musical comedy. Included are occasional BBC World Theatre presentations, Gilbert Highet's "People, Places and Books," among others.

The station airs eleven to fourteen daily newscasts edited from Associated Press and city news bureaus. Newscasts average twelve minutes in length but vary according to the amount and the importance of the news. In the morning, newscasts are forty-five minutes apart and average seven minutes in length. Throughout the rest of the day, the news is broadcast approximately every three hours and averages about fifteen minutes, although the news may run twenty minutes or more on a hot news day. The announcer also has been known to report, "There really isn't anything of significance in today's news; here is the weather." The station does not chase fire engines. It tries to report only the significant, that which will make a dent in history. WFMT listeners are more apt to hear about the actions of the Supreme Court than a robbery, a school board meeting before a car wreck.

The station really does not have a news department. The music announcers also do the news. But they are serious about the news, and they have more time than the standard DJ who has to integrate eighteen spots, fifteen 2½-minute records, and a personality into his program. They present the news rather than report it, and they present almost no actuality reports. The newscasts are presented intelligently, calmly, and without commercial interruption. They try to be thorough without being wordy. The station does not editorialize.

WFMT will interrupt the regular programing for bulletins. It was one of the first stations to announce the Senate's rejection of Harold Carswell's nomination to the Supreme Court. The announcement of a Nobel Prize winner would be considered bulletin material, as would many other significant but not necessarily sensational events. Also, the station carries all major presidential news conferences.

The music is mostly scheduled by the program director, although the 6 A.M. to 9 A.M. segment is improvised by the announcer on duty. Since the five announcers rotate, the segments will vary according to the personality of the host. The morning segment includes shorter, brighter selections than those at other times. The announcers are personal but do not make a big issue of giving their names and the show titles at each change of shift. They do give their names on occasion; they do have identity. But they try not to force it.

The music includes fewer selections from the common repertoire than many serious music stations play. The station plays a higher proportion of newer music and pieces seldom heard. The station makes personal statements with its musical selection. It tries to influence the direction of public taste.

WFMT sells program sponsorship as well as spots. The limit of four minutes per hour also includes one-hour protection from competitive accounts. The station claims it turns down more clients than it accepts. All spots are either rewritten or edited by station personnel. All are low-key in presentation. WFMT has two rates—one for standard advertisers and a lower rate for cultural advertisers. The lower-rate spots can be pre-empted, and program sponsorship takes preference over spots. The station designates two time classifications—*A* and *B*. *A* time is Monday through Friday from 6 A.M. to 9 A.M. and 5 P.M. to midnight, and Saturday and Sunday from 6 A.M. to midnight. Class *B* time is Monday through Friday from 9 A.M. to 5 P.M. Midnight to 6 A.M. has been sold on a five-year, half-million dollar contract to a financial institution. During that time period, the sponsor has requested only one commercial per hour, even though he could have four. The selling is done by one salesman, the station manager, and national and regional reps. Not many radio stations can be almost entirely sold out with only one full-time salesman.

The promotion effort consists of low-key, on-air reminders about upcoming program features, unusual help from the print media (the station is the darling of the press), and the *WFMT Guide*. The station also has exceptionally good sales promotion brochures and handouts that tell a success story effectively and impressively.

The *WFMT Guide* is much more than a program guide. It has become the city magazine. Although magazine competitors have tried to serve the area with publications that offered articles on local issues and events including entertainment and eating-out guides, all have folded. The *Guide* contains WFMT's program schedule, including a list of musical selections to be programed. It also gives the schedule of educational television channels 11 and 20. It includes articles about the arts and Chicago, a list of interesting places to visit, a selective dining guide, an entertainment guide (especially cultural), and advertising. The magazine is published monthly, costs five dollars per year, and makes a profit. The station manager is the publisher.

The station started in 1951 with a small budget and high standards. (The first announcer hired was Mike Nichols.) Since 1958, the station has been in the black. The staff has grown to twenty-five. When founder Bernard Jacobs' health began to decline, he decided to hand-pick the group to whom he would sell. He chose WGN Continental Broadcasting to continue the tradition he had started. WGN is affiliated with the *Chicago Tribune*. Although WGN's stations are among the best run in the country, the proposed sale to the conservative *Tribune* worried many of the more liberal members of the community. A campaign was conducted against the sale in hopes that the FCC would not approve it, but the sale was approved. WGN put about $250,000 into the station, improving its physical plant, before donating the station to the Chicago Educational Television Association. Now, the ownership is by a nonprofit association, but the station's policies remain as commercial and as lucrative as ever. Profits go to further educational television in Chicago. The radio station retains its same management and policies. It also retains the same quality staff, which has seen little turnover. The station is nonunion. The manager and program director both do programs, and the staff has freedoms it would not have in a union shop.

Station management feels that entertainment and fun are needed in the radio station. The station manager and program director, while encouraging the announcers to provide lighter moments throughout the program day, are themselves alternate hosts of the Saturday "Midnight Special." This show is filled with programing that either does not fit into other programs or simply "feels good." Jazz, blues, comedy, satire, and especially folk music fill this slot. Songs by Jacques Brel, Malvina Reynolds, Tom Lehrer, Odetta, and Josh White, among others, will be heard. Also heard might be a piece of progressive rock music or poetry by e. e. cummings.

The radio station once ran a newspaper ad thanking all of the people who have made the station a success. On the list were Johann Sebastian Bach, Wolfgang Amadeus Mozart, Engelbert Humperdinck the composer, T. S. Eliot, W. C. Fields, Bob Newhart, Mike Nichols and Elaine May, Béla Bartók, "and a host of others too numerous to mention."

WFMT sponsors include especially financial institutions, real-estate developers and apartment-building owners, and travel-oriented firms. The sponsors also include every major utility in Chicago, more than thirty restaurants, plus major department stores. About fifty-four percent of the male audience have family incomes of $15,000 or more; fifty-six percent of adult male listeners are in professional or technical occupations. Nearly sixty-five percent of all adult listeners are college educated. About eighty-four percent of the listeners are in the 25-to-49 age range.

The technical quality of WFMT is among the best in the industry. The physical plant in an attractive setting on North Michigan Avenue is not large but is impressive.

WFMT is a station that has built up expectations from its audience. It evolved slowly and had to prove itself over time. Now, it has a halo effect about it because it has a reputation, tradition, and quality standards that the listeners of its area respect. Duplicating these efforts could not be done overnight, and perhaps these same tactics would not transfer to another market. But the station's type of integrity and its attitude toward the listener, along with its sensitivity to local conditions, have made it a pattern for other adventurous and uncompromising broadcasters. WFMT is an unusual and remarkable radio station.

Profile 13

Call Letters and Location: KMET–FM – Los Angeles, California
Owner and Affiliation: Metromedia Radio–Independent
Classification and Power: Class B–58 kw

KMET, Metromedia's Los Angeles FM station, was one of the first progressive rock stations in the country and has been one of a small number to retain essentially the same format since those early days of what was then called "underground" radio. Calling such a radio station "underground" is really absurd. Its announcers are union. It is licensed by the federal government, plays records that can be purchased in any shopping center, advertises products that can be purchased by anyone, and is owned by a capitalistic firm that also owns billboards, magazines, television stations, a motion picture company, and a lot of real estate. As Eldridge Cleaver said, "How can it be underground if everyone can hear it?" "Underground" was a slogan. To be sure, some of the early stations had a revolutionary aura about them, but more a pro-marijuana than a pro-bomb kind of revolution.

Tom Donahue, of San Francisco's KSAN (also owned by Metromedia) and before that of San Francisco's KMPX and Los Angeles's KPPC, is often credited with being the father of progressive rock radio. He noted some very obvious and basic things. One was that a number of record albums that were selling a large number of copies were not being played on radio stations. Another was that a lot of the audience was outgrowing bubblegum rock but was still interested in music that could be their very own. They also were not yet ready to fully embrace a 9 to 5 job and all of what traditionally went with that. Donahue further noted that two of their major complaints about radio were getting hyped by bubblegum-type announcers and by a horde of commercials. He incorporated these things he noticed into a new kind of radio station, daring and rebellious and a little forbidden at that time, which of course made it all the more desirable to a segment of society. Donahue was successful with his new venture, and a lot of others copied many of the trappings, but most such stations folded for lack of financial support. The more moderate of them retained many of the trappings but softened the sound, played the more commercial cuts from the albums, and became more mainstream rock. The most progressive and most experimental stations were gradually pushed aside by stations that were more moderate.

Even on those that retained their more progressive elements, the acid rock elements have waned and the attempts to see how many of the forbidden four-letter words can be aired have eased (as has shock at public use of them).

KMET has changed with the times, so that while they are still one of the more progressive stations in their market, they are not as experimental as they were in 1970. This is partly because of the recognition of what their audience wants and partly because their own success has spawned so many imitators and near imitators. They have been beaten in the audience ratings and advertiser appeal by ABC's KLOS. They have a strong competitor in KWST, which may be more progressive than KMET. KNX–FM's soft rock sound, used by all of the CBS–FM stations, has attracted its share of audience. At a given time there are usually two or three other stations also trying to appeal to the 18-to-25 audience segment. It is an audience segment that is served by more stations than the Los Angeles market can economically support. The fact that KMET has survived means that it is a strong competitor.

In 1970, KMET would have played The Rolling Stones along with Miles Davis, Jimmy Rushing, Bessie Smith, Zubin Mehta conducting the Los Angeles Philharmonic in Tchaikovsky's *1812 Overture*, Billie Holliday or Leadbelly, and current album rock bestsellers. The mix is much less adventuresome today. The music used to be totally free-form. Today the air people still pick their own music, but they have a policy book and a music list of sorts. Bestselling current albums make up the bulk of programing. People who program the music are still made aware of station policy through a process of socialization more than edict. Staff meetings are now less apt to be discussion groups and gripe sessions. The station still needs on-air people who know the catch phrases, the fads, the music, and the feelings of their segment of the listening public more than it needs announcers with pear-shaped tones. The overall approach is more formatted than it used to be, partly because the people in management have more experience doing this kind of radio, with track records in several major markets to refer to when trying to make decisions about what will work. Along with the specific do's and don'ts, especially important for this kind of radio is for management and on-air people to have a feel for the music and its audience. Much of it cannot be articulated.

At one time the station tried automation. When the automation was dropped the ratings went up. Then for a time the automation was used for the all-night program. In 1972, the automation was dropped totally. Management feels that intimacy and one-to-one contact are important and that their audience is less likely to listen to a station if they know it is automated.

The station broadcasts full-time in matrix quad stereo. Station manager Dave Moorehead feels that quad has not been significant in attracting audience. At first they heavily promoted the fact that they were quad. They got little obvious reaction. They had planned to go discrete quad in 1977, but decided to wait for further standardization by equipment manufacturers and other technological developments, feeling it just too uncertain and not worth it yet.

KMET used to be concerned that its type of station attracted many more males than females. For a time they tried playing more oldies, out of the belief that females would be more attracted by the familiar. They still have many more male listeners and have decided to spend less time worrying about it.

Commercials are limited to nine minutes an hour, or ten units, and are generally clustered in groups of three. The biggest advertisers are record stores, entertainment (clubs, concerts, and films), and clothing shops. While Cal Stereo and the Wherehouse are among the high-volume advertisers, more automotive and other more traditional radio advertisers have begun to advertise in recent years. Station management feels that the integration of spots and program material is less a problem than it was in 1970, because advertisers are more understanding and listeners are not as militantly anti-commercial as they were.

News consists of five minutes of on-the-air reporting during the morning and afternoon, with occasional news specials as needed. Associated Press, UPI, and City News Service are utilized. They do Sunday night and Saturday morning call-in talk shows, and air the *King Biscuit Flower Hour* on Saturdays at 11 P.M.

Record sales influence but do not totally dictate air play. The station tries to read, interpret, and reflect audience tastes. Artists that may be selling a lot of records may not be played if it is felt that they are not right for the station. Emotional content, tempo, time of day, and music styles are factors in music selection. Programs are looked upon by station personnel as a form of artistic expression. They believe that their music should have intensity, sincerity, and enthusiasm, and that it have something to say as valid and significant as the poetry of Robert Frost or Emily Dickinson. Deejays are expected to be brief in introducing the music.

The music has changed from '50s good-time rock-and-roll and the unremitting grimness of '60s rock. Cross-fertilization has made country, jazz, and mainstream-pop part of rock and rock part of the others. The Brigham Young University marching band uses amplified guitars and rock rhythms! Carmen McRae sings songs by rock artists in her club dates. Dorothy Collins sings songs by Stevie Wonder at state fairs. But the KMET's of the world are not content to become the middle of the mainstream. They remain somewhat *avant-garde.* If KMPC plays their records, they are likely to stop playing those records. If one of their performers gets a slot on a prime-time television show, he is less apt to be played on progressive radio stations. They are critical of artists who "sell out," which is sometimes about the same thing as being discovered by the mass audience. Exclusivity is part of the appeal.

Much of hard rock music remains rebellious. It is used heavily by college youth, but its roots are anti-intellectual. Bad grammar and harsh, crude, violent sounds with excesses in sound level characterize much of the music of our ultra-sophisticated computer age. The performers sing in "down home" accents, rejecting educated speech and trained voices and conventional manners. "Honesty" and "reality" are words much admired in rock music circles, but performers from England and the Bronx alike affect Mississippi delta accents. Also, while many of the feelings expressed are sympathetic to the common person, the progressive rock stations are really a form of elitist radio.

KMET is housed with sister stations KTTV television and KLAC (country) radio in an attractive new complex called Metromedia Square, in Los Angeles. While it does not often make the top ten stations overall, it and sister stations across the country remain provocative, viable, pacesetting radio stations.

Profile 14

In this profile, the station is not identified. If it were, some of the more personal information, which gives a feeling for some of the realities of the business, might have to be withheld.

A town of 8,000 is served by two radio stations. The one which has become dominant in recent years is run by a young man who grew up in the town, earned a college degree in broadcasting at a state university, and returned to be employed by the station. He soon became the station manager and has been gradually buying what has become controlling interest in the station. Besides the manager there are only three full-time employees, but other part-time help. The manager opens the station up six days a week, hosting the morning program from 5:30 to 9:00. At 6:30 in the morning, a newsman comes on duty, works until nine, sells advertising time in midday, and returns in the late afternoon to do newscasts again. Midday program-hosting is done by the traffic manager (female). Midday news and afternoon deejaying are done by the third full-time employee. Evenings and weekends are handled by part-time help. There are obviously no unions, and an informal personal relationship exists among the employees, each of whom gets an opportunity for a range of experience and has a major responsibility for keeping the station on the air.

The programing is mostly country music. At noon there is a swap-and-shop program in which people call up on the telephone and are heard on the air. The major morning and afternoon newscasts are mostly from wire copy, with some editing and writing of local stories and telephone beeper reports. Country music is played from 5:30 A.M. to 7 P.M., but at night a young black man plays music by black artists, mostly rhythm and blues. Weekends are country.

The music is loosely formatted. The approach is personality radio, in which the personalities produce as well as host their programs. The station attempts to keep current and play popular selections more often than older hits or other music, but management realizes that listeners have fewer choices and tend to listen longer to one station than they might in a major fragmented market, so the station plays more music than some larger-market stations might. The manager and the morning newsman are good friends, have nicknames for each other on the air, and have a loose, casual relationship. They joke back and forth and occasionally "put the audience on." A regular feature of the morning is the topic of the day, in which the manager invites listener opinion. People phone in their opinions, which are recorded by the newsman and dropped in between records and commercials. If there is a really hot topic *no* records may be played, but the usual day is music, news, and opinions dropped in several times an hour.

Ratings are not as important here as in larger cities. In a small town, people have a better feeling for the public pulse. There are fewer choices for advertisers. Repeat business is necessary, since there are not many clients to choose from. Servicing the account includes personally writing the copy in most cases. Personal contact with clients and advertiser success are especially important in getting repeat business. Two examples of the nature of these relationships follow.

One of the best of the station's clients is a drugstore. The drugstore has done most of its advertising for a long time on this station. In the years the store has advertised, its share of the market has increased dramatically. Its successes have resulted in larger advertising budgets. One morning the station manager called on the drugstore owner. Instead of the usual friendliness of the store owner, there was tight-lipped silence—not even acknowledgment that the station manager was there.

After a couple of unsuccessful attempts to find out what was the matter, the store owner said he would talk to the manager in the back. The manager found out in considerable detail and with some heat what was wrong. The manager is a member of a service club which sponsors a beauty contest each year. The previous evening, this year's contest had been emceed by the station manager. The previous year the drug store owner's daughter had won the contest. This year his younger daughter had been first runner-up. The station manager had to convince this drugstore owner that he was just the emcee and not a judge, that his mixing up her introduction slightly was just a slip of the tongue and was in no way intentional and was unlikely to have swayed the judges, and that without a doubt the druggist's daughter was the prettiest girl in the whole county.

Another long-time client is a grocery store. The grocery store owner is a deacon in the church that the manager attends. This grocery store, like nearly all stores in the area, is not open for business on Sunday. Recently, a large chain supermarket opened, giving the existing store tougher competition than it has ever had. This chain store stays open on Sunday. It also buys time on the radio station to tell everybody that it stays open on Sunday. The other store owner tells the station manager that he is canceling his advertising. He further asks the manager to editorialize on his station against stores being open on Sunday. What would you do? Many other businessmen in the town are certainly in sympathy with the store owner. The manager and the store owner have a relationship at church and are personal friends. On the other hand, the chain store usually does not advertise on radio, and it has been a personal victory for the manager that he could convince their advertising agency that his station was a dominant advertising medium in its market area and was important to their advertising strategy. Profit margins in small-town radio stations are seldom large. They cannot afford to lose many clients. In this case, it took a lot of talking to keep both stores on the air, including revised commercials by the first store to tell its story.

Evening programing has been something of a problem also. A large percentage of the area is black. The station manager feels that he has a commitment to them, especially since his area is not served by a large number of stations. So he hired a young black man to program and host the evening programing, featuring music that would primarily appeal to blacks. The person he found was desirable in three ways. He was local (the manager likes to have employees who know and really care about the area), he was easy to work with, and he had talent for doing the program. There was a problem, however. He wrote bad checks all over town, including many businesses advertising on the station. The station manager talked to the employee, who promised he would do better but kept writing bad checks. In order to solve the problem, the manager got him a better-paying job in a larger market, but then he had the problem of finding a good locally-oriented black air personality. Obviously, such problems are not confined to any one group. It is a problem of small-town radio, and some not-so-small towns.

Routine engineering problems are handled by the station manager and the afternoon deejay. Serious problems are handled on a contract basis by an engineer who works for a station in an adjacent market.

Profile 15

Call Letters and Location: KSL–Salt Lake City, Utah

Owner and Affiliation: KSL, Incorporated (Bonneville)–CBS Radio

Classification and Power: Class I A–50 kw

The following is a brief profile of a promotion campaign, to be read as a case study supplementing the chapter on promotion. The campaign was locally originated, professionally executed, and provides an example of what can be done at the local station level in a medium-sized market.

KSL is a 50,000-watt, clear-channel radio station in Salt Lake City—a market of approximately 600,000 people. KSL has the highest ad rate, the foremost tradition, the strongest public service image, the strongest news image, and the biggest share of the national-spot business of any station in its market. In 1966, the station, simultaneously with the hiring of Bob Pusey as promotion manager, decided to start a new promotion campaign. The old promotion theme, though it had served well, seemed to management to be a little stale. The station thought a brightening of its image was in order.

Pusey came up with a theme around which to coordinate the entire campaign. The theme, which initially struck the competition and the employees alike as being a little pretentious, was "Home of Radio." The idea had a number of overtones. It included the impression that KSL was in a class by itself, that KSL was "real radio" and the other stations were something less. Also, it was felt that "home" is a strong, positive word that affects people like "mother" and "beauty." It exudes wholesome warmth. The station was attempting to reach a wide part of the audience spectrum by playing music of a wide variety, trying to keep a balance between music that would be current and fresh while not offending the older, more conservative elements. Balance was also being sought between music, news, conversation, sports, public service, humor, and other elements. The station felt that "Home of Radio" would have appeal to all audience groups—to a wide spectrum of the listening public. It also was felt that the theme could be used for a long period of time with variations, and it could be used visually in an interesting way.

The first step in the new campaign was to romance the employees of the station. The plans were unveiled at a dinner for the employees held in a pleasant atmosphere at one of Salt Lake City's better restaurants. The employees were complimented for their fine efforts in the past. Then, a presentation was made that was intended to sell the employees on the idea while informing them of the scope of plans for using the new theme.

Once the employees were sold, the promotion began. A graphic artist and a printing firm assisted in designing and producing a new logo. They incorporated a roof over the station's call letters and a microphone. The new logo appeared on all stationery, letterheads, business cards, envelopes, and mail pieces to clients and the national sales representative. New signs with the logo were painted on the station doors as well as on staff cars. All stationery was water-marked with the logo. The office door of each department head had a new sign with the name of the office holder under the "Home of Radio" logo.

An advertising agency was used to assist the station in off-air promotion. Newspaper ads were purchased regularly, pushing special program efforts, personalities, the news effort, a play-by-play sports program, awards the station had won, or some news scoop. Institutional ads were purchased in a regional magazine. Similar ads were purchased in theater programs as well as in programs at university and professional sports events.

KSL's sister television station and FM station exchanged promotional announcements. The radio stations plugged TV programs. The TV station promoted both radio stations, most often with voice-over-slides announcements. Radio station personnel were booked for appearances on TV shows, and TV personnel did guest shots on radio.

KSL got involved in a number of public service ventures, sometimes with the TV station on joint ventures and sometimes alone. The station offered standard, commercial-type announcements for free, plus short program interviews, personalized air-personality appeals, public appearances, editorials, and even money to assist in the ventures. Special efforts included a summer jobs-for-youth campaign. The station used air appeals to encourage businesses to find a place for full- or part-time summer jobs for youth. Personal appeals were mailed to businesses, asking their executives to promote the idea to the various clubs of which they were members. KSL set an example by making room in the station for summer jobs for young people. The employment commission made personnel at the employment office available to handle the station's effort.

The station engaged in another effort with Utah State University, sponsoring a homemaker's symposium of three days' duration. The symposium offered some entertainment for a small fee, but mostly a series of workshops and lectures in child psychology, homemaking, and nutrition. The university provided many, though not all, of the experts. The station personnel helped coordinate the program and provide publicity. Local and national experts participated in the program, which was received favorably by the people who attended.

The station's on-air promotion included announcements, mostly ten seconds in length, about programs or personalities other than the one on the air at the time. Some of the announcements involved elaborate production, with special effects, music, and sometimes multiple voices. A guide sheet, which contained catch phrases for use by announcers with station identifications, time, temperature, weather, and other announcements, was placed in the control room and updated frequently.

The station did not use singing jingles for station IDs. The station had no strong aversion to jingles, but it had not found a syndication series it liked and had not wanted to spend the money to create an original series.

The station was cautious of contests and had used very few. So many other stations in the market had used a variety of contests that KSL seemed different because it was not contest-oriented. The station had tried two contests, one in which the listeners had to write a humorous story. Even though the grand prize was fairly large, the mail response was not strong, probably because of the work involved in entering the contest. Mostly, the contest was one the on-air people could have fun with. The other contest was simple to enter, with a grand prize large enough for incentive, and response was fairly good. The station still was ambivalent about contests.

Pusey designed a portable "Home of Radio" to represent KSL. An old truck was purchased, cut down, and adapted to carry a brightly colored house with the KSL roof. The house had many colored panels that opened, and the chimney was fixed so that smoke would pour out. This house was used at special events that were broadcast by the station. At football games, for instance, it was placed beyond the end zone within sight of the crowd. When the home team scored, it would let off smoke. Sirens would wail. Balloons would come out of the panels. Fireworks would go off. The team mascot could make its entrance out of the house. Pusey even hoped that the school band could make its entrance to the field through the "Home of Radio," but the band would not fit because of the balloons. In order to get hundreds of balloons ready for halftime, two men had to work frantically using an air compressor. Getting the necessary permits to move the house on the highways and to park it at desired locations, plus such tasks as blowing up the balloons, made the fun idea a lot of work.

The program director and promotion director both knew the entertainment editor at one of the city's two major newspapers. Both tried to maintain friendly relations with him and keep him informed on newsworthy developments at the station. The other newspaper was reluctant to give time to broadcasting, so no such liaison was attempted with it, although the station did purchase ads in both papers.

In the area of sales promotion, the air personalities became more involved than they ever had been before. For a period of time, the air personalities spent every Wednesday with the salesmen on calls to clients and agencies. This was to serve two functions. First, it would show the client that the station cared a little extra and would let clients meet the air people; it also added glamor to the sales beat. Second, it made the air personalities more aware of the sales problems and tended to give them a more personal interest in the clients and in the products they were pushing on the air. Salesmen and air personalities wore their KSL blazers every Wednesday.

"Speculation commercials" were made with great care. (These are hypothetical commercials used to demonstrate to a client the ideas the salesman has and to give the client an idea of how they actually will sound on the air. Speculation spots are used more often in the direct sale than in the sale that goes through an ad agency.)

Elaborate brochures and mail pieces were prepared for the national rep. The sales manager made repeated calls and trips to the rep offices. The station also provided a number of air checks for the rep and agencies. (The air check is a tape recording of an actual program, usually done in the recording studio and without the knowledge of the people on the air at the time. Sometimes, air checks will be edited and put into composite form to give a cross section of the station's sound. At other times, they will include merely a half-hour or an hour of a program as it was broadcast.)

When a member of the national rep office who had not visited the station before was a guest of the station, a special effort was made to have him meet the key members of the staff, to sell him on the station, and to make him feel that the people in the station personally cared about him. The station's personnel attempted not only to show him that the station was a good one but to build a bond of friendship between them. This was done with meetings, lunches, and tours. One national rep was met at the airport with a limousine and a band, and his hotel room was rigged with a tape-recorded message from his wife. This personal treatment was a sincere attempt to make friends with business associates, and it also was good business.

This is by no means an exhaustive list or a diary of a promotion campaign, but it gives the essence of one campaign effort at an adult, popular music, strong personality, strong news operation. Not all of the promotion was new in the "Home of Radio" campaign. The theme has since been changed to KSL–Radio West. No campaign that is static can maintain success.

APPENDIX A

The Radio Code

Preamble

In 1937 a major segment of U.S. commercial radio broadcasters first adopted industry-wide standards of practice. The purpose of such standards then, as now, is to establish guideposts and professional tenets for performance in the areas of programming and advertising content.

Admittedly, such standards for broadcasting can never be final or complete, because broadcasting is a creative art, always seeking new ways to achieve maximum appeal and service. Therefore, its standards are subject to periodic revision to reasonably reflect changing attitudes in our society.

In 1945 after two years devoted to reviewing and revising the 1937 document, new standards were promulgated. Further revisions were made in subsequent years when deemed necessary. The objectives behind them have been to assure that advertising messages be presented in an honest, responsible and tasteful manner and that broadcasters, in their programming, tailor their content to meet the needs and expectations of that particular audience to which their programming is directed.

The growth of broadcasting as a medium of entertainment, education and information has been made possible by its commercial underpinning. This aspect of commercial broadcasting as it has developed in the United States has enabled the industry to grow as a free medium in the tradition of American enterprise. The extent of this freedom is underscored by those laws which prohibit censorship of broadcast material. Rather, those who own the nation's radio broadcasting stations operate them—pursuant to this self-adopted Radio Code—in recognition of the needs of the American people and the reasonable self-interests of broadcasters and broadcast advertisers.

The Radio Broadcaster's Creed

We Believe:

That Radio Broadcasting in the United States of America is a living symbol of democracy; a significant and necessary instrument for maintaining freedom of expression, as established by the First Amendment to the Constitution of the United States;

That its contributions to the arts, to science, to education, to commerce, and therefore to the public welfare have the potential of influencing the common good achievements of our society as a whole;

That it is our obligation to serve the people in such manner as to reflect credit upon our profession and to encourage aspiration toward a better estate for our audiences. This entails making available to them through all phases of the broadcasting art such programming as will convey the traditional strivings of the U.S. towards goals beneficial to the populace;

The Radio Code (Twentieth Edition, June 1976) is reprinted here by permission of the National Association of Broadcasters.

That we should make full and ingenious use of the many sources of knowledge, talents and skills and exercise critical and discerning judgment concerning all broadcasting operations to the end that we may, intelligently and sympathetically:

Observe both existing principles and developing concepts affecting our society;

Respect and advance the rights and the dignity of all people;

Enrich the daily life of the people through the factual reporting and analysis of news, and through programming of education, entertainment, and information;

Provide for the fair discussion of matters of public concern; engage in works directed toward the common good; and volunteer our aid and comfort in times of stress and emergency;

Contribute to the economic welfare of all by expanding the channels of trade, by encouraging the development and conservation of natural resources, and by bringing together the buyer and seller through the broadcasting of information pertaining to goods and services.

Toward the achievement of these purposes we agree to observe the following:

I. Program Standards

A. News

Radio is unique in its capacity to reach the largest number of people first with reports on current events. This competitive advantage bespeaks caution—being first is not as important as being accurate. The Radio Code standards relating to the treatment of news and public events are, because of constitutional considerations, intended to be exhortatory. The standards set forth hereunder encourage high standards of professionalism in broadcast journalism. They are not to be interpreted as turning over to others the broadcaster's responsibility as to judgments necessary in news and public events programming.

1. *News sources* Those responsible for news on radio should exercise constant professional care in the selection of sources—on the premise that the integrity of the news and the consequent good reputation of radio as a dominant well-balanced news medium depend largely upon the reliability of such sources.

2. *News Reporting* News reporting should be factual, fair and without bias. Good taste should prevail in the selection and handling of news. Morbid, sensational, or alarming details not essential to factual reporting should be avoided. News should be broadcast in such a manner as to avoid creation of panic and unnecessary alarm. Broadcasters should be diligent in their supervision of content, format, and presentation of news broadcasts. Equal diligence should be exercised in selection of editors and reporters who direct

news gathering and dissemination, since the station's performance in this vital informational field depends largely upon them.

3. *Commentaries and Analyses* Special obligations devolve upon those who analyse and/or comment upon news developments, and management should be satisfied completely that the task is to be performed in the best interest of the listening public. Programs of news analysis and commentary should be clearly identified as such, distinguishing them from straight news reporting.

4. *Editorializing* Broadcasts in which stations express their own opinions about issues of general public interest should be clearly identified as editorials.

5. *Coverage of News and Public Events* In the coverage of news and public events broadcasters should exercise their judgments consonant with the accepted standards of ethical journalism and should provide accurate, informed and adequate coverage.

6. *Placement of Advertising* Broadcasters should exercise particular discrimination in the acceptance, placement and presentation of advertising in news programs so that such advertising is clearly distinguishable from the news content.

B. Controversial Public Issues

1. Radio provides a valuable forum for the expression of responsible views on public issues of a controversial nature. Controversial public issues of importance to fellow citizens should give fair representation to opposing sides of issues.

2. Requests by individuals, groups or organizations for time to discuss their views on controversial public issues should be considered on the basis of their individual merits, and in the light of the contributions which the use requested would make to the public interest.

3. Discussion of controversial public issues should not be presented in a manner which would create the impressions that the program is other than one dealing with a public issue.

C. Community Responsibility

1. Broadcasters and their staffs occupy a position of responsibility in the community and should conscientiously endeavor to be acquainted with its needs and characteristics to best serve the welfare of its citizens.

2. Requests for time for the placement of public service announcements or programs should be carefully reviewed with respect to the character and reputation of the group, campaign or organization involved, the public interest content of the message, and the manner of its presentation.

D. Political Broadcasts

1. Political broadcasts, or the dramatization of political issues designed to influence voters, shall be properly identified as such.

2. Political broadcasts should not be presented in a manner which would mislead listeners to believe that they are of any other character.

(Reference: Communications Act of 1934, as amended, Secs. 315 and 317, and FCC Rules and Regulations, Secs. 3.654, 3.657, 3.663, as discussed in NAB's "Political Broadcast Catechism & The Fairness Doctrine.")

3. Because of the unique character of political broadcasts and the necessity to retain broad freedoms of policy void of restrictive interference, it is incumbent upon all political candidates and all political parties to observe the canons of good taste and political ethics, keeping in mind the intimacy of broadcasting in the American home.

E. Advancement of Education and Culture

1. Because radio is an integral part of American life, there is inherent in radio broadcasting a continuing opportunity to enrich the experience of living through the advancement of education and culture.

2. Radio broadcasters, in augmenting the educational and cultural influences of the home, schools, religious institutions and institutions of higher education and other entities should:
    (a) be thoroughly conversant with the educational and cultural needs and aspirations of the community served;
    (b) develop programming consonant with the stations particular target audience.

F. Religion and Religious Programming

1. Religious programming shall be presented by responsible individuals, groups or organizations.

2. Radio broadcasting reaches audiences of all creeds simultaneously. Therefore, both the advocates of broad or ecumenical religious precepts, and the exponents of specific doctrines, are urged to present their positions in a manner conducive to listener enlightenment on the role of religion in society.

G. Responsibility Toward Children

Broadcasters have a special responsibility to children. Programming which might reasonably be expected to hold the attention of children should be presented with due regard for its effect on children.

1. Programming should be based upon sound social concepts and should include positive sets of values which will allow children to become responsible adults, capable of coping with the challenges of maturity.

2. Programming should convey a reasonable range of the realities which exist in the world to help children make the transition to adulthood.

3. Programming should contribute to the healthy development of personality and character.

4. Programming should afford opportunities for cultural growth as well as for wholesome entertainment.

5. Programming should be consistent with integrity of realistic production, but should avoid material of extreme nature which might create undesirable emotional reaction in children.

6. Programming should avoid appeals urging children to purchase the product specifically for the purpose of keeping the program on the air or which, for any reason, encourage children to enter inappropriate places.

7. Programming should present such subjects as violence and sex without undue emphasis and only as required by plot development or character delineation.

   Violence, physical or psychological, should only be projected in responsibly handled contexts, not used to excess or exploitatively. Programs involving violence should present the consequences of it to its victims and perpetrators.

   The depiction of conflict, and of material reflective of sexual considerations, when presented in programs designed primarily for children, should be handled with sensitivity.

8. The treatment of criminal activities should always convey their social and human effects.

H. Dramatic Programming

1. In the design of dramatic programs it is in the interest of radio as a vital medium to encourage those that are innovative, reflect a high degree of creative skill, deal with significant moral and social issues and present challenging concepts and other subject matter that relate to the world in which the listener lives.

2. Radio programming should not only reflect the influence of the established institutions that shape our values and culture, but also expose the dynamics of social change which bear upon our lives.

3. To achieve these goals, radio broadcasters should be conversant with the general and specific needs, interests and aspirations of all the segments of the communities they serve.

4. Radio should reflect realistically the experience of living, in both its pleasant and tragic aspects, if it is to serve the listener honestly. Nevertheless, it holds a concurrent obligation to provide programming which will encourage positive adjustments to life.

   In selecting program subjects and themes, great care must be exercised to be sure that treatment and presentation are made in good faith and not for the purpose of sensationalism or to shock or exploit the audience or appeal to prurient interests or morbid curiosity.

5. In determining the acceptability of any dramatic program, especially those containing elements of crime, mystery, or horror, consideration should be given to the possible effect on all members of the listening audience.

   In addition, without sacrificing integrity of presentation, dramatic programs on radio shall avoid:

   (a) the presentation of techniques of crime in such detail as to be instructional or invite imitation;

(b) presentation of the details of violence involving the excessive, the gratuitous and the instructional;

(c) sound effects calculated to mislead, shock, or unduly alarm the listener;

(d) portrayals of law enforcement in a manner which does not contribute to its proper role in our society.

I. General

1. The intimacy and confidence placed in radio demand of the broadcaster, the networks and other program sources that they be vigilant in protecting the audience from deceptive broadcast practices.

2. Sound effects and expressions characteristically associated with news broadcasts (such as "bulletin," "flash," "we interrupt this program to bring you," etc.) shall be reserved for announcement of news, and the use of any deceptive techniques in connection with fictional events and non-news programming shall not be employed.

3. The broadcasters shall be constantly alert to prevent inclusion of elements within programming dictated by factors other than the requirements of the programming itself. The acceptance of cash payments or other considerations in return for including the choice and identification of prizes, the selection of music and other creative programming elements and inclusion of any identification of commercial products or services, trade names or advertising slogans within the programming are prohibited unless consideration for such inclusion is revealed to the listeners in accordance with Sections 317 and 508 of the Communications Act.

4. Special precautions should be taken to avoid demeaning or ridiculing members of the audience who suffer from physical or mental afflictions or deformities.

5. The broadcast of gambling sequences deemed necessary to the development of plot or as appropriate background is acceptable only when presented with discretion and in moderation, and in a manner which would not excite interest in, or foster, betting nor be instructional in nature.

6. Quiz and similar programming that is presented as a contest of knowledge, information, skill or luck must, in fact, be a genuine contest and the results must not be controlled by collusion with or between contestants, or by any other action which will favor one contestant against any other.

7. Contests may not constitute a lottery.

8. Listener contests should not mislead as to the nature or value of prizes, likelihood of winning, nor encourage thoughtless or unsafe acts.

9. No programming shall be presented in a manner which through artifice or simulation would mislead the audience as to any material fact. Each broadcaster must exercise reasonable judgment to determine whether a particular method of presentation would constitute a material deception, or would be accepted by the audience as normal theatrical illusion.

10. Legal, medical and other professional advice will be permitted only in conformity with law and recognized ethical and professional standards.

11. Narcotic addiction shall not be presented except as a destructive habit. The use of illegal drugs or the abuse of legal drugs shall not be encouraged or be presented as desirable or socially acceptable.

12. Material pertaining to fortune-telling, occultism, astrology, phrenology, palmreading, numerology, mind-reading, character-reading, or subjects of a like nature, is unacceptable if it encourages people to regard such fields as providing commonly accepted appraisals of life.

13. Representations of liquor and smoking shall be de-emphasized. When represented, they should be consistent with plot and character development.

14. Obscene, indecent or profane matter, as proscribed by law, is unacceptable.

15. Special sensitivity is necessary in the use of material relating to sex, race, color, age, creed, religious functionaries or rites, or national or ethnic derivation.

16. The presentation of marriage, the family and similarly important human relationships, and material with sexual connotations, should not be treated exploitatively or irresponsibly, but with sensitivity.

17. Broadcasts of actual sporting events at which on-the-scene betting is permitted by law should be presented in a manner in keeping with federal, state and local laws, and should concentrate on the subject as a public sporting event.

18. Detailed exposition of hypnosis or material capable of having an hypnotic effect on listeners is forbidden.

19. Any technique whereby an attempt is made to convey information to the listener by transmitting messages below the threshold of normal awareness is not permitted.

20. The commonly accepted standards of humane animal treatment should be adhered to as applicable in programming.

21. Broadcasters are responsible for making good faith determinations on the acceptability of lyrics under applicable Radio Code standards.

22. Guests on discussion/interview programs and members of the public who participate in phone-in programs shall be treated with due respect by the program host/hostess.

    Interview/discussion programs, including telephone participation programs, should be governed by accepted standards of ethical journalism. Any agreement substantively limiting areas of discussion/questions should be announced at the outset of the program.

23. The standards of this Code covering programming content are also understood to include, wherever applicable, the standards contained in the advertising section of the Code.

24. To assure that broadcasters have the freedom to program fully and responsibly, none of the provisions of this Code should be construed as preventing or impeding broadcasts of the broad range of material necessary to help broadcasters fulfill their obligations to operate in the public interest.

II. Advertising Standards

Advertising is the principal source of revenue of the free, competitive American system of radio broadcasting. It makes possible the presentation to all American people of the finest programs of entertainment, education, and information.

Since the great strength of American radio broadcasting derives from the public respect for and the public approval of its programs, it must be the purpose of each broadcaster to establish and maintain high standards of performance, not only in the selection and production of all programs, but also in the presentation of advertising.

This Code establishes basic standards for all radio broadcasting. The principles of acceptability and good taste within the Program Standards section govern the presentation of advertising where applicable. In addition, the Code establishes in this section special standards which apply to radio advertising.

A. General Advertising Standards

1. Commercial radio broadcasters make their facilities available for the advertising of products and services and accept commercial presentations for such advertising. However, they shall, in recognition of their responsibility to the public, refuse the facilities of their stations to an advertiser where they have good reason to doubt the integrity of the advertiser, the truth of the advertising representations, or the compliance of the advertiser with the spirit and purpose of all applicable legal requirements.

2. In consideration of the customs and attitudes of the communities served, each radio broadcaster should refuse his/her facilities to the advertisement of products and services, or the use of advertising scripts, which the station has good reason to believe would be objectionable to a substantial and responsible segment of the community. These standards should be applied with judgment and flexibility, taking into consideration the characteristics of the medium, its home and family audience, and the form and content of the particular presentation.

B. Presentation of Advertising

1. The advancing techniques of the broadcast art have shown that the quality and proper integration of advertising copy are just as important as measurement in time. The measure of a station's service to its audience is determined by its overall performance.

2. The final measurement of any commercial broadcast service is quality. To this, every broadcaster shall dedicate his/her best effort.

3. Great care shall be exercised by the broadcaster to prevent the presentation of false, misleading or deceptive advertising. While it is entirely appropriate to present a product in a favorable light and atmosphere, the presentation must not, by copy or demonstration,

involve a material deception as to the characteristics or performance of a product.

4. The broadcaster and the advertiser should exercise special caution with the content and presentation of commercials placed in or near programs designed for children. Exploitation of children should be avoided. Commercials directed to children should in no way mislead as to the product's performance and usefulness. Appeals involving matters of health which should be determined by physicians should be avoided.

5. Reference to the results of research, surveys or tests relating to the product to be advertised shall not be presented in a manner so as to create an impression of fact beyond that established by the study. Surveys, tests or other research results upon which claims are based must be conducted under recognized research techniques and standards.

C. Acceptability of Advertisers and Products

In general, because radio broadcasting is designed for the home and the entire family, the following principles shall govern the business classifications:

1. The advertising of hard liquor shall not be accepted.

2. The advertising of beer and wines is acceptable when presented in the best of good taste and discretion.

3. The advertising of fortune-telling, occultism, astrology, phrenology, palm-reading, numerology, mind-reading, character-reading, or subjects of a like nature, is not acceptable.

4. Because the advertising of all products and services of a personal nature raises special problems, such advertising, when accepted, should be treated with emphasis on ethics and the canons of good taste, and presented in a restrained and inoffensive manner.

5. The advertising of tip sheets and other publications seeking to advertise for the purpose of giving odds or promoting betting is unacceptable.

    The lawful advertising of government organizations which conduct legalized lotteries is acceptable provided such advertising does not unduly exhort the public to bet.

    The advertising of private or governmental organizations which conduct legalized betting on sporting contests is acceptable provided such advertising is limited to institutional type announcements which do not exhort the public to bet.

6. An advertiser who markets more than one product shall not be permitted to use advertising copy devoted to an acceptable product for purposes of publicizing the brand name or other identification of a product which is not acceptable.

7. Care should be taken to avoid presentation of "bait-switch" advertising whereby goods or services which the advertiser has no intention of selling are offered merely to lure the customer into purchasing higher-priced substitutes.

8. Advertising should offer a product or service on its positive merits and refrain from discrediting, disparaging or unfairly attacking competitors, competing products, other industries, professions or institutions.

   Any identification or comparison of a competitive product or service, by name, or other means, should be confined to specific facts rather than generalized statements or conclusions, unless such statements or conclusions are not derogatory in nature.

9. Advertising testimonials should be genuine, and reflect an honest appraisal of personal experience.

10. Advertising by institutions or enterprises offering instruction with exaggerated claims for opportunities awaiting those who enroll, is unacceptable.

11. The advertising of firearms/ammunition is acceptable provided it promotes the product only as sporting equipment and conforms to recognized standards of safety as well as all applicable laws and regulations. Advertisements of firearms/ammunition by mail order are unacceptable.

D. Advertising of Medical Products

Because advertising for over-the-counter products involving health considerations is of intimate and far-reaching importance to the consumer, the following principles should apply to such advertising:

1. When dramatized advertising material involves statements by doctors, dentists, nurses or other professional people, the material should be presented by members of such profession reciting actual experience, or it should be made apparent from the presentation itself that the portrayal is dramatized.

2. Because of the personal nature of the advertising of medical products, the indiscriminate use of such words as "safe," "without risk," "harmless," or other terms of similar meaning, either direct or implied, should not be expressed in the advertising of medical products.

3. Advertising material which offensively describes or dramatizes distress or morbid situations involving ailments is not acceptable.

E. Time Standards for Advertising Copy

1. The amount of time to be used for advertising should not exceed 18 minutes within any clock hour. The Code Authority, however, for good cause may approve advertising exceeding the above standard for special circumstances.

2. Any reference to another's products or services under any trade name, or language sufficiently descriptive to identify it, shall, except for normal guest identification, be considered as advertising copy.

3. For the purpose of determining advertising limitations, such program types as "classified," "swap shop," "shopping guides," and "farm auction" programs, etc., shall be regarded as containing one and one-half minutes of advertising for each five-minute segment.

F. Contests

1. Contests shall be conducted with fairness to all entrants, and shall comply with all pertinent laws and regulations.

2. All contest details, including rules, eligibility requirements, opening and termination dates, should be clearly and completely announced or easily accessible to the listening public; and the winners' names should be released as soon as possible after the close of the contest.

3. When advertising is accepted which requests contestants to submit items of product identification or other evidence of purchase of products, reasonable facsimiles thereof should be made acceptable. However, when the award is based upon skill and not upon chance, evidence of purchase may be required.

4. All copy pertaining to any contest (except that which is required by law) associated with the exploitation or sale of the sponsor's product or service, and all references to prizes or gifts offered in such connection should be considered a part of and included in the total time limitations heretofore provided. (*See Time Standards for Advertising Copy.*)

G. Premiums and Offers

1. The broadcaster should require that full details of proposed offers be submitted for investigation and approval before the first announcement of the offer is made to the public.

2. A final date for the termination of an offer should be announced as far in advance as possible.

3. If a consideration is required, the advertiser should agree to honor complaints indicating dissatisfaction with the premium by returning the consideration.

4. There should be no misleading descriptions or comparisons of any premiums or gifts which will distort or enlarge their value in the minds of the listeners.

Regulations and Procedures

The following Regulations and Procedures shall obtain as an integral part of the Radio Code of the National Association of Broadcasters:

I. Name

The name of this Code shall be the Radio Code of the National Association of Broadcasters, hereinafter referred to as the Radio Code.

Definitions: Wherever reference is made to programs it shall be construed to include all program material including commercials.

II. Purpose of the Code

The purpose of this Code is cooperatively to establish and maintain a level of radio programming which gives full consideration to the educational, informational, cultural, economic, moral and entertainment needs of the American public to the end that more and more people will be better served.

III. The Radio Code Board

Section 1. Composition There shall be a continuing Committee entitled the Radio Code Board.[1] The Code Board shall be composed of 11 members. Members of the Radio Board shall not be eligible to serve on the above specified Board. The Chairperson and members of the Code Board shall be appointed by the President of the NAB, subject to confirmation by the Radio Board, and may include no more than two members as representatives of subscribing nationwide radio networks. Due consideration shall be given, in making such appointments, to factors of diversification, such as market size, geographical location, network affiliation, class of broadcast service, etc. The Board shall be fully representative of the radio industry. All Code Board members shall be selected from subscribers to the Radio Code. In every odd-numbered year, four members shall be appointed for two-year terms; in every even-numbered year, five members shall be appointed for two-year terms provided, however, that network representatives be rotated on an annual basis. Appointments become effective at the conclusion of the annual NAB convention of the year in which appointments are made.

A. *Limitation of service* A person shall not serve consecutively as a member of the Board for more than two two-year terms or for more than four years consecutively provided, however, that appointment to fill an unexpired term shall not count toward the limitation of service as previously stated.

Network representatives on the Radio Code Board shall be limited to non-consecutive two-year terms; provided, in the first year of such representation one network member may be appointed for a one-year term and one for a two-year term. Thereafter, all network members may be appointed for two-year terms. Any one network representative may be reappointed following an interim two-year period.

A majority of the membership of the Radio Code Board shall constitute a quorum for all purposes unless herein otherwise provided.

Section 2. Authorities and responsibilities The Radio Code Board is authorized and directed:

(1) To recommend to the Radio Board amendments to the Radio Code; (2) to consider in its discretion, any appeal from any decision made by the Code Authority Director with respect to any matter which has arisen under the Code, and to suspend, reverse, or modify any such decision; (3) to prefer formal charges, looking toward the suspension or revocation of the subscription and/or the authority to use the Radio Code Audio and Visual Symbols, to the Radio Board concerning violations and breaches of the

---

[1] The Radio Board of the NAB shall have power: "to enact, amend and promulgate Radio Standards of Practice or Codes, and to establish such methods to secure observance thereof as it may deem advisable;—." By-Laws of the National Association of Broadcasters, Article VI, Section 8, B. Radio Board.

Radio Code by a subscriber; (4) to be available to the Code Authority Director for consultation on any and all matters affecting the Radio Code.

A. *Meetings*   The Radio Code Board shall meet regularly semi-annually on a date to be determined by the Chairperson. The Chairperson of the Board may, at any time, on at least five days' written notice, call a special meeting of the Board.

IV. Code Authority Director

Section 1. Director   There shall be a position designated as the Code Authority Director. This position shall be filled by appointment of the President of NAB, subject to the approval of the Board of Directors.

Section 2. Authority and responsibilities   The Code Authority Director is responsible for the administration, interpretation and enforcement of the Radio Code. In furtherance of this responsibility he/she is authorized and directed:

(1) To maintain a continuing review of all programming and advertising material presented over radio, especially that of subscribers to the Radio Code of NAB; (2) to receive, screen and clear complaints concerning radio programming; (3) to define and interpret words and phrases in the Radio Code; (4) to develop and maintain appropriate liaison with governmental agencies and with responsible and accountable organizations and institutions; (5) to inform, expeditiously and properly, a subscriber to the Radio Code of complaints or commendations, as well as to advise all subscribers concerning the attitudes and desires program-wise of accountable organizations and institutions, and of the American public in general; (6) to receive and monitor, if necessary, any certain series of programs, daily programming, or any other program presentations of a subscriber, as well as to request recorded material, or script and copy, with regard to any certain program presented by a subscriber; (7) to reach conclusions and make recommendations or prefer charges to the Radio Code Board concerning violations and breaches of the Radio Code by a subscriber; (8) to recommend to the Code Board amendments to the Radio Code; (9) to take such action as may be necessary to enforce the Code, including revocation of subscription as hereinafter provided in Chapter V, Section 4.

A. *Delegation of powers and responsibilities*   The Code Authority Director shall appoint such executive staff as is needed, consistent with resources, to carry out the above described functions, and may delegate to this staff such responsibilities as he/she may deem necessary.

V. Subscribers

Section 1. Eligibility   A. Any individual, firm or corporation which is engaged in the operation of a radio broadcast station or radio network; or which holds a construction permit for a radio broadcast station within the United States or its dependencies, shall, subject to the approval of the Radio Board, as hereinafter provided, be eligible to subscribe to the Radio Code of the NAB to the extent of one subscription for each such station or network, or each station which holds a construction permit; provided, that a non-radio member of NAB shall not become eligible via Code subscription to receive any of the member services or to exercise any of the voting privileges of a member.

B. The Radio Code Board may recommend categories of affiliate subscribers as may be desired, together with applicable fees for such affiliate subscriptions.

Section 2. Certification of subscription Upon subscribing to the Code there shall be granted forthwith to each such subscribing station authority to use such copyrighted and registered audio and visual symbols as will be provided. The symbols and their significance shall be appropriately publicized by the NAB.

Section 3. Duration of subscription Subscription shall continue in full force and effect until there has been received a written notice of resignation or until subscription is revoked by action of the Code Authority, the Radio Code Board or the Radio Board of Directors.

Section 4. Revocation of subscription Any subscription and/or the authority to utilize the above-noted symbols, may be voided, revoked or temporarily suspended for radio programming, including commercial copy, which, by theme, treatment or incident, in the judgment of the Code Authority constitutes a continuing, willful or gross violation of any of the provisions of the Radio Code; provided, however, that the following conditions and procedures shall govern:

A. *Conditions precedent* Prior to Revocation of Subscription, the Code Authority (1) Shall appropriately inform the subscriber of any and all complaints and information it possesses relating to the programming of said subscriber, (2) Shall have reported to, and advised, said subscriber by analysis, interpretation, recommendation or otherwise, of the possibility of a violation or breach of the Radio Code, and (3) Shall have served upon the subscriber by registered mail a Notice of Intent to Revoke Subscription; such Notice shall contain a statement of the grounds and reasons for the proposed revocation, including appropriate references to the Radio Code and shall give the subscriber 30 days to take such action as will satisfy the Code Authority. During this interim period the Code Authority may, within its sole discretion, reconsider its proposed action based upon such written reply as the subscriber may care to make, or upon such action as the subscriber may care to take program-wise, in conformance with the analysis, interpretation or recommendation of the Code Authority. If upon termination of the 30 day period, no such action has been taken or the subscriber has not requested a hearing, as hereinafter provided, his/her subscription to the Code shall be considered revoked.

B. *Time* In the event that the nature of the program in question is such that the Code Authority deems time to be of the essence, the Code Authority may limit the time in which compliance must be made, provided that a time certain in which subscriber may reply is included in the Notice of Intent, and provided further that the Code Authority's reasons therefor are specified in its Notice of Intent to Revoke Subscription.

C. *Hearing* The subscriber shall have the right to a hearing before the Code Board by requesting same and by filing an answer within 20 days of the date of receipt of the Notice of Intent. Said answer and request for hearing shall be directed to the Chairperson of the Code Board with a copy to the Code Authority.

D. *Waiver* Failure to request a hearing shall be deemed a waiver of the subscriber's right thereto. If a hearing is requested, action of the Code Authority is suspended pending decision of the Code Board.

E. *Designation* If hearing is requested by the subscriber, it shall be designated as promptly as possible and at such time and place as the Code Board may specify.

F. *Confidential status* Hearings shall be closed; and all correspondence between a subscriber and the Code Authority and/or the Code Board concerning specific programming shall be confidential; provided, however, that the confidential status of these procedures may be waived by a subscriber.

G. *Presentation; representation* A subscriber who has exercised his/her right to a hearing, shall be entitled to effect presentation of his/her case personally, by agent, by attorney, or by deposition and interrogatory.

H. *Intervention* Upon request by the subscriber-respondent or the Code Authority, the Code Board, in its discretion, may permit the intervention of one or more subscribers as parties-in-interest.

I. *Transcript* A stenographic transcript record may be taken if requested by respondent and shall be certified by the Chairperson of the Code Board to the Office of the Secretary of the National Association of Broadcasters, where it shall be maintained. The transcript shall not be open to inspection unless otherwise provided by the party respondent in the proceeding.

J. *Code authority; counsel* The Code Authority may, at its discretion, utilize the services of an attorney from the staff of the NAB for the purpose of effecting its presentation in a hearing matter.

K. *Order of procedure* At hearings, the Code Authority shall open and close.

L. *Cross-examination* The right of cross-examination shall specifically obtain. Where procedure has been by deposition or interrogatory, the use of cross-interrogatories shall satisfy this right.

M. *Presentation* Oral and written evidence may be introduced by the subscriber and by the Code Authority. Oral argument may be had at the hearing and written memoranda or briefs may be submitted by the subscriber and by the Code Authority. The Code Board may admit such evidence as it deems relevant, material and competent, and may determine the nature and length of the oral argument and the written argument or briefs.

N. *Transcriptions, etc.* Records, transcriptions, or other mechanical reproductions of radio programs, properly identified, shall be accepted into evidence when relevant.

O. *Authority of Presiding Officer of Code Board* The Presiding Officer shall rule upon all interlocutory matters, such as, but not limited to, the admissibility of evidence, the qualifications of witnesses, etc. On all other matters, authority to act shall be vested in a majority of the Code Board unless otherwise provided.

P. *Continuances and extensions* Continuance and extension of any proceeding or for the time of filing or performing any act required or allowed to be done within a specific time may be granted upon request, for a good cause shown. The Code Board or the Presiding Officer may recess or adjourn a hearing for such time as may be deemed necessary, and may change the place thereof.

Q. *Findings and conclusions* The Code Board shall decide the case as expeditiously as possible and shall notify the subscriber, Code Authority, and the Radio Board in writing, of the decision. The decision of the Code Board shall contain findings of fact with conclusions, as well as the reasons or bases therefor. Findings of fact shall set out in detail and with particularity all basic evidentiary facts developed on the record (with appropriate citations to the transcript of record or exhibit relied on for each evidentiary fact) supporting the conclusion reached.

R. *Disqualification* Any member of the Code Board may disqualify himself/herself, or upon good cause shown by any interested party, may be disqualified by a majority vote of the Code Board.

S. *Review* A request for review of the Code Board's decision may be filed by the subscriber with the Radio Board. Such petition for review must be served upon the Chairperson of the Radio Board within 10 days after receipt by the subscriber of the Code Board's decision.

T. *Penalty, suspension of* At the discretion of the Code Board, application of any penalty provided for in the decision may be suspended until the Radio Board makes final disposition of the Petition for Review. The entire record in the proceedings before the Code Board shall be certified to the Radio Board. The review will be limited to written statements and no provision is made for further oral argument.

U. *Final decision* The Radio Board shall have the discretion upon review to uphold, reverse, or amend with direction the decision of the Code Board. The decision of the Radio Board is final.

Section 5. Additional procedures When necessary to the proper administration of the Code, additional rules of procedure will be established from time to time as authorized by the By-Laws of the NAB; in keeping therewith, special consideration shall be given to the procedures for receipts and processing of complaints and to necessary rules to be adopted from time to time, taking into account the source and nature of such complaints; such rules to include precautionary measures such as the posting of bonds to cover costs and expenses of processing same; and further provided that special consideration will be given to procedures insuring the confidential status of proceedings relating to Code observance.

Section 6. Amendment and review The Radio Code may be amended from time to time by the Radio Board which shall specify the effective date of each amendment; provided, that said Board is specifically charged with review and reconsideration of the entire Code, its appendices and procedures, at least once each year.

Section 7. Termination of contracts All subscribers on the air shall be in compliance at the time of subscription to the Code.

VI. Rates

Each subscriber shall pay fees in accordance with such schedule, at such time, and under such conditions as may be determined from time to time by the Radio Board (*See Article VI, Section 8, B. Radio Board By-Laws of the NAB*).

APPENDIX B

Broadcast
Advertising Manual:
A Guide to
Using Radio

Checklist for Planning and Executing a Broadcast Campaign

1. Set campaign goals and budget as far in advance as possible. Next, break budget into monthly departmental budgets.

2. Consult with stations on best contracts available for the amount of budget you're spending with them.

3. Use Weekly Broadcast Planner (which follows) to plan by weeks. The store manager, advertising manager, and departments using broadcast should get a copy so everyone will know when spots are to be aired.

4. Select stations for items, events, or institutional spots that will reach the target audience you're aiming for.

5. Decide on ideal times of the day to run spots, then get availabilities from stations to see if they can be worked out. The farther ahead you plan, the better time slots you'll get from stations.

6. Get a confirmation or contract from the stations before the schedule begins. This should include dates, time of day, and costs.

7. Write your commercials or have your agency or the station write them, when you are not using materials from the corporate office.

8. Check spots on the air to see how they look and/or sound.

9. Stations will submit an affidavit of performance or bill at the end of the month. The FCC requires stations to keep a "log" of daily broadcasts and exact time each spot was aired.

10. Check affidavit to see that your spots ran at correct times. If for some reason they did not (without your prior approval), you're entitled to "make-good" spots at times comparable to the ones you asked for. If the wrong commercial copy ran at the right time, you're still entitled to a "make-good" commercial.

This report (August 1, 1970) was prepared by the Radio Advertising Bureau, Inc., and is reprinted by permission of the Bureau.

Weekly Broadcast Planner

Items	Stations	Spot Cost	Spot Length	Number of Spots						
				Sun.	Mon.	Tue.	Wed.	Thu.	Fri.	Sat.

Introduction

The backbone of retail advertising efforts for major retailers is still the newspaper medium. However, our customers' interests and our business are constantly changing—so is the effectiveness of newspaper advertising. Several key factors point this up:

> In many major markets, while population has grown, newspaper circulation has either declined or remained stable. The result: a decrease in coverage. This decrease *could* be offset by using a number of different metropolitan daily and suburban papers, but would probably be accompanied by sizable increases in dollar expenditures and duplication of readers.
>
> Current statistics tend to show that readership of newspapers among the younger segment of the population has declined.
>
> Data indicates that an increasing segment of the population commutes to work by car. Their opportunity to read either a morning or evening paper is drastically reduced; their time spent reading is less.
>
> Indications are that an all-too-high percentage of the population (in many markets) do not read *any* major daily newspaper *at all!* One example of this is a current study of Chicago papers conducted by W. R. Simmons & Associates. Results showed that 30 percent of the adults (age 18 and over) in the Chicago Metropolitan area *did not read any of the four major daily newspapers* the day before they were interviewed.

We all know that an ad can be effective only if it reaches the customer. When one medium does only part of the job, other media must be used to bridge the gap. Radio may be your answer. This manual is designed to be used like a textbook and a working reference when you use radio advertising.

1. Advantages of Radio Advertising

There are some 5,500 radio stations in this country that have the ability to transmit your messages to prospects. Although your merchandise or services cannot be visibly portrayed through this medium, you will find it offers these distinct advantages over other media.

> Listeners *"identify"* with certain stations or personalities— *radio is the most personal of advertising media.*
>
> Personality is communicated as an integral part of the advertising message.
>
> Ideas can be presented rapidly and in continuity form.
>
> The reception of advertising is conditioned by program content.
>
> The listener can be stimulated to become involved through his imagination.

There is voluntary attention (although in varying degrees) and instantaneous communication.

The ground rules for effective radio advertising are very much similar to those of other media: buy your time properly and economically, attempting to reach the right audience at the right time at the right location, with messages that tell your story. The following sections should help you do your job easier and more effectively.

2. Planning a Campaign

What do you want radio to accomplish? Your goals in using radio should be clearly established before you embark on a radio campaign. Your goals will determine the kind of radio commercials you use—whether image, event, items, departmental promotion, or services and the stations best suited to run them on. Possible goals might include:

	Commercial Approach
Reaching new customers not now shopping with you	Image
Establishing a reputation for good values	Image
Enhancing your image as a store that's fun to shop in	Image
Building excitement for monthly sales	Events
Increasing store traffic with special/regular items	Items
Building merchandise categories: Jr., Young Men's, Appliances, Garden Shoppe, TBA	Merchandise category
Selling store services: Parking, Night Openings	Services

Stores that use radio most effectively employ all five of these radio techniques in a carefully planned campaign. Not necessarily one objective at a time. For instance, image and item can be combined in a commercial using the basic sound-logo and live item copy; a department can be featured with an example of an item that's timely; an event commercial can build excitement in the sound-logo as it says that your store is a fun place to shop.

The most important things to remember are: establish your radio goals, make a plan for accomplishing them, and then check periodically to see what kind of job you're doing. Now for successful techniques in promoting your image, events, items, departments, and services.

Special Events

Probably more locations use radio for special events than any other purpose. It's easy to understand why: Radio does three important things for special events. It gets the store news out to customers, builds excitement and a desire to shop the sale, and increases store traffic.

Another unique advantage of using radio for special events is radio's economy, which enables you to reach customers multiple times, for less money, reminding them to come to the store.

A. Kinds of Events to Use

Three different kinds of special events are naturals for radio:

> Sales featuring savings for limited time only
>
> Non-price events: Housewares Shows, Appliance Fairs, Fashion Shows
>
> Special Interest Events: Teen Shows, Career Girl Clubs, Baby Shows, Senior Citizen Events—all lend themselves well to radio promotion because of radio's ability to select just the customers you want to come in for the event

B. Buying Time for Special Events

Vertical saturation is a plan many stores use to buy time for their special events. This means commercials are bought heavily two days before a sale and on the sale day itself on a variety of stations. Horizontal saturation is the way to buy for items, image, or categories.

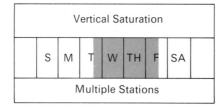

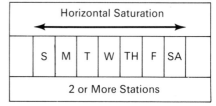

For a week-long sale you might use the vertical buying plan and add another day's saturation on Sunday evening and Monday to give the sale another punch. Your depth of saturation will be determined by the importance of the event. A week-long sale will, of course, have a bigger radio budget than a "housewares" promotion.

C. Copy for Special Events

The copy for events will build excitement and traffic and can mention specific on-sale items (no more than three to a 60-second commercial seem to work best). Some stores use 10-second ID's as well as their basic saturation of a 60-second commercial. Building excitement can be accomplished in several intriguing ways with radio:

> Live copy on strong items that are exciting in themselves
>
> Taped commercials done on the floor by the radio station during the event
>
> Slice-of-life taped copy with imaginary shoppers discussing the values
>
> Humorous approaches
>
> Remote radio broadcasts directly from the selling floor

D. Rules to Remember in Planning Radio Events

Buy enough radio to reach your customers several times and make the sale sound like it shouldn't be missed.

Write exciting copy; use one of the approaches above to get the sale out of *"just another sale"* rut.

Don't use too many items in event commercials—your newspaper ad can list the items. Radio should motivate your customers to shop—*immediately*—before the best items are gone.

Merchandise Items

A study was done in Cleveland by Radio Advertising Bureau to see if Radio could sell regularly priced, specific items as well as newspapers were known by stores to do. The answer was that radio does! Radio, intelligently used, pulled dollar-for-dollar results just as good as newspapers. Here are some other planning tips from the Cleveland study to use in advertising our merchandise on the air:

1. Items must be carefully chosen to fit the stations on which you run them. Running an electric guitar on an older-profiled station is a disastrous waste of radio money.
2. High and low priced merchandise sells well on radio.
3. Minute commercials work best.
4. Two items can be used in a minute commercial, but items should be related by who buys them, department or price.
5. Item advertising is more flexible on radio. If competition undersells on an item, you can change the price or substitute another item (if you don't want to break the price). Or if the weather changes suddenly (snow, rain, heat wave), you can change your radio item just as suddenly.
6. Radio results cumulate. The longer you've been on the air, the better your radio results will be because your customers will learn to listen for your news.

Selecting Radio Items

Since every merchandise category has been successful on radio, don't let preconceived notions get in the way. Like . . . *an announcer can't sell girdles.* Many have done an excellent job, some with a humorous approach, some completely ad lib.

Another preconceived notion to forget in buying radio: High-priced merchandise won't sell on radio. Radio programing attracts every income group, and here are some items that have repeatedly done outstandingly on radio:

Major appliances

Carpets

Fur coats

Diamonds

Men's suits

Price leaders are good item choices when you're getting a sale swinging and want to build traffic. Otherwise, consider your whole merchandise assortment as potential radio items.

Just three *don'ts* in selecting radio items:

1. Don't ask radio to sell what no other medium can sell—out-of-season or out-of-fashion or overpriced items.

2. *Don't ask radio to introduce new items that customers aren't familiar with.* One of radio's plusses is that it summons up mental images in the customer's mind. But if no image is available, you've lost a prospect and wasted radio money. Let one of the visual media introduce brand new items.

3. Don't mismatch items with stations. Use a station your target customer tunes in to.

Image

Radio has helped stores in:

Attracting younger/older customs

Correcting mistaken ideas about merchandise—it's cheap/expensive

Updating an old-fashioned image

Projecting store's service facilities

Radio commercials through the use of music, voices, sincerity, a sense of humor, the radio personality endorsement can change how your customers and potential customers think about you. And naturally when you make your claim good, they'd rather shop with you.

Merchandise Categories

Other symptoms of the changing times are changing merchandise patterns in the stores, more youth-oriented fashions and home furnishings; more recreational equipment; more personalized beauty care departments; more luxury kitchen appliances; more activity in TBA areas and garden shops with more leisure time away from work.

All of these categories present unique selling possibilities on radio. First to inform the customers that the departments are there and then to tell them about the new and interesting merchandise. The next step is that the customer comes in to see for herself and is sold on being your customer. And radio's economical frequency advantage gives you several chances to talk about your departments to the same customer.

Category, or departmental, radio selling is an informal and effective way to acquaint customers with news and change in the store. It also enhances your image as a good place to shop.

Services

Stores services aren't the easiest idea to get across in print. Parking, late openings, credit plans, branch locations usually end up at the bottom of the page in small print and are lost. Yet services are valuable additions to your merchandising operation, and your customers should know what you do for them . . . because you care.

Regular item commercials, sale events, or departmental spots can be tagged with the news that you are open *tonight* until nine or "Use your charge plate . . . and just say charge it!" Bonus tags that pay off in what customers think about you . . . and what they *do*.

3. Develop Your Objectives

Organize your radio campaign just as you would a campaign to be run through any other mass media. Give it careful thought, know what you want to accomplish, then implement your plan through a positive set of objectives. Make these factors an integral part of your plan:

Know What You Want to Accomplish

Determine whether you want to:

Increase store traffic

Increase departmental traffic

Sell specific merchandise

Promote leaders

Build store image

Introduce new services

Promote special non-price events

Build an image for a certain category of merchandise, such as more youthful fashions, higher-priced furnishings, and so on

Know Where to Reach Prospects

In pre-TV days, radio was a far different advertising medium than it is today. Then, radio's audience was primarily stationary; most listening was in the living room or bedroom. The audience sought long segments of programing—drama, music and variety, and comedy. Personalities became national celebrities and household heroes.

Today, radio's audience is on the move, whether from room to room, across town, or from city to city.

Personalities are *now* likely to be *local celebrities and personal favorites*. No longer able to attract the same large audiences by the appeal of major programs, radio today selects its listeners on the basis of the general appeal of its total sound. This is a complex balance, usually, which includes the type of programing, the personalities of announcers, the pacing of the program units, the balance of various kinds of program material, and the manner in which the audience becomes involved.

The variety of radio station programing is wide in most markets and features programs that appeal to every customer group individually. You won't have all these choices in every market, but in many markets there will be stations classified like this:

Middle-of-the-Road Music

News

Conversation and Talk

Country-Western Music

Contemporary (Top-40, etc.)

Good Music (Semiclassical, Standards, etc.)

Within these broad program formats there may be elements of other formats. A middle-of-the-road music station may carry traffic reports and in-depth news, a news station may play music for some of its program day, and a country-western station may feature strong sports coverage.

Some stations in smaller markets may program all six of the above formats in the course of a day, but a station builds its programing around a specific listener group it wants to reach.

Know Whom You Want to Reach

By listening to your local stations, you can make some extremely educated guesses about which of your customers are attracted to which station. And this is the basis of targeting customer groups with merchandise that's specifically geared for them. For instance, a younger audience probably likes contemporary music more than do older people. The reverse is true of middle-of-the-road music. Conversation programs tend to appeal to housewives who use radio as a companion medium; news is popular with men.

Radio research is far from exact in auditing the types of listeners, the degree of attention, or the number of people listening. None of the present methods employed in assaying the radio audience is able to measure each of these dimensions. The buyer is faced with sifting through a series of probabilities presented by the analysis of available research, the study of other evidences presented by stations themselves and objective analysis.

The number and type of commercials accepted and amount of on-air station promotion are very important considerations. Stations that do not overcommercialize and engage in only moderate promotion offer a much more desirable selling climate. Competitive product protection and commercial rotation are also considered.

The number and type of advertisers (particularly local advertisers) using a station can frequently provide a good indication of a station's effectiveness. Those outlets that receive the greatest proportion of local advertising dollars are usually those that produce the greatest consumer response. In addition, the kinds of advertisers using a station reflect upon the image projected by the station.

Many other considerations also go into an evaluation of an individual station. Quality of station management, recognition by the NAB (National Association of Broadcasters) Code. Interest in retaining a client's advertising as reflected by continuous efforts to improve schedules, proper rotation of announcements ordered by broad time period, and actual delivery of schedules precisely as ordered are all important considerations that are involved in an overall appraisal of individual stations.

Other important clues to the type of audience likely to be attracted to a station arc: material bearing on the community stature of the station, the type of mail elicited from listeners, the character of the station's own promotion, etc.

Further, most station representatives can tell you the audience his station is trying to reach. He wants you as a repeat customer, and it is not in his best interest to cause you to advertise the wrong items on his station.

Based on a gross evaluation of all stations in a market, gleaned by reviewing such information as is outlined above, the buyer will then narrow down the available choices to those stations considered suitable for the commercials and for the planned marketing objectives. These stations will then be reviewed further, and will be asked for specific time availabilities, plans, costs, and outlines of merchandising assistance. Many times you will find it necessary to use more than one station (possibly three or four) for a specific promotion in order to reach a large enough segment of the radio audience. In all too many major markets, individual stations just do not have the *"pulling power."*

Know When to Reach Prospects

Having made some generalizations on selecting station programs that will reach customers, there's another element to be considered in buying time to advertise merchandise and that is *when* the customers you want to reach will be available in the radio audience. The *"radio day"* looks like this:

Category	Class	Time	Comparable rate
Morning Drive Time	AA	6 A.M.–10 A.M.	Most Expensive
Housewife Time	B	10 A.M.–4 P.M.	Third Most Expensive
Evening Drive Time	A·	4 P.M.–7 P.M.	Second Most Expensive
Evening Time	C	7 P.M.–Midnight	Fourth Most Expensive
After Midnight	D	Midnight–6 A.M.	Least Expensive

The fact that morning drive is the most expensive in the radio day indicates that you reach most customers from 6 to 10 A.M. This is radio's prime time. You get women fixing breakfast, teens at breakfast, men driving to work, and career women during morning drive time. All departments with male-female appeal would go well here: home furnishings, major appliances, home modernizing, recreational, automotive, and appeal. But maybe you don't want to reach men; you have an item that's mostly bought by women. Housewife time accumulates a lot of women at home, and you can reach them less expensively from 10 A.M. to 4 P.M. Apparel, home furnishings, recreation, and major appliances are good housewife choices.

Men, of course, are again in the radio audience during evening drive time and so are students out of school. All merchandise departments should be considered. Evening time is good for reaching hobbyists at home, people out driving, and younger people studying, so consider young apparel and family items for evening time. Weekend time, when families get together, is exceptionally good for joint-decision merchandise items and usually is priced advantageously.

Know How Long Your Radio Advertising Can Be

Radio advertising is sold in denominations (units) of 60 seconds, 30 seconds, and 10 seconds. By far the most popular with advertisers is the 60-second for two reasons:

1. You have time enough to present a complete selling message along with your identifying sound-logo and . . .
2. 30-second spots cost about 80 percent of 60-second ones, although only half the time is purchased.

Ten-second commercials are mostly ID's to promote a sale or other feature.

Radio commercials come in a variety of patterns. They can be 60 seconds of straightforward copy read live or adlibbed by the station announcer, or 60 seconds of prerecorded tape. Or they can be a combination of these. Say a tape of your sound-logo (which corresponds to your logo in newspaper ads) that identifies you, a middle section of live-selling copy and your sound-logo ending.

This last commercial pattern is called a doughnut because there's a hole in the middle for live copy. A doughnut commercial might sound like this:

Sound Logo 20 Seconds	Live Copy 35 Seconds	Sound Logo 5 Seconds

The corporate office furnishes sound-logo tape and periodic scripts and tapes for local use.

4. How to Stretch Your Radio Budget

The price of a commercial varies from market to market and station to station because the cost is based on the total audience reached by the commercial. This, in turn, is influenced by the population of your market, the popularity of your local stations, and their selling power.

In most markets (except for the largest ones) you will buy radio at the local retail rate. This corresponds to the way you buy your newspaper space—as a local advertiser you are entitled to the lowest rate the station offers. The one-time rate will be even less expensive when you buy commercials in quantity lots, just as your newspaper space costs less when you buy more lines.

An explanation of buying plans follows, but, first, the other ways radio is sold are through *national spots*, for advertisers whose agencies buy nationwide in specified markets, and *network spots*, where national advertisers buy all the affiliates that a network has to offer across the country.

Many stations in large markets have a single-rate policy, which means that local and national spots are sold for the same price.

Efficient Ways to Buy Radio Time

One of the great advantages of radio advertising is its cost efficiency (economy), which means that radio reaches more people more times for the same budget. Radio is bought most efficiently when you plan ahead to take advantage of the attractive spot packages most stations offer to good users. Planning ahead also lets you "look-up" the time periods you'll want to use for your spots. Here are some typical time buying plans that stations offer:

A. Contract Rates

These are based on the total number of spots you contract for in a year. This plan is most like newspaper contracts (or discounts) because the more spots/lines/inches you buy during the year the cheaper the units become. (Like all other media contracts, radio contracts should be co-signed by the retail sales promotion media office.)

B. Package Plans

Package plans apply to weekly spot buys. For instance, you can buy a 12-spot or 24-spot package of spots at a much lower spot cost than the one-time spot rate. Package plans allow you to buy radio heavily when you need lots of support for events and selling seasons; use less time at other periods.

C. Total Audience Plans

Such plans are available from stations for weekly, monthly, yearly periods. Your spots are rotated in all the station's time periods so that you reach the station's total listening audience during the course of a specific time period.

D. Run of Schedule (ROS)

This type of plan means you pay minimum spot cost for best available times that station can schedule your spots.

E. End Rate

If your radio campaign is a consistent one, well planned in advance, you'll probably be able to buy at the station's "end rate," which is the lowest rate at which the stations sell time. (See your local station rate cards for multiple-spot plans available.)

Spot Adjacencies and Fixed Times

Many stores like to run some of their radio spots adjacent to popular radio features or at a fixed time each day. These advantageous positions are sometimes sold at a premium spot rate or are included in your contract, depending on the station's rate card. It's necessary to plan ahead to secure adjacencies and fixed times because the number of these spots available (called availabilities) are limited.

Program Sponsorship

Spot schedules have become the most popular use of radio by advertisers, but some stations still offer programs of lengths that vary from five minutes to an hour or more. A popular local program might well be a good investment for you. The disadvantage, of course, is lack of flexibility in that more of your budget will be channeled into one time period on one station.

The stations you select to advertise on will assign salesmen to you in the same way you have a salesman from the paper. This salesman can be very helpful in explaining his station rate card and advantageous packages, helping you schedule spots, lending a hand with your radio copy (perhaps having his own copy department write the copy), and coming up with promotional ideas to make your special events successful.

5. Running a Radio Advertising Campaign

Radio is most effective when it's an integral part of a store's advertising campaign—budgeted and planned well in advance. The radio budget should be a planned expenditure similar to your newspaper, television, circular, and other store media budgets. The size of the radio budget will be a direct reflection of your goals in using radio—enough to accomplish what radio can do for you best, bearing in mind the cumulative effects of using radio consistently.

Who Runs Radio Advertising

A. The Store

In zone or ROS stores radio advertising becomes a regular assignment of store personnel: store manager, merchandise managers, assistant managers, or advertising manager. In metro districts it is a function of the advertising department. This means that the advertising manager performs all the radio functions from budgeting with management, selecting items in connection with department managers, scheduling, writing copy (or having it written by radio stations), alerting departmental people on run of commercials, checking bills, and assessing radio results.

B. Advertising Agency

Some of our locations have a local agency that handles their radio advertising. An agency will handle creative concepts, help to work out your budgeting, schedule spots with stations, write copy, and check bills.

Often agencies come to the store for the advertising meeting where radio campaign and items are decided on and talk with department managers about merchandise benefits. They also have periodic meetings with store management to discuss the performance of the radio program.

Usually the agency fee is paid by the radio stations you're using, though in some cases the agency charges a fee for services.

C. Store/Station

Many stores rely heavily on local station salesmen in using radio. Stations help stores to set budgets, attend advertising meetings, help select items and promotions to go on the air, have their station copywriters prepare radio copy, and schedule time on the station. The store is then responsible for checking station bills and assessing radio results—often in consultation with their station salesmen.

Scheduling Radio

Radio—unlike newspapers which can add extra pages for advertisers—has set a number of commercial availabilities in each hour of programing and cannot expand its advertising time beyond this. So try to schedule your spots far enough in advance to get the times and the stations that you want to use.

The person handling radio will consider the departments running spots on a weekly or monthly basis (the weekly planner form is useful in this planning) and select stations and times of the day the spots should be aired. He gives the station individual scheduling requests, which they check with their time availabilities and come back to him with a confirmation of schedule, listing specific copy if different items are running.

At the same time radio copy should go to the station. Radio's flexibility allows last-minute copy changes, but it's a good idea to have the copy at the station so the announcer can go over it in advance of broadcast. It's not always possible for stations to change your time slots because of their availabilities. But they'll make every effort to if they can.

6. Tips on Writing Radio Commercials

One of the most important reasons for the success of any advertising medium is the copy—it's often the difference between customers coming in to shop or not coming in and often the reason they get there.

Writing radio copy is the same as writing newspaper copy in some ways. For instance, the copywriter should know what he's writing about. All the available merchandise information should be gathered and time should be spent by the writer in talking to the merchandiser, sales people—even customers—on why they sell and buy what they do. This research into our merchandise will make your copy believable.

But there are some significant ways that writing good radio copy differs from writing newspaper ads.

A. Write Like You Talk, Not Like You Write

Radio is heard, not seen. This means your radio copy should be more conversational, more vernacular than written prose.

B. Use Short, Easy-to-Understand Sentences or Phrases

Make every word count; do not use unnecessary and alliterative adjectives unless you would really *say it* that way.

C. Use Action Words

This is also the way you speak. You don't say, *"There's an exciting sale today."* You say, *"Get to our sale!"* . . . *It's exciting!"* Action words motivate action, which is your prime concern as a radio writer.

D. Slant Copy for Target Customer

Decide who you're selling the merchandise to and talk to her or him—nobody else. Use your customer's language.

E. Emphasize Customer Benefits, Play Down Details

This is a rule that should be used more often in newspaper copy, but it's even more vital in radio. You're playing to the ear which must immediately relate to "What does this mean to me?" In terms of happiness, fashion, family, convenience, etc., or else it switches you off. A recital of "buttons down the front," "five lovely pastels" or a referral to fabric content are not the way to go in radio. Capture your target customer with the benefit for *her* or *him*. Then enlarge on it.

F. Mention Your Name as Many Times as You Can

Then listeners who've tuned in late will know where they can find your merchandise, sale, or service.

G. Listen to Your Copy before It Goes on Radio

This is very important, and too infrequently practiced. It's not enough to read through radio copy for typos or difficult phrases; you should read it aloud to yourself to see how it sounds, if it rings true, if it is hard to pronounce. If it isn't right, then you can rework it. Other ideas are to have someone else read this copy to see if it "plays" or to read it into a tape recorder and play it back.

7. Assessing Radio Results

You want to know how any advertising medium is working for your store —particularly a relatively new one—and there are several ways to gauge radio results.

Keep track of sales results on your weekly radio schedules as you do in your newspaper ad record book, noting the cost of the radio time and the merchandise sold. This record will guide you in selecting future radio items.

Some stores that have added radio to their newspaper advertising examine last year's sales and compare them with this year's when radio was added.

Of course, if you run radio and newspaper ads for the same items, you won't be able to tell which of the two brought the results, but you can compare last year's sales figures to get an idea.

Probably the best way—outside of sales figures—to evaluate radio results are periodic radio reviews by management and those concerned with producing the radio advertising. You might want to ask these questions:

Are new customers shopping here?

Are you spending less to reach new customers?

Are your customers better acquainted with departments? With services?

Are you building volume in areas you've concentrated on in radio?

Are you selecting the best stations for each item? The best day parts? Taking advantage of radio personalities?

Building total store volume?

Giving customers new ideas about you?

Remember, radio results are both immediate—in next day store traffic—and cumulative by having a continuing radio program that customers come to listen for on "their" radio stations. By careful evaluation of radio results to date you have both these radio benefits and more.

APPENDIX C

The FCC's 1960 Programing Policy Statement

On October 3, 1957, the Commission's Network Study Staff submitted its report on network broadcasting. While the scope and breadth of the network study as set forth in Order Number 1 issued November 21, 1955 encompassed a comprehensive study of programming, it soon became apparent that due to factors not within the control of the staff or the committee consideration of programming would be subject to substantial delay making it impracticable that the target dates for the overall report could be met in the program area. The principal reasons were: (a) the refusal of certain program distributors and producers to provide the committee's staff with certain information which necessitated protracted negotiations and ultimately legal action (FCC v. Ralph Cohn, et al., 154 F. Supp. 899); and (b) the fact that a coincidental and collateral investigation into certain practices was instituted by the Department of Justice. Accordingly the network study staff report recommended that the study of programming be continued and completed. The Director of the Network Study in his memorandum of transmittal of the Network Study Report stated:

> The staff regrets that it was unable to include in the report its findings and conclusions in its study of programming. It is estimated that more than one-fourth of the time of the staff was expended in this area. However, the extended negotiations and litigation with some non-network program producers relative to supplying financial data necessary to this aspect of the study made it impossible to obtain this information from a sufficient number of these program producers to draw definitive conclusions on all the programming issues. Now that the Commission's right to obtain this information has been sustained, it is the hope of the staff that this aspect of the study will be completed and the results included in a supplement to the report. Unless the study of programming is completed, the benefit of much labor on this subject will have been substantially lost.

Report and Statement of Policy re: Commission en banc Programming Inquiry (FCC 60–970, July 29, 1960).

As a result on February 26, 1959, the Commission issued its "Order for Investigatory Proceeding," Docket No. 12782. That Order stated that during the course of the Network Study and otherwise, the Commission had obtained information and data regarding the acquisition, production, ownership, distribution, sale, licensing, and exhibition of programs for television broadcasting. Also, that that information and data had been augmented from other sources including hearings before Committees of Congress and from the Department of Justice, and that the Commission had determined that an overall inquiry should be made to determine the facts with respect to the television network program selection process. On November 9, 1959, the proceeding instituted by the Commission's Order of February 26, 1959 was amended and enlarged to include a general inquiry with respect to programming to determine, among other things, whether the general standards heretofore laid down by the Commission for the guidance of broadcast licensees in the selection of programs and other material intended for broadcast are currently adequate; whether the Commission should, by the exercise of its rule-making power, set out more detailed and precise standards for such broadcasters; whether the Commission's present review and consideration in the field of programming and advertising are adequate, under present conditions in the broadcast industry; and whether the Commission's authority under the Communications Act of 1934, as amended, is adequate, or whether legislation should be recommended to Congress.

This inquiry was heard by the Commission *en banc* between December 7, 1959, and February 1, 1960, and consumed 19 days in actual hearings. Over 90 witnesses testified relative to the problems involved, made suggestions and otherwise contributed from their background and experience to the solution of these problems. Several additional statements were submitted. The record in the *en banc* portion of the inquiry consisted of 3,775 pages of transcript plus 1,000 pages of exhibits. The Interim Report of the staff of the Office of Network Study was submitted to the Commission for consideration on June 15, 1960.

The Commission will make every effort to expedite its consideration of the entire docket proceeding and will take such definitive action as the Commission determines to be warranted. However, the Commission feels that a general statement of policy responsive to the issues in the *en banc* inquiry is warranted at this time.

Prior to the *en banc* hearing, the Commission had made its position clear that, in fulfilling its obligation to operate in the public interest, a broadcast station is expected to exercise reasonable care and prudence with respect to its broadcast material in order to assure that no matter is broadcast which will deceive or mislead the public. In view of the extent of the problem existing with respect to a number of licensees involving such practices as deceptive quiz shows and payola which had become apparent, the Commission concluded that certain proposed amendments to our Rules as well as proposed legislation would provide a basis for substantial improvements. Accordingly, on February 5, 1960, we adopted a Notice of Proposed Rule Making to deal with fixed quiz and other non-bona fide contest programs involving intellectual skill. These rules would prohibit the broadcasting of such programming unless accompanied by an announcement which would in all cases describe the nature of the program in a manner to sufficiently apprise the audience that the events in question are not in fact spontaneous or actual measures of knowledge or intellectual skill. Announcements would be made at the beginning and end of each program. Moreover, the proposed rules would require a station if it obtained such a program from networks, to be assured similarly that the network program has an accompanying announcement of this nature. This, we believe, would go a long way toward preventing any recurrence of problems such as those encountered in the recent quiz show programs.

We have also felt that this sort of conduct should be prohibited by statute. Accordingly, we suggested legislation designed to make it a crime for anyone to wilfully and knowingly participate or cause another to participate in or cause to be broadcast a program of intellectual skill or knowledge where the outcome thereof is prearranged or predetermined. Without the above-described amendment, the Commission's regulatory authority is limited to its licensing function. The Commission cannot reach networks directly or advertisers, producers, sponsors, and others who, in one capacity or another, are associated with the presentation of radio and television programs which may deceive the listening or viewing public. It is our view that this proposed legislation will help to assure that every contest of intellectual skill or knowledge that is broadcast will be in fact a bona fide contest. Under this proposal, all those persons responsible in any way for the broadcast of a deceptive program of this type would be penalized. Because of the far reaching effects of radio and television, we believe such sanctions to be desirable.

The Commission proposed on February 5, 1960 that a new section be added to the Commission's rules which would require the licensee of radio broadcast stations to adopt appropriate procedures to prevent the practice of payola amongst his employees. Here again the standard of due diligence would have to be met by the licensee. We have also approved on February 11 the language of proposed legislation which would impose criminal penalties for failure to announce sponsored programs, such as payola and others, involving hidden payments or other considerations. This proposal looks toward amending the United States Code to provide fines up to $5,000 or imprisonment up to one year, or both, for violators. It would prohibit the payment to any person or the receipt of payment by any person for the purpose of having as a part of the broadcast program any material on either a radio or television show unless an announcement is made as a part of the program that such material has been paid for or furnished. The Commission now has no direct jurisdiction over the employees of a broadcast station with respect to this type of activity. The imposition of a criminal penalty appears to us to be an effective manner for dealing with this practice. In addition, the Commission has made related legislative proposals with respect to fines, temporary suspension of licenses, and temporary restraining orders.

In view of our mutual interest with the Federal Trade Commission and in order to avoid duplication of effort, we have arrived at an arrangement whereby any information obtained by the FCC which might be of interest to FTC will be called to that Commission's attention by our staff. Similarly, FTC will advise our Commission of any information or data which it acquires in the course of its investigations which might be pertinent to matters under jurisdiction of the FCC. This is an understanding supplemental to earlier liaison arrangements between FCC and FTC.

Certain legislative proposals recently made by the Commission as related to the instant inquiry have been mentioned. It is appropriate now to consider whether the statutory authority of the Commission with respect to programming and program practices is, in other respects, adequate.

In considering the extent of the Commission's authority in the area of programming it is essential first to examine the limitations imposed upon it by the First Amendment to the Constitution and Section 326 of the Communications Act.

The First Amendment to the United States Constitution reads as follows:

> Congress shall make no law respecting an establishment of religion or prohibiting the free exercise thereof; or abridging the freedom of speech, or of the press; or the right of the people peaceably to assemble, and to petition the Government for a redress of grievances.

Section 326 of the Communications Act of 1934, as amended, provides that:

> Nothing in this chapter shall be understood or construed to give the Commission the power of censorship over the radio communications or signals transmitted by any radio station, and no regulation or condition shall be promulgated or fixed by the Commission which shall interfere with the right of free speech by means of radio communication.

The communication of ideas by means of radio and television is a form of expression entitled to protection against abridgement by the First Amendment to the Constitution. In *United States* v. *Paramount Pictures,* 334 U.S. 131, 166 (1948) the Supreme Court stated:

> We have no doubt that moving pictures, like newspapers and radio are included in the press, whose freedom is guaranteed by the First Amendment.

As recently as 1954 in *Superior Films* v. *Department of Education,* 346 U.S. 587, Justice Douglas in a concurring opinion stated:

> Motion pictures are, of course, a different medium of expression than the radio, the stage, the novel or the magazine. But the First Amendment draws no distinction between the various methods of communicating ideas.

Moreover, the free speech protection of the First Amendment is not confined solely to the exposition of ideas nor is it required that the subject matter of the communication be possessed of some value to society. In *Winters* v. *New York,* 333 U.S. 507, 510 (1948) the Supreme Court reversed a conviction based upon a violation of an ordinance of the City of New York which made it punishable to distribute printed matter devoted to the publication of accounts of criminal deeds and pictures of bloodshed, lust or crime. In this connection the Court said:

> We do not accede to appellee's suggestion that the constitutional protection for a free press applies only to the exposition of ideas. The line between the informing and the entertaining is too elusive for the protection of that basic right. . . . Though we can see nothing of any possible value to society in these magazines, they are as much entitled to the protection of free speech as the best of literature.

Notwithstanding the foregoing authorities, the right to the use of the airwaves is conditioned upon the issuance of a license under a statutory scheme established by Congress in the Communications Act in the proper exercise of its power over commerce.[1] The question therefore arises as to whether because of the characteristics peculiar to broadcasting which justifies the government in regulating its operation through a licensing system, there exists the basis for a distinction as regards other media of mass communication with respect to application of the free speech provisions of the First Amendment? In other words, does it follow that because one may not engage in broadcasting without first obtaining a license, the terms thereof may be so framed as to unreasonably abridge the free speech protection of the First Amendment?

We recognize that the broadcasting medium presents problems peculiar to itself which are not necessarily subject to the same rules governing other media of communication. As we stated in our Petition in *Grove Press, Inc.* and *Readers Subscription, Inc.* v. *Robert K. Christenberry* (Case No. 25,861) filed in the U.S. Court of Appeals for the Second Circuit,

> radio and TV programs enter the home and are readily available not only to the average normal adult but also to children and to the emotionally immature. . . . Thus, for example, while a nudist magazine may be within the protection of the First Amendment . . . the televising of nudes might well raise a serious question of programming contrary to 18 U.S.C. 1464. . . . Similarly, regardless of whether the "four-letter words" and sexual description, set forth in "Lady Chatterley's Lover," (when considered in the context of the whole book) make the book obscene for mailability purposes, the utterance of such words or the depiction of such sexual activity on radio or TV would raise similar public interest and Section 1464 questions.

Nevertheless it is essential to keep in mind that "the basic principles of freedom of speech and the press like the First Amendment's command do not vary."[2]

Although the Commission must determine whether the total program service of broadcasters is reasonably responsive to the interests and needs of the public they serve, it may not condition the grant, denial or revocation of a broadcast license upon its own subjective determination of what is or is not a good program. To do so would "lay a forbidden burden upon the exercise of liberty protected by the Constitution."[3] The Chairman of the Commission during the course of his testimony recently given before the Senate Independent Offices Subcommittee of the Committee on Appropriations expressed the point as follows:

> Mr. Ford: When it comes to questions of taste, unless it is downright profanity or obscenity, I do not think that the Commission has any part in it.
>
> I don't see how we could possibly go out and say this program

---

[1] *NBC* v. *United States*, 319 U.S. 190 (1943).

[2] *Burstyn* v. *Wilson*, 343 U.S. 495, 503 (1952).

[3] *Cantwell* v. *Connecticut*, 310 U.S. 926, 307 [*sic*].

is good and that program is bad. That would be a direct violation of the law.[4]

In a similar vein Mr. Whitney North Seymour, President-elect of the American Bar Association, stated during the course of this proceeding that while
the Commission may inquire of licensees what they have done to determine the needs of the community they propose to serve, the Commission
may not impose upon them its private notions of what the public ought to
hear.[5]

Nevertheless, several witnesses in this proceeding have advanced persuasive arguments urging us to require licensees to present specific types
of programs on the theory that such action would enhance freedom of expression rather than tend to abridge it. With respect to this proposition we
are constrained to point out that the First Amendment forbids governmental interference asserted in aid of free speech, as well as governmental
action repressive of it. The protection against abridgement of freedom of
speech and press flatly forbids governmental interference, benign or otherwise. The First Amendment "while regarding freedom in religion, in speech
and printing and in assembling and petitioning the government for redress
of grievances as fundamental and precious to all, seeks only to forbid that
Congress should meddle therein." (*Powe* v. *United States*, 109 F. 2nd 147)

As recently as 1959 in *Farmers Educational and Cooperative Union of
America* v. *WDAY, Inc.* 360 U.S. 525, the Supreme Court succinctly stated:

> . . . expressly applying this country's tradition of free expres-
> sion to the field of radio broadcasting, Congress has from the
> first emphatically forbidden the Commission to exercise any
> power of censorship over radio communication.

An examination of the foregoing authorities serves to explain why the
day-to-day operation of a broadcast station is primarily the responsibility
of the individual station licensee. Indeed, Congress provided in Section 3(h)
of the Communications Act that a person engaged in radio broadcasting
shall not be deemed a common carrier. Hence, the Commission in administering the Act and the courts in interpreting it have consistently maintained
that responsibility for the selection and presentation of broadcast material
ultimately devolves upon the individual station licensee, and that the fulfillment of the public interest requires the free exercise of his independent
judgment. Accordingly, the Communications Act "does not essay to regulate
the business of the licensee. The Commission is given no supervisory control over programs, of business management or of policy. . . . The Congress intended to leave competition in the business of broadcasting where
it found it. . . ."[6] The regulatory responsibility of the Commission in the
broadcast field essentially involves the maintenance of a balance between
the preservation of a free competitive broadcast system, on the one hand,
and the reasonable restriction of that freedom inherent in the public interest standard provided in the Communications Act, on the other.

---

[4] Hearings before the Subcommittee of the Committee on Appropriations,
United States Senate, 86th Congress, 2nd Session on H.R. 11776 at page 775.

[5] Memorandum of Mr. Whitney North Seymour, Special Counsel to the National
Association of Broadcasters at page 7.

[6] *FCC* v. *Sanders Brothers*, 309 U.S. 470 (1940).

In addition, there appears a second problem quite unrelated to the question of censorship that would enter into the Commission's assumption of supervision over program content. The Commission's role as a practical matter, let alone a legal matter, cannot be one of program dictation or program supervision. In this connection we think the words of Justice Douglas are particularly appropriate.

> The music selected by one bureaucrat may be as offensive to some as it is soothing to others. The news commentator chosen to report on the events of the day may give overtones to the news that pleases the bureaucrat but which rile the . . . audience. The political philosophy which one radio sponsor exudes may be thought by the official who makes up the programs as the best for the welfare of the people. But the man who listens to it . . . may think it marks the destruction of the Republic. . . . Today it is a business enterprise working out a radio program under the auspices of government. Tomorrow it may be a dominant, political or religious group. . . . Once a man is forced to submit to one type of program, he can be forced to submit to another. It may be but a short step from a cultural program to a political program. . . . The strength of our system is in the dignity, resourcefulness and the intelligence of our people. Our confidence is in their ability to make the wisest choice. That system cannot flourish if regimentation takes hold.[7]

Having discussed the limitations upon the Commission in the consideration of programming, there remains for discussion the exceptions to those limitations and the area of affirmative responsibility which the Commission may appropriately exercise under its statutory obligation to find that the public interest, convenience and necessity will be served by the granting of a license to broadcast.

In view of the fact that a broadcaster is required to program his station in the public interest, convenience and necessity, it follows despite the limitations of the First Amendment and Section 326 of the Act, that his freedom to program is not absolute. The Commission does not conceive that it is barred by the Constitution or by statute from exercising any responsibility with respect to programming. It does conceive that the manner or extent of the exercise of such responsibility can introduce constitutional or statutory questions. It readily concedes that it is precluded from examining a program for taste or content, unless the recognized exceptions to censorship apply: for example, obscenity, profanity, indecency, programs inciting to riots, programs designed or inducing toward the commission of crime, lotteries, etc. These exceptions, in part, are written into the United States Code and, in part, are recognized in judicial decision. See Sections 1304, 1343, and 1464 of Title 18 of the United States Code (lotteries; fraud by radio; utterance of obscene, indecent or profane language by radio). It must be added that such traditional or legislative exceptions to a strict application of the freedom of speech requirements of the United States Constitution may very well also convey wider scope in judicial interpretation as applied to licensed radio than they have had or would have as applied to other communications media. The Commission's petition in the

---

[7] *Public Utilities Commission* v. *Pollak*, 343 U.S. 451, 468, Dissenting Opinion.

Grove case, *supra,* urged the court not unnecessarily to refer to broadcasting, in its opinion, as had the District Court. Such reference subsequently was not made though it must be pointed out there is no evidence that the motion made by the FCC was a contributing factor. It must nonetheless be observed that this Commission conscientiously believes that it should make no policy or take any action which would violate the letter or the spirit of the censorship prohibitions of Section 326 of the Communications Act.

As stated by the Supreme Court of the United States in *Joseph Burstyne, Inc.* v. *Wilson, supra:*

> . . . Nor does it follow that motion pictures are necessarily subject to the precise rule governing any other particular method of expression. Each method tends to present its own peculiar problem. But the basic principles of freedom of speech and the press, like the First Amendment's command, do not vary. Those principles, as they have frequently been enunciated by this Court, make freedom of expression the rule.

A review of the Communications Act as a whole clearly reveals that the foundation of the Commission's authority rests upon the public interest, convenience and necessity.[8] The Commission may not grant, modify or renew a broadcast station license without finding that the operation of such station is in the public interest. Thus, faithful discharge of its statutory responsibilities is absolutely necessary in connection with the implacable requirement that the Commission approve no such application for license unless it finds that "public interest, convenience, and necessity would be served." While the public interest standard does not provide a blueprint of all the situations to which it may apply, it does contain a sufficiently precise definition of authority so as to enable the Commission to properly deal with the many and varied occasions which may give rise to its application. A significant element of the public interest is the broadcaster's service to the community. In the case of *NBC* v. *United States,* 319 U.S. 190, the Supreme Court described this aspect of the public interest as follows:

> An important element of public interest and convenience affecting the issue of a license is the ability of the licensee to render the best practicable service to the community reached by broadcasts. . . . The Commission's licensing function cannot be discharged, therefore, merely by finding that there are no technological objections to the granting of a license. If the criterion of "public interest" were limited to such matters, how could the Commission choose between two applicants for the same facilities, each of whom is financially and technically qualified to operate a station? Since the very inception of federal regulation by radio, comparative considerations as to the services to be rendered have governed the application of the standard of "public interest, convenience, or necessity."

Moreover, apart from this broad standard which we will further discuss in a moment, there are certain other statutory indications.

It is generally recognized that programming is of the essence of radio

---

[8] Secs. 307(d), 308, 309, *inter alia.*

service. Section 307(b) of the Communications Act requires the Commission to "make such distribution of licenses . . . among the several States and communities as to provide a fair, efficient, and equitable distribution of radio service to each of the same." Under this section the Commission has consistently licensed stations with the end objective of either providing new or additional programming service *to* a community, area or state, or of providing a new or additional "outlet" for broadcasting *from* a community, area, or state. Implicit in the former alternative is increased radio reception; implicit in the latter alternative is increased radio transmission and, in this connection, appropriate attention to local live programming is required.

Formerly by reason of administrative policy, and since September 14, 1959, by necessary implication from the amended language of Section 315 of the Communications Act, the Commission has had the responsibility for determining whether licensees "afford reasonable opportunity for the discussion of conflicting views on issues of public importance." This responsibility usually is of the generic kind and thus, in the absence of unusual circumstances, is not exercised with regard to particular situations but rather in terms of operating policies of stations as viewed over a reasonable period of time. This, in the past, has meant a review, usually in terms of filed complaints, in connection with the applications made each three year period for renewal of station licenses. However, that has been a practice largely traceable to workload necessities, and therefore not so limited by law. Indeed the Commission recently has expressed its views to the Congress that it would be desirable to exercise a greater discretion with respect to the length of licensing periods within the maximum three year license period provided by Section 307(d). It has also initiated rulemaking to this end.

The foundation of the American system of broadcasting was laid in the Radio Act of 1927 when Congress placed the basic responsibility for all matter broadcast to the public at the grass roots level in the hands of the station licensee. That obligation was carried forward into the Communications Act of 1934 and remains unaltered and undivided. The licensee, is, in effect, a "trustee" in the sense that his license to operate his station imposes upon him a non-delegable duty to serve the public interest in the community he had chosen to represent as a broadcaster.

Great confidence and trust are placed in the citizens who have qualified as broadcasters. The primary duty and privilege to select the material to be broadcast to his audience and the operation of his component of this powerful medium of communication is left in his hands. As was stated by the Chairman in behalf of this Commission in recent testimony before a Congressional Committee:[9]

> Thus far Congress has not imposed by law an affirmative programming requirement on broadcast licenses. Rather, it has heretofore given licensees a broad discretion in the selection of programs. In recognition of this principle, Congress provided in section 3(h) of the Communications Act that a person engaged in radio broadcasting shall not be deemed a common carrier. To

---

[9] Testimony of Frederick W. Ford, May 16, 1960, before the Subcommittee on Communications of the Committee on Interstate and Foreign Commerce, United States Senate.

this end the Commission in administering the Act and the courts in interpreting it have consistently maintained that responsibility for the selection and presentation of broadcast material ultimately devolves upon the individual station licensee, and that the fulfillment of such responsibility requires the free exercise of his independent judgment.

As indicated by former President Hoover, then Secretary of Commerce, in the Radio Conference of 1922–25:

> The dominant element for consideration in the radio field is, and always will be, the great body of the listening public, millions in number, country wide in distribution. There is no proper line of conflict between the broadcaster and the listener, nor would I attempt to array one against the other. Their interests are mutual, for without the one the other could not exist.
>
> There have been few developments in industrial history to equal the speed and efficiency with which genius and capital have joined to meet radio needs. The great majority of station owners today recognize the burden of service and gladly assume it. Whatever other motive may exist for broadcasting, the pleasing of the listener is always the primary purpose. . . .
>
> The greatest public interest must be the deciding factor. I presume that few will dissent as to the correctness of this principle, for all will agree that public good must ever balance private desire; but its acceptance leads to important and far-reaching practical effects, as to which there may not be the same unanimity, but from which, nevertheless, there is no logical escape.

The confines of the licensee's duty are set by the general standard "the public interest, convenience or necessity."[10] The initial and principal execution of that standard, in terms of the area he is licensed to serve, is the obligation of the licensee. The principal ingredient of such obligation consists of a diligent, positive and continuing effort by the licensee to discover and fulfill the tastes, needs and desires of his service area. If he has accomplished this, he has met his public responsibility. It is the duty of the Commission, in the first instance, to select persons as licensees who meet the qualifications laid down in the Act, and on a continuing basis to review the operations of such licensees from time to time to provide reasonable assurance to the public that the broadcast service it receives is such as its direct and justifiable interest requires.

Historically it is interesting to note that in its review of station performance the Federal Radio Commission sought to extract the general principles of broadcast service which should (1) guide the licensee in his determination of the public interest and (2) be employed by the Commission as an "index" or general frame of reference in evaluating the licensee's discharge of his public duty. The Commission attempted no precise definition of the components of the public interest but left the discernment of its limit to the practical operation of broadcast regulation. It required existing stations to report the types of service which had been provided and called on the public to express its views and preferences as to programs and other

---

[10] Cf. Communications Act of 1934, as amended, *inter alia*, Secs. 307, 309.

broadcast services. It sought information from as many sources as were available in its quest of a fair and equitable basis for the selection of those who might wish to become licensees and the supervision of those who already engaged in broadcasting.

The spirit in which the Radio Commission approached its unprecedented task was to seek to chart a course between the need of arriving at a workable concept of the public interest in station operation, on the one hand, and the prohibition laid on it by the First Amendment to the Constitution of the United States and by Congress in Section 29 of the Federal Radio Act against censorship and interference with free speech, on the other. The Standards or guidelines which evolved from that process, in their essentials, were adopted by the Federal Communications Commission and have remained as the basis for evaluation of broadcast service. They have in the main, been incorporated into various codes and manuals of network and station operation.

It is emphasized, that these standards or guidelines should in no sense constitute a rigid mold for station performance, nor should they be considered as a Commission formula for broadcast service in the public interest. Rather, they should be considered as indicia of the types and areas of service which, on the basis of experience, have usually been accepted by the broadcasters as more or less included in the practical definition of community needs and interests.

Broadcasting licensees must assume responsibility for all material which is broadcast through their facilities. This includes all programs and advertising material which they present to the public. With respect to advertising material the licensee has the additional responsibility to take all reasonable measures to eliminate any false, misleading, or deceptive matter and to avoid abuses with respect to the total amount of time devoted to advertising continuity as well as the frequency with which regular programs are interrupted for advertising messages. This duty is personal to the licensee and may not be delegated. He is obligated to bring his positive responsibility affirmatively to bear upon all who have a hand in providing broadcast matter for transmission through his facilities so as to assure the discharge of his duty to provide acceptable program schedule consonant with operating in the public interest in his community. The broadcaster is obligated to make a positive, diligent and continuing effort, in good faith, to determine the tastes, needs and desires of the public in his community and to provide programming to meet those needs and interests. This again, is a duty personal to the licensee and may not be avoided by delegation of the responsibility to others.

Although the individual station licensee continues to bear legal responsibility for all matter broadcast over his facilities, the structure of broadcasting, as developed in practical operation, is such—especially in television —that, in reality, the station licensee has little part in the creation, production, selection, and control of network program offerings. Licensees place "practical reliance" on networks for the selection and supervision of network programs which, of course, are the principal broadcast fare of the vast majority of television stations throughout the country.[11]

In the fulfillment of his obligation the broadcaster should consider the

---

[11] The Commission, in recognition of this problem as it affects the licensees, has recently recommended to the Congress enactment of legislation providing for direct regulation of networks in certain respects.

tastes, needs and desires of the public he is licensed to serve in developing his programming and should exercise conscientious efforts not only to ascertain them but also to carry them out as well as he reasonably can. He should reasonably attempt to meet all such needs and interests on an equitable basis. Particular areas of interest and types of appropriate service may, of course, differ from community to community, and from time to time. However, the Commission does expect its broadcast licensees to take the necessary steps to inform themselves of the real needs and interests of the areas they serve and to provide programming which in fact constitutes a diligent effort, in good faith, to provide for those needs and interests.

The major elements usually necessary to meet the public interest, needs and desires of the community in which the station is located as developed by the industry, and recognized by the Commission, have included: (1) Opportunity for Local Self-Expression, (2) The Development and Use of Local Talent, (3) Programs for Children, (4) Religious Programs, (5) Educational Programs, (6) Public Affairs Programs, (7) Editorialization by Licensees, (8) Political Broadcasts, (9) Agricultural Programs, (10) News Programs, (11) Weather and Market Reports, (12) Sports Programs, (13) Service to Minority Groups, (14) Entertainment Programming.

The elements set out above are neither all-embracing nor constant. We re-emphasize that they do not serve and have never been intended as a rigid mold or fixed formula for station operations. The ascertainment of the needed elements of the broadcast matter to be provided by a particular licensee for the audience he is obligated to serve remains primarily the function of the licensee. His honest and prudent judgments will be accorded great weight by the Commission. Indeed, any other course would tend to substitute the judgment of the Commission for that of the licensee.

The programs provided first by "chains" of stations and then by networks have always been recognized by this Commission as of great value to the station licensee in providing a well-rounded community service. The importance of network programs need not be re-emphasized as they have constituted an integral part of the well-rounded program service provided by the broadcast business in most communities.

Our own observations and the testimony in this inquiry have persuaded us that there is no public interest basis for distinguishing between sustaining and commercially sponsored programs in evaluating station performance. However, this does not relieve the station from responsibility for retaining the flexibility to accommodate public needs.

Sponsorship of public affairs, and other similar programs may very well encourage broadcasters to greater efforts in these vital areas. This is borne out by statements made in this proceeding in which it was pointed out that under modern conditions sponsorship fosters rather than diminishes the availability of important public affairs and "cultural" broadcast programming. There is some convincing evidence, for instance, that at the network level there is a direct relation between commercial sponsorship and "clearance" of public affairs and other "cultural" programs. Agency executives have testified that there is unused advertising support for public affairs type programming. The networks and some stations have scheduled these types of programs during "prime time."

The Communication Act[12] provides that the Commission may grant con-

---

[12] Section 308(a).

struction permits and station licenses, or modifications or renewals thereof, "only upon written application" setting forth the information required by the Act and the Commission's Rules and Regulations. If, upon examination of any such application, the Commission shall find the public interest, convenience, and necessity would be served by the granting thereof, it shall grant said application. If it does not so find, it shall so advise the applicant and other known parties in interest of all objections to the application and the applicant shall then be given an opportunity to supply additional information. If the Commission cannot then make the necessary finding, the application is designated for hearing and the applicant bears the burden of providing proof of the public interest.

During our hearings there seemed to be some misunderstanding as to the nature and use of the "statistical" data regarding programming and advertising required by our application forms. We wish to stress that no one may be summarily judged as to the service he has performed on the basis of the information contained in his application. As we said long ago:

> It should be emphasized that the statistical data before the Commission constitute an index only of the manner of operation of the stations and are not considered by the Commission as conclusive of the over-all operation of the stations in question.
>
> Licensees will have an opportunity to show the nature of their program service and to introduce other relevant evidence which would demonstrate that in actual operation the program service of the station is, in fact, a well rounded program service and is in conformity with the promises and representations previously made in prior applications to the Commission.[13]

As we have said above, the principal ingredient of the licensee's obligation to operate his station in the public interest is the diligent, positive, and continuing effort by the licensee to discover and fulfill the tastes, needs, and desires of his community or service area, for broadcast service.

To enable the Commission in its licensing functions to make the necessary public interest finding, we intend to revise PART IV of our application forms to require a statement by the applicant, whether for new facilities, renewal or modification, as to: (1) the measures he has taken and the effort he has made to determine the tastes, needs and desires of his community or service area, and (2) the manner in which he proposes to meet those needs and desires.

Thus we do not intend to guide the licensee along the path of programming; on the contrary the licensee must find his own path with the guidance of those whom his signal is to serve. We will thus steer clear of the bans of censorship without disregarding the public's vital interest. What we propose will not be served by pre-planned program format submissions accompanied by complimentary references from local citizens. What we propose is documented program submissions prepared as the result of assiduous planning and consultation covering two main areas: first, a canvass of the listening public who will receive the signal and who constitute a definite public interest figure; second, consultation with leaders in community life—public officials, educators, religious, the entertainment media,

---

[13] Public Notice (98501), Sept. 20, 1946, "Status of Standard Broadcast Applications."

agriculture, business, labor—professional and eleemosynary organizations, and others who bespeak the interests which make up the community.

By the care spent in obtaining and reflecting the views thus obtained, which clearly cannot be accepted without attention to the business judgment of the licensee if his station is to be an operating success, will the standard of programming in the public interest be best fulfilled. This would not ordinarily be the case if program formats have been decided upon by the licensee before he undertakes his planning and consultation, for the result would show little stimulation on the part of the two local groups above referenced. And it is the composite of their contributive planning, led and sifted by the expert judgment of the licensee, which will assure to the station the appropriate attention to the public interest which will permit the Commission to find that a license may issue. By his narrative development, in his application, of the planning, consulting, shaping, revising, creating, discarding and evaluation of programming thus conceived or discussed, the licensee discharges the public interest facet of his business calling without Government dictation or supervision and permits the Commission to discharge its responsibility to the public without invasion of spheres of freedom properly denied to it. By the practicality and specificity of his narrative the licensee facilitates the application of expert judgment by the Commission. Thus, if a particular kind of educational program could not be feasibly assisted (by funds or service) by educators for more than a few time periods, it would be idle for program composition to place it in weekly focus. Private ingenuity and educational interest should look further, toward implemental suggestions of practical yet constructive value. The broadcaster's license is not intended to convert his business into "an instrumentality of the federal government";[14] neither, on the other hand, may he ignore the public interest which his application for a license should thus define and his operations thereafter reasonably observe.

Numbers of suggestions were made during the *en banc* hearings concerning possible uses by the Commission of codes of broadcast practices adopted by segments of the industry as part of a process of self-regulation. While the Commission has not endorsed any specific code of broadcast practices, we consider the efforts of the industry to maintain high standards of conduct to be highly commendable and urge that the industry persevere in these efforts.

The Commission recognizes that submissions, by applicants, concerning their past and future programming policies and performance provide one important basis for deciding whether—insofar as broadcast services are concerned—we may properly make the public interest finding requisite to the grant of an application for a standard FM or television broadcast station. The particular manner in which applicants are required to depict their proposed or past broadcast policies and services (including the broadcasting of commercial announcements) may, therefore, have significant bearing upon the Commission's ability to discharge its statutory duties in the matter. Conscious of the importance of reporting requirements, the Commission on November 24, 1958 initiated proceedings (Docket No. 12673) to consider revisions to the rules prescribing the form and content of reports on broadcast programming.

---

[14] "The defendant is not an instrumentality of the federal government but a privately owned corporation." *McIntire* v. *Wm. Penn Broadcasting Co.*, 151 F. 2d 597, 600.

Aided by numerous helpful suggestions offered by witnesses in the recent *en banc* hearings on broadcast programming, the Commission is at present engaged in a thorough study of this subject. Upon completion of that study we will announce, for comment by all interested parties, such further revisions to the present reporting requirements as we think will best conduce to an awareness, by broadcasters, of their responsibilities to the public and to effective, efficient processing, by the Commission, of applications for broadcast licenses and renewals.

To this end, we will initiate further rule making on the subject at the earliest practicable date.

Separate Statement of Commissioner Hyde

I believe that the Commission's "Interim Report and Statement of Policy" in Docket No. 12782 misses the central point of the hearing conducted by the Commission en banc, December 7, 1959, to February 1, 1960.

It reiterates the legal position which was taken by the Federal Radio Commission in 1927, and which has been adhered to by the Federal Communications Commission since it was organized in 1934. This viewpoint was accepted by the executives of the leading networks and by most other units of the broadcasting industry as well as the National Association of Broadcasters. The main concern requiring a fresh approach is what to do in the light of the law and the matters presented by many witnesses in the hearings. This, I understand, is to be the subject of a rule-making proceeding still to be initiated. I urged the preparation of an appropriate rule-making notice prior to the preparation of the instant statement.

I also disagree with the decision of the Commission to release the document captioned "Interim Report by the Office of Network Study, Responsibility for Broadcast Matter, Docket No. 12782." Since it deals in part with a hearing in which the Commission itself sat en banc, I feel that it does not have the character of a separate staff-study type of document, and that its release with the Commission policy statement will create confusion. Moreover, a substantial portion of the document is concerned with matter still under investigation process in Docket 12872. I think issuance of comment on these matters under the circumstances is premature and inappropriate.

APPENDIX D

Federal Communications Commission

Ascertainment of Community Problems by Broadcast Applicants

Title 47—Telecommunication

CHAPTER 1—FEDERAL
COMMUNICATIONS COMMISSION
[FCC 75-1361; Docket No. 19715]

PART 1—PRACTICE AND
PROCEDURE

First Report and Order

In the matter of ascertainment of community problems by broadcast applicants.

1. The Commission has before it a *Further Notice of Inquiry and Proposed Rulemaking,* 53 FCC 2d 3 (1975), in the above-captioned proceeding, and 51 comments in response thereto.

2. This proceeding was initiated by a *Notice of Inquiry,* 40 FCC 2d 379 (1973), to develop standards for the ascertainment of community problems and needs by commercial broadcast license applicants.[1] Renewal applicants are presently required to follow the guidelines set forth in the *Primer on Ascertainment of Community Problems by Broadcast Applicants,* 27 FCC 2d 650, 36 F.R. 4092 (1971), which was intended to apply to them until separate procedures were developed. Based upon comments received in response to the initial *Notice of Inquiry, supra,* the Commission made specific proposals regarding ascertainment by license renewal applicants, which were set forth in the *Further Notice,* released on May 15, 1975 (40 FR 22091).

Summary of Action Taken

3. We have considered the roles and functions of the radio and television media in discharging their statutory responsibilities for service in the public interest and how the execution of those responsibilities might be affected by variations in station and market size, station formats and numbers of outlets in a given market. We have determined that television and radio differ in substantial and meaningful ways, but that these differences do not call for different standards of community ascertainment. On the other hand, such distinctions as station size and format may reasonably affect the way in which common ascertainment standards are met, as well as the manner in which programming responsive to ascertained problems is designed and carried out.

Reprinted from the *Federal Register,* vol. 41, no. 4 (Wednesday, January 7, 1976).

[1] Ascertainment guidelines and reporting methods for non-commercial educational licensees have been set out for comment in *Ascertainment of Community Problems by Noncommercial Educational Broadcast Applicants,* 54 FCC 2d 766 (1975).

4. We are eliminating the requirement that an applicant compile a compositional survey. In its place the licensee must maintain, in its public file, a listing of certain demographic aspects of its city of license, including total population figures, numbers and proportions of males, females, minorities, youth and the elderly. Also, we have compiled a list of structural and institutional elements common to most communities and are requiring licensees to interview leaders in each of these elements. No *minimum* number of interviews has been established—the key remaining the representativeness of the leaders interviewed—but we have established a reasonable number of interviews which, if performed, would preclude any challenge to the gross quantitative sufficiency of the licensee's leader survey. Up to 50 percent of these interviews may be conducted by non-management level employees under proper supervision. We seek to emphasize that the other half or more of such interviews conducted by management should be allocated in such a way as to bring the officials and principals of a station into contact with a variety of leaders—particularly those who speak for the interests of racial and ethnic minorities and women.[1a] We are retaining face-to-face interviewing as a staple of leader consultations, but are liberalizing the format of these interviews to allow licensees to include less formal contacts with leaders in their leadership surveys.

5. We expect that the ascertainment process will be continuous throughout the license term, but are requiring the licensee to submit its community leader checklist only with its renewal application. Summaries of these interviews are to be placed in the public file. From these interviews and whatever other input the licensee receives, the licensee must present programming to meet some community problems. We are extending to all licensees the current requirement that television licensees annually list no more than 10 problems they have discovered and the programs broadcast to meet these problems. These annual lists will be kept in the public file and submitted to the Commission with the licensee's renewal application. Further, we are retaining the requirement that licensees conduct general public surveys of their community. These surveys may be conducted at any time during the license term and are to be placed in the licensee's public file together with a narrative statement of the sources consulted and the methods followed in conducting the survey.

6. We will adopt our proposed small market exemption which excludes all stations located in communities with populations of 10,000 or fewer persons, but not within a Standard Metropolitan Statistical Area, from certain ascertainment requirements. Licensees of these stations, however, are still required to remain conversant with community problems. The exemption merely allows the licensee to choose the method by which he will become aware of these problems. Further, licensees in these small markets are required to prepare annual problems-programs lists and to submit them to the Commission with their renewal application. (Para. 5, *supra*)

7. In the discussion which follows, we will set out each specific proposal from the *Further Notice*, an analysis of the comments thereupon, and our conclusions. Included as Appendix A are certain changes in § 1.526 of the Rules, while Appendix B is the new *Primer on Ascertainment of Community Problems by Commercial Broadcast Renewal Applicants*.[2]

The Roles of Radio and Television

8. In the *Further Notice*, we acknowledged the differing roles of radio and television in serving the public. We stated our belief, however, that the differences in the two media did not provide a basis for departing from the basically similar ascertainment *standards* applied to both kinds of commercial broadcast facilities. 53 FCC 2d at 6.[3] Comments were made by a number of parties insisting that there

---

[1a] See Q. and A's 4 and 13(a), 1971 *Primer, supra.*

[2] This proceeding is being kept open because there are some additional alterations to the *Primer* which we believe worthy of consideration with respect to applicants other than renewal candidates. These changes will be set out for comment later.

[3] Apart from these standards, however, we stated that "a station with few employees, for instance, cannot be expected to conduct a community survey as extensive as its larger television counterpart (footnote omitted). Similarly, how a licensee of a radio station decides to respond to the many conflicting and competing problems and needs of the public within its service area may differ substantially from the manner in which its television counterpart serves the public." 53 FCC 2d at 6.

are differences between radio and television translatable into differing ascertainment requirements for each medium. These are stated mainly in terms of economic and manpower resources available (Brandon-Robinson Radio Corporation and RKO–General, Inc.), as well as greater variety in formats available in radio (American Broadcasting Companies, Inc.). The differences are said to be such that the ascertainment requirements should be lessened for radio licensees.

9. Specifically, Storer Broadcasting Company suggests that the general public survey be eliminated entirely, and that radio licensees be required to conduct only one community leader survey during the entire license period, and file only one set of documents (the leader survey form and the problems-programs list). Midwest Radio-Television, Inc. suggests that the annual lists of problems and programs be dispensed with entirely for radio. ABC submits that if the Commission is unable to outline different procedures for radio, then there should be "* * * different levels of application unique to radio * * *" of the proposed procedures. Specifically, the numbers of leaders to be contacted should be significantly reduced for radio licensees, and only one triennial list of problems and programs ought to be filed.

10. The comments are more detailed, but nevertheless essentially repetitive of the materials before us when the *Further Notice* was issued. We thus have decided to leave unaltered our decision to treat radio and television in the same manner in their ascertainment requirements for the reasons set forth in the *Further Notice*, 53 FCC 2d at 6. We believe, however, that the effect of the procedures adopted here—some of them modified beyond the extent proposed in *Further Notice*—frequently will be beneficial to those smaller-staff, smaller-market licensees with lesser financial and personnel resources to draw upon for ascertainment. This is particularly true of the "small-market" exemption (Paras. 47–55, *infra.*), which covers roughly 25% of all commercial radio and TV stations presently licensed (only a handful of these being TV stations, however).

Ascertainment Guidelines for Renewal
Applicants: Continuous Ascertainment

11. We have stated our opinion that renewal applicants ought to ascertain throughout their license terms. 53 FCC 2d at 9. Continuous ascertainment is not new in concept but dates at least from the *Report and Statement of Policy Re: Commission en banc Programming Inquiries*, 25 Fed. Reg. 7291, 20RR 190, (1960) (hereinafter *Programming Policy Statement*). The novelty of the proposal in the *Further Notice* had to do with the continuity or periodicity of the reporting of ascertainment efforts, in contrast to the *Primer's* requirement that surveying be accomplished within six months of the filing of the renewal application. Requiring a licensee to record its ascertainment continuously or periodically throughout the license term received both support and opposition in the current round of comments. The National Organization for Women pointed out that one benefit of continuous ascertainment would be the spreading of the licensee's interest and involvement in the community through the entire term. CBS, Inc. says that it is more realistic to conduct an ascertainment continuously, and that the burdens imposed upon both the licensee and its interviewees will be alleviated through this stretching out, rather than being so tightly concentrated as is presently the case. McClatchy Newspapers states that it has followed the continuous ascertainment principle (as well as many of the other proposals in the *Further Notice*) for some time, and has found the approach to be valuable in establishing guidelines for programming. Heart O'Wisconsin Broadcasters, Inc. supports the concept because the listing of past programming with needs already discovered is more meaningful than attempting to propose programming for problems and needs which may exist at the time discerned, but not by the time the programming responses are made. Finally, the National Black Media Coalition supports the principle, but does not believe that the remainder of the proposals in the *Further Notice* are designed adequately to assure its effectiveness.

12. Opponents of continuous ascertainment, including several multiple station owners—e.g., Wendell Mayes, Jr. and John Quinlan Hearne—believe that continuous ascertainment will result in additional burdens upon licensees and upon the renewal process of the Commission, with no resulting increase in available information. They say that licensees are in such a position in the community that they hear about, or are aware of, all community problems and needs. Mr. Mayes believes further that the proposal will result not in continuous ascertainment, but in disjointed, periodic ascertainments. Similarly, Capitol Broadcasting Company, Inc. states that a licensee will never be able to get a single comprehensive

picture of community problems and needs, but only fragmented glimpses. Finally, the Office of Communication of the United Church of Christ (UCC) argues that ascertainment is intended to be a prospective device for discovering community problems and needs with a view toward what programs will be proposed to serve those problems and needs.

13. The Commission is of the view that the principle of ascertainment throughout the license term is sound, and that the recording and reporting of those community survey efforts should complement the principle. At the same time, we have no desire to create three entire ascertainments—i.e., one for each of the yearly reports proposed in the *Further Notice*. Our aim, instead, was to enable the licensee to report the same single, continuous effort in three annual segments instead of one voluminous exposition near the end of the license term. We find persuasive, however, the argument that, under annual reporting as proposed in the *Further Notice*, *expectations* of what is required yearly—e.g., numbers of community leader interviews—will tend to rise until they approximate the levels of the current three-year effort. We are provided no comments, and we perceive no public interest reasons, why ascertainment reporting should triple in size and effort. Accordingly, we are adjusting our proposals to head off any such proliferation of community surveying and attendant paper work.

14. We shall expect a distribution of ascertainment effort throughout the license term (the exception being the general public survey, which may be done at a single discrete time during the license period). As is set forth in paragraph 19, *infra*, the licensee will be expected to achieve a representative survey of community leaders from the elements appearing on the community leader checklist (paragraph 16, and Appendix D) over the entire license period, rather than apportioning the contacts into particular time frames, such as the annual period of the *Further Notice*. Thus the change we make goes to periodicity, not continuity. We expect the licensee's ascertainment to be continuous, and believe that both timely performance and sustained evaluation of the leader surveying will be enhanced through the required deposit in the public file of information—such as that contained on the Community Leader Contact Form (Appendix E)—within a reasonable time after the contact has been completed. (See discussion at Paras. 38–39, *infra*.)

15. UCC is correct that *Primer* ascertainment has looked from presently discerned problems and needs toward future programming to treat some of those problems. This is so because the *Primer* was designed to apply to new applicants for broadcast facilities and proposals for prospective programming to meet current problems were, *inter alia*, considered in determining whether a grant of license was in the public interest. The *Primer* was not designed to apply to renewal applicants who have operated stations in their communities and, thus, already have ascertained community needs and problems and are programming to them throughout their license terms. Nonetheless, this prospective element is retained under our proposals for continuous ascertainment, since earlier interviews provide problems-needs responses that may be the basis for later programming. In fact, ascertainment remains up-to-date if done in this fashion throughout the license term. However, ascertainment is chiefly a means to the end of better programming service to a community, not an end in itself. *Programming Policy Statement, supra*. The retrospective nature of the suggested problems-programs list for radio stations—like its predecessor for television stations, which has been requested of licensees since January 16, 1974—is one means of evaluating periodically the effectiveness of an ascertainment's programming results. This yearly look backward at problems and illustrative programming which treated them is, we believe, particularly appropriate for renewal applicants, who must "run on their records." *Office of Communication of the United Church of Christ v. F.C.C.*, 359 F. 2d 994 (D.C. Cir. 1966) at 1007. In sum, we do not think that the introduction of a retrospective element into an ascertainment scheme which is also prospective will detract from the purposes and effect of either community ascertainment or of the programming which is ascertainment's chief goal. Indeed, this method—which requires the licensee to prepare annually a list of problems and programs designed to meet those problems—will give rise to timely responses to current community problems.

Community Leader Checklist

16. In an effort to simplify the compositional study required by the 1971 *Primer*, and to lend greater certainty to the survey coverage of a community of license, we

proposed to substitute a "Community Leader Checklist" of "common socioeconomic elements" we believed would be found in most communities but which, in any event, could be added to or subtracted from to match the peculiarities of any broadcaster's own service area. 53 FCC 2d at 12. The Community Leader Checklist received generally favorable comments. CBS argues however, that the Checklist has the disadvantage of freezing the licensee's perceptions of the community. UNDA–USA says that the Checklist unduly narrows the scope of leader consultations from their present level. Other problems cited are the lack of a category, "Others," in which a licensee could enumerate contacts with leaders of elements peculiar to the community he serves but not found on the Checklist, and the possibility of confusion resulting from the overlap of some of the elements on the list. RKO-General notes the same difficulty, and says that the Commission should make clear that the licensee's discretion will control the inclusion of a particular leader in a given category. NOW states that there should be included a requirement that the licensee include the total number of women as well as minority persons interviewed in each category of the Checklist. Storer opposes some of the categorization, saying that "public health" and "safety and welfare" should be separated.

17. Additionally, ABC supports specification of key elements within the community as an effective guide for ascertainment. ABC opposes, however, the concept and need for a Checklist, claiming this will merely increase the paperwork burden on licensees. ABC suggests a simple "yes-no" question in the renewal application to reflect the licensee's confirmation of contacts with leaders in each element, or the inclusion of the list of elements in the renewal application itself. John Quinlan Hearne also says that the checklist can be improved by recombination and re-ordering of the categories. NBMC supports the principle, but points out that the listing of elements should be done alphabetically. The Commission should also clearly state its expectations that minority persons are to be contacted in all categories, as well as the one labeled "minority and ethnic groups." NBMC also says that there should be a separate column in the form to indicate the number of minority persons in each category. NBC, on the other hand, submits that the Commission should make clear that licensees are *not* required to interview one minority person in each category, either annually or over the three-year license period. Finally, the Gay Coalition Task Force on the Media requests inclusion of the homosexual community in the list of common elements.

18. After consideration of all comments, we shall adhere to our decision to employ a Community Leader Checklist (Appendix D) as a means of assuring licensee contacts with a representative cross-section of community leaders, while at the same time relieving them of the burdens and uncertainties involved in the *Primer's* compositional study.[4] The Checklist is—with a few modifications adopted from the comments—thorough enough for most communities and yet not overly detailed. The checklist provides a general framework to the licensee, who must complete the details by contacting leaders within categories found in the community served. A licensee is permitted to show that one or more of these categories is not present in its community.

19. Among the commenters' suggestions we shall adopt are: (a) alphabetical listing of the elements; and (b) inclusion of a separate reporting category for women (the numbers of leaders contacted in all elements who are women) matching that for minorities. We have also included a category, "Other." This latter addition is intended to make allowances for certain elements not on the Checklist but peculiar to a given community, which the licensee could, at its own option, contact because of the size and/or influence of these elements. We do not wish the flexibility introduced by the "Other" category, however, to destroy the essential uniformity and common applicability of the Checklist by leading to disputes over whether a licensee should have perceived as significant in its community some element not otherwise covered on the Checklist. We intend, therefore, that if a licensee conducts interviews in all Checklist categories that apply in its community, its coverage of all significant elements will not be open to question. Whether the interviews performed in each element actually establish representativeness would depend not only on coverage, but on such above-mentioned factors as size and/or influence of these elements in the community. (See discussion of numbers at para. 27, *infra*).

---

[4] We note that currently all licensees will have performed a compositional study at some point either as purchasers or applicants for new facilities.

20. It is evident from the comments that clarification is necessary upon some additional matters. First is whether licensees are required to include women and members of minority groups in their contacts within each element of the community contained in the Community Leader Checklist. Licensees should be aware, from five years of practice under the 1971 *Primer*, that community leader surveys are to be representative of the significant elements in a community. *Primer*, Questions and Answers 13(a) and 16. If women as women, or women's groups as such, are significant, they should be represented in the survey; and the same is true for minority individuals and groups. But representativeness does not mean mathematically precise mirroring of the proportions of women and minorities in the community's population. What is true for the overall community leader survey is even more pertinent in considering the several topical elements of the Checklist. That is, it seems quite possible for a leader survey adequately to represent leadership by females and minority persons in an entire community without necessarily interviewing a woman or a minority individual in every Checklist element. Females and minorities may predominate in certain areas of community leadership, but they may be absent from others.

21. A further matter of possible confusion is the placement of leaders in particular categories. It is possible that one community leader could speak for more than one element from the Checklist. If so, should such a person be counted in more than one element? We believe that where the leader, in discussing community problems and needs, may fairly be said to have spoken for more than one element, that person may be included in all relevant categories. We will rely upon the licensee's discretion in this matter. Conceivably, that discretion might be abused if a single person were made to stand for too much of a community's opinion of problems and needs. But we will not draw that line in the abstract.

Number of Leaders To Be Contacted

22. We proposed in the *Further Notice* that the licensee's certification, in its renewal application, for consultation with "one or more" community leaders in each of the Checklist categories annually would "create a presumption of the adequacy of this part of the community leader ascertainment, rebuttable only by a clear and convincing showing to the contrary." 53 FCC 2d at 13. Our intent was to set some minimal standard of continuity, or at least periodicity (i.e., annual), and we attempted to make clear that tripling this yearly number of contacts over the triennial term was neither a requirement nor a guarantee—neither floor nor ceiling—of representativeness for the community leader survey. *Ibid.* at 14. A number of commenting parties (RKO-General, CBS, Dempsey & Koplovitz) requested clarification as to the number of community leader interviews giving rise to the presumption of adequacy for that portion of the ascertainment. Confusion is said to result from our reference to both quantitative (one leader per element per year) and qualitative ("representativeness") standards, and to two different time periods—one year and three years. RKO-General says that one leader contacted in each category annually should be sufficient. On the other hand, if a "representativeness" test is to be applied, and no number specified, then the criteria for that test, as well as some irreducible minimum number of total contacts, should be stated.

23. NBMC states the contrary proposition, that one leader in each category should not be sufficient to create a presumption, because no single element in a community is so homogeneous that a single leader can speak for the entire group. NBMC also argues that, should a minimum number be established, there should be a higher number for large VHF television stations than for other broadcast facilities. CBS submits that, if a test of representativeness is to be used, licensees be able to meet such a requirement over the entire three-year license term, rather than annually. Midwest Radio-Television argues that the entire idea of a presumption of adequacy based upon minimum numbers reduces to a "ritual dance" what is otherwise a meaningful experience for licensees. Midwest observes that one contact of a leader in agriculture could be virtually meaningless in a large metropolitan area, and a single contact insufficient in a farm community. NOW says that the presumption of adequacy is an improper abandonment of the principle in the *Programming Policy Statement, supra,* that the chief ingredient of the licensee's service in the public interest is the ascertainment and meeting of community problems and needs. NOW also notes that there is no way of determining the relative importance of each element in the community, other than leaving this matter to the licensee's discretion, which NOW disapproves.

24. NAB argues that the Commission has said it is not getting into a "numbers

game" when, in fact, it is. NAB also believes that the Commission is not actually relaxing any requirements or burdens upon licensees. ABC faults our failure to establish a minimum number of leaders to be contacted as being a numbers game without rules, subjecting a licensee to second-guessing by public interest groups and ultimately by the Commission. It is said that minimum numbers are necessary as a guideline, and that such guidelines could be correlated to the size of the SMSA, or the population of the community of license (where not located within an SMSA).

25. The comments received have caused us to reconsider as well-intentioned but unwise our efforts to place a floor under numbers of community leaders to be consulted. We sought to introduce a measure of predictability concerning ascertainment's quantitative aspects—a certain stability of expectation which would benefit both broadcasters and their citizen-evaluators. The magnitude and diversity of critical comment this inspired leads us to doubt the benefit in any change from the *Primer's* focus on a community leader ascertainment representative of all "significant elements" in the community—without reference to any "set number or formula." *Primer*, Question and Answer 14. We are inclined to agree, upon reflection, with the comment of Midwest Radio-Television that any effort to establish a presumptively adequate minimum number of leader consultations in each element—this number being the same for all communities, despite the varying importance of given elements in different cities—tends to place ritual ahead of representativeness.

26. We shall add a modicum of certainty to the leader ascertainment, however, by stating explicitly what we consider to be reasonable numbers of consultations which licensees in communities of varying sizes are expected to undertake during the license term. A licensee may conduct fewer interviews than set out in the table below, but a licensee who performs that number of interviews will be free of any question as to the gross quantitative sufficiency of its community leader survey. The relative coverage given to the several significant elements found on the Community Leader Checklist—i.e., whether representativeness has been achieved—would still be open to inquiry or challenge.

27. The following table of numbers of leader interviews takes into account several comments responsive to the *Notice* and *Further Notice*, as well as our own experience under the 1971 *Primer*:

Population of city of license:	Number of consultations
10,001 to 25,000	60
25,001 to 50,000	100
50,001 to 200,000	140
200,001 to 500,000	180
Over 500,000	220

Level of Consultations

28. The *Further Notice* proposed to modify the requirement of the 1971 *Primer* that all community leader interviews be conducted by principals or management personnel of a broadcast station. We suggested that up to 50 percent of such interviews ought to be permitted by non-managers or non-principals, if the licensee chose, so long as, during the three-year license term, principals or managers conducted at least one interview in each element of the Checklist. We further provided for supervision by principals or managers of leader surveying done by non-management station personnel. 53 FCC 2d 16. There was general agreement among the commenting parties for allowing 50% of the consultations with community leaders to be conducted by non-managerial employees of the licensee, so long as they are operating under the control of, and reporting results to, management personnel. For example, CBS states that this approach is more realistic, and will permit an increased scope of contacts. ABC, while supporting the relaxation, argues that the conditions imposed, particularly our admonition that one or more contacts within each element should be by a principal or manager, are unnecessarily restrictive, and minimize the benefits gained. In addition, ABC says that there should be no limitation upon the types of employees permitted to conduct ascertainment interviews, a point echoed by Haley, Bader and Potts, who express the hope that such persons as chief engineers, traffic directors and office managers would also qualify. RKO-General says that the limitation to 50% of the interviews by non-management employees is arbitrary so long as the control requirements are adhered to.

29. NOW, on the other hand, opposes interviews by non-management employees (as does NBMC), pointing out that such persons are not in decision-making positions, and rarely are able to influence major programming decisions. NOW urges that the burden upon licensees, if any, is a cost of doing business which must be accepted. Finally, NOW urges that, should the Commission decide to permit other employees to be involved, at the very least they should be employees in the upper levels, and not, for example, secretaries or maintenance workers.

30. Nothing in the comments on this point causes us to change our previous determination that non-managerial personnel ought to be permitted a degree of involvement in the ascertainment of community leaders, if the licensee chooses. Such participation constitutes an option, not a requirement. We reiterate the importance of leader contacts by principals and managers, and have decided to adopt the recommendations of the *Further Notice* that these decisionmakers should account for at least 50 percent of total leader interviews. We shall also adhere to the idea of managerial supervision for non-management interviewing. We have decided to withdraw, however, from the *Further Notice's* suggestion that there be at least one management interview in every applicable element of the Checklist. Instead, we wish to recognize that contact by a station's principals and officials may be more important for some elements than for others. We reaffirm, in this connection, the 1971 *Primer's* emphasis on contacts with leaders who represent the interests of racial and ethnic minorities and, by extension, of women. 27 FCC 2d at Q. & A. 4 and 13(a).

Format of Leader Consultations

31. Of several means for executing community leader interviewing, the *Further Notice* recommended that "face-to-face" should remain the "staple," but suggested that such sessions need not be pre-arranged or otherwise steeped in formality. Other methods mentioned included joint surveys by several broadcasters serving the same community, as well as telephone interviewing and even "on-air" discussions of problems and needs with leaders guesting on programs. 53 FCC 2d at 17.

32. Comment was generally favorable, to the effect that these relaxations from the *Primer* would result in more extensive and meaningful efforts on the part of the licensee, and ultimately in better programming for the public. (CBS, WKJB AM–FM, Inc. and ABC) The Greater Portland Radio Broadcasters Association noted that it has conducted joint leader surveys in the past (as well as individual surveys by member stations) and that this has worked to the benefit of both broadcasters and leaders. RKO-General made the additional request that jointly owned stations in the same market be allowed to conduct a single ascertainment for all stations so owned. McKenna, Wilkinson, Kittner (MWK) want us to make clear that other than "face-to-face" interviewing is not "inferior."

33. NAB, on the other hand, characterized the changes as slight, not truly a relaxation of the formalities of the *Primer*. NBMC believes that citizen advisory panels would be a better approach to community ascertainment. It argues that use of the telephone should not be allowed and that "town hall" and broadcast ascertainment methods should be used only to supplement face-to-face contacts, which it believes remain necessary. The Office of Communication, United Church of Christ (UCC), states that, while formality does not mean a "Victorian drawing room," it does mean something to impress the importance of the event on all parties concerned, which would be lost if any of the additional methods are allowed. Brandon-Robinson Broadcasting Corporation faults the proposed allowances as being still too rigid and formalistic, stating that a completely informal process would achieve the best results.

34. The comments generally supported our proposals for liberalizing the format of leader interviews, and we have found nothing in opposition which causes us to alter these aspects of ascertainment for renewal applicants. By retaining face-to-face interviewing as a "staple" of leader consultations, we intend no label of inferiority for other methods. We appreciate UCC's concern that only a relatively formal contact will impress the parties with the importance of their undertaking. However, as we stated in the *Further Notice*, informal encounters might be equally fruitful, or more so, on any given occasion. 53 FCC 2d at 17. There is nothing wrong with the NBMC suggestion for citizen panels in supplemental ascertainment. Indeed, some licensees already are using them. To rely wholly upon such bodies, however, might affect both the representativeness of the in-

terviewees and the independence of their responses. *Southern California Broadcasting Association, Inc.,* 30 FCC 2d 705 (1971). In any event, we see no reason to require citizen panels.

General Public Survey

35. The 1971 *Primer* provided for licensee interviews with a "random sample" of members of the general public in the community served—in addition to consultations with community leaders. *Primer* Q. & A. 13(b). The *Further Notice* declined to recommend deleting or substantially modifying this requirement, as some commenters urged, "in the absence of a clear demonstration that public surveying is unwarranted." 53 FCC 2d at 21. In the latest round of comments, the public survey met with positive responses from some licensees (e.g. Metromedia and CBS), but negative reactions from others. Among the latter, Storer repeated earlier comments that the public survey should be eliminated as time-consuming, burdensome and unproductive. ABC suggests that the function of public surveying essentially is fulfilled, continuously, by the semi-monthly announcements of renewal filings and of general trusteeship obligations recently introduced in §§ 1.580 and 73.1202 of the rules. Metromedia would like it made clear that only one survey of the public need be done over the three-year license term, and Media Statistics —a commercial organization specializing in public sampling—believes that, as a check upon the possible introduction of unfavorable variables interviews with the public should take place during a fixed time period as required under the *Primer.* The Greater Portland Radio Broadcasters' Association, noting that its members have conducted joint public surveys, and that this has lessened the burdens on licensees and achieved positive results, invites us to grant specific permission for such an approach. Midwest Radio-Television asks whether the Commission intends any distinction in the use of the terms "interview" and "consult" as applied to ascertainment surveys. Greater Media, Inc. suggests that the public survey should be permitted to consist of questions asked over the air, and responses to the station by telephone or mail. It argues that this approach would permit use of a readily available source of respondents—the station's listeners.

36. These comments, while diverse, present no clear weight of opinion for or against the general public survey, and tend to reinforce the tentative conclusion of the *Further Notice* that it ought to remain substantially unchanged from the practices developed under the 1971 *Primer.* We have discussed our reasons for believing that one-time surveying of the public may be more consonant with the idea of "randomness" than continuous public interviewing, 53 FCC 2d at 21, but we see no reason to bar more frequent or periodic surveying if rough randomness can be maintained. In response to ABC's point regarding the Section 1.580 and 73.1202 announcements, as well as Greater Media's suggestion, we stated in the report and order adopting on-air notices that they were not to be considered substitutes for ascertainment, *Formulation of Rules and Policies Relating to the Renewal of Broadcast Licenses,* 43 FCC 2d at 10 (1973). While responses of listeners may supplement ascertainment in making the broadcaster more aware of his community, we suspect that total reliance on such responses might not only introduce distortion or bias into the sampling but probably would produce more comments on program preferences than on the real matter of ascertainment —community problems and needs. *Primer,* Question and Answer 18. Answering Greater Portland's request for approval of joint public surveying, we see no reason why such methods could not comply with the 1971 *Primer.* Public interviewing may be done by a station's employees, or by an outside individual or organization having professional competence in the general field of polling, working under the licensee's supervision. We caution that if an association of broadcasters were to coordinate the surveying, it must somehow provide not only for the requisite technical expertise, but also for adequate supervision by each licensee taking part. A mere pooling of employees from each participating station to do the work of all—having among them no particular professional expertise—would not be sufficient, we believe. As we understand the *Primer,* a licensee may choose to survey the public by using either its own employees or an outside expert. But the employee-pooling arrangement described above would not insure every station a survey done by its own staff, nor would it guarantee professional competence. For the benefit of Midwest Radio-Television we have used the words "interview" and "consult" interchangeably so far as ascertainment is concerned—in the past and in this document.

Documentation

37. *Community Leader Checklist.* Our decision, after review of all comments, not to require annual reporting of numbers of community leader interviews is discussed at Paras. 13–14, *supra.* In keeping with that decision, a single Checklist covering the three-year license term would be submitted with the license renewal application and simultaneously deposited in the public file. (See amendments to § 1.526, Appendix D) As previously noted, we make this change not out of any desire to retreat from the continuity of ascertainment espoused in the *Further Notice,* but to alleviate any concern or expectation on the part of broadcasters or citizens that three years' worth of ascertainment need be done by licensees every year. More important than quantities of leader interviews, we believe, are the timeliness and quality of the contacts, which should be enhanced by continuous interviewing, duly reported and filed in some fashion such as that suggested on the sample Community Leader Contact Form (Appendix E).

38. *Leader Contact Form.* In the *Further Notice,* we suggested a form for reporting community leader contacts which would provide more information to the licensee and the public, but which could serve its chief purpose simply through deposit in the station's public file and ordinarily would not have to be filed with the Commission. Radio licensees presently send with their renewal applications lists of leaders identified by name, organization and position of leadership.[5] We proposed adding to the description of the contact its date, time and place, and the problems and needs disclosed; the name of the interviewer, and the interviewer's supervisor, if any; and, finally, the date of review of the record of consultation by a principal or manager of the licensee. However, absent complaint or dispute involving the leader ascertainment, this information ordinarily would not be required by the Commission, and would not have to be submitted with a renewal application. 59 FCC 2d at 23. Many broadcast commenters expressed concern that linking leaders' names with the community problems and needs they identified would tend to inhibit their candor and reduce their willingness to participate in the ascertainment process. Westinghouse adds that the Commission expressed similar concern in its report and order adopting the 1971 *Primer,* and should have no reason to alter that view now. Storer thinks information about the leader-interviewee could be kept in the public file, and even suggests adding biographical data, but believes the problems and needs disclosed by that interviewee ought to be maintained separately and not be traceable to the spokesman. UCC objects to our proposal that the licensee be permitted 45 days after a community leader interview to deposit the record of the contact in the public file. It claims that a station doing numerous interviews near renewal filing time might not have to deposit forms until some time after the application had been sent to the Commission. Some broadcasters, on the other hand, suggest 45 days might not be enough time to prepare records for deposit where, for example, they derive from a joint survey not entirely under the control of any single licensee.

39. We acknowledge our earlier concern over the possibly inhibitory effect upon ascertainees if the problems they discern in the community were to be linked with their names. 27 FCC 2d at 671. Our conclusion then, however, was that "the choice of attributing specific comments to community leaders is a matter left to the applicant and the particular leader." (*Id.*) We adhere to that view. Any leader wishing his or her opinions of problems and needs to remain undisclosed may request confidentiality—and this may be noted on the contact form or other record of the interview. Frankly, we expect such requests will be rare. Most interviewees will not be strangers to the limelight, and will be accustomed to speaking to and for the public. The exposure of their views of community problems in a broadcast station's public file is not likely to restrain them overmuch. In view of our acknowledgment in the *Further Notice* of the wishes of some citizen-commenters for more and better ascertainment documentation at the local level, 53 FCC 2d at 23, we prefer to make the content of leader interviews public unless some restriction is requested.[6] Regarding Storer's suggestion for more bio-

---

[5] Television licensees, however, may simply certify that the appropriate ascertainment materials have been placed in the public file. *Formulation of Rules and Policies Relating to the Renewal of Broadcast Licenses,* 43 FCC 2d at 48 (1973).

[6] There is no requirement, in any event, that a contact record's summary of problems and needs contain direct quotes. Paraphrase, rather than confidentiality, may be the only protection needed in many situations.

graphical data on interviewees, that is a matter for station representatives and their leader-contacts to decide. With respect to the period within which interview records should be available through the public file, we shall draw back from any specified number of days and simply require deposit within a reasonable time—which we would perceive to be no more than 30 to 45 days in most cases. To meet UCC's concern, we shall require that any interview for which credit is sought on a renewal application be recorded and available in the public file no later than the day the renewal application itself is filed with the Commission (and, of course, simultaneously deposited in the public file).

40. *Annual Problems-Programs Lists.* The *Further Notice* proposed that radio licensees deposit yearly in their public files a list of no more than 10 significant problems and needs existing in their service areas during the preceding 12 months, and a related list of illustrative programming presented during that period to treat those problems and needs. Placement in the station file would occur on the anniversary date of the filing of the renewal application, and upon sending of the application to the Commission, all such annual problems-programs lists from the term about to expire would be transmitted with it. 53 FCC 2d, 8, 23, 30. A similar requirement already obtains for television licensees. Section 1.526(a)(9) of the Rules, 47 C.F.R. 1.526(a)(9). Several broadcast multiple owners asked for clarification, in that we variously referred to "most significant problems" (53 FCC 2d at 8), simply "problems" (*Id.* at 23) or, in the text of the proposed rule, "significant problems." (*Id.* at 30). They urge that the reference be stated "problems," since the broadcaster has the discretion and the duty to evaluate their significance, in any event. Westinghouse praises the Commission for abandoning the prospective view currently followed under the *Primer*, i.e., the licensee must project programming to deal with problems and needs determined by an ascertainment which actually took place in the preceding license period. It is said to be more realistic to consider problems and responsive programs in retrospect. NBMC, on the other hand, opposes this retrospective approach. It argues that the link between problems and future programs is necessary in order to make the determination that a licensee will adequately serve the community in the coming license period. NBMC contends that there will be no way of determining a promise-versus-performance violation and such programming proposals as are made will be baseless. NBMC adds that the problems-programs list itself would discriminate against minorities because it is the problems and needs of the majority which will, quite naturally, be the "most significant." A number of parties fault the Commission for omissions or exclusions of certain types of programming from proposed § 1.526(a)(9), which may be counted as treating community problems and needs. RKO-General calls our omission of public service announcements "inappropriate." CBS argues that the Commission should reconsider its proposed exclusion of "ordinary news inserts," claiming that news is a valuable means of dealing with community problems, that there are First Amendment problems in making such an exclusion, and that this discriminates against radio stations with all-news formats. This point is also made by Channel Two Television Co., KPRC Radio Co. and WTVY, Inc. NAB, in supporting the problems-programs list, says that this is really the only material which should be required for ascertainment and that it should be triennial rather than annual, because 12 months is too short a time for a full overview of all problems and all responsive programs. NAB says that the yearly term invites shortsighted attacks by groups who are unable to see the broader range of community problems, or the overall programming of a station during the entire license term.

41. We shall clarify that the intent of our proposal, as stated in the draft amendment to § 1.526(a)(9), was to ask for up to 10 "significant" problems found in the licensee's service area during the 12 months prior to compilation and deposit of the list in the station's public file. The broadcaster wishing to depict his service in a favorable light, we suspect, would want to avoid listing "insignificant" problems anyway. On the other hand, we see no reason to invite dispute, and Commission second-guessing, as to whether five or seven or 10 problems on a given station's list truly were the "most significant" of the past year. "Significant" strikes the desirable balance between meaningful recording of service rendered and the licensee's discretion to evaluate not only the significance of a problem but its feasibility of treatment by the licensee's particular station.

42. At paragraph 15, *supra*, we have already responded to NBMC's concerns over the retrospective nature of the problems-programs list. We repeat that the renewal ascertainment proposed in the *Further Notice*, and adopted here, remains prospective, chiefly through the newly continuous recording of that process, and that the

look back each year at the problems-programs performance provides an effective means for both broadcasters and citizens to evaluate the end and aim of ascertainment—namely, programming. With regard to NBMC's comment on promise versus performance evaluation (para. 40), it should be clear that the purpose of regulation is not the maintenance of "violations." If it is found to be in the public interest to change somewhat the nature of a broadcaster's "promises" regarding his programming, then we ought not refrain from making that change simply because the measure of performance to meet that promise also will be modified somewhat.[7] We suggest that a yearly problems-programs listing in the public file will give the citizen more information, not less, and that the citizen's ability to evaluate a broadcaster's service will be enhanced rather than diminished. We reject NBMC's contention that "majority" problems will turn out to be the "significant" ones chosen for treatment by the broadcasters, to the exclusion of minority service. We repeat our observation from the *Further Notice* that "ascertainment constitutes an effort to dig beneath the surfaces of majority opinion and conventional wisdom to discover and deal with needs that might not otherwise be exposed." 53 FCC 2d at 27. Noting that the problems-programs list would be required of *all* licensees, even those in smaller markets who were proposed for exemption from other ascertainment reporting, (see paras. 47–54, *infra*), we stated:

> The exempt licensee who fails * * * to program for [minorities]— notably the racial minorities protected under the Civil Rights Acts of 1964 and 1972, as well as our own rules—weakens [the] hypothesis [that he knows his community thoroughly], to the point which may cause us to inquire further into his trusteeship of a scarce broadcast frequency. (citations omitted) *Id.* at 28.

43. We shall also decline to credit announcements (such as PSA's) and ordinary "news inserts" (see Section 1.526 (a)(9) of the rules) for purposes of the problems-programs list. There is no need for this Commission to defend the importance it attaches to news broadcasts in serving the community of license. It is also plain that we value public service announcements. While news inserts and announcements can sometimes respond to problems and needs, the ordinarily do not possess the length or depth to proceed toward a meeting or solution of problems. For this purpose, we seek *programs*. It is clear from the *Further Notice* that our concept of a "program," particularly on radio, is flexible enough to accommodate even the all-news station, 53 FCC 2d at 6, and that no licensee which takes seriously its non-entertainment programming obligations will have any trouble finding matter for its problems-programs list. As to NAB's suggestion that the list should be triennial rather than annual in scope, we are not persuaded. While we have elected to change the Community Leader Checklist from annual to triennial (see paras. 13–14, *supra*), the rationale applied in modification of that document does not hold for the problems-programs list. The latter possesses a limit of no more than 10 significant problems for each yearly list, while, theoretically at least, there are no ceilings on leader interviews. More importantly, ascertainment remains *continuous*, in the resolution reached here, whether interviews are counted every year or every three years. And the problems-programs list, as an evaluative tool for broadcaster and citizen respecting the programming results of a continuous ascertainment, rightly deserves more "continuity," or frequency, than the triennial compilation would provide. As for the NAB's concern with the broad overview of a licensee's program service, presumably that is met through appending to the renewal application problems-programs lists from each year of the expiring term —not to mention other information of three-year scope found in the same application.

44. *Demographic Data.* The *Further Notice* proposed replacement of the present *Primer's* "compositional study" with a checklist of institutional structural elements common to most comcapsuled briefly by certain statistical that the demographic aspects of the former compositional study could be capsuled briefly by certain statistical information maintained in the licensee's public file. 53 FCC 2d at 12, 31. A number of comments noted confusion in the *Further Notice* as to

---

[7] Under the present renewal application (FCC Form 303), of course, the licensee makes a number of representations about his programming, and some of these would continue to be made in the revised form (303-R) on which comment has been sought. *Revision of FCC Form 303*, 52 FCC 2d 184 (1975).

whether demographic information is to be prepared and kept for the community of license or for the broadcaster's entire service area. Storer and RKO-General stated that "service area" is too broad and difficult to determine, and the requirement should be stated in terms of community of license only. ABC notes that, while the proposal is an improvement over what is presently required, the Commission appears to be indicating that two sets of data are to be maintained, one for the community of license and one for the service area. It adds that the language stated in the proposed rule, "service area," is preferable and would avoid the necessity of separate compilations.

45. We agree that our discussion in the *Further Notice* was not clear on the areas for which demographic data was to be maintained. In view of the *Primer's* restriction to "community of license" for the compositional study, and in view of the likely variability—or unavailability—of data for "service areas" which cut across city, county and even state lines, we shall confine our public-file requirement to community of license also. Since the deposit of this data in the file is achieved by rule, we need a clarity which "service area" cannot provide.[8] At the same time, we think it appropriate to remind the licensee that if it undertakes to serve specific areas with definable populations outside its community of license, it might wish, optionally, to accumulate demographic data useful to the ascertainment and serving of those outside areas. Whether this optional or extra data is placed in the public file would be for the licensee to decide. Finally, while U.S. Census statistics are perhaps the most generally reliable, we do not wish to preclude licensees from the use of other information they have reason to believe accurate.

46. *Public Survey Description.* The *Further Notice* proposed placement in the public file of a "brief narrative statement covering the techniques and results" of the general public survey, such placement to be within 45 days of the survey's completion. 53 FCC 2d at 24. ABC suggests that the narrative statement consist only of the technique followed to obtain randomness. It claims that the description of results has led to present difficulties with special interest groups, who insist that their particular viewpoint did not receive adequate representation or attention by the station. ABC says it would be sufficient for the results of the survey to be simply available to the licensee, while the problems and needs so discovered could be traced in the annual lists of community problems. We believe that licensees should familiarize themselves with, and share with the public, the methods employed to achieve rough randomness for their general public surveys and the results in terms of problems and needs ascertained. The same information is available for community leader consultations, and we perceive no reason for dissimilar treatment here. We shall, in this connection, retreat from the specified 45-day grace period for filing this information after completion of the public survey, and substitute a "reasonable time" requirement as has been adopted for community leader interview data. We repeat our belief, however, that 45 days—or perhaps a bit longer for more extensive surveys in larger cities—should be an ample period within which to assemble and file the survey results. Moreover, we caution—again as with community leader data—that general public survey results for which credit is sought on a renewal application should be deposited in the public file no later than the date the application is submitted to the Commission.

Small Market Exemption

47. In the *Further Notice,* we suggested a test of the hypothesis that "the broadcaster in the smaller community knows his town thoroughly, not only its majorities but also its minority elements." 53 FCC 2d at 28. We proposed that commercial radio and television stations licensed to such communities be exempt from all Commission inquiry into the manner in which they become aware of community problems and needs. We offered tentatively "to define a small community of license as one with a population of 10,000 or less (as enumerated in the 1970 U.S. Census) and which is located outside all officially designated Standard Metropolitan Statistical Areas (SMSA's)." *Id.* at 27. We invited comment, however, on "whether the 10,000 figure is an appropriate cutoff," noting that this would exempt from ascertainment reporting "approximately 1900 commercial radio stations and 14 commercial TV stations." *Id.* As we stated in the *Further Notice,* we

---

[8] No such problem exists for interviews with leaders representing areas outside the community of license. Their addresses or affiliations can be identified with reasonable certainty.

believe that licensees in these communities must continue to maintain their awareness of local problems and needs. For the purpose of this test, however, we shall avoid any inquiry into *how* the licensee discerned which particular problems would be covered. *Id.* at 26.

48. Several commenting parties agreed with this exemption, but requested that it be extended to communities of populations larger than 10,000. NAB, Station KYMN and Central Broadcasting Company proposed a limit of 20,000; Bluestem Broadcasting Company proposed 20–24,000; Pappas Electronics at least 25,000 but preferably 50,000,[9] as did Dempsey and Koplovitz; while Brandon-Robison Broadcasting Corporation and KLIC, Inc. suggested a 100,000 limit. The reasons stated for raising the exemption were essentially similar. For instance, the NAB claims that a community of 20,000 has the same attributes as that of a community of 10,000. The station is equally likely, it is said, to have a thorough knowledge of the community based upon the licensee's presence there, and the importance of the station to the community. Such licensees are also as likely to know and understand the problems of minorities within the community. In addition, stations in such communities tend to have small staffs, thus making the burdens of ascertainment great. Finally, the station and its staff are equally as likely to be actively involved in their communities. Dempsey and Koplovitz points out that it would make sense to raise the figure to 50,000, in order to make this criterion of ascertainment comport with the size of community which has been deemed determinative by the Commission in the *Suburban Communities Policy Statement*, 2 FCC 2d 190 (1965). Brandon-Robison notes that communities of up to 100,000 have the same kinds of information flow into and out of the station, with regard to community problems, and community leaders in such places tend to be business leaders, with whom the station personnel are in constant contact. Finally, as KYMN notes, it is the only station licensed to serve a community of 10,230 (Northfield, Minnesota), about which the station says "we are the community."

49. The confinement of the exemption to communities not located within SMSA's also received opposition. Dempsey and Koplovitz states that SMSA's contain many small noncontiguous communities which are entities unto themselves, and cannot be arbitrarily considered mere bedroom communities. NAB makes the same point, saying that the Commission's determination "defies reality." NAB argues that a station licensed to such a community is licensed to serve that community, has only the maximum power required to do so, and if the concern is that such stations are really serving the adjacent metropolitan center, then there is cause to believe that the Commission's suburban communities policy is being violated on a large scale, which simply is not the case.

50. On the other hand, there is opposition to the entire concept of the exemption. NOW points out that all stations have the same obligation to serve in the public interest, regardless of size or location. The exemption allegedly would effectively prevent public interest groups from performing their function of monitoring and analyzing the station's performance. Finally, the Commission would not be able to make the statutorily required finding that the licensee has served in the past, and will likely continue to serve, the public interest, because the basic information for making this determination would not be available. NBMC opposes the exemption, arguing that small communities are particularly dependent upon their broadcast stations, and thus the obligations of those stations are great. In addition, the problems of achieving interchange between the station and minority groups within the community are oftentimes particularly acute in these smaller communities. NBMC argues that the exemption violates the constitutional requirement of equal protection of the laws, in that the public—and particularly minorities in small communities—are not to receive the full protection and benefits of ascertainment. Finally, both public interest groups and the Commission will lose a means by which they may measure the performance of small-market stations. UCC urges that stations in small communities have at least as much need to be fully aware of the community and its problems as stations in any larger community.

51. Finally, proposals are made for additional exemptions to be applied to ascertainment reporting. Southern Broadcasting suggests an exemption for all licensees, regardless of location or size, if they have received regular renewals of

---

[9] Pappas adds that 50,000 would be a valid cut-off because the federal government has defined such a population as being a "small community" for urban renewal assistance purposes.

their licenses—including the most recent ones—without major problems from the community or regulatory agencies. Spanish International Communications requests a special exemption for stations serving minority audiences. Such stations should be allowed to ascertain and serve only that audience, and exempted from making an ascertainment survey of the entire community. The station would, however, be able to obtain a broader view of the community by selecting spokesmen from outside the specialized audience served, but not on the scale presently required.

52. In the *Further Notice* we gave two criteria we thought the exemption level should satisfy: first, it should "create a large enough sample of 'exempt' licensees to make the experiment meaningful;" and second, it should keep the size of the exempt community "such as to admit of a reasonable assumption that the broadcaster knows his town thoroughly." 53 FCC 2d at 27. While we do not pretend to be statisticians, we believe that the approximately 1900 stations (virtually all radio) that would be exempted as licensed to communities of 10,000 or less outside all SMSA's is a sufficient sample, constituting some 25 percent of all commercial radio and TV stations presently licensed. This is not to say that the sample could not be enlarged, of course, and for that purpose we invited comment on other feasible cutoffs. We have found that the opponents of the small-market exemption do not dispute on statistical grounds, but dislike the concept altogether. Thus, no commenter attempted to demonstrate that a non-metropolitan community of 10,000 or less was not small enough to permit of the "reasonable assumption" noted above. On the other hand, many commenters suggested that communities are "knowable" well above 10,000. When the special pleading is removed from these comments—i.e. from licensees who fall rather narrowly outside the exemption and want to be included—the chief rationale for raising the exemption level appears to be the creation of a sample not only larger, as such, but more diverse and therefore potentially more informative to our proposed experiment. It is asserted, for example, that a greater number of multi-station and multi-owner communities would come into the sample. Similarly, since to retain the outside-SMSA restriction would be to rule out every broadcast facility in such megalopolitan areas as the New York–Washington corridor, why not remove the restriction and permit the sample to include some of those mid-Atlantic seaboard stations. (See especially the comments of Central Broadcasting Co.)

53. We have decided to stick with the exemption parameters in the *Further Notice* —stations licensed to communities of 10,000 or fewer persons not located in any SMSA. We are not attempting to define "small town" by this action.[10] Indeed, we acknowledge that there may be many communities of more than 10,000 population, some of them even lying within SMSA's, that are as knowable to a broadcaster as many of the communities where stations will be exempt from ascertainment reporting. But, as a test, we must draw a line somewhere. No commenter specifically opposed the 10,000 cutoff, although some attacked the exemption generally. As for the invitation of those favoring exemption to increase the size and diversity of the experimental sample, we have already observed the rough statistical adequacy of the approximately 1900 stations licensed to communities of 10,000 or less outside SMSA's. Moreover, without pretending to scientific rigor, we suspect that the more diverse a sample is, the less it may tell us—rather than more—because of the difficulty of identifying, much less controlling, the greater number of variables. Finally, Central Broadcasting Co. appears to have misunderstood our reference to "bedroom" suburbs and the knowledge of them possessed by the average resident. 53 FCC 2d at 27. Opposing the SMSA restriction, Central states that the metropolitan or non-metropolitan character of a small community is irrelevant to the question of whether a broadcaster can come to know the community well; and, in any event, it is the broadcaster, rather than the bedroom community's residents, whose degree of knowledge is at issue. Despite its imprecision, our use of the term bedroom suburbs was intended to identify a familiar phenomenon in metropolitan areas—namely, that many of the inhabitants live and work in different sectors of the metropolis, sometimes far removed. To this extent, we meant to suggest, it is harder for a broadcaster or for any citizen to get to know the community and its people. Indeed, the fund of common interests and in-

---

[10] At the same time, we cannot accept the suggestion of Pappas (Note 9, *supra*) that we import into our field of regulation a measure of community size used in determining eligibility for certain forms of federal assistance by other agencies whose missions are distinctly different from the mission of the FCC.

formation frequently is less for suburbanites than for individuals who both live and work in smaller, non-metropolitan communities. We believe that for the limited experimental purpose in which we apply it, the definition of a small community as one lying outside all SMSA's is sound, and we shall retain it as proposed.[11]

54. We believe that our discussion of the problems-programs list at Paragraphs 13 and 42, *supra*, disposes of NOW's and NBMC's concerns that citizens would be left with no way to evaluate the performance of a station in an exempt community. Moreover, we fail to understand how the modification of a policy—ascertainment—not established by any law, but instead falling within the discretion left to the Commission by the Communications Act of 1934, as amended, could deny equal protection of law to any citizen or group of citizens. We repeat that if the exempt licensee fails to carry out programming obligations toward significant minorities in his community, the administrative sanctions we possess should suffice to remedy the situation far in advance of any denial of constitutional rights. We wish to emphasize the following from the *Further Notice:*

> At its best, ascertainment constitutes an effort to dig beneath the surfaces of majority opinion and conventional wisdom to discover and deal with needs that might not otherwise be exposed. We expect all licensees to strive for that ideal, including those small market licensees who would be exempted from most reporting requirements under the experiment proposed herein. For the purpose of this experiment, we will accept as a given the hypothesis that the broadcaster in the smaller community knows his town thoroughly, not only its majorities but also its minority elements. The exempt licensee who fails, during this period of testing, to program for the latter—notably the racial minorities protected under the Civil Rights Act of 1964 and 1972, as well as our own rules—weakens this hypothesis, to the point which may cause us to inquire further into his trusteeship of a scarce broadcast frequency. (Citations omitted) *Id.* at 27.

55. Finally, we decline to explore Southern Broadcasting's suggestion that licensees be relieved of ascertainment on "good behavior," so to speak; and likewise elect not to extend, beyond the flexibility of the current *Primer* (Questions 25 and 32) the specialization of ascertainment for specialized formats, as urged by Spanish International. We repeat our conclusion from the *Further Notice* that "all broadcast licensees have the same basic obligation to discover and fulfill the problems, needs and interests of the public within their service areas"—through ascertainment and programming. 53 FCC 2d at 6.

Summary and Conclusions

56. The above represents the Commission's view on ascertainment by commercial broadcast license renewal applicants. These views have been restated in a *Renewal Primer* (Appendix B) and effectuating provisions added to Section 1.526 of the rules. Such new forms as are required will be adopted, subject to General Accounting Office approval, in Docket 20419.[12] The *Renewal Primer*, the revised § 1.526(a) of the rules and the new forms will become effective February 6, 1976 for licensees whose authorizations expire December 1, 1976, and for all licensees whose

---

[11] The suggestion by several broadcasters or their representatives that the SMSA restriction is inconsistent with the Commissions' suburban communities policy is not only unpersuasive but out of date. First of all, the policy, when fully operative, had the effect of forcing a suburban applicant to prove that he really meant to serve the suburb in which he applied, and not a nearby large city. What this demonstration would have to do with how well the suburban licensee could come to know his community later is unclear. In any event, the Commission recently has decided to diminish substantially the application of the suburban communities policy; *AM Assignment Standards*, 54 FCC 2d 1 (1975); and any relevance it might have had to this proceeding is correspondingly reduced.

[12] See *Revision of FCC Form 303*, 52 FCC 2d 184 (1975).

[13] We recognize that the Commission will be receiving applications from licensees whose expiring terms fall partly under these new ascertainment policies and rules and partly under the older guidelines of the 1971 *Primer*. We intend to review each portion of such a term by the standards then applicable. It should be noted that the small-market exemption is not available for licensees whose terms expire prior to December 1, 1976. With respect to the annual problems-programs list to be newly required of radio licensees, we shall not expect any radio licensee to deposit such a list in its public file prior to August 1, 1976, which is the deadline for the submission of renewal applications by licensees whose terms expire December 1, 1976. This ensures the better part of a year of notice to all affected licensees. Thus, a licensee whose

authorizations expire thereafter.[13] Renewal applicants whose licenses expire prior to that date will be expected to follow the existing guides set forth in the original *Primer*.

57. This proceeding will be held open so that further consideration may be given to matters contained in the original *Primer*, as it applies to applicants for new or changed facilities. This proceeding is also being held open to further test the small market exemption, which we propose to revisit roughly three years from the time the first renewal applications are filed under the *Renewal Primer*.[14]

58. Accordingly, *it is ordered*, pursuant to the authority contained in sections 4 (i) and 303 of the Communications Act of 1934, as amended, That § 1.526(a) *is amended* as set forth in Appendix A effective February 6, 1976 (effective for licensees whose authorizations expire on or after December 1, 1976. Renewal applicants whose licenses expire prior to that date will be expected to follow the existing guides set forth in the original *Primer*.

59. *It is further ordered*, That the attached *Renewal Primer* (Appendix B), is adopted.

Adopted: December 15, 1975.

Released: January 7, 1976.

(Secs. 4, 303, 48 Stat., as amended, 1066, 1082; 47 U.S.C. 154, 303).

FEDERAL COMMUNICATIONS COMMISSION,[15]

[SEAL] VINCENT J. MULLINS,
Secretary.

Appendix A

In consideration of the foregoing Part I of Chapter I of Title 47 of the Code of Federal Regulations is amended as follows:

1. In § 1.526, paragraph (a) and subparagraph (a)(9) are revised, subparagraphs (11) & (12) added, and the note following to become Note 1, and a Note 2 added to read as follows:

**§ 1.526   Records to be maintained locally
for public inspection by applicants,
permittees, and licensees.**

(a) *Records to be maintained.* Every applicant for a construction permit for a new station in the broadcast services shall maintain for public inspection a file for such station containing the material in subparagraph (1) of this paragraph, every permittee or licensee of a section in the broadcast services shall maintain for public inspection a file for such station containing the material in subparagraphs (1), (2), (3), (4), (5), (6), (7) and (9) of this paragraph, and every permittee or licensee of a commercial television station shall maintain for public inspection a file for such station containing the material in subparagraph (8) of this paragraph: *Provided, however,* That the foregoing requirements shall not apply to applicants for or permittees or licensees of television broadcast translator stations, FM broadcast translator stations, or FM broadcast booster stations. The material to be contained in the file is as follows:

*   *   *   *   *

(9) To be placed in the public inspection file every year, on the anniversary date on which the station's renewal application would be due for filing with the Commission, a listing of no more than ten significant problems and needs of the area served by the station during the preceding twelve months. In relation to each problem or need cited, licensees and permittees shall indicate typical and illustrative programs or program series, excluding ordinary news inserts of breaking events (the daily or ordinary news coverage of breaking newsworthy events), which

---

term expires on June 1, 1978, for example, would be expected to deposit lists on his "anniversary" filing dates of February 1, 1977 and February 1, 1978, but would not have to deposit a list on February 1, 1976.

[14] The Commission will conduct studies to analyze and evaluate whether this exemption in fact has served the public interest.

[15] Commissioner Hooks concurring and issuing a statement; Commissioner Robinson dissenting and issuing a statement. Both statements were filed as part of the original document.

were broadcast during the preceding twelve months in response to those problems and needs. Such a listing shall include the title of the program or program series, its source, type, brief description, time broadcast and duration. The third annual listing shall be placed in the station's public inspection file on the due date of the filing of the station's application for renewal of license. Additionally, upon the filing of the station's application for renewal of license, the three annual problems-programs listings shall be forwarded to the Commission as part of that application. The annual listings are not to exceed five pages, but may be supplemented at any time by additional material placed in the public inspection file and identified as a continuation of the information submitted to the Commission.

*   *   *   *   *

(11) Each licensee or permittee of a commercially operated radio or television station (except as provided in Note 2, below) shall place in the station's public inspection file appropriate documentation relating to its efforts to interview a representative cross-section of community leaders within its service area to ascertain community problems and needs. Such documentation shall be placed in the station's public inspection file within a reasonable time after the date of completion of each interview but in no event later than the due date for filing the station's application for renewal of license and shall include: (a) the name, address, organization, and position or title of the community leader interviewed; (b) the date, time and place of the interview; (c) the name of the principal, management-level or other employee of the station conducting the interview; (d) the problems and needs discussed during the interview or, when the interviewee requests that his/her statements be held in confidence, that request shall be noted; and (e) for interviews conducted by non-principals or non-managers, the date of review of the interview record by a principal or management-level employee of the station. Additionally, upon the filing of the application for renewal of license each licensee shall forward to the Commission as part of the application for renewal of license a checklist indicating the numbers of community leaders interviewed during the current license term representing the several elements found on the form; provided that, if a community lacks one of the enumerated institutions or elements, the licensee or permittee should so indicate by providing a brief explanation on its checklist.

(12) Each licensee or permittee of a commercially operated radio and television station (except as provided in Note 2, below) shall place in the station's public inspection file documentation relating to its efforts to consult with a roughly random sample of members of the general public within its service area to ascertain community problems and needs. Such documentation shall consist of: (a) information relating to the total population of the station's city of license including the numbers and proportions of males and females; of minorities; of youth (17 and under); and of the elderly (65 and above); (b) a narrative statement of the sources consulted and the methods followed in conducting the general public survey, including the number of people surveyed and the results thereof. Such documentation shall be placed in the public inspection file within a reasonable time after completion of the survey but in no event later than the date the station's application for renewal of license is filed. Upon filing its application for renewal of license, each licensee and permittee must certify that the above-noted documentation has been placed in the station's public inspection file.

*   *   *   *   *

Note 1 * * *
Note 2: Subparagraphs (a)(11) and (a)(12) above shall not apply to commercial radio and television stations within cities of license which (1) have a population, according to the immediately preceding decennial U.S. Census, of 10,000 persons or less; and (2) are located outside all Standard Metropolitan Statistical Areas (SMSA's), as defined by the federal Bureau of the Census.

Appendix B: Primer on Ascertainment
of Community Problems by
Broadcast Renewal Applicants

Introduction

The principal ingredient of a licensee's obligation to operate in the public interest is the diligent, positive and continuing effort by the licensee to discover and fulfill the problems, needs and interests of the public within the station's service area. *Statement of Policy Re: Commission En Banc Programming Inquiry*, 25 Fed.

Reg. 7291, 20 RR 1901 (1960). In the fulfillment of this obligation, the licensee must consult with leaders who represent the interests of the community and members of the general public who receive the station's signal. *1960 Programming Policy Statement, supra.* This Primer provides guidelines for the licensee of a commercial broadcast station to follow in conducting these consultations. The types of consultations required can best be summarized in a question and answer format.

A. General

Question 1. When must the community survey be conducted?

Answer. The licensee's obligation is to ascertain the problems, needs and interests of the public within the station's service area on a *continuing* basis. The licensee, therefore, must make reasonable and good faith efforts to ascertain community problems, needs and interests throughout the station's license term.

Question 2. What area should the community survey encompass?

Answer. The licensee is obligated to provide service to the station's entire service area. As a practical matter, however, it is realized that the service contours of a station cover a substantial geographical area. Thus, the licensee is permitted to place primary emphasis on the station's city of license and secondary emphasis outside that area. In any event, no community located more than 75 miles from the city of license need be included in the licensee's survey. Further, if a licensee chooses not to serve a community within the station's contours, a brief statement should be placed in the station's public inspection file explaining the reason(s) therefor.

Question 3. What is the purpose of the community survey?

Answer. The purpose of the community survey is to discover the problems, needs and interests of the public as distinguished from its programming preferences. However, a licensee may, if it wishes, also seek to discover the public's programming preferences.

Question 4. Who must be consulted during the community survey?

Answer. The licensee must interview leaders who represent the interests of the service area and members of the general public.

Question 5. Must a compositional study of the community be conducted?

Answer. A special compositional study of the community need not be conducted. We have identified typical community institutions and elements normally present in most communities and we expect the licensee to utilize this listing in conducting its community leader survey. (See Question and Answer 7, below.) We recognize that all communities are not the same and that other significant institutions or elements may be indigenous to a particular community. However, if a licensee interviews a representative sample of leaders from among the elements in this listing that apply to its community, its coverage of all significant elements will not be open to question. The licensee may, at its option, interview leaders within elements not found on this list.

Question 6. Must the licensee obtain demographic data relating to its community of license?

Answer. A licensee should have on file information relating to the population characteristics of its city of license. The population data required can be extracted from the U.S. Census Bureau's *County and City Data Book* and *General Population Characteristics* (two separate publications), or similarly reliable reference material. The information needed relates to the total population of the city of license; the numbers and proportions of males and females, of minorities, of youths (age 17 and under), and of the elderly (age 65 or older). Inclusion of data on portions of the station's service area outside the city of license is optional.

B. Community Leader Survey

Question 7. What community leaders should be consulted?

Answer. The community leaders consulted should constitute a representative cross-section of those who speak for the interests of the service area. This requirement may be met by interviews within the following institutions and elements commonly found in a community: (1) Agriculture; (2) Business; (3) Charities; (4) Civic, Neighborhood and Fraternal Organizations; (5) Consumer Services; (6) Culture; (7) Education; (8) Environment; (9) Government (local, county, state & federal); (10) Labor; (11) Military; (12) Minority and ethnic groups; (13) Organizations of and for the Elderly; (14) Organizations of and for Women; (15) Organizations of and for Youth (including children) and Students; (16) Professions; (17) Public Safety, Health and Welfare; (18) Recreation; and (19) Religion. A licensee is permitted to show that one or more of these institutions or elements is not present in its community. At its option it may also utilize the "other" category to interview leaders in elements not found on the checklist.

Question 8. If a licensee interviews in all of the above categories will the licensee be considered to have contacted all the significant groups in its community?

Answer. The Checklist is thorough enough for most communities and yet not overly detailed. Interviews in all of its elements will establish the requisite coverage of significant community groups. Whether this coverage is also representative will depend on such factors as number of interviews in each element, size and influence of that element in the community, etc. A licensee is permitted to show that one or more of these categories is not present in its community. It may also, at its option, interview leaders in other categories which may not be found on the Checklist.

Question 9. How many community leaders should be consulted?

Answer. A licensee should consult with leaders on a continuous basis. The Commission's concern, in this regard, is not one of numbers but of representativeness. The licensee's reasonable and good faith discretion as to how many community leaders should be interviewed to establish representativeness will be accorded great weight. However, we have established a reasonable number of interviews (see table below) that a licensee may conduct during the license term, if it wishes to remove any question as to the gross quantitative sufficiency of its community leader survey. Fewer interviews may be conducted if, in the exercise of its discretion, a licensee determines that a lesser number results in a leadership survey that is representative of its service area.

	Number of
Population of city of license:	*Consultations*
10,001 to 25,000	60
25,001 to 50,000	100
50,001 to 200,000	140
200,001 to 500,000	180
Over 500,000	220

Question 10. What leaders in each significant institution or element should be consulted?

Answer. There are many community leaders in each of the enumerated institutions and elements. Due to the physical impossibility of interviews with all community leaders, and the practical impossibility of requiring interviews with leaders based on some ratio to population of their constituencies, each licensee is accorded wide discretion in determining what leaders in each of the institutions or elements should be interviewed from time to time. The leadership of some institutions or elements (e.g., government) may remain relatively stable throughout the license term and, thus, interviews with such leaders on several occasions can be expected. In this respect, each consultation with a community leader constitutes a separate ascertainment interview. The licensee should, of course, make reasonable and good faith efforts to consult with various leaders in each significant institution or element and not limit the consultations to the same leaders throughout the license term.

Question 11. Who can conduct the community leader consultations?

Answer. Principals, management level and other employees of the station may conduct the community leader consultations. (See Question and Answer 12, below.) When such interviews are conducted by non-management level employees, their efforts must be under the direction and supervision of a principal or management level employee. Also, the results of the interview must be reported to a principal or management level employee within a reasonable period of time after the consultation.

Question 12. Since non-management level employees may conduct community leader interviews, is it necessary for principals and management level employees to be involved in the consultations at all?

Answer. Yes. Community leader consultations may be conducted by any employee who the licensee believes is qualified for the assignment. However, a substantial degree of participation, as interviewers, by principals and management level employees is still necessary. Accordingly, 50 per cent of all interviews must be conducted by management level employees.

Question 13. Can a professional research firm conduct the community leader survey on behalf of the licensee?

Answer. No. The licensee is expected on its own behalf to consult with a cross-section of community leaders who represent the interests of the service area. Thus, a professional research firm cannot be used for this purpose.

Question 14. Must the community leader interviews take place in a formal meeting called for the specific purpose of inquiring about community problems, needs and interests?

Answer. The interview process allows for a multiplicity of dialogue techniques. Such interviews, for example, may take place during a meeting called for the specific purpose of discussing community problems, needs and interests, or in a business meeting with a community leader by a principal, management level or other employee of the licensee where community problems, needs and interests are also the subject of discussion. Additionally, such an interview may take place during community leader luncheons, joint consultations (see Question and Answer 15, below), on the air broadcasts (see Question and Answer 16, below), and during news interviews. In any event, appropriate documentation must be obtained (see Question 18, below).

Question 15. Are joint consultations between licensees and community leaders permitted?

Answer. Joint consultations between licensees and community leaders are permitted, provided: (i) each community leader who participates is on a roughly equivalent plane of interest or responsibility; (ii) each community leader is given ample opportunity to freely present his or her opinions as to community problems, needs and interests; and (iii) each licensee participating is given ample opportunity to question each leader.

Question 16. Can community leader interviews taking place during an on-the-air broadcast be used as evidence of a licensee's ascertainment process?

Answer. Ordinarily, a licensee should not rely on this method to ascertain community problems. When, however, such an on-the-air interview reveals a community problem, need or interest which results in the consideration of a future program concerning that problem, need or interest, the consultation may be used as evidence of the licensee's ascertainment efforts.

Question 17. Can community leaders be interviewed via telephone?

Answer. Face-to-face interviews should be the staple of the licensee's ascertainment process. The limited use of the telephone to conduct community leader interviews is permitted, particularly in areas outside the community of license, and other situations where reasons of convenience, efficiency or necessity might apply. However, a licensee should not, through over-reliance on ascertainment by telephone, abuse the flexibility that this medium gives the station.

Question 18. What documentation is required to be placed in the station's public inspection file regarding community leader interviews?

Answer. Within a reasonable time after completion of an interview, which we perceive ordinarily to be 30 to 45 days, the licensee must place in its public inspection file information identifying: (a) the name and address of the community leader consulted; (b) the institution or element in the community represented; (c) the date, time and place of the interview; (d) problems, needs or interests discussed during the interview (unless the leader requests that his comments be kept confidential); (e) the name of the licensee representative conducting the interview; and (f) where a non-manager performed the interview, the name of the principal or management level employee who reviewed the completed interview record. No credit will be given for interviews placed in the public file after the date on which the licensee's renewal application is filed with the Commission.

Question 19. What documentation relating to the community leader interviews must be submitted with the station's application for renewal of license?

Answer. Upon the filing of an application for renewal of license, the licensee must certify that the documentation noted in Question and Answer 18, above, has been placed in the station's public inspection file at the appropriate times. Additionally, the licensee must submit as part of its renewal application a checklist indicating the number of community leaders interviewed during the license term in the enumerated categories set forth at Question and Answer 7 above. If one or more of the institutions or elements is not present in the community, a brief explanation must be included with the checklist.

C. General Public Survey

Question 20. With what members of the general public should consultations be held?

Answer. A random sample of members of the general public should be consulted. For our purposes, a random sampling may be taken from a general city telephone directory or may be done on a geographical distribution basis by means of "man-in-the-street" interviews or questionnaires collected by the licensee. These techniques are illustrative, not exhaustive. Whatever survey technique is utilized by the licensee, there must be a full description of the methodology used to assure a roughly random sampling of the general public and an indication of the total number of general public interviews conducted by that survey technique.

Question 21. What is the purpose of the general public survey?

Answer. Here, again, the primary purpose of the general public survey is to discover the community problems, needs and interests of the public as distinguished from its programming preferences. (See Questions and Answers 3 and 4 above.)

Question 22. How many members of the general public should be surveyed?

Answer. No set number or formula has been adopted. A sufficient number of members of the general public should be consulted to assure a generally random sample. The number, of course, will vary with the size of the community in question.

Question 23. When should the general public survey be conducted?

Answer. Either throughout the license term or within some specific period during the license term, at the licensee's option. In either event, appropriate documentation must be placed in the station's public file within a reasonable time after its completion, which we perceive ordinarily to be 30 to 45 days, but in no event later than the date on which its renewal application is filed with the Commission.

Question 24. Who should consult with members of the general public?

Answer. Principals, station employees, or a professional research or survey service. If consultations are conducted by employees who are below the management level, the consultation process must be supervised by principals or management level employees.

Question 25. What documentation concerning the general public survey is required?

Answer. Each licensee must place in the station's public inspection file a narrative statement concerning the method used to conduct the general public survey, the number of people consulted, and the ascertainment results of the survey. (See also the reference to demographic data in Q. and A. 6).

Question 26. What documentation relating to the general public survey must be filed with the station's application for renewal of license?

Answer. Upon the filing of an application for renewal of license, the licensee must certify that the documentation noted in Question and Answer 25, above, has been placed in the station's public inspection file. No other submission is necessary unless specifically requested by the Commission.

D. Programming

Question 27. Must all community problems revealed by the licensee's consultations with community leaders and members of the general public be treated by the station?

Answer. In serving the needs of its community, a licensee is not required to program to meet all community problems ascertained. There are a number of problems which may deserve attention by the broadcast media. The evaluation of the relative importance and immediacy of these many and varied problems, and the determination of how the station can devote its limited broadcast time to meeting the problems that merit treatment, is left to the good faith judgment of the licensee. In making this determination, the licensee may consider the programming offered by other stations in the area as well as its station's program format and the composition of its audience. With respect to the latter factor, however, it should be borne in mind that many problems affect and are pertinent to diverse groups within the community. All members of the public are entitled to some service from each station. While a station may focus relatively more attention on community problems affecting the audience to which it orients its program service, it cannot exclude all other members of the community from its ascertainment efforts and its nonentertainment programming. Indeed, many special interests may be adequately dealt with in programming which has a wide range of appeal.

Question 28. Must all community problems revealed by the ascertainment consultations be included in the licensee's showing placed in the public inspection file?

Answer. Yes. The purpose of the community leader and general public consultations is to elicit from those interviewed what they believe to be the community's problems, needs and interests. All ascertained community problems should, therefore, be reflected in the community leader contact reports and in the general public narrative retained in the station's public inspection file.

Question 29. In what form may matter be broadcast to treat ascertained community problems, needs and interests?

Answer. Programs, news and public service announcements. This includes station editorials, ordinary and special news inserts, program vignettes, and the like. (But see Question and Answer 33 below regarding the exclusion from the yearly problems-programs list of announcements and ordinary news inserts of breaking events.)

Question 30. Can a licensee use only news and public service announcements to treat community problems, needs and interests?

Answer. Not necessarily. It is the responsibility of the individual licensee to determine the appropriate amount, kind, and time period of broadcast matter which should be presented in response to the ascertained problems, needs and interests of its community and service area. Where the licensee, however, has chosen a brief and usually superficial manner of presentation, such as news and public service announcements, to the exclusion of all others, a question could be raised as to the reasonableness of the licensee's action. The licensee would then be required to clearly demonstrate that its single type of presentation would be the most effective method for its station to respond to the community's ascertained problems.

Question 31. When should matter broadcast in response to the community's ascertained problems, needs and interests be presented?

Answer. The Commission does not prescribe the time of day at which specific program matter responsive to the community's ascertained problems should be broadcast. Rather, the licensee is expected to schedule the time of presentation based upon its good faith judgment as to when the broadcast reasonably could be expected to be effective.

Question 32. If a licensee utilizes a specialized program format—such as all-news, classical music, religious—must it present broadcast matter to meet community problems, needs and interests?

Answer. Yes. It is the responsibility of the licensee to be attentive and responsive to the problems, needs and interests of the public it is licensed to serve. The licensee's choice of a particular program format does not alter its obligation to meet community problems, needs and interests. The manner in which the licensee presents such responsive programming may, of course, be tailored to the particular format of the station. (See, however, Question and Answer 27, above.)

Question 33. What documentation must be placed in the station's public inspection file regarding the licensee's efforts to program to meet ascertained community problems, needs and interests?

Answer. Each year on the anniversary date of the filing of the station's application for renewal of license, the licensee must place in its public inspection file a list of no more than ten significant problems, needs and interests ascertained during the preceding twelve months. Concerning each problem, need or interest listed the licensee must also indicate typical and illustrative programs broadcast in response to those problems, needs and interests indicating the title of the program or program series, its source, type, a brief description thereof, time broadcast and duration. Such programs do not include announcements (such as PSA's) or news inserts of breaking events (the daily or ordinary news coverage of breaking newsworthy events).

Appendix C: Parties Filing Comments

1. William Armstrong (President of KOSI, Aurora, Colorado).
2. American Broadcasting Companies, Inc.
3. Ben Hill Broadcasting Co. (WBHB, Fitzgerald, Georgia).
4. Bluestem Broadcasting Co., Inc. (KVOE and KLRF(FM), Emporia, Kansas).
5. Brandon-Robison Broadcasting Corp. (WYAM, Bessemer, Alabama).
6. Capitol Broadcasting Co., Inc. (WRAI–TV and WRAL–FM, Raleigh, North Carolina).
7. Carthage Broadcasting Co. (KDMO, KRGK(FM), Carthage, Missouri).
8. CBS, Inc.
9. Central Broadcasting Co. (WCGC, Belmont, North Carolina).
10. Channel Two Television Co. and KPRC Radio Co. (KPRC–TV and KPRC, Houston, Texas).
11. J. B. Crawley (WCND, Shelbyville, Kentucky; WPTN–AM–FM, Cookeville, Tennessee; WMSK, Morganfield, Kentucky).
12. Dempsey & Koplovitz.
13. Gay Coalition Task Force on the Media.
14. Simon Geller (WVCA–FM, Gloucester, Massachusetts).
15. General Electric Broadcasting Co., Inc.
16. Greater Media, Inc.
17. Greater Portland Radio Broadcasters' Association.
18. Haley, Bader & Potts.
19. John Quinlan Hearne (shareholder of Santa Monica Broadcasting Co., licensee of KSRF, Santa Monica, California).
20. Heart O' Wisconsin Broadcasters, Inc. (WISM and WISM–FM, Madison, Wisconsin).
21. Mary Ann Heller.
22. Joint Comments of Radio Licenses.
23. Joint Comments of Television Licenses.
24. KCOK, Inc.; Concerned Communications Corp.; C & M Broadcasting, Inc.; Paulina Broadcasting Corp.; and KQEN Broadcasting, Inc.
25. KLIC, Inc. (KLIC, Monroe, Louisiana).
26. KYMN Radio (KYMN, Northfield, Minnesota).
27. Mark Media, Inc. (WKYK, Burnsville, North Carolina; WCSL, Cherrysville, North Carolina; WKKR, Pickens, North Carolina; and WKHJ, Holly Hall, South Carolina).
28. Wendell Mayes, Jr. (of the Wendell Mayes stations).
29. McClatchy Newspapers.
30. Media Statistics, Inc.
31. Metromedia, Inc.
32. Midwest Radio-Television, Inc. (WCCO AM/FM/TV, Minneapolis, Minnesota).
33. National Association of Broadcasters (NAB).
34. National Black Media Coalition (NBMC).
35. National Broadcasting Co., Inc. (NBC).
36. National Organization for Women (NOW).
37. National Urban League, Inc.
38. Office of Communication of the United Church of Christ (UCC).
39. Ozark Broadcasting Corp. (WZOK and WOAB–FM, Ozark, Alabama).
40. Pappas Electronics, Inc. (KGEN and KBOS–FM, Tulare, California).
41. Progressive Broadcasting Co. (KCCO, KRCG–FM, Lawton, Oklahoma).
42. Public Interest Research Group; the California Citizen Action Group; The Connecticut Citizen Action Group; the Missouri Public Interest Research Group; the North Carolina Public Interest Research Group; the New Jersey Public Interest Research Group; and the Oregon Student Public Interest Research Group.
43. Radio Station WKJB AM–FM, Inc. (Mayaguez, Puerto Rico).
44. RKO General, Inc.

45. Southern Broadcasting Co.
46. Spanish International Communications Corp.
47. Storer Broadcasting Co.
48. UNDA–USA (National Association for Broadcasters and Allied Communicators).
49. West Virginia Radio Corp. (WAJR and WAJR–FM, Morgantown, West Virinia).
50. Westinghouse Broadcasting Co., Inc.
51. WTVY, Inc. [WTVY(TV) and WTVY–FM, Dothan, Alabama].

APPENDIX D: SAMPLE—COMMUNITY LEADER ANNUAL CHECKLIST

Institution/Element	Number	Not Applicable (Explain briefly)
1. Agriculture		
2. Business		
3. Charities		
4. Civic, Neighborhood and Fraternal Organizations		
5. Consumer Services		
6. Culture		
7. Education		
8. Environment		
9. Government (local, country, state & federal)		
10. Labor		
11. Military		
12. Minority and ethnic groups		
13. Organizations of and for the Elderly		
14. Organizations of and for Women		
15. Organizations of and for Youth (including children) and Students.		
16. Professions		
17. Public Safety, Health and Welfare		
18. Recreation		
19. Religion		
20. Other		
While the following are not regarded as separate community elements for purposes of this survey, indicate the number of leaders interviewed in all elements above who are:		
(a) Blacks		
(b) Hispanic, Spanish speaking or Spanish–surnamed Americans.		
(c) American Indians		
(d) Orientals		
(e) Women		

APPENDIX E: SUGGESTED LEADER CONTACT FORM

Date:

Name and address of person contacted: _____

_____

_____

Organization(s) or group(s) represented by person contacted: _____

_____

_____

Date, time and place of contact: _____

_____

Method of contact: _____

_____

Problems, needs and interests identified by person contacted: _____

_____

_____

_____

_____

_____

_____

_____

_____

_____

_____

_____

Name of interviewer _____

Reviewed by _____ Position _____

Date _____

APPENDIX E

Music
Glossary

The following glossary is intended to give a comprehensive identification of legitimate music terms used in radio broadcasting to describe music policy. Terms which are particularly subjective in character, such as "lush background music," or which are technical distinctions, such as "aria da capo" versus "through-composed aria," are purposely omitted since their inclusion would only obscure the objective of this glossary.

Undoubtedly there will be much music which can be properly classified in several categories (see Table 1): a Mozart symphony might be regarded as symphonic music, classic music, or general orchestral music, and performed by either a chamber group or a symphony orchestra. Likewise, calypso might fall under categories of folk music, ethnic music, trend music, or current hits. In such cases the general nature of a program will not be determined by individual pieces but rather by the common characteristics of several different pieces. Thus, Harry Belafonte, Theodore Bikel, and Peter, Paul and Mary would constitute a folk music grouping; Harry Belafonte, Xavier Cugat, and Stan Getz playing "Girl from Ipanema" might form a Latin (ethnic) group.

This glossary will best serve its purpose if each part is read in its entirety rather than as single entries. The following outline should be helpful in showing the overall organization of this project (see also Table 1).

Type of Music

Popular music Music considered to be primarily of entertainment value to a relatively large general public. Commercial success is not necessary. Under the broad heading Popular Music fall the following categories:

Current hits Popular music regardless of types which are currently commercially successful. Other terms include "Top-20," "Top-40," "Pop Hits," and "Top Pops."

From *Spot Radio Rates & Data* (July 1, 1971), pp. 11–14. Music glossary prepared for Standard Rates & Data Service by James Hopkins and Theodore Ashford, School of Music, Northwestern University. Reprinted here by permission.

Table 1 Broadcast Music Terms

Performance Medium

Type of Music	Vocal — Ensemble	Vocal — Solo	Instrumental — Ensemble	Instrumental — Solo

Vocal — Ensemble columns: Small group, Chorus, combo, With instrumental, With orchestra, etc.
Vocal — Solo columns: With piano, organ, etc., With chorus, With vocal and inst. ensemble, With instrumental ensemble, With piano, organ, etc., Combo
Instrumental — Ensemble columns: Dance band, "Big" band, Military or symphonic band, Symphony orch., orchestra, Chamber (small), String orchestra, Chamber ensemble, Inst. w/orchestra, Instrument w/piano
Instrumental — Solo columns: Electronic, Piano, Organ, Other (guitar, harp, etc.)

Type of Music — Serious Music *(Not necessarily limited to a specific historical or compositional type, nor to any particular medium)*:

- Current hits
- Trend music
- General popular music
  - Film music
  - Show tunes
  - Standards
  - Jazz-oriented
  - Country rock
  - "Middle-of-the-road"
- Jazz
  - Dixieland
  - Swing
  - Modern
  - Popular
- Folk music
- Rock
  - Progressive rock
- Rhythm and blues
- Country and western

Type of Music — Popular Music:

By stylist (historical) type:
- Light classic
- Pre-baroque
- Baroque
- Classic
- Romantic
- Modern

By type of composition:
- Solo or chamber forms
- Concerto
- Orchestra music
  - (Symphony, ballet, symphonic, poem, etc.)
- Opera, operetta
- Oratorio, cantata
- Motet, madrigal, etc.
- Songs, arias

- Ethnic
- Religious
  - (Sacred)
  - Gospel
  - Spiritual
- Novelty

Trend music Popular music that fits well technically into one of the other categories, but because of its association with a particular trend, fad, or era is classed by itself. This does *not* apply to current trends (see above). Examples include "Roaring Twenties music," "Charleston," "Barbershop," "Calypso," "Cha-cha," and "Boogie-woogie."

General popular music Popular music which is not suitably classed as "Rock," "Folk," "Country and Western," or "Jazz," because it contains a mixture of several different styles.

Film music Popular music written for or taken from a motion picture. This music can be instrumental or vocal or a number of pieces which are either. This is a source category and will include music which is classified elsewhere, e.g., the film score from a motion picture could also be mainstream jazz.

Showtunes (broadway) Popular music taken from theatrical productions, current or otherwise. This music can be vocal or instrumental or a combination. The music may be original soundtracks (original cast) or arrangements of music from theatrical productions. This is also a source category and will include music which is classified elsewhere. The difference between this category and the film music category is slight. In many cases, the music is identical (e.g., *West Side Story, Sound of Music,* and *My Fair Lady*).

Standards Popular music which at one time was either a current hit (see above) or popular music which is included because of its long-term popularity. Technically, this category may contain other types of music, *the arrangements usually defining the type.* The prime interest in a standard is its melody and lyrics as opposed to a particular arrangement. This category and the trend music category will in many cases overlap, since a given trend will have reached a certain popularity. Categories have been constructed to be inclusive, and music which fits into a more specialized category should be placed in that category. For example, there was an Elvis Presley trend; in addition, many of his selections were current hits; however, a more appropriate designation in his case would be "Rock."

Jazz-oriented Popular music whose accompaniment or whose style shows a jazz influence. This category contains primarily vocal (see jazz). Examples include Frank Sinatra, Jack Jones, and Nancy Wilson.

Country rock-oriented Popular music whose accompaniment or whose style shows a rock or country influence (see "Rock," "Country and Western"). This category includes mostly vocals.

Middle-of-the-road Popular music whose accompaniment or whose style shows no specific influence to any degree.

Jazz Popular music, vocal or instrumental which is characterized by all or most of the following features: (1) syncopated or intricate rhythms; (2) improvisation;[1] (3) intricate harmonic and melodic activity; (4) virtuosic instrumentalists and vocalists; (5) a form which consists of a statement of a theme, subsequent improvisation around the melody and harmonic patterns, and a return to the initial theme.

Of great interest to jazz composition are the performer(s) and performance rather than the actual composition. For example, one is generally more interested in Louis Armstrong than in the actual piece being performed.

---

[1] There are two types of improvisation, and their distinction is a necessity in the understanding of the various categories of jazz. True improvisation is spontaneous, unrehearsed in the ordinary sense, and original in its musical content (melody, harmony, rhythm, timbre of performing instrument, etc.) There are varying degrees of true improvisation, judged by the amount of variation from the original music content and the amount of complexity imposed on the original music ideas. There also exists pseudo-improvisation, which is distinct from true improvisation by all or some of the following features: (1) passages which are copies of earlier true improvisations; (2) passages which are carefully prepared to sound like true improvisations; and (3) passages which do not alter or vary the musical content to any significant degree.

In addition, one is also interested in the improvisations of a performer and his display of virtuosity.

Jazz was and is essentially a developing area of music, and certain phases of its development have become trends and have certain stylistic features which overlap and are present in other styles.

Dixieland Music associated with the early development of jazz containing the features discussed above with very little complexity. Its features also include simple and folk-like melodies and harmonies, and emphasized bass line, regular rhythmic accents usually 4–4 time, and the improvisation of several performers simultaneously. Typical instrumentation includes tuba, banjo, trumpet, clarinet, trombone, and piano. Authentic Dixieland dates as early as 1902 and includes music with such descriptive titles as "Barrel-house," "New Orleans Jazz," and "Traditional." Examples include Joe Oliver, Turk Murphy, and Jelly Roll Morton. Modern Dixieland employs more contemporary melodies (sometimes standards) and instrumentation with the not always obvious feature of pseudo-improvisation. An example is Al Hirt.

Swing In general jazz music associated with the *swing* era, dating from the 1930s through the 1940s. The music is usually associated with big bands (e.g., Tommy Dorsey, Glenn Miller) but smaller groups as well (e.g., Benny Goodman). There are many present-day groups playing in the same style (e.g., Ray McKinnly, Tex Beneke). Largely intended for dancing, the rhythm remains very simple and regular, and there is a great emphasis of smoother and more melodic lines. The improvisations are generally conservative, performed by one player at a time, and the overall volume (loudness) of such groups is much less than with Dixieland in general.

Modern jazz In general, jazz as it has developed since 1948–49 to the present, although there are examples which date earlier. Increasing attention is paid to the arrangements, intricate melodic lines, and harmonic patterns, as well as a concentration of activity centered around the rhythm section consisting of drums, string bass, piano, and/or guitar. There are four subdivisions of this category.

Mainstream jazz Jazz in which melodic and harmonic elements are akin to popular standards but with the following additional characteristics: (1) improvisation, (2) more equal balance between the primary activity (melody, instrumentalist, vocalist, etc.) and the accompaniment. Instrumentation varies from small groups to big bands, either with or without vocalist(s). The term "West Coast Jazz" has often been used to describe this type, although this category includes music which would not generally be considered to be West Coast Jazz. The term "West Coast Jazz" and its antithesis "East Coast Jazz" were originally coined to distinguish between jazz as performed by "white" musicians (West Coast) and that played by Negro musicians (East Coast), the former supposedly more intellectual and concerned with lyrical melodies and subtle harmonies, the latter supposedly more concerned with a dominating rhythm section and a forceful manner of playing. Mainstream jazz may be either if its requisites are fulfilled. The distinction between mainstream jazz and the categories which follow is based upon the lack of certain dominating features present in the others. Examples of mainstream jazz include Gerry Mulligan, Stan Kenton, Dave Brubeck (see Pop Jazz), Oscar Peterson, June Christy, and Bill Evans.

Bop (*bebop*) Bop is essentially an offshoot of earlier mainstream jazz and is generally associated with developments of the early 1950s in which improvisation reached a high degree of complexity. The emphasis was such that often the music consists of nothing more than a set of harmonic progression around which a soloist improvised. In vocal music of this sort, it was frequently the case that the vocalist improvised in the manner of an instrumentalist, using nonsense syllables in the place of words. "Themes" very often consisted of little more than earlier improvisations around some standard song. Examples include Charlie Parker, Sonny Stitt, and Dizzy Gillespie.

Hard jazz Jazz very much in the style of mainstream with greater emphasis on a strong and driving rhythm section, but with as much emphasis on the soloist and improvisation. The term "East Coast" is often used to mean *Hard Jazz* (see above), although the term Hard Jazz is more inclusive. Hard Jazz is often blues-oriented. Examples include Horace Silver, Ray Charles (see Rhythm and Blues), Jimmy Smith, and Cannonball Adderly.

Experimental jazz Jazz of varying characteristics which employs a good deal of experimentation with compositional techniques, and which has either never reached a level to become a phase, or else which is still too new to make such a decision.

Popular jazz Jazz which may be in the style of any of the above, but which has reached a relatively wide public acceptance. The reasons for public acceptance may vary (e.g., in the case of Stan Getz, the Bossa Nova; in the case of Ramsey Lewis, the strong rock beat). Examples include Dave Brubeck on "Take Five" and Vince Guaraldi on "Cast Your Fate to the Wind." This category does not usually include vocalists (see General popular music, Jazz-oriented).

Folk music Music which is most often in ballad style reflecting trends, culture, and/or beliefs of the common people, or providing social comment. The music is characterized by a simple melody and accompaniment. Often a guitar or other strummed instrument. Although this basically implies a solo singer, this category would also include larger ensembles whose arrangement does not destroy the basic simplicity of style. *Authentic Folk Music* employs folk songs predominantly of anonymous authorship, but songs such as "Scarlet Ribbons" which are in similar style are included also. Examples of performers of Authentic Folk Music include Pete Seeger, Josh White, and Theodore Bikel. *Contemporary Folk Music* generally employs more recently composed melodies, modern instrumentation, and arrangements with a greater emphasis on rhythm. *Folk Rock* is primarily contemporary folk music, sometimes authentic folk music, with a very strong rock influence. The rhythm is predominant and the arrangements may include trumpets, trombones, saxophones, and/or violins. Examples include the Mamas and the Papas, Sonny and Cher, and some Beatles recordings (e.g., "Norwegian Wood"). Country and Western, Ethnic Folk Songs, and Rhythm and Blues qualify in this category, but because of their special characteristics are placed into separate categories elsewhere.

Rock (rock-and-roll) Popular music, usually vocal and with a vocal line described as having lyrics of the non-ballad type, employing a great deal of repetition of words, especially those of a percussive nature (e.g., rock, blues, etc.), and with little or no attention paid to grammatical correctness. The music itself is characterized by strong driving rhythms, fragmentary melodic lines, and with little attention paid to refined arrangements or tone quality. In addition, the usual instrumentation includes electronically amplified instruments (electric guitar, electric bass, etc.), a wind instrument (often tenor saxophone), and drums. Especially prominent are the numerous effects employed in the recordings—many electronically produced (echo). *Hard Rock* and *Pop Rock* are subcategories, the distinction between the two being a matter of degree. The overall sound of the former is generally much more coarse and spontaneous (unrehearsed), and it is not unusual to find screaming and shouting on the part of the performers. *Pop Rock* employs the same basic sound, but often instrumentation includes trumpets, violins, etc., and tends toward a more polished performance for a wider audience (e.g., Twist, Go-Go, etc.).

Progressive rock   Also called Art Rock or New Rock. A type of popular music in which the integration or influence of different styles is not so characteristic as the actual presence of diverse styles usually simultaneously, and in nearly "pure" form. These different styles would include, for example, jazz, rhythm-blues, orchestral music, ethnic music (e.g., Indian), electronic music, and church music. Very often the pieces are sectional, each section shifting to a different mood, tempo, or style. This is in contradistinction to popular music which is predominantly one style but shows the influence of other styles, such as in Jazz Rock or Folk Rock. The rhythm and rhythm section sound employed in this music are most usually derived from other rock types, hence the term "rock." In many cases, however, examples can be found which have an extremely remote connection to other rock types. Examples would include Richard Harris's "MacArthur Park," Mason William's "Classical Gas," and also selections of artists such as Simon and Garfunkel, Blood, Sweat and Tears, and the Beatles.

Rhythm and blues   A ballad type song originated by the American Negro, and in this sense, folk in content. Often considered to be a type of rock, because of the strong rhythmic pulse and the general lack of polish, but the distinction lies in its content. *Modern Rhythm and Blues* often employs large ensembles and vocal background. Examples include Ray Charles and Lou Rawls. There is a close relationship between rhythm and blues and jazz, featuring singers who concentrate on blues type songs. The presence of other characteristics usually determines which category is appropriate. For example, Joe Williams, a singer of blues type songs, primarily sings with jazz accompaniment, and most probably his records would fall into the jazz category.

Country and western   A general category of music which is often characterized by a particular timbre including instruments such as bass, banjo, violin (solo), plus vocalist or vocal groups. The melodies and harmonies are simple and straightforward. The performances often incorporate regional characteristics either in subject matter (in this sense folk-like) or in instrumentation or vocal quality.

Country music   Music of the peoples of rural areas, although there are degrees according to the amount of urbanization. Often connected with and suitable for country dancing. In this category fall Hillbilly, Grand Ole Opry, Mountain Music, and Blue Grass Music, this distinction lying in the degree of urbanization and the presence of particular regional characteristics. It is again pointed out that certain songs and performances are actually authentic folk music and the selection of categories must be made on the basis of dominating features. For example, most of Burl Ives' songs would be authentic folk as opposed to country.

Modern country music Music retaining many of the predominant features of country music in general but which incorporates the current techniques of instrumentation and arranging. Different from general popular music, country rock-oriented in the degree of influence from country music in general.

Western Western music is literally music in the style of the ballad written about western subject matter. To a large extent this definition will encompass many authentic folk songs. The performance relies heavily on strummed instruments, often electrically amplified. It is not unusual to find amplified Hawaiian guitars and ukuleles in these performances.

Semiclassic (light) Refers either to (a) a serious composition which has become very well known to the general public because of its especially appealing or attractive nature, e.g., Debussy's *Clair de Lune*, Rachmaninoff's *Piano Concerto No. 2*, etc.; (b) a style in which a particular piece, of either serious or popular origin, is set. Usually an arrangement in this style introduces certain performance techniques (runs, florid arpeggios, etc.) or orchestrations, particularly a rather full texture, which are traditionally associated with serious music.

Serious music Music which is considered as being written especially for its aesthetic value as perceived through performance or listening, in contrast to that which is essentially written for entertainment and/or to accompany another activity. Other terms used to describe serious music include "classical," "good," "highbrow," "art," and "long-hair."

Grouping by Historical Era

Pre-baroque music Used here to include serious occidental music written before about 1600. Stylistic terms include Gregorian chant, Middle Ages, Romanesque, Gothic, and Renaissance. Palestrina and Machaut are representative composers.

Baroque music Serious music of the period c. 1600–1750. Representative composers include Monteverdi, Vivaldi, Handel, and J. S. Bach.

Classic music Generally, serious music written c. 1750–1830, and especially including the Viennese composers, Mozart, Haydn, early Beethoven, and Schubert. The term "classic" should not be confused with the less specific "classical," used to describe all serious music regardless of the historical style. The term "classical" is best avoided entirely.

Romantic music Generally, serious music written c. 1820–1900, especially including the works of Berlioz, Mendelssohn, Schumann, Chopin, Liszt, Wagner, Brahms, Tschaikovsky, and Mahler. It may also be applied to such Impressionist composers as Debussy and Ravel. The term is often used to describe popular music whose text deals with love, etc. The latter application to "romantic mood" music should be avoided.

Modern (serious) music Commonly used to include serious music written since c. 1910. Well-known composers include Stravinsky, Bartók, Schoenberg, Hindemith, and Barber. The term "contemporary" is also frequently used.

Classification by Type of Composition

Solo or chamber forms Types of music most frequently played by solo instruments or small instrumental ensembles; used here to refer to serious music exclusively. Among the most common specific names for such music are: Sonata, Minuet, Rondo, Suite, Prelude, Fugue, Toccata, Nocturne, Rhapsody, Theme and Variations, Etude, plus such dance names as Polonaise, Mazurka, etc.

Concerto A composition, usually in three movements or sections, for a solo player and orchestra. Pieces of this type date from the Baroque era to the present. (Occasionally, the title is applied to quite a different performance media such as Concerto for Orchestra, Organ Concerto, etc.)

General orchestra music Includes all serious music played by orchestras, especially symphonies, ballet, and symphonic poems.

Symphony A composition for orchestra, usually in four movements or sections. True symphonies date from the Classic period to the present, although such terms as "sinfonia" are encountered in earlier orchestral music.

Ballet Literally, the theatrical performance of a dancing group with costumes and scenery, to the accompaniment of music, but without singing or spoken word. As used here, the term applies particularly to the music which accompanies such a performance. Usually, this music is composed for orchestra and consists of numerous separate pieces, e.g., "The Nutcracker Suite." The majority of the well-known ballets have been written since 1800.

Symphonic poem Also known as the *Tone Poem;* this is a name given to a type of orchestral music which is distinguished by its association with a poetic or descriptive idea, e.g., "Don Quixote," "The Pines of Rome," etc. Most symphonic poems are from the latter half of the Romantic period.

Incidental music Instrumental music designed to be performed during a play. Properly speaking, the term does not include the music which is played before or between acts (overture, entr'acte), although it now generally includes all music associated with a play, e.g., Mendelssohn's "A Midsummer Night's Dream."

Suite A collection of separate pieces designed to be played in succession as a single work, similar to the various movements of a symphony or sonata. The term has specific reference to a type of instrumental form common in the Baroque era, but is often used to refer to free succession of movements of different types, frequently derived from incidental music (Grieg's "Peer Gynt Suite") or from ballet (Tschaikovsky's "Nutcracker Suite").

Opera A drama, either tragic or comic, sung (usually) throughout, with appropriate scenery and acting, to the accompaniment of an orchestra.

Operetta Literally, a short opera; the term is commonly used to describe a theatrical piece of relatively light and often sentimental character in simple and popular style, containing spoken dialogue, music, dancing, etc. Johann Strauss, Jr. (*Die Fledermaus*) and Arthur Sullivan in collaboration with W. S. Gilbert (*The Mikado*) are among the best-known writers of this form.

Oratorio A large-scale work for voices and orchestra, based on text of religious or contemplative character; but works based on a scriptural or liturgical text (Mass, Requiem, Passion) are usually not included under the category of oratorio.

Cantata A composite form, especially in the Baroque era, consisting of vocal solos, duets, choruses, etc., accompanied by instruments. The text may be secular or sacred; the latter differs from the oratorio in its smaller dimensions and in its having (usually) less narrative and a more continuous text.

Song A short composition for solo voice, usually but not necessarily accompanied, based on a poetic text, and (usually) composed so that the music enhances the text rather than overshadows it; often called by the term "Art Song." Lied: a song in the German vernacular especially from the nineteenth century.

Aria An elaborate solo song (occasionally for two solo voices, i.e., duet) with instrumental accompaniment. The aria may be a single piece, or be extracted from a composite form such as opera or oratorio. It differs from the song or Lied in that it is usually of greater length, nonstrophic, and emphasizes purely musical design and expression, often at the expense of the text.

Recitative A vocal style designed to imitate and to emphasize the natural inflections of speech, usually accompanied by a small group of instruments. The recitative rarely occurs as a separate piece; instead, it is usually found before an aria, duet, etc., of an opera or cantata.

Motet Usually an accompanied choral composition based on a Latin sacred text. The term also applies to similar settings of secular texts, or to settings for soloists rather than chorus. Also, some motets call for instrumental accompaniment.

Madrigal A composition for unaccompanied voices, usually one to a part, using a secular text and most often employing imitative counterpoint.

Anthem A choral composition written to English words from sacred sources; it holds a position in Anglican and Protestant churches similar to that of the motet in Roman rites; usually, the anthem is accompanied, preferably by the organ, and may include parts for solo singers.

Chorale The hymn tunes of the German Protestant Church; the term is also applied to a style characterized by the various parts (usually four) moving together as chords, i.e., hymn style.

Ethnic music The music of a particular race or nation which incorporates the characteristics of that race or nation in language, melodic and harmonic style, instrumentation, rhythms, and customs. This category of music will include all types of music. Specifically ethnic music will probably fall either into a *general popular* category or into a *folk* category.

Religious music A general term applied to any music which, by nature of its text, deals with religious subjects, usually the Christian faith. By extension, the term is also used for nonvocal music with similar meditative, musical characteristics, instrumental arrangements of vocal religious music, or music played by instruments characteristic of churches (i.e., the organ or carillon). Religious music may be either church music or non-church music.

Sacred music Generally, a music of a devotional or religious nature; this term is used especially for religious music of a serious type, e.g., a mass, motet, etc., as opposed to that of a more popular appeal, e.g., a gospel song or spiritual.

Gospel song A composition for either solo voice or ensemble which emphasizes a personal religious experience, hence, a song written from a "manward" point of view to, rather than about, Jesus or God. Stylistically, such music is usually either in smooth, close harmony in a moderately slow tempo (inspirational) or a rather vigorous hand-clapping rhythm (southern style); often the congregation participates freely.

Spiritual A religious folk-song of the kind originated by the American Negro during slavery days; also, the style of such songs. Spirituals may be either solo or ensemble, accompanied or unaccompanied.

Novelty A category which includes all music (though primarily popular), which is distinguished from the specific category of composition because of unusual performance qualities. Generally, pieces in this category create a musically humorous effect, e.g., Jonathan and Darlene Edwards, Mrs. Miller, etc.

Performance Media

Instrumental

Electronic instruments Modern instruments which are capable of producing an infinite number of sounds and are especially useful for creating sounds not available through traditional means. Electronic music is a 20th-century development; it may include traditional sounds, e.g., Concerto for Tape Recorder and Orchestra. Electronic instruments usually do not include such instruments as the organ or electronic piano, whose sound is merely imitative.

Chamber ensemble An instrumental combination ranging from two to about twenty-five players; typical groups include trios, string quartets and quintets, and groups as large as the chamber orchestra, the latter usually including only one player to a part. Chamber music, the repertoire of such groups, is limited to serious music.

String orchestra An ensemble of string instruments ranging in size from about 15 to "101" players; the literature ranges from early Baroque music up to and including arrangements of popular music, the latter usually characterized by lush, full sounds. Besides members of the violin and viol families, string orchestras may include the piano, harp, or various solo wind or brass instruments.

Symphony orchestra A large ensemble of instruments (as distinct from the "chamber" or "small" orchestra) consisting of about 60 to 100 players who are divided into four groups: strings, wood winds, brass, and percussion. The repertoire may include Baroque music, though it generally begins with Classic music and continues to the present.

Military band A moderately large ensemble composed primarily of brass and percussion instruments, which, however, may also include piccolos, saxophones, bagpipes, and other instruments suited to outdoor playing.

Symphonic band A large ensemble composed of wood winds, brasses, and percussion instruments, and often including also string bass, piano, or harp. The original repertoire dates from the nineteenth century, and arrangements include earlier music as well as popular music. The term "concert band" is often used to refer to this ensemble.

Dance band Usually, an ensemble which performs popular music and ranges in size from about ten to twenty players. It is composed mainly of wood wind and brass instruments, plus piano, bass, and percussion. Often, a few violins are added (e.g., by Lawrence Welk) which do not alter the basic characteristic sound.

Big band A term used to mean an ensemble similar to a dance band, which, however, emphasizes the performance of jazz for listening.

Combo An abbreviation of "combination," meaning a small group, two to about seven players, which usually includes percussion (rhythm), bass, and/or piano, plus a solo wind and/or brass instrument, especially saxophone and trumpet. Contemporary combos may include more unusual instruments such as the flute or oboe. The repertoire is essentially popular in nature, as distinct from chamber music.

Vocal

Chorus A large (usually more than twelve) body of singers who perform in ensembles usually with several singers assigned to each part. The term includes "choir," traditionally a chorus associated with a particular church. Choral music ranges from the very earliest pre-baroque period to the present day, and includes serious music, both sacred and secular, as well as popular music.

A cappella Choral singing without instrumental accompaniment, especially typical of pre-baroque music.

"Vocal group" A small ensemble of singers, usually only one performer to a part, which performs primarily popular music. Such groups would include the Swingle Singers and Four Freshmen as well as barbershop quartets.

APPENDIX F

Radio
Glossary

(Abbreviations are listed at the beginning of each letter)

AFM   The American Federation of Musicians, a union.

AFTRA   The American Federation of Television and Radio Artists, a union for announcers and singers.

AM   Amplitude modulation. A method of transmitting radio signals.

AOR   Stands for Album Oriented Rock or Adult Oriented Rock. A type of station format frequently referred to in recent years as "mellow" rock.

ASCAP   American Society of Composers, Authors, and Publishers. One of the two major music licensing agencies. (*See* BMI.)

Account   A client, an advertiser.

Across-the-board   A strip show. One aired at the same time daily (at least five days a week).

Ad lib   Improvise. An unprepared remark, sound effect, or piece of music.

Affidavit   A sworn statement that commercials were on the air in certain time periods.

Affiliate   An independent station that forms part of a network.

Ambience   Reverberant sound, such as the reflected sound of the concert hall, that gives a recording the feel of a live performance.

Atmosphere   The sound elements that establish a mood or locale of a production.

Attenuation   Diminution of sound intensity.

Audio   Sound.

Audition A tryout performance. Also a checking of material before airing.

Availabilities Unsold time slots where commercials can be placed.

BMI Broadcast Music Incorporated. One of the two major music licensing agencies. (*See* ASCAP.)

BTA Best time available. Also called ROS, or run of schedule. This means that the station may schedule an advertiser's commercials in the best available time that is left in the station's schedule. Spots bought under a BTA contract are low-cost and can be a good buy if the station has many availabilities. However, if a station has few availabilities these spots are unlikely to run in anything other than fringe time.

Background Sound used to heighten atmosphere or mood, displayed in a secondary perspective. Abbreviated BG.

Back-time Timing an element from the end rather than the beginning. Often a record will be dead-rolled (started on the turntable but with the sound volume turned off) and faded up in the middle so that it will end at the desired time—for example, to join a network newscast or to finish at the end of a commercial.

Baffles Sound-absorbing panels used in recording studios to increase the acoustic separation of musical instruments and to prevent one instrument's sound from being picked up on another instrument's microphone.

Balance The proper volume relationship. The desired blending of sounds to accomplish the desired end.

Barter Paying for goods through advertising rather than money. It also means airing programs which contain some commercials and some availabilities without paying directly for the program.

Beat A one-count pause. Also a segment of a measure of music.

Bias current Used to reduce distortion in audio recording. A high-frequency current, called the bias current, is recorded along with the other material. The bias setting of the recorder affects the sensitivity to what is recorded, the overall signal-to-noise ratio, frequency response, and distortion. If the bias setting of the playback unit is different from the unit used for recording, or if the bias setting of a brand of tape is different from a recorder, the incompatibility can result in inferior quality recordings.

Bidirectional mike One with two live faces or pickup areas.

Billboard An announcement of elements or programs to follow.

Bit A small part. Also a routine.

Bite it off Cut off music or other sound cleanly and sharply.

Blasting Distorting of sound due to excess volume.

Blend   Balance. A desired combination of sound. A sound mix.

Blow   Completely lose self-control. A major fluff.

Board   An audio console.

Board fade   Fading sound from all sound sources simultaneously, accomplished by using a master gain control. It also means fading electronically rather than changing mike position.

Boom   A mike stand with a long arm holding the mike.

Booth   Announce booth. A small room separate from the control room.

Break up   When an announcer loses self-control and giggles or laughs.

Bridge   To make a transition between scenes. Also a piece of music used to make a transition.

Build   Increase of emotional excitement by acceleration of tempo, intensity, or volume. This can be accomplished by the writing, acting, music, and sound effects.

Canned   Recorded.

Cans   Headphones.

Capstan   Part of a tape recorder. The capstan is rotated by a motor which works at constant speed. Audio tape passes between the capstan and the capstan roller to move the tape across the tape head to the take-up reel.

Cardioid mike   One with approximately a heart-shaped pickup pattern.

Channel   A radio frequency on which a station is licensed to broadcast. The word is also used to refer to an input or output circuit on a console. It also refers to one track of a multi-track tape.

Character   A performer other than a leading lady or leading man. The old, the young, the eccentric, those with unusual voices or unusual accents.

Clear channel station   One with an unduplicated frequency at night and 50,000 watts of power. Only twelve stations are truly unduplicated with non-directional nighttime signals. An additional number have 50,000 watts but directional signals and other stations on the same channel in other parts of the country.

Climax   The pay-off. The point of greatest emotional intensity to which a program or program element has built.

Cold   Without rehearsal. Without preliminary buildup.

Commentator   A newscaster who injects personal opinion.

Composite   A mixed audio track. One which has combined several elements on one track.

Compresser An automatic fader. When the sound level reaches a certain peak, a compressor automatically fades the volume down to an acceptable level. If the compression ratio is large enough, the compressor is called a limiter.

Condenser microphone A microphone which uses electrostatic rather than electromagnetic principles. It uses two very thin plates, one movable and one fixed, to form a capacitor. Such microphones need their own power supplies. They can be very high-quality but are less rugged than dynamic mikes.

Console A sound-mixing panel which an engineer or operator uses to mix and control sound. An audio board.

Contemporary music The term has many and varied meanings in current radio. It is frequently used to refer to current popular music of whatever kind is selling records. It is just as often used as a synonym for rock music. It is often used as a kind of slogan indicating that a certain station is playing current music and that other stations not playing the same brand of music are old hat. The term is also used in serious music circles to describe twentieth-century compositions. Actually, there are many forms of contemporary music: rock, jazz, mainstream pop, classical, and country.

Continuity A catch-all term for written radio. Commercial copy, scripts for programs (if any), public service announcements, and promotions to be read all can be called continuity.

Control room The room in which the engineer or operator mixes the sounds from tape recorders, microphones, turntables, and other sources.

Co-op An advertising procedure which combines a local and national advertiser's messages into one announcement for which they share the cost.

Cost per thousand The cost of reaching 1,000 persons with a radio commercial. For example, if 5,000 persons are listening and a commercial cost $15, the CPM (cost per thousand) is $3.

Coverage area The geographical area reached by a given station, based on the station's signal.

Cross fade Fading in the sound from one source while fading out the sound from another source.

Cue A direction to proceed. It could be a hand signal, a light, or a previously agreed upon sound signal. The term also refers to an audition system for "cuing up" records or tapes, feeding sound through a cue speaker so that a record or tape can be started at just the right time.

Cumulative audience (cume) The number of different persons reached by a radio station's programing in a specified time period, such as a week (called a weekly cume).

Cushion Optional material that can be used or eliminated near the end of a program in order to fit into a tight time-frame. Also called a pad or a fill.

Cut   Stop. It also means to eliminate some element, to cut it. A third usage of the word refers to a track on a sound recording, as the first cut on an album or tape. A fourth usage is to make a recording. To cut a spot is to record it. It also means to eliminate it. Context determines the meaning.

Cut in   To interrupt. Also to include a local element into a network program, such as to include a local commercial at the appropriate place in a network newscast. The local element is called a cut-in.

Cut off   To cut off is to stop or to switch off. A cut-off refers to a cough box, a button or switch that shuts off the mike while an announcer clears his throat or coughs.

DB   Short for decibel, a measure of sound volume.

Dampen   To cut down reverberation. It can mean to add sound-absorbing material to a studio. It can also mean to touch the edge of a chime or gong to prevent it from reverberating freely.

Dead air   Silence. Often caused by human error, but it can be caused by equipment failure.

Dead mike   A microphone that will not pick up sound, either because it is faulty or not plugged in.

Dead side   The sound of a microphone that does not pick up sound.

Decibel   A measure of sound volume which uses a logarithmic scale to express sound volume in workable figures.

Degausser   A demagnetizer. Passing an audio tape or magnetized object through a magnetic field of sufficient strength to leave a magnetic pattern essentially random is called degaussing. It is a quick manner of erasing an audio tape. A degausser should not be used close to a tape recorder or it may magnetize the record head in an undesirable manner.

Discrete quad   Transmission of four separate signals to achieve quadraphonic sound, as opposed to matrix quad which reduces the four signals to two before transmission, relying on an encoder to return the signal to four channels at reception.

Dolby   A widely used system for electronically reducing unwanted noise in order to mtaintain the highest possible sound quality.

Donut   A commercial in which live copy runs between an opening and close of a produced commercial, often a singing jingle. Also called a sandwich.

Dub   A tape copy. Used as both a noun and verb.

Dynamic Mike   A moving coil mike, pressure actuated. A fine coil of wire is attached to a delicate diaphragm in a permanent magnetic field. Basic pressure mikes are inherently omnidirectional.

Earphones Also called headphones or cans. Used when extraneous sounds interfere with hearing, or when it is necessary to hear other sound elements in front of a live microphone.

Echo The reflection or return of sound after a delay. It can be accomplished with an echo chamber or electronic reverberation device.

Echo chamber A room with highly reflective walls, no two of which are parallel, which has a speaker and microphone in it. Used for adding presence or natural echo effects.

End rate The lowest rate at which a station offers commercial time.

Engineer The term can refer to a person who maintains equipment, but also to a person who operates a board.

Equalization Altering the frequency response of an amplifier so that certain frequencies are more or less pronounced than others. It can be used to give control over harmonic balance or timbre of instrumentation.

Establish Present a sound just long enough to identify it or to establish a mood.

Ethnic radio A station format aimed at one or more ethnic groups, usually focusing on racial identity, language, or cultural heritage.

FM Frequency modulation. Form of sound transmission characterized by line-of-sight high fidelity signal.

Fade To reduce in volume, either electronically or by moving away from the live portion of the mike. Also called fade down or fade out. To increase sound is to fade in or fade up.

Fake To improvise or simulate a sound. Also to carry on as if prepared when in reality unprepared.

Fat To be fat is to run overtime. It can also mean well-prepared, as with sure-fire jokes or easy lines.

Fidelity Exactness of sound reproduction.

Fill To add material to use up all the time. The material added is also called fill.

Filter A device used to change sound quality by eliminating sound frequencies.

Fixed position A spot presented at a specific time (such as just before the 7 A.M. news) and usually sold at a premium price.

Flight The period during which an advertiser runs his spots if not a 52-week advertiser, such as a fall flight, specific weekly flight, etc.

Fluff A mistake ("Ladies and gentlemen, the president of the United States, Hoobert Hever").

Format   The type of programing. Also, specific prescribed ingredients that make up a sound hour or a program.

Free-lance   A person who is not a staff member but who is employed on a special assignment basis.

Frequency   The number of times a listener is in a radio audience in a week. Also the number of times a sound wave passes through all of its values between its maximum positive and negative excursions and returns to its starting value. Each complete fluctuation is called a cycle, and the accepted unit of cycles per second is called hertz (Hz). The term also refers to the assigned channel of a station.

Gain   Volume.

Gross rating points   Take the quarter-hour rating for the time period when each scheduled commercial of a specified advertiser aired, add the ratings up, and you have the gross rating points. As an example, say that an advertiser ran four spots. The quarter-hour ratings for each were 4, 3.5, 3.5, and 4. The gross rating points in this limited example would be 15.

Highs   Upper sound registers. High frequencies. Highs can be eliminated or enhanced with filters.

Homes using radio (HUR)   In ratings, the percentage of all homes that are turned to radio at a specified time period.

Hook   A surprise ending, or an interesting opening, or a repetitive musical phrase designed to attract a listener or to impress an item on one's consciousness.

Horizontal buy   A continuing radio campaign with commercials placed throughout the week. (*See also* Vertical saturation.)

Hot mike   One that is turned on and ready for operation. The opposite of a cold or dead mike.

IBEW   The International Brotherhood of Electrical Workers. Some sound engineers belong to this union.

ID   Station identification. In advertising terms, a ten-second commercial that keeps an advertiser's name before the public.

IPS   Inches per second. Most audio recording in radio stations has for years been 7½ ips, although newer formats are used for specific purposes. Generally, the higher the recording speed, the greater the fidelity of the recorded sound. Recording studios using multi-track formats often record at 15 ips and sometimes at 30 ips. Tapes maintained to keep a record of station programing (where fidelity is less important) may run at 1⅞ or even 15⁄16 ips.

Impedance   A rating used to match the signal-providing capability of one device (such as a microphone) with the signal-drawing requirements of another device (such as a tape recorder). Impedance is measured in ohms and its symbol is Z. Generally speaking, high-impedance mike lines are more susceptible to pickup of electrostatic noise, such as that caused by fluorescent lights and motors. Low-impedance mike lines are fairly insensitive to such electrostatic pickup, but are more sensitive to induced hum pickup from power lines. Use of differing cables and other devices can make maximum use of each type of microphone, but top signal quality can be achieved only where compatible impedances are present in appropriate electronic devices.

Independent   A station not affiliated with a network.

Input   A sound source coming in to a console or other equipment.

Institutional   A type of advertising which promotes the corporate image rather than selling specific products.

Kill   Stop. Cancel. If you kill a mike you turn it off. If you kill a program you take it off the air.

Lead-in   Set the scene. The material used to set the scene is also called a lead-in.

Leakage   Escaping sound going where it is not wanted, such as through a microphone, a tape recorder, or a channel on a console.

Level   Volume.

Limiter   An electronic device used to prevent sound level from getting so high that it causes overloading of the amplifiers.

Live   Not recorded. In FCC terms, a disc jockey show is not considered live, even though the disc jockey is not recorded, because the majority of the program, the recorded music, is not live.

Live copy   Copy read by the announcer as it airs, in contrast to recorded spots.

Live mike   One that is turned on and functioning.

Live studio   One that is on the air. Also one that is acoustically reverberant.

Live tag   A message added by the announcer to a recorded commercial. Often used to give a daily special or to add a specific address when a central office provides a tape to be used for many stores.

Log   A station's record of its programing, including legal identification, programs, commercials, and public service announcements. Technical logs are also required for monitoring transmitter performance. Both logs are required by the FCC but would be good business practice even if they were not required.

Logo   Short for logotype. Often used to mean a visual signature, a graphic identity. Can also be used to include sound signatures.

Lows Low sound frequencies.

MC Master of ceremonies.

MOR Middle-of-the-road. A term used to describe radio stations which play a wide spectrum of mainstream pop music. Most stations playing such music do not call themselves MOR, preferring such descriptive terms as pop-standard, adult contemporary, adult popular music, or similar. There must be at least a dozen other terms used to describe variations of this form of radio.

Make-good An announcement run to replace an originally scheduled spot which was missed, run at the wrong time, or otherwise messed up.

Master The original taped (sometimes disc) production. Could refer to the negative mold from which records are pressed. Also refers to Master Control.

Master control The control room through which all station originations pass.

Matrix quad A system of quadraphonic sound in which four original channels are reduced to two. Through use of a decoder, the encoded signals are returned to four channels. (*See* Discrete quad.)

Mix Blend sound from two or more sources.

Mixer A console. An audio control board.

Monaural Single-channel sound.

Monitor A control room speaker. To monitor means to listen.

Montage A succession of short scenes or effects used for rapid presentation of events, or used to obtain an emotional effect by the particular blending of the elements.

NABET National Association of Broadcast Employees and Technicians. One of the most common unions for technicians.

NPR National Public Radio, the noncommercial government-funded network.

Narrator An announcer or actor who presents information used to summarize, to bridge breaks in dramatic time elements, to bridge like program elements together, or to lead into a story situation.

Natural sound The use of real sound, as crowd noise at a sports event. Such sound can often add atmosphere and credibility to a production. Some productions are most effective if done in controlled studio environments, while others may make effective use of sounds at remote locations.

Nemo Remote broadcast. Programing originating from outside the station.

Network Networks originate programs from one location which are broadcast simultaneously on two or more stations. These can be ongoing or special networks. The program can be distributed by lines leased from AT&T, by microwave, or by satellite. Prior to 1977, the FCC required network exclusivity in a given market. This was changed when the FCC decided that Associated Press and UPI news services were networks, allowing these and other networks to air on more than one station in a market if they wished.

Noise Any undesired sound. Usually it refers to unplanned sound which interferes with radio's planned sound, such as cross talk, leakage, and static.

Nondirectional A microphone that is not limited to picking up sound from any specific direction.

Off mike At a distance or direction from the mike resulting in presence that is not clear or foreground.

On mike At the appropriate distance and direction from a mike which gives a live, foreground presence.

On the nose On time.

Open cold To begin without music, sound, or preliminary introduction.

Open end Programing with only a middle, like so much of modern radio. An open end program may also be one that does not need to end at a specific time, such as an open-forum special-issue program. An older use of the term means a recorded syndicated program with the commercial positions left open. It also means a commercial which has room at the end for a tag.

Output A sound source leaving a console.

Overdubbing If a recording is made on one channel of a multi-track tape and then one or more additional tracks are recorded separately, this is overdubbing. When played back, all of the tracks are in synchronization. In this way a few voices or instruments can become a chorus or orchestra, or it can be a way of minimizing the effect of one person's mistake on others. Modern recording may use as many as 64 separate tracks, allowing elaborate sound mixes and, when desired, the opportunity for multitalented people to play many roles in an orchestra.

Pad Cushion or fill.

Participating program A program having more than one sponsor.

Perspective The placement of sound in relation to the microphone. Its perceived location.

Pick it up Increase the pace.

Pickup To start again from a particular location, as in recording a commercial. Also a received radio transmission.

Playback   Auditioning of something previously recorded.

Pot   Short for potentiometer. Fader. Volume control.

Pre-empt   To replace a regularly scheduled program or spot with special programing.

Premium rate   An extra charge for especially valuable time. This could be for special events coverage, for fixed position spots, etc.

Presence   Perspective. Sound quality in relation to its location.

Print through   Unwanted transfer of a signal from one layer of tape. Tapes with thinner backings and high-output oxide coatings tend to print through more than others. Print-through also increases with length of storage and increased temperature. Also, storing tape tails out and rewinding just before playback makes the effect less noticeable.

Public service announcement   A free announcement given to support some nonprofit activity.

Punch   To deliver a line with added force or energy.

Quadraphonic   Four-channel sound.

RADAR   Radio's All Dimension Audience Research. A continuing survey of national listening habits conducted for ABC, CBS, Mutual, and NBC by Statistical Research, Inc.

Rate holder   A spot run to preserve the conditions of a contract. For instance, many stations give a price break for 52-week advertisers. A given advertiser may want to concentrate his advertising in specified periods for a seasonal business, but he may run one spot per week for the remainder of the year so that he can get the 52-week discount. It may be to his advantage to run a few commercials he really does not need.

Rating   The percent of the total audience (potential listeners) tuned to a specific station at a given time.

Rating service   A company such as Arbitron, Pulse, The Source, Mediastat, or Hooper which measures radio listening.

Reach   The number of households or individuals a given station, program, or commercial reaches in a given time period. Along with frequency, it is an important measure for advertiser evaluation of the station's audience.

Rebate   An extra discount on radio time given when an advertiser uses more commercials than his original contract required, allowing him to qualify for a better rate.

Remote   A broadcast originating outside the station.

Resonance   Body or fullness of sound.

Reverberation Reflected sound blending with immediate sound to provide an altered sound quality. Echo.

Ribbon mike Velocity mike, one with a thin metal ribbon suspended between poles of a magnet to sense the sound. These are inherently bidirectional.

Ride gain To adjust faders constantly to maintain optimum transmission level.

Room tone The sum total of the sound characteristics of a room. In recording, the microphone picks up not only the sound recorded but the room in which it is recorded.

Run of schedule The same as Best Time Available. Abbreviated ROS.

Run through First rehearsal using facilities.

Schmaltz A highly sentimental performance.

Segue To play two pieces of music back to back without interruption.

Sets in use The number of radios turned on in a given market at a given time.

Share of audience The percent of those listening to radio in a given market that are tuned to a specific station.

Short rate The opposite of rebate. An extra charge for radio time assessed when an advertiser uses fewer commercials than his original contract required, dropping him to a higher ad rate.

Signature A theme, sound, or catch phrase used for identification. A sound logo.

Sotto voce A direction to speak softly.

Sound head A device that activates sound, such as the device that senses the impulses on magnetic tape and plays them.

Sound truck A movable console containing turntables, controls, and capability for generating sound effects. Not often used in contemporary recording and production.

Speaker Short for loudspeaker. A speaker reverses the action of the microphone.

Splash tank A water container used for generating sound effects such as swimming, bodies falling into the water, etc.

Sponsor One who underwrites a particular program and presents his commercial messages in the program. Not all advertisers are sponsors, since most advertisers buy spot availabilities only.

Spot   Spot announcement. A commercial.

Stand by   An alert that one is about to go on the air or will begin recording.

Station break   The call letters and location of a station. FCC rules specify that these should be given once each hour at the top of the hour. Most stations do not need encouragement to identify themselves. Also called a station identification.

Stereophonic   Sound of two or more channels.

Stet   A proofreading term meaning to let stand as originally written.

Sting   A sharp and emphatic musical punctuation. Also called a stab.

Stretch   Slow down.

Studio fade   When the performer moves away from the mike, as opposed to a board fade.

Sweetener   A track that is added to an already existing track to reinforce some part of the sound. Commonly done to television comedy shows on the laugh or applause tracks.

System cue   Network identification, frequently given as a cue for local stations to run a local commercial or to let them know that the broadcast is completed. Example: "This is the Golden West Radio Network."

TF or TFN   'Til forbid or 'til further notice. An advertising schedule without a fixed expiration date.

TIS   Travelers information service. Often called roadside radio. Low-power government-funded noncommercial stations using AM frequencies 530 and 1610 to present public information to travelers, such as road conditions, directions to parking lots, etc.

TWX   A teletype machine. Pronounced twix.

Tag   An announcement given live and added to a recorded spot.

Take   A specific recording of a sound sequence.

Talent   Any air performer or presenter, whether they really have talent or not.

Theme   A piece of music used for identification purposes. Themes were common on older network radio programs and deejay shows. Only occasionally used today.

Throw it away   Give a line in an offhand manner, to speak without emphasis.

Tight   Strict time deadlines. Without dead air. Also nervous.

Tone   The timbre of a specific sound depending on its frequency vibration.

Track   The sound on one channel of a tape.

Type   Type cast. Stereotyping. Limiting a performer to one kind of role. Also, fitting a performer to a role for which he or she is suited.

Unidirectional mike   One with a pickup pattern that works in only one direction.

VU meter   VU stands for volume units. Also called a VI meter, for volume indicator. A sensitive meter in the audio console which measures the volume of sound passing through the console. It is more accurate than relying on the human ear alone. It allows the board operator to adjust the volume of in-studio monitors, thus changing the apparent loudness of the program, while having an accurate indicator of what the true volume is. Newer and more sophisticated sound systems frequently use a device that shows sound volume in the form of a moving bar graph using lights rather than the older waving needle.

Velocity mike   Ribbon mike.

Vertical saturation   The slotting of many commercials on one or several stations during a short time period to expose a large number of listeners to a repeated message, such as to announce a sale. (*See also* Horizontal buy.)

Walla walla   Crowd noise. Random indistinct conversation which gives the effect of a crowd.

Selected
Bibliography

Books

Allen, Steve, *The Funny Men*, Simon and Schuster, New York, 1956. Dated, but many excellent observations about humor and humorists.

Asher, Thomas R., and J. Victor Hahn, *Broadcast Media Guide for Candidates*, Media Access Project, Washington, D.C., 1910 N Street, N.W., 1974. Written for the political candidate but useful inside the station as well.

Ashley, Paul P., *Say It Safely*, University of Washington Press, Seattle, 1976. A short, readable book.

The Associated Press, *Broadcast Style Book*, New York. A short, useful manual for newswriters.

The Editors of BM/E Magazine, *FM Radio Station Operations Handbook*, Tab Books, Blue Ridge Summit, Pa., 1973. The emphasis is on technical operations.

Barnouw, Erik, *A History of Broadcasting in the United States*, Oxford University Press, New York, 1966. The most complete history of broadcasting in America. Very readable. In three volumes.

Barton, Roger, *Advertising Agency Operations and Management*, McGraw-Hill, New York, 1955. Dated, but useful for understanding how an ad agency operates.

Barton, Roger (ed.), *Handbook of Advertising Management*, McGraw-Hill, New York, 1970. Edited collection of massive proportions. 37 authors writing treatises on various advertising subjects.

Bauer, Raymond A., and Stephen A. Greyser, *Advertising in America: The Consumer View*, Division of Research, Graduate School of Business Administration, Harvard University, Cambridge, Mass., 1968. The most comprehensive survey of American advertising attitudes available.

Blake, Reed H., and Edwin O. Haroldsen, *A Taxonomy of Concepts in Communication*, Hastings House, New York, 1975. A summary of communication theory.

Chester, Giraud, Garnet R. Garrison, and Edgar E. Willis, *Television and*

Radio, 4th Edition, Appleton-Century-Crofts, New York, 1971. Covers many areas.

Coddington, R. H., *Modern Radio Broadcasting,* Tab Books, Blue Ridge Summit, Pa., 1970. Centers on the small station.

Cone, Fairfax M., *With All Its Faults: A Candid Account of Forty Years in Advertising,* Little, Brown, Boston, 1970. Deals primarily with Foote, Cone and Belding Advertising Agency.

Denisoff, R. Serge, *Solid Gold: The Popular Record Industry,* Transaction Books, New York, 1976. Inside the record industry and its gatekeepers.

Dolan, Robert Emmett, *Music in Modern Media,* G. Schirmer and Co., New York, 1967. About recording, with emphasis on music recording.

Dunning, John, *Tune in Yesterday: The Ultimate Encyclopedia of Old-Time Radio, 1925–1976,* Prentice-Hall, Englewood Cliffs, N.J., 1976. Comprehensive listing of programs and a narrative discussion of their casts and role in radio development.

Emery, Walter, *Broadcasting and Government,* Michigan State University, East Lansing, 1961. Deals primarily with the FCC.

Ennes, Harold E., *AM/FM Broadcast Operations,* Howard W. Sams, Indianapolis, 1966. Practical discussion of equipment and operational techniques in layman terms.

Friendly, Fred W., *The Good Guys, the Bad Guys, and the First Amendment: Free Speech vs. Fairness in Broadcasting,* Random House, New York, 1976. An analysis of the Fairness Doctrine and the legal cases that have shaped it.

Green, Maury, *Television News: Anatomy and Process,* Wadsworth, Belmont, Calif., 1969. About television; not all useful for radio, but some excellent material not as well stated elsewhere.

Guimary, Donald L., *Citizens Groups and Broadcasting,* Praeger Special Studies, New York, 1975. A study of the impact of citizens groups on radio and television stations.

Head, Sydney A., *Broadcasting in America,* 3rd Edition (revised and enlarged), Houghton Mifflin, Boston, 1976. An updating of the best book about the social framework and organization of American broadcasting.

Hale, Julian, *Radio Power: Propaganda and International Broadcasting,* Temple University Press, Philadelphia, 1975. Examines past and present use of radio for propaganda, including the Nazi model, communist uses, Voice of America, BBC, clandestine radio.

Hall, Claude, and Barbara Hall, *This Business of Radio Programming,* Billboard, New York, 1977. Focuses on the disc jockey and program director, includes interviews previously printed in *Billboard* magazine.

Heighton, Elizabeth J., and Don R. Cunningham, *Advertising in the Broadcast Media,* Wadsworth, Belmont, Calif., 1976. Excellent book covering the subject matter fully.

Hennessy, Bernard C., *Public Opinion,* 2nd Edition, Wadsworth, Belmont, Calif., 1970. Includes 70 pages on media and media-caused opinion change.

Hiebert, Ray E., and Carlton E. Spitzer, *The Voice of Government,* John Wiley, New York, 1968. Emphasis on public information and the relation of politics to media in public relations.

Hilliard, Robert L. (ed.), *Radio Broadcasting*, Hastings House, New York, 1974. Various authors contribute chapters on elements of radio production.

Hilliard, Robert L., *Writing for Television and Radio*, Hastings House, New York, 1976. Practice materials and script form for various kinds of writing.

Hoffer, Jay, *Radio Production Techniques*, Tab Books, Blue Ridge Summit, Pa., 1974. Really a book on station operations.

House Commerce Committee, *Review of Federal Communications Commission Activities—1969*, Government Printing Office, Washington, D.C., 1970. Shows some of the strain the FCC is under.

Hyde, Stuart W., *Television and Radio Announcing*, Houghton Mifflin, Boston, 1971. Comprehensive, with solid approach and good practice materials.

Institute for Broadcast Financial Management, *Accounting Manual for Broadcasters*, IBFM, Suite 308, 360 North Michigan Ave., Chicago, Ill. 60601. Provides guidelines and financial reporting forms.

Kahn, Frank J. (ed.), *Documents of American Broadcasting*, Appleton-Century-Crofts, New York, 1968. A good collection of readings about basic legal decisions involving broadcasting.

Klapper, Joseph, *Effects of Mass Communication*, Free Press, Glencoe, Ill., 1960. Provides a perspective on how communications affect the public.

Kleppner, Otto, *Advertising Procedure*, Prentice-Hall, Englewood Cliffs, N.J., 1966. Helpful in relating radio to advertising.

Koenig, Allen E. (ed.), *Broadcasting and Bargaining: Labor Relations in Radio and Television*, The University of Wisconsin Press, Madison, 1970. The only book that covers unions in broadcasting, including history, background, federal actions, arbitration, and current problems.

Kohlmeier, Louis, *The Regulators: Watchdog Agencies and the Public*, Harper & Row, New York, 1970. Discusses and critiques all federal regulatory groups.

Lasswell, H. D., R. D. Casey, and B. L. Smith (eds.), *Propaganda and Promotional Activities: An Annotated Bibliography*, University of Chicago Press, Chicago, 1969.

Levinson, Harry, *Exceptional Executive: A Psychological Conception*, Harvard University Press, Cambridge, Mass., 1968.

Lichty, Lawrence W., and Joseph M. Ripley, *American Broadcasting: Introduction and Analysis—Readings*, College Printing, Madison, Wisc., 1969. An extensive collection of materials on programing and audiences of broadcasting.

Macdonald, Jack, *The Handbook of Radio Publicity and Promotion*, Tab Books, Blue Ridge Summit, Pa., 1970. A catalog of promotion ideas.

Milam, Lorenzo W., *Sex and Broadcasting*, Book People, 2940 7th, Berkeley, Calif., 1975. Serious comments on operation of noncommercial radio, interspersed with off-the-wall humor.

Miles, Donald, *Broadcast News Handbook*, Howard W. Sams and Co., Indianapolis, 1975. Basics of radio news gathering and presentation.

National Association of Broadcasters, *Political Broadcast Catechism and the Fairness Doctrine*, Washington, D.C., 1966. A guide to working with "equal time" and fairness.

National Association of Broadcasters, *Standard Definitions of Broadcast Research Terms*, January 1967. Very useful guide to ratings.

National Association of Broadcasters, *Radio Today*, 1970. A short book summarizing a nationwide survey of audience attitudes toward radio.

National Association of Broadcasters, *Broadcast Self-Regulations*, 1971. Contains advertising guidelines and NAB Code Authority interpretations.

National Association of Educational Broadcasters, *Hidden Medium: Educational Radio*, Washington, D.C., 1968. Discussion of potential of public radio; survey of station resources and practices prior to the birth of national public radio.

Nisbet, Alec, *The Technique of the Sound Studio*, 2nd Edition (revised and enlarged), Hastings House, New York, 1970. Very British but good information.

Office of Telecommunications Policy, *The Radio Frequency Spectrum: United States Use and Management*, Washington, D.C., 1970. Invaluable guide to current spectrum assignment policy.

Oringel, Robert S., *Audio Control Handbook*, Hastings House, New York, 1974. Introduction to some of the hardware found in the radio studio.

Passman, Arnold, *The Deejays*, Macmillan, New York, 1971. An informal history of the disc jockey.

Peck, William A., *Anatomy of Local Radio-TV Copy*, Tab Books, Blue Ridge Summit, Pa., 1968. Short, easy to read; much useful information for a beginning copywriter.

Peck, William A., *Radio Promotion Handbook*, Tab Books, Blue Ridge Summit, Pa., 1968. Breezy, easy to read; some useful information.

Pike and Fischer, *Radio Regulation*, Washington, D.C., 1945. The most complete reference for regulations of broadcasting. An expensive service not found in all libraries.

Practicing Law Institute, *Business and Legal Problems of Television and Radio*, New York, 1971. Authors are from legal staffs of CBS, NBC, and FCC.

Quaal, Ward L., and Leo A. Martin, *Broadcast Management*, Hastings House, New York, 1969. A practical overview of management concerns.

Ray, Verne M., *FM Radio Station Operations Handbook*, Tab Books, Blue Ridge Summit, Pa., 1966. One of few books dealing with FM and small stations.

Reinsch, J. Leonard, and Elmo Ellis, *Radio Station Management*, Harper & Row, New York, 1960. Excellent for overall understanding of radio.

Robinson, Sol, *Broadcast Station Operating Guide*, Tab Books, Blue Ridge Summit, Pa., 1969. Helpful for the small station manager.

Rosden, George, and Peter Rosden, *The Law of Advertising*, Matthew Bender, New York, 1974. Two volumes. Costs $97.50 with an annual update for $20 per year. Volume one covers issues, volume two the Federal Trade Commission and its jurisdiction and regulations.

Routt, Edd, *The Business of Radio Broadcasting*, Tab Books, Blue Ridge Summit, Pa., 1972. Good overview of station management procedures and operations.

Runstein, Robert E., *Modern Recording Techniques*, Howard W. Sams and Co., Indianapolis, 1975. An excellent book on audio recording.

Seehafer, Gene F., and Jack W. Laemmar, *Successful Television and Radio Advertising*, McGraw-Hill, New York, 1959. Old book, but solid, basic information.

Senate Commerce Committee, *The Campaign Broadcast Reform Act of 1969*. Government Printing Office, Washington, D.C., 1969. Though dealing with specific legislation, illuminates the broadcasting-political advertising issue.

Shemel, Sidney, and M. William Krasilovsky, *This Business of Music* (2 vols.), Billboard, New York, 1964 and 1967. A pair of books that provides a thorough look at the music industry. Some of the material is useful for the radio station.

Sparks, Kenneth R., *A Bibliography of Doctoral Dissertations in Television and Radio*, 3rd Edition, School of Journalism, Syracuse University, Syracuse, N.Y., 1971. Contains about 880 titles. Masters level work not covered.

St. John, Robert, *Encyclopedia of Radio and Television Broadcasting*, Cathedral, Milwaukee, 1967. For reference.

Summers, Robert E., and Harrison B. Summers, *Broadcasting and the Public*, Wadsworth, Belmont, Calif., 1966. Good background book for understanding relationships between broadcaster and public.

Udell, Gilman, G., *Radio Laws of the United States*, Government Printing Office, Washington, D.C., 1968. All legislation on broadcast regulations from 1910 Wireless Act to latest Communications Act amendments.

UNESCO, *World Communications: A 20 Country Survey of Press, Radio, Television, Film*, U.S. distribution by Unipub, New York, 1975. The standard reference for comparative media information on virtually all the countries of the world.

United Press International, *Broadcast Style Book*, UPI, New York. A frequently updated handbook for broadcast news writing.

Vainowski, Robert, *In Our View*, Tresgatos Enterprises, 2019 Monroe St., Belmont, Calif. 94002, 1976. A manual for ascertainment and editorializing.

Wainwright, Charles Anthony, *The Television Copy Writer*, Hastings House, New York, 1968. British, but useful for Americans too.

Warner, Daniel S., *Marketing and Distribution*, McGraw-Hill, New York, 1969. Exhaustive text relating distribution to media and marketing planning.

Warner, Harry P., *Radio and Television Land*, M. Bender, Albany, N.Y., 1948. Standard reference book on broadcast law.

Warner, Harry P., *Radio and Television Rights*, M. Bender, Albany, N.Y., 1953. Deals with copyrights and trademarks as these pertain to broadcasting.

Wattenberg, Ben, *The Real America*, Doubleday, Garden City, N.Y., 1974.

A demographic analysis of the U.S. population and where it is headed. The information is from U.S. government statistical abstracts.

Wells, Robert D. (ed.), *Life Style and Psychographics*, American Marketing Association, 1974. Background for understanding the audience and advertising approaches.

Wilde, Larry, *How the Great Comedy Writers Create Laughter*, Nelson-Hall, 1977. Wilde draws on his own experience and interviews with leading comedy writers in an attempt to tell how to create laughter.

Willis, Edgar E., *Writing Television and Radio Programs*, Holt, Rinehart and Winston, 1967. Primarily dramatic writing, but an excellent source book for broadcast writing generally. One of the few textbooks in broadcasting that has anything about writing humor.

Woram, John M., *The Recording Studio Handbook*, Sagamore Publishing Co., 1120 Old Country Road, Plainview, N.Y., 1976. For those with engineering interest in recording practices.

World Radio and TV Handbook, Billboard Publications, New York. Comes out annually. Standard guide to the frequencies and hours of operation of international broadcasters.

Wright, Charles, *Mass Communication: A Sociological Perspective*, Random House, New York, 1975. An update of the classic 1959 book.

Periodicals

Advertising Age, 630 Third Ave., New York, N.Y. 10017. Current news and issues in advertising.

Advertising News of New York (ANNY), 12 E. 46th St., New York, N.Y. 10022. Current news, especially about people in advertising.

Annual Report, Federal Communications Commission, Washington, D.C. 20554. A yearly summary of FCC actions, including data about the status of American broadcasting.

Billboard, 165 West 46th St., New York, N.Y. 10036. Oriented toward record sales and the record industry.

Broadcasting, 1735 DeSales St., N.W., Washington, D.C. 20036. The prime source of news about radio; publishes a yearbook, also.

Broadcast Management/Engineering, 820 Second Ave., New York, N.Y. 10017. The most useful source for keeping abreast of technical developments; need not be an engineer to understand it.

Broadcast Programming and Production, Box 2449, Hollywood, Calif. 90028. One of the best sources of current radio programing practices. Contains more substance than those publications that worry about which records will be hits.

Client, Dr. Don R. DeDuc, Department of Communication Arts, University of Wisconsin, Madison, Wis. 53706. Legal articles and references.

College Radio, 305 Communications Building, Oklahoma State University, Stillwater, Okla. 74074. Oriented toward student-operated stations.

Columbia Journalism Review, Graduate School of Journalism, Columbia University, New York, N.Y. 10027. Excellent source of articles on current issues in journalism.

Communication News, Harbrace Publications, 402 W. Liberty Dr., Wheaton, Ill. 60187. More broad-based than broadcasting. News of voice, signal, and data communication.

FM Atlas and Station Directory, Available from Bruce Elving, P.O. Box 24, Adolph, Minn. 55701. Location, programing, and reception data on FM stations in the United States, Canada, and Mexico.

Freedom of Information Center Reports, Journalism Department, University of Missouri, Columbia, Mo. 65201.

Hall Radio Report, 30 Ten O'Clock Lane, Weston, Conn. 06880. Deals with radio only, includes current news and rating summaries. Weekly.

Journal of Broadcasting, Temple University, Philadelphia, Pa. 19122. The journal of the Association for Professional Broadcast Education; deals with both commercial and educational stations.

Journal of Communications, The Annenberg School of Communications, University of Pennsylvania, 3620 Walnut St., Philadelphia, Pa. 19174. One of the best research oriented journals.

Journalism Quarterly, School of Journalism, University of Iowa, Iowa City, Iowa 52240. Excellent source for a wide range of scholarly articles about mass communications.

Marketing/Communications, Marcel Dekker, 95 Madison Ave., New York, N.Y. 10016. Helpful for understanding the commercial side of broadcasting.

Mass Media Booknotes, Christopher Sterling (ed.), Department of Radio-Television-Film, Temple University, Philadelphia, Pa. 19122.

Media Agencies Clients (MAC), 6565 Sunset Blvd., Los Angeles, Calif. 90028. The West Coast version of ANNY.

National Radio Trader, P.O. Box 1147, Mount Vernon, Wash. 98273. A newsletter for tape collectors.

Public Telecommunications Review, 1346 Connecticut Ave., N.W., Washington, D.C. 20036. Covers a wide range of educational and instructional uses of media.

Radio Quarterly Report, Bob Hamilton, Radio Reports, 1608 Argyle St., Hollywood, Calif., 90028. Chronology of events, station and personnel listings, compilation of programing and service sources. Issued sporadically in the past, planned for quarterly release.

Sales Management, 630 Third Ave., New York, N.Y. 10017. Includes a yearbook; useful data for market analysis and sales data.

SAM, 16 W. Erie St., Chicago, Ill. 60610. The Midwestern issue of ANNY.

Spot Radio Rates and Data, 5201 Old Orchard Road, Skokie, Ill. 60076. Ownership, advertising rates, and policies of all American commercial stations.

Television/Radio Age, 1270 Avenue of the Americas, New York, N.Y. 10020. Another excellent source for news about the electronic media.

Variety, 154 W. 46th St., New York, N.Y. 10036. Along with *Broadcasting,* the most complete news source covering industry problems; trends, and developments.

Trade Associations and Professional Societies

These groups offer interaction among members who have common interests and concerns. They act as lobby groups. They act to promote high standards in their industry. Many issue journals or other publications. Members exchange ideas and share friendships and business interests.

Acoustical Society of America, 335 E. 45th St., New York, N.Y. 10017.

Advertising Council, 825 Third Avenue, New York, N.Y. 10022.

Alpha Epsilon Rho (national honorary broadcasting society), College of Journalism, University of South Carolina, Columbia, S.C. 29208.

American Advertising Federation, 1225 Connecticut, N.W., Washington, D.C. 20036.

American Association of Advertising Agencies, 200 Park Avenue, New York, N.Y. 10017.

American Women in Radio and Television, 1321 Connecticut Ave, N.W., Washington, D.C. 20036.

Association for Broadcast Engineering Standards, Inc., 1730 M St., N.W., Suite 700, Washington, D.C. 20036.

Association of National Advertisers, 155 E. 44th St., New York, N.Y. 10017.

Audio Engineering Society, 60 E. 42nd St., New York, N.Y. 10017.

BCA Credit Information, Inc., 370 Lexington Ave., New York, N.Y. 10017.

Broadcast Education Association, Offices with the NAB.

Broadcasting Foundation of America, Suite 1810, 52 Vanderbilt Ave., New York, N.Y. 10017.

Broadcasters Promotion Association, Box 5102, Lancaster, Pa. 17601.

Broadcast Pioneers, 40 West 57th St., New York, N.Y. 10019.

Clear Channel Broadcasting Service, 1776 K St., N.W., Washington, D.C. 20006.

Country Music Association, 1511 Sigler St., Suite 111, Nashville, Tenn. 37203.

Federal Communications Bar Association, Box 32251, Washington, D.C. 20007.

Hollywood Radio and Television Society, 1717 N. Highland Ave., Hollywood, Calif. 90028.

Institute of Broadcast Financial Management, 360 N. Michigan, Chicago, Ill. 60601.

Intercollegiate Broadcast System, Box 592, Vails Gate, New York, N.Y. 12584.

International Radio and Television Society, 420 Lexington Ave., New York, N.Y. 10017.

National Association of Broadcasters, 1771 N St., N.W., Washington, D.C. 20036.

National Association of Educational Broadcasters, 1346 Connecticut Ave., N.W., Washington, D.C. 20036.

National Black Media Coalition, 2027 Massachusetts Ave., Washington, D.C. 20036.

National Broadcast Editorial Association, 514 W. 57th St., New York, N.Y. 10019.

National Radio Broadcasters Association, 1705 DeSales St., N.W., Washington, D.C. 20036.

Radio Advertising Bureau, 555 Madison Avenue, New York, N.Y. 10016.

Radio Television News Directors Association, 1735 DeSales St., N.W., Washington, D.C. 20036.

Society of Professional Journalists, Sigma Delta Chi, 35 E. Wacker Dr., Chicago, Ill. 60601.

Women in Communications, 8305A Shoal Creek Boulevard, Austin, Tex. 78758.

INDEX